FRED CUMBERLAND: BUILDING THE VICTORIAN DREAM

GEOFFREY SIMMINS

Fred Cumberland: Building the Victorian Dream

UNIVERSITY OF TORONTO PRESS
Toronto   Buffalo   London

© University of Toronto Press Incorporated 1997
Toronto Buffalo London
Printed in Canada

ISBN 0-8020-0679-5

Printed on acid-free paper

Canadian Cataloguing in Publication Data

Simmins, Geoffrey
Fred Cumberland : building the Victorian dream

Includes bibliographical references and index.
ISBN 0-8020-0679-5

1. Cumberland, Frederic William, 1821–1881.   2. Cumberland,
Frederic William, 1821–1881 – Catalogues raisonnés.
3. Architecture, Modern – 19th century – Ontario.
4. Architects – Canada – Biography.   I. Title.

NA749.C85S55 1997   720′.92   C97-930679-5

University of Toronto Press acknowledges the financial assistance to its
publishing program of the Canada Council for the Arts and
the Ontario Arts Council.

This book has been published with the help of a grant from the Humanities
and Social Sciences Federation of Canada, using funds provided by the
Social Sciences and Humanities Research Council of Canada.

Publication has been made possible, in part, by a grant provided by the
Office of the Vice-President (Research), The University of Calgary, through
the Publication Subvention program administered by the
University Research Grants Committee.

This book is dedicated to the Victorian spirit.

CONTENTS

PART ONE: LIFE AND TIMES

PART TWO: ARCHITECTURAL CASE STUDIES

PART THREE: *CATALOGUE RAISONNÉ* OF CUMBERLAND'S WORKS

PREFACE

Fred Cumberland, perhaps the leading Canadian architect of his generation, was also the epitome of the mid-Victorian man of business – vital and opinionated, hard-working, and forceful to the point that some feared him. Born in England and trained there, Cumberland found his way along circuitous paths to the British Admiralty drafting rooms. There he chafed under a system that allowed only inch-by-inch progress through the ranks, and he eventually opted to emigrate to Canada. The move to a new country afforded him ample opportunities to establish himself as an independent architect and businessman – initially created by his notable social connections but subsequently because of his considerable talents as a designer and a promoter. In Toronto alone, and in ten short years, he designed the county courthouse, the Anglican cathedral and a separate cemetery chapel, the Normal School, the post office, the registry office, the Mechanics' Institute, law courts, various houses for the city's leading citizens – and the largest university in all of Canada. After this remarkable career as an architect he gravitated toward railway management and, eventually, politics.

That Cumberland was ambitious, more so than most men, cannot be doubted. He would not have left the security of the British Admiralty had he not been. He moved to Canada because he was convinced that only here could he achieve his full potential. In 1854 he wrote a revealing letter to his wife in which he promised that if she would but 'give [him] four more years

I will give you a butler and an estate: and we will gang [sic] merrily in independent comfort with M.P.P. stuck to our tails!'[1]

In his prime, Cumberland was a man of Dickensian dimensions. In appearance he resembled no one so closely as Sir Charles Barry, the beefy, mutton-chopped mid-Victorian English architect who peers from photographs with the same vital, impatient intensity to which photographs of Cumberland attest. Cumberland knew Barry, admired him, and even went to the same school as one of his sons. Barry embodied Cumberland's own quintessentially mid-Victorian qualities – a hard-nosed business sense combined with a strong dash of artistic talent and a penchant for hard work. Like Barry, Cumberland was a vigorous and determined businessman who just happened to be an architect. He also resembled Barry in that he could be a faithful yet demanding colleague as well as an implacable enemy. Cumberland probably would have wished to be considered Barry's Canadian counterpart.

Cumberland was also Dickensian in spirit. He might even be compared to Mr Gradgrind, the unsympathetic character in Charles Dickens's *Hard Times* (published in 1854, at the peak of Cumberland's career).[2] Gradgrind was heartless and base in pursuit of his high ideals, sentimental yet ruthless, and Cumberland appears to have had more than his share of Gradgrind's brand of moralizing in his judgments of others. Cumberland, however, was liked and respected by the men in his employ. He was also a gregarious gourmand who enjoyed a full house as much as a glass of good wine, and his letters reveal that he could be a kind man. He could also give free rein to a tenderness and thoughtfulness that belied his Gradgrindian exterior.

This book is divided into three parts. Part One offers a study of Cumberland's life and times (including chapters on his political career and work as a railway manager). Part Two examines his architectural career. Part Three is a *catalogue raisonné* of all of his architectural designs.

Did Cumberland abandon architecture, or did he simply move on to other challenges after designing buildings for the most significant cultural institutions in his adopted country? Did he adhere to ideals about Canadian society, about its progress, that his architecture would have served to promote? What drove him? These are the principal questions addressed by this biography.

ACKNOWLEDGMENTS

I am particularly grateful to the Cumberland family descendants, Mrs Nancy Redner and Gordon deSaint Wotherspoon, both of whom obligingly provided access to documents in their collections.

I acknowledge my indebtedness to a fellowship from the Social Sciences and Humanities Research Council of Canada, which made it possible for me to conduct research.

I appreciated the opportunity to talk about Cumberland with Frederick Armstrong and Peter Baskerville, who wrote the entry on Cumberland for the *Dictionary of Canadian Biography*, and I thank Professor Baskerville for sending me a copy of his paper on Cumberland's railway management style. I have taken Professor Baskerville's views into account in the chapter on Cumberland's railway career. Malcolm Thurlby generously shared with me his extensive knowledge of medieval architectural history.

Many archivists in Canada and the United Kingdom offered help, and my sincere thanks go to them all. William H. Cooper is responsible for the Horwood Collection of architectural drawings in the Archives of Ontario, and we spent many hours together going over the Cumberland drawings in that collection. Leon Warmski, who is with the Manuscript Division of the Archives of Ontario, encouraged my research and helped me with various aspects of the Cumberland family papers, which he catalogued. The late John Crosthwait of the Metropolitan Toronto Reference Library's Baldwin Room helped a great deal with Toronto history.

In preparing Part Three of this book, the *catalogue raisonné*, I was generously assisted by Robert Hill, Shirley Morriss, Kent Rawson, Douglas Richardson, and, again, William H. Cooper and John Crosthwait. I owe a particularly significant debt to Stephen Otto, who frequently sent me nuggets of information otherwise impossible to obtain. I thank this community of scholars for their encouragement and generosity. Part Three incorporates information from Shirley Morriss's catalogue of the works of Cumberland, contained in her exemplary University of Toronto MA thesis. The thesis, completed in 1976, was the first attempt to prepare a catalogue of Cumberland's works, but unfortunately was written just before the Horwood drawings came to light. Morriss generously shared with me research materials not drawn on in her thesis, and in 1991 we collaborated on an exhibition of Cumberland's architectural drawings at the Lynnwood Arts Centre in Simcoe.

I would also like to thank the following people: Anthony Adamson, who shared with me some of his thoughts on Cumberland's work; Barry Baldwin, for help with Latin; Carl Berger, whose stimulating book on mid-Victorian Canada strongly influenced my own views on the period; Angela Carr, who reviewed the section on Osgoode Hall; William Cooke, archivist, St James's Cathedral, Toronto; Jonathan Franklin, British Architectural Library, Royal Institute of British Architects; Elaine Granatstein, Engineering Library, University of Toronto; J. Brian Henley, Special Collections Department, Hamilton Public Library; Ellen McIntosh, Lynnwood Arts Centre; Philip Oldfield, librarian, University of Toronto, for information on natural history publications; Edward Phelps, librarian, University of Western Ontario; Henri Pilon, archivist, Trinity College; David Roberts, manuscript editor, *Dictionary of Canadian Biography*, for detailed information on the Moberly family; Roy Schaeffer, archivist, Osgoode Hall; Howard Shubert, for his encouragement and friendship; the late Prudence Tracy, editor, University of Toronto Press, who believed in the project and helped me remain focused on it; R.G. Turvey, superintendent, St James's Cemetery and Crematorium; Juta Upshall; and William Westfall, for information on Ontario history.

Thanks are also due to Joan Bulger and Suzanne Rancourt, Prudence Tracy's successors as editors of this project at the University of Toronto Press. Finally, I must thank Howard Baker, a meticulous and thoughtful copy-editor, who improved the book in matters of both style and substance.

ABBREVIATIONS

AO	Archives of Ontario
C & R	Cumberland & Ridout
C & S	Cumberland & Storm
CFP	Cumberland Family Papers
DCB	*Dictionary of Canadian Biography*
DPW	Department of Public Works
FWC	Frederic William Cumberland
Horwood	J.C.B. and E.C. Horwood Collection (Archives of Ontario)
MTL/BR	Metropolitan Toronto Library/ Baldwin Room
NAC	National Archives of Canada
UCA	University College Archives (University of Toronto)
UCC	Upper Canada College
UTA	University of Toronto Archives

PART ONE: LIFE AND TIMES

CHAPTER ONE

Early Life in Ireland and England

In the spring of 1869, Fred Cumberland, weary of politics and in poor health, took a recuperative holiday in Cuba. A diary chronicled his reactions to the trip.[1] While on board ship to Cuba, Cumberland met an Irish steward who had grown up in the same suburb of Dublin, Rathmines. A little more than a mile south of St Stephen's Green, Rathmines was one of the fashionable suburbs on Dublin's south side that had been developed during the early nineteenth century. It was a brisk walk of about twenty minutes from Dublin Castle, where Cumberland's father Thomas had been employed. The steward, whose name was John Kane, exclaimed, 'Rathmines? Did you know Rathmines, your honour?' The memory of the place awoke in Cumberland a mood of sentimental reflection:

Rathmines! I repeople it with my earliest loves, my oldest & still greenest friendships, and I picture it in black, the moment & the spot which told me of my dead mother. 'Did you know Rathmines yr Honor?' said Kane as he startled me back from the past – so near & yet so far – so sweet & yet so sorrowful. So sitting upon my portmanteau I told John Kane of how my childhood & my school days & my youth were fashioned there and we fraternized over the dear old memories – and there away out at sea in a western hemisphere thousands & thousands of miles from home & parted from all kindred, we chatted & joked & laughed & sighed by turns, John Kane and I, all by ourselves, and all about Rathmines.[2]

This diary entry was the only known occasion on which Frederic Cumberland – whom all knew as Fred – wrote of his childhood in Dublin, and indeed the only mention of his mother and her death. Nor are there more than passing references to his early years in his letters to his wife; all that is known of that period of his life must be reconstituted from other similarly accidental remarks.

The Cumberland family can be traced through documentary sources as far as Fred's paternal grandfather Thomas, but no further with any certainty.[3] In December 1786 Thomas Cumberland appears in the records of the remote Yorkshire village of Kippax as a witness at a wedding.[4] Thomas apparently had two sons, John, later active in London's theatre world,[5] and Thomas, father to Fred. The younger Thomas seems also to have lived in Kippax, where he was employed as a clerk and factotum by the Rev. A.H. Cathcart, vicar of the parish. Fred's mother was Elizabeth Stevens, whose family seems to have been from Buckinghamshire. Thomas and Elizabeth were married on 20 January 1811 at Old Wolverton, Buckinghamshire.[6] The couple had six children from 1811 to 1820, five of them in Kippax. Fred was the youngest child, born after the family had moved to London in 1819.[7] He arrived on 10 April 1820 and was baptized in St Margaret's Church, Westminster.[8]

Fred's father Thomas was then employed in the Colonial Office in London, probably as a clerk.[9] Sometime around 1826, Thomas left the Colonial Office for Ireland to serve under Lord

1.1 Portrait of Frederic Cumberland, age 15, 1834. By Edward Matthew Ward. Cumberland family collection, Port Hope, Ontario. Photo by W. Edward Hunt

Stanley, most likely as Stanley's private secretary.[10] Thomas was employed at Dublin Castle, then the headquarters of the British administration in Ireland. What precisely he did cannot be determined, for the documentary record is seemingly incomplete. Thomas's signature appears in December 1826 on a few chits for office supplies, which supports the assumption that he worked as a clerk or secretary. Thomas received a total of £325 between 5 August 1830 and 24 December 1832, apparently as salary. Strangely, there are no other documents firmly connecting Thomas with Dublin during those years. While it remains uncertain whether Thomas and his family were in Ireland throughout the period from 1826 to early 1834, when Thomas returned to London, it seems reasonable to assume that they were.

Little is known, either, about Fred Cumberland's early life while in Dublin, save for the oft-repeated information that he attended the collegiate school of the Rev. Dr Wall, Fellow of Trinity College, Dublin.[11] Nothing is known of this school. In 1834 Thomas commissioned the artist Edward Matthew Ward (1816–79), later a member of the Royal Academy, to paint portraits of Fred (fig. 1.1) and his brother Charles; at that time the Cumberland family was said to be living at Dublin Castle. (The portraits are still extant in the collections of the Cumberland descendants in Canada.) That the family could afford portraits of the boys suggests that they were fairly well off, or at least that Thomas harboured ambitions for his two sons. At some point during the Dublin years, although precisely when is unknown, Fred's mother died.[12]

When Thomas moved back to London in 1834 he enrolled Fred in King's College, a good London school favoured by middle-class parents.[13] Boys who attended King's College frequently went on to become apprentices to engineers and architects. Fred followed a curriculum that included religious instruction, sacred history, English composition, Greek, Latin, English history, French, writing, arithmetic, drawing, and geography. In 1834 he was the top student in French – which is all that is known about his school record. Fred left the school at the beginning of Lent Term 1835.[14] A short stay of this sort was not unusual; those boys who spent more time there were normally aiming to enter Oxford or Cambridge.[15]

Fred's drawing teacher was the talented yet penurious John Sell Cotman (1782–1842) who in 1834 took up the post of professor of drawing at King's College.[16] Cotman was a distinguished water-colourist of the Norwich School, who had produced the etchings for some lavish publications on Norman monuments in England and France, such as Dawson Turner's *Sepulchral Brasses in Norfolk and Suffolk* (1819) and *Architectural Antiquities of Normandy* (1822). But the surviving Cumberland drawings from the 1830s show little evident of Cotman's influence; they are dry, competent stylistic exercises with no trace of Cotman's fluidity of line or dramatic treatment of light and shade.

In April 1836 Fred Cumberland signed papers of indenture with William Tress, an undistinguished London architect and surveyor known today mostly for his designs for railway buildings in southern England.[17] Tress had been a pupil of Sir William Tite, architect of the Royal Exchange.[18] Tress designed All Saints' Church in Islington, consecrated in 1838, and the London Fever Hospital, erected after 1846.[19] All Saints' was an unprepossessing structure. The English architectural critic Harry Stuart Goodhart-Rendel described it as 'A mean box with a sort of show east front; quite awful but perhaps cheap.'[20]

The agreement with Tress stated that Cumberland was 'to learn the Art or Profession of an Architect or Surveyor, for the term of four years.' Until the dissolution of the agreement Cumberland was required to reside with Tress.[21] The indenture papers mention no specific duties, but from Cumberland himself, writing in 1852, we have it that Tress was working on projects related to surveys for various railways.[22] Cumberland assisted Tress in his work.[23]

Two student sketch-books exist from this period of Cumberland's apprenticeship with Tress. One sketch-book sheet is dated 30 January 1838, and another 30 April, and therefore provide a general date for the sketch-books as a whole.[24] The drawings are dry and academic exercises, filled with precise copies of existing buildings and architectural details. The manner of delineation is precise and spiritless – an approach that belies any connection with his former teacher Cotman's evocative and heavily textured etchings, and seems instead more suited to engraving.

Cumberland was learning architecture directly from books; in May 1839 he obtained from Lord Stanley a letter of introduction to the librarian of the British Library reading room. Stanley requested that Cumberland be granted access to 'some valuable works on architecture,'[25] but which ones he saw is unknown.

The arrangement with Tress lasted until January 1840, after which Cumberland continued his studies in the office of an architect and surveyor identified only as Mr Jackson. The early 1840s were an unsettled period for Cumberland, a time when his commitment to architecture wavered. Early in 1842, for instance, he asked the Duke of Wellington for a letter of recommendation for entry into the East India Company. Why

he chose the duke is not known. The duke's response contained the following frosty comments: 'We cannot say of any Gentleman that which he does not know to be true. We cannot recommend to the E. India Company over which establishment he has neither control nor influence that Mr. Cumberland should be employed in their military service.'[26]

Perhaps disheartened by the duke's response, Cumberland gravitated back to the fields in which he had received training. In September 1842 he obtained steady employment with the British Admiralty at Chatham, on England's east coast. He was 'appointed Draughtsman in the Civil Architects Department in H.M. Dockyards, Chatham, on trial for six months, [where he] is reported by the officer on charge of that department to be in every way qualified for the situation, and that his character and abilities are very good.'[27] His duties eventually included superintending the construction of dry docks and sea walling.[28]

When Cumberland moved to Chatham to take up his appointment, he began to write to Wilmot Mary Bramley, to whom he had recently become engaged.[29] Wilmot, the youngest of nine children, was the daughter of Hollingworth Bramley of Kentish Town, London. Many of the letters between Cumberland and Wilmot have survived. The letters are lively and ardent, and provide detailed insights into the hopes and aspirations of the young couple.[30] The rest of this chapter will quote extensively from these letters, as a means of introducing the reader to Fred Cumberland as a person.

Cumberland and Wilmot were in many ways a typical Victorian couple: they attended church services, discussed the sermons they heard, and went on walks. Cumberland vaunted – but self-deprecatingly – his athletic abilities in cricket, running, and other activities. In one letter he remarked, 'I am fond of all manly exercise tho' I excel in none.'[31] They exchanged presents: she gave him a pair of slippers, and he gave her a prayer book.

They also discussed literature. Cumberland disapproved of Frances Trollope's *Vicar of Wrexhill* (1837),[32] saying that although he had finished the book, 'it was not admiration that led me on it was curiosity. How any woman could write such a work I cannot think. There is no *effort* at a moral – deceit & depravity are depicted with a lightness that disgusts & there is such lowly profanity in every page of the book as would disgrace a heathen. It cannot be a dangerous book, for none – but a Frenchman – could smile at it. I really think that if I were to meet Mrs. Trollope I could spit at her – much as she condemns the practice among Americans.'[33] Such disapproving comments might make Cumberland sound like a prude, or perhaps merely a bore, but he was neither. His letters include numerous examples of sharply observed characterizations that are sometimes ribald in tone and yet also frequently witty and romantic. During the years of courtship in particular they are touchingly gallant.

Cumberland and Wilmot were a typical Victorian couple in another sense: they both came from large families that did not have the means to assist them financially in their marriage. And so the two lived in different cities – he in Chatham, she in Kentish Town – wrote letters, and dreamed of marriage.

The letters provide ample information about what Cumberland's duties for the Admiralty were like, and also about the future couple's families. Working for the Admiralty was drudgery. Cumberland's immediate supervisor, John Fincham, frequently denied him leave, or granted it grudgingly. On one occasion when Fincham granted leave, he pompously informed Cumberland, 'Take what you like Cumberland but don't forget that I want you & that note is made of the amount of leave taken & it weighs when promotion is sought.'[34] Cumberland was kept busy in a variety of ways, sometimes outside of regular hours. Early in July 1843, for instance, he wrote to Wilmot apologizing for not responding to her latest letter, explaining that his supervisor had called on him and asked him to do extra work outside of office hours: 'John Fincham came to me at nine o'clock & from that time till now I have had no peace. He is publishing a work on Naval Architecture & I have been with him the Evening assisting him in arranging & correcting the proofs.'[35] And yet Fincham rarely gave him

time off as compensation. Such experiences made Cumberland very unhappy. In July 1843 he wrote, 'There are many things I could wish changed – and one is that I was at home instead of here. I hate the place & heartily wish I had never seen it.'[36]

As they dealt with the impediments to being together, and exchanged confidences concerning their families, the couple were strengthened in their resolve to marry. They were annoyed about being apart, and in July 1843 contemplated with pleasure a plan to spend two days together in Gravesend, a few miles from Chatham.

There may be much to lament but the possession of your affection would counterbalance a *world* of troubles. I am not forgetful of the responsibility of having won it & this it is that frightens me sometimes. I almost tremble when I think how many people there are who can gratulate [*sic* – an archaic word meaning congratulate] with good fortune but cannot sympathise with failure – but I told you in my last that I loved the bright side of a picture – o let us turn over the leaf & only wonder if it would be possible to forget one's present enjoyments so far as to allow anxieties about what are not yet even shadows to overcome our appreciation of them. 'What will not even the *gentlest* spirits do, when strong affection stirs their courage up' which proposition I take to be very encouraging. I am not one of 'the gentlest spirits' no more was Atlas – he threw the world over his shoulder why should not I make the attempt.[37]

In August they were able to spend a week's holiday together. Wilmot's family acted as complaisant chaperons. During the week the couple discussed their marriage plans. On returning to Chatham, Cumberland wrote to Wilmot:

This ended the most delightful and the happiest week that ever I spent & I owe you all a deep debt of gratitude ... As you said we had previously seen so little of each other that we were quite strangers than we ought to have been & now that we *have* been together I hope & *jolly believe* that our affection has been so much strengthened that we can better afford to be separated if it must be so.[38]

By return post she sent him a present. He hastened to respond to her token of love:

You ask me for a corner of my heart – you have it all. There is no wish or thought which does not belong to you & it is my greatest joy my most treasured blessing to know that our feelings are reciprocal. If we live there will be a day when we shall look back and be proud of our constancy. *Then* we shall be reaping its fruits in perfect unity. Each the delight & comfort of the other & equally grateful to the guiding hand that brought us together. This is what I hope & what I will strive to attain ... The threads of our lives are intertwined & I would rather mine should snap than be unravelled.[39]

Such ardency, however, did not make them abandon their common sense. They had realized for some time that Cumberland's salary would scarcely permit them to marry immediately. Cumberland complained that he was 'all but powerless'; no post would open up unless some superior might 'superannuate ... and make me Civil Architect.'[40] And this was unlikely.

By the late fall of 1843, they had begun to investigate opportunities in Canada. The alternative to emigration would be a long engagement – a prospect neither favoured. In a reflective letter written in November, Cumberland cited the Victorian novelist Bulwer-Lytton, who recommended against long engagements.[41] In considering whether emigration was possible, Cumberland wrote:

So pass we on to matter of fact [as opposed to the speculative world of novelists] and first of all to the Cumberland Trans Atlantic House and Home Seeking Speculation. I have written to Killaly[42] asking all the questions which I considered necessary to insure a prudent and correct decision – I have asked him with whom the patronage is lodged, what the probable progression under Government what the chance of private practice & other queries of a professional nature and soon like Rip van Winkle I will draw on my Cap of Patience and go to sleep till the answer comes and if your deserts avail me, or my own anxiety can coax the shafts of fate into an adventurous course then shall we succeed.[43]

In another letter of the same month, he confided to Wilmot that the idea of Canada had entered his spirit. Late one night, he revealed, he 'had a delightful walk home over the lanes in the moonlight & frost. It was gloriously cold & my fingers were crying Canada! the tips were so cold.'[44]

But this initial plan to emigrate led nowhere, presumably because Cumberland could not see a reasonable position available in Canada. As a result, he redirected some of his hopes toward the Royal Dockyards and advancement in government service, and managed to obtain a promotion and a transfer to the larger dockyards at Portsmouth, where his new duties carried substantially greater responsibilities and a correspondingly higher salary. In September 1844 he conveyed to Wilmot some welcome news: 'My appointment has arrived and I am ordered to repair to Portsmouth on the 30th ulto., on which day I am to be relieved here. My pay is to be £180 without deductions ... and I am to rank as assistant to the Royal Engineer Commanding.'[45] He was to have a small staff of two junior draftsmen and a clerk. The prospect made him somewhat nervous, because these men were his seniors 'both of *age* and *service* so that I doubt not their jealousies will beget many difficulties. I am well pleased with these arrangements as I think my chances are better by remaining in the office than taking the practical supervision of the works.'[46]

Cumberland's optimism radiated from a letter written just before he was to take up his new position. The letter also conveyed the extent to which he felt a sense of duty and obligation to make a secure future for himself and Wilmot:

I had plenty to think of darling & to think of with delight – you are so kind & devoted and so entirely my own that I revel in the ideas of our approaching happiness – but not without giving a fair share of consideration to the new responsibilities which are to be incurred, or without praying that I may be found equal to them – However much we may desire our early marriage it would be very wrong not to look cautiously forward – this done – as it already has been in a principal degree – to our own satisfaction, we may start with every hope and a comfortable security. Upon these matters I think your brother Tom and I agree – and I shall always be happy to have the advantage of his advice, and to counsel with him as to the best means of securing your happiness – upon which by the by, insofar as duty & its conscientious discharge is concerned, we cannot differ – for duty like truth has but one face.[47]

The optimism accompanying the transfer and the increase in pay and responsibility soon gave way to a stronger and stronger conviction that it would still not be possible for a married man to live in any style on his salary. And despite being involved in assisting the director of the dockyards with a variety of publishing projects for the Corps of Royal Engineers, he still found his prospects for advancement in the near future dim.[48]

Despite the uncertainties they faced, Cumberland and Wilmot married on 30 September 1845 in Saint Pancras, Old Church, London.[49] Shortly after, they moved to Portsea and had a son, Frederick Barlow, who was christened on 16 October 1846 in St Mary's, Portsea.[50] His birth caused the couple to renew with vigour their efforts to emigrate to Canada. In 1834 Wilmot's sister Matilda had married Thomas Gibbs Ridout (1792–1861), the astute and influential Cashier (senior officer) of the Bank of Upper Canada.[51] They had established themselves in Toronto, where they eventually had six sons and five daughters. Wilmot's sister Julia Elizabeth had married Thomas's cousin, Joseph Davis Ridout, and had likewise moved to Toronto.[52] Thomas often visited England, and during one visit in early 1847 he encouraged the Cumberlands to move to Toronto.

In March 1847 Cumberland wrote to Ridout at length on this proposal:

After long hesitation and many postponements, I have at last determined to write to you with reference to a project about which we have all been talking a great deal tho' hitherto without result. Since you were here Willy and I have been turning our eyes towards Canada and indulging our idle hours with visions most enticing and aerial Castles most capricious: and if the indulgence has not yet been very profitable it has at least prompted the propriety

of further enquiry, that we may either content ourselves with the realities at home or seek at once for better things abroad.[53]

Cumberland was particularly anxious to determine whether a spirit of free enterprise reigned in Canada, or whether he would be impeded by bureaucracy and inertia, as he had been in England:

Is there a probability for much activity in Engineering Works and if so will their control & supervision be entrusted to Government servants or to private practitioners ...
... Government employment is out of the question. It is bad enough at home, and *I* have had enough of it. It is a bar to all spirit of enterprise and a clog upon industry, for the best man seldom has the most credit or the highest pay. I have almost worn out the brim of my hat in the Service, and having learnt my lesson in it as a drudge, I desire to apply it elsewhere independently.

Although Cumberland believed in advancing by one's own merits, he was unwilling to emigrate without an introduction to the society he would be entering. Ridout, with his established social connections, was a necessary element in the plan:

A great inducement towards my starting in Canada would of course be the advantage of your introduction and the benefit of your advice. I should certainly not undertake the effort as a Stranger. I could not afford to wait to gather the necessary knowledge of the province & the people, a knowledge that in some degree is absolutely necessary to judge where, with whom and how one's fortune could best be pushed.

Cumberland assured Ridout that he would be a worthy recipient of any aid Ridout could give him:

You will very fairly ask: If there be sufficient practice am I prepared to pursue it? On this point I feel no alarm. My opportunities have been so varied that I am 'a Jack of all Trades' & yet I hope *not* a master of none. No man can be an unprejudiced judge of his own ability, & so I would rather rely on what high authorities have said of me than on my own puffing, & as I am desirous that you should be fully acquainted with my position that you may better judge of my prospects, I enclose copies of letters referring to the point.[54]

The rest of the letter discussed the probable expenses of emigrating; Cumberland was understandably reluctant to subject his family to privations. He therefore asked for Ridout's opinion on whether the move would enhance his financial standing. His government salary was £180, which could be increased by private commissions, 'making as £210 my present maximum income!'[55] Cumberland considered this to be insufficient. Nor would matters improve rapidly, for he faced 'a very meagre prospect of *slow* promotion.' His income was sufficient for his family's current needs, but it would surely not be if he and his wife were to have more children – as he fully expected would happen, 'as we have no reason for supposing that we are less prolific than the rest of our fruitful family!' He added that

This is a source of great anxiety to me & makes me most heartily desirous of striking into some new path which would at least give me an opportunity of providing by energy and perseverance for our increasing wants; and altho' I am determined to be prudent in effecting any change, I should be content for a year or two if I could cover my expenses that thereafter I might reap the benefits which would be a fair requital for the exertions made ... I work hard, and if I went to Canada should work harder; I leave no stone unturned if there by any profit in turning it.

This letter provides ample evidence of Cumberland's ambitious outlook, yet reveals him to have been a cautious and prudent man, particularly where his young family was concerned.

Ridout wrote back immediately with warm encouragement for the Cumberlands' plans. Cumberland had asked Ridout for a candid opinion on whether Ridout would be able to promote Cumberland's interests without compromising those of Tom Ridout Jr, who was also an architect-engineer. Cumberland also

had delicately suggested that a partnership with Tom could alleviate any such conflict: 'my more mature experience & my readiness to take the field at once & so secure what is going for both would be a set off against the value & influence of Tom's name.' The elder Ridout saw no impediment to promoting the interests of both men, and encouraged a partnership. He also invited the Cumberlands to live with the Ridouts until they established themselves. Cumberland responded in June, thanking Ridout effusively:

Willy and I have determined to avail ourselves of your most hospitable invitation for which, lest I should fail, I will not now attempt to make sufficient acknowledgment. It clears our path of so much difficulty at the outset, and seems so much like opening to us the warmth of home that we have almost ceased to fear & have nearly taught ourselves to regard our emigration rather as a change of firesides than as a search for a new one.[56]

Staying with the Ridouts was desirable from a financial point of view because the Cumberlands had little ready cash and few assets: 'You are no doubt aware that my own personal possessions are pretty nearly represented by a 0.' Cumberland proposed to take out a loan of £400, with his wife's eventual inheritance as collateral. Professional books and instruments, he continued, would represent their greatest expense, as 'it would be a false economy to take a bad supply.' Cumberland had seen Tom Ridout Jr in London, where Tom was then studying, and they had discussed the prospects of partnership in Canada, although they intended to defer to Ridout Sr concerning the specific nature of their business association.

At about the same time, Tom informed his parents in Toronto that the Cumberlands were nearly ready to emigrate. Wilmot's mother (Tom's grandmother) was resigning herself to the reality of losing another child to a new country:

The Cumberlands have very serious thoughts of going out now, I don't think my grandmother half likes parting with Willie, she is afraid she will never see her again. They will have a great deal to do before they can leave. I suppose they will come down to London for two or three weeks. Fred sent my Father a letter up to Mr. Shawbridge[57] to read and ask his advice with regard to raising the necessary money. It will be delightful for you having Willy and when Aunt Julia returns ... you will have a large party out there.[58]

It is not known exactly when the Cumberlands left for Canada or by what route. Cumberland's letter to Ridout Sr stated that they planned to leave in mid-August and there is no reason to assume otherwise. They probably sailed aboard the *Victoria*, as Cumberland mentioned that ship in a later letter.[59] It has been stated that they emigrated by way of New York City and the Erie Canal and that the journey took six weeks. This cannot be corroborated but seems likely enough.[60] By the fall of 1847 they were in Toronto – and, it seems safe to assume, were royally welcomed by Ridout Sr, Wilmot's sisters Matilda and Julia, and the rest of the large Ridout clan.

Soon after arriving in Toronto, Cumberland set out to find work as an architect – at first on his own, and later in partnership with Tom Ridout Jr. Within a few years his success had exceeded even his most optimistic expectations. Tracing his steps during the early years in Canada will be the goal of the next chapter.

CHAPTER TWO

Constructing a Canadian Career:
The First Years in Toronto

Under the heading 'Immigrants,' the following terse notice appeared in the *Toronto Examiner* on 15 September 1847, around the time that the Cumberlands arrived in the city:

300 indigent Scotch arrived this morning. Sent to hospital, 31. Emigrant fever hospital: number at last return: 533: admitted 26, died 9, left six, remaining 544. Number of emigrants arrived at the Port of Toronto up to the 6th instant: 31,563.[1]

The 'fever' was typhus. On 22 September the *Examiner* reported on a meeting held at the City Hall two days before, during which the problems caused by the great influx of immigrants were discussed. So many immigrants were diseased that the rest of the population was at risk. The numbers of patients entering the local hospitals were so great that one hospital lost track of 500 patients, for as soon as the patients were well enough to go they would leave the hospital without notifying the authorities, and their beds would be filled so fast that their names would not be taken off the lists.[2] Nor did matters improve as the fall brought cooler weather. As late as 27 October the *Examiner* commented on the 'filth and indecency' of the immigrant sheds.[3]

In October Toronto also received a visit from the new governor general, the Earl of Elgin. His visit brought lustre to the colony and the newspapers covered it at great length. The governor general was shown Toronto's most notable newer buildings, and met a number of its leading citizens, among whom were the Cumberlands and the Ridouts. Thus we know that the Cumberlands were in the city by October 1847, and that they were enjoying the social advantages of being connected with a well-established family in the city, unlike the thousands of impoverished newcomers who arrived the same year.[4]

Some insight into the privileged world inhabited by families such as the Ridouts can be obtained from the letters of the young lawyer Larratt Smith. In trying to convince an English cousin to emigrate to Canada, Smith provided an enthusiastic portrait of Toronto in 1847, saying that the city offered ample material comforts to those who could afford them:

Canada is not such a wilderness as some might imagine, and when you tread the gas lit streets of Toronto, and look into as many handsome shops with full length plate glass windows as there are in Bristol or London you will not look upon us as many of your countrymen do, when you see steamer after steamer entering our noble bay as comfortable as magnificent in their internal arrangements, the bay wharves, the thousands and thousands of passengers hourly arriving from the United States and all ports, the electric Telegraph almost from one end of the Province to the other every moment conveying intelligence with the rapidity of thought, you will have reason to be proud of your country and of her glorious dependencies, if you never were before, and to thank God that you were born an Englishman.[5]

Juxtaposing Smith's letter and the reports of the governor general's visit against accounts of the immigrant sheds is here intended to demonstrate something more than simply that inequities existed in Toronto during this period. During the nineteenth century cities all over the world were governed by a sort of Social Darwinism: if one did not rise, one surely sank. Nor was Cumberland particularly privileged. Having borrowed against his wife's small inheritance to emigrate, he was not much better off than some of the immigrants in the sheds and hospitals. All he had was an introduction to the social circle of people such as Larratt Smith and the governor general's party. This explains why Cumberland was so determined to succeed. What fuelled his ambition was partly a desire to aspire to the level of those who might expect to be presented to the governor general, and partly a desire to distance himself and his family from the spectre of the unfortunates who sickened amid the squalor of the sheds and hospitals.

Canada in the late 1840s and early 1850s needed immigrants, particularly educated middle-class ones such as Cumberland. This was an era of important administrative reforms and institutional developments, which saw the development of Responsible Government and the first steps toward realization of the dream of a transcontinental nation.[6] Toronto itself changed in a number of ways that were particularly auspicious for an immigrant with architectural training, as developments in education and government opened up new opportunities for architectural practice.[7] The year 1849 saw the passage of Robert Baldwin's Municipal Corporations Act, which established a county-based system of local government, and created a need for new county courthouses, three of which were designed by Cumberland in 1848-52. Baldwin was also the author of the University of Toronto Act of 1850, which secularized the formerly Anglican King's College. The University of Toronto, freed from sectarian religious debates, became a public university,[8] with Cumberland as its architect.[9] In the area of elementary-school education, a thorough transformation took place under the energetic initiative of Egerton Ryerson, the Methodist advocate of public education who in 1844 was appointed superintendent of education for Canada West (the former Province of Upper Canada). By 1848 Ryerson had advanced the cause of public elementary schools to such an extent that he was able to obtain funding for the construction of a teacher-training institution, the Toronto Normal School, also designed by Cumberland. Another important development for architects was the creation of the Province of Canada in 1841. From 1841 to 1844 Kingston was the province's seat of government, after which the government moved to Montreal, where it stayed until a mob set fire to the Parliament Buildings in April 1849. Toronto was next, and in 1849-50 there was a flurry of activity to make the city's buildings suitable for government occupancy, and it was Cumberland who was responsible for all the renovation work. The capital moved to Quebec in 1851, went back to Toronto in 1855, and then was removed to Quebec a second time in 1859. Finally, Ottawa was chosen as the permanent capital, and the peregrinations ceased.[10] Another opportunity for designing buildings in Toronto came when the city suffered a terrible fire in April 1849. Many new commercial buildings were required, and the fire also resulted in the destruction of St James's Anglican Cathedral. An open competition was held to design a new cathedral, and Cumberland won it.

Architecture was not the only field to be stimulated by legislative action. The railways also benefited from legislation, and railway development created further architectural possibilities. In 1852 Francis Hincks, co-premier of the Province of Canada, created a Municipal Loan Fund. This grew out of an earlier initiative, the Guarantee Act of 1849, whereby the government guaranteed the payment of interest of up to six per cent on loans for all railways of seventy-five miles or longer. The guarantee applied once half the construction of a railway was completed. Then, in 1851, the government passed a law that not only guaranteed principal as well as interest for certain designated trunk lines but also allowed the railway companies to raise capital by issuing provincial bonds. Following the passage of this act, many new railway ventures were launched – so many in fact that eventually large public debts were accumulated. The construction of the Northern Railway – the

2.1 Frederic Cumberland. Proposed Town Hall, St Catharines, 1848. Competition drawing of plan and front and flank elevations. Horwood (67)4

company in which Cumberland was to play such an important role – would likely not have been possible had it not been for the Hincks initiative. All of this will be discussed at greater length in chapter 5.

The point of reciting these details is to indicate the extent to which Cumberland's career as an architect and railway manager was inextricably linked with the growth of crucial Canadian institutions. Had conditions not been ripe in Canada West for the legislative developments outlined above, it is doubtful that Cumberland would have enjoyed the career success he did.

Cumberland's first official appointment after his arrival in Toronto came in January 1848 when he was appointed district surveyor of the Home District, the predecessor to York County, whose seat of government was Toronto.[11] His title was somewhat misleading, for the job principally entailed architectural work on public buildings. Cumberland's duties as district surveyor were varied, as his letters to Toronto City Council reveal.[12] Not only was he responsible for maintaining local public buildings, he also served as a corresponding secretary for the

Home District Council. In February 1849, for instance, Cumberland wrote to the mayor of Toronto suggesting that with plans for the construction of a new lunatic asylum in the works, the city would find it of 'great public advantage' to use the soon-to-be-vacated temporary lunatic asylum as a minimum-security jail for minor offenders. On 31 October 1849, and again on 2 and 13 November, Cumberland wrote to the mayor concerning the placement of extra gas lamps near the Parliament Buildings and Elmsley Villa, which was then being fitted up for use by the governor general. While such letter-writing may not have required a great deal of talent, Cumberland handled his duties competently and with dispatch.

Cumberland's other activities during his first few years in Toronto are somewhat obscure. The office journals of his fellow architect (and later rival) John Howard contain several references to Cumberland from April 1848 to June 1849.[13] Both Cumberland and Howard were hired by several insurance companies to assess buildings damaged in the Toronto fire of April 1849. In examining the damage to the City Hall,

Howard represented the city, Cumberland a private insurance company.[14]

Cumberland was reappointed district surveyor in 1849, and in 1850 became county engineer for York County.[15] He was by then responsible principally for supervising the construction and maintenance of government buildings in the county, including Elmsley Villa, the Parliament Buildings, and Old Government House (also known as Elmsley House). Such duties constituted the bulk of his work as county engineer for some years to come. Cumberland's annual report for 1853 (to offer an example of the kind of work he was doing) contained detailed recommendations concerning improvements to streets, to the courthouse, and to the jail.[16] The jail – the city's third, a structure designed by John Howard and constructed in 1838 – occupied much of his time. Already by the late 1840s it was in poor repair, and Cumberland was constantly working on it.

Cumberland's work as district surveyor (and later as county engineer) provided him with some degree of financial stability, and he soon began to look for private architectural commissions. In April 1848 he placed a notice in the *Globe* advertising his services as a civil engineer and architect. In June he entered a competition to design a new market building and town hall for St Catharines.[17] His drawings for this competition still survive, and they are his first known Canadian architectural designs (fig. 2.1). In connection with the competition Thomas Gibbs Ridout wrote a letter of introduction for Cumberland in which he remarked, '[Cumberland] is an Engineer and Architect by Profession, and has first rate testimonials and being a competitor for the design required for the St. Catherine [*sic*] Town Hall and Market he takes over with him the drawings that he has executed for the inspection of your Board of Police, which he would be very glad to shew to you in the first place. All he asks is a fair field which I am sure that you will give him but being a stranger yet in the Country having only come out last year he feels rather diffident in ushering himself forward where he is not known.'[18] The letter is interesting because it provides an example of Cumberland drawing on the aid of his well-con-

nected relations. But Ridout's efforts were to no avail, for the judges chose a design by Kivas Tully. This was the only known occasion on which Cumberland tried to use his family connections to obtain a commission; in the future he found work solely through his own efforts (although it surely did not hurt to be known in Toronto as a relation of the Ridout family).

If obtaining commissions for public buildings proved elusive at first, Cumberland soon obtained a number of private commissions. These initially consisted of renovations to existing works. In 1848–9, for instance, he designed additions and alterations to the Toronto residences of Justice R.B. Sullivan and J.H. Hagarty, among others. By 1850–1 he had established himself well enough to be doing architectural work for a number of private clients and companies, among them the Canada Company and the *Guardian* newspaper office. Not surprisingly, he was responsible for renovations to the residence of his brother-in-law, Thomas Gibbs Ridout, and to the Toronto office of the Bank of Upper Canada. He was able to rise so quickly in part because he faced little opposition. In 1850–1 only eight other Toronto architects advertised in the *Canada Directory*. Cumberland's rivals were John Howard, F.F. Passmore, William Thomas, John Tully, Kivas Tully, W.W. Fraser, Joseph Sheard, and Thomas Young,[19] and among this group Cumberland rapidly became the dominant figure.

During his early years in Toronto Cumberland was quite willing to undertake subcontracts for other architects. In 1850, for instance, he worked as John Howard's assistant on a commission for the Toronto Lunatic Asylum. Cumberland was responsible for designing outbuildings and a brick wall. He also executed temporary works in Toronto, for instance in August 1850, when William Thomas's St Lawrence Hall was decorated for a visit by dignitaries from Buffalo. The decorations included an evergreen-covered arcade some five hundred feet long connecting St Lawrence Hall with the City Hall. The *British Colonist* was extremely complimentary about Cumberland's contribution:

Much praise is due to Mr. Cumberland, and Messrs.

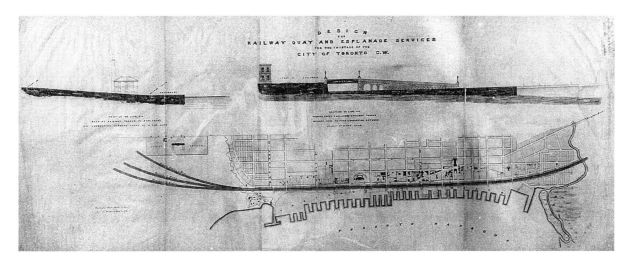

2.2 Frederic Cumberland and Sandford Fleming(?). 'Design for Railway Quay and Esplanade Services for the Frontage of the City of Toronto,' 1853. Horwood (68)1

Jacques & Hay [the city's leading furniture makers], for the very tasteful way in which the room was decorated ... it was certainly a matter of some delicacy to arrange matters so as to give the two countries their due place and prominence; but, we are glad to say, that no herald or master of the ceremonies, however skillful, could have made a more appropriate and courteous display of the several flags, armorial bearings, and other insignia of England and America, than they did on this occasion.

Everything seemed to have been studied with the nicest taste, so as to do every honour and pay every consistent compliment due to our distinguished guests. The British and American flags stood lovingly side by side, and long may they remain so. The English lion and the Columbian eagle sat peacefully in each others [sic] embrace as if conscious of their united power, and as if declaring to the whole world that while united 'touch us who dare.'[20]

Cumberland at first maintained his office in his residence, 4 Duke Street (now Adelaide Street East). Although he lived well to the east of Yonge Street and the present-day downtown, 4 Duke Street was then a central address. In the 1840s the city core was east of Church Street. Duke Street crossed New Street (now Jarvis Street), one block east of Church, and lay only two blocks above Palace Street (now Front

Street), then as today one of the city's main east-west streets. The Cumberlands lived on Duke Street until 1859, when they moved to a new house well to the west of the heart of the city. Thomas Gibbs Ridout lived nearby, on the northeast corner of Duke and George streets, where the main office of the Bank of Upper Canada was located.[21] In July 1848 Cumberland set up an office in the basement of the District Court House,[22] which he was still occupying in 1850–1.[23]

After winning the competition to rebuild St James's Cathedral – the design for which will be discussed in chapter 12 – Cumberland realized that he would need to take on a partner. We have already seen that he had long considered going into partnership with Thomas Ridout Jr, who had been in England furthering his studies but in late 1849 was expected to return to Toronto imminently. A press report stated that Ridout had been in England 'engaged in the study of his profession, where he enjoyed advantages unobtainable in this country.'[24] On 1 January 1850 Cumberland advertised the formation of a partnership with Tom,[25] although Tom did not actually return to Toronto until April.

Cumberland & Ridout was responsible for an impressive list of commissions during the early 1850s. In addition to the partnership's crowning success – St James's Cathedral – Cumberland designed Toronto's Normal School, the Haldimand County Courthouse and Jail, the York County Courthouse, the Hamilton Central School, the Church of the Ascension in Hamilton, and St James's Parochial School in Toronto.

Public commissions eventually started to flow in as well. During this period the buildings on which Cumberland worked included the Home District Registry Office, in 1848–9. He also prepared detailed designs for the Hamilton Courthouse and Jail, although these were not executed.[26] In addition to their architectural practice, Cumberland and Ridout were jointly appointed as York County's county engineers in 1851 and 1852.[27]

In 1852 Cumberland, buoyed by the degree of his success, attempted to gain an academic post, a goal that would have been inconceivable in England. In February he applied unsuccessfully to the University of Toronto for the position of professor of engineering.[28] In July he was appointed chief engineer of the Ontario, Simcoe and Huron Railroad Union Company.[29] Assuming the duties of chief engineer seems to have inspired him to reorganize his architectural practice. On 1 July 1852, following a brief period of solo practice, Cumberland announced in the newspapers that his partnership with Ridout had ended and that any business of the old firm would be executed by the new partnership of Cumberland & Storm. Cumberland's reason for ending the partnership with Ridout seems to have been pragmatic: the English-born, Canadian-raised William George Storm (1826–92) was a more capable architect than Ridout, and would become by far the more significant of Cumberland's two partners.[30] Already by August 1852, the new firm was making tender calls.[31] As had been the case earlier with Ridout, Cumberland and Storm served jointly as York County's county engineers (in 1852–3).[32] Cumberland & Storm soon undertook ambitious projects such as the Seventh Toronto Post Office in 1852–3, the Mechanics' Institute, Osgoode Hall, and University College. Storm's contribution to the firm will be discussed in more detail in chapter 9.

By the end of 1852, Cumberland and his partners had made an obvious – and well-regarded – contribution to the architectural character of the city. An anonymous Montreal *Herald* correspondent wrote that

It is about twelve months since the writer was in that city [Toronto], and in that short time, the beauty of the principal streets has been very greatly increased. St. James's Church had been completed [with the exception of the spire, which was completed by Henry Langley in 1873] and added to it, some pretty school buildings [the Parochial School] and other dependencies. This church, built of white brick, for which Toronto is famous, is decidedly the most beautiful and appropriate religious structure to be seen in Canada. In the order of Civil Architecture, the new Court House deserves notice. It promises to be as fine a structure, in its own kind, as the Church.[33]

The writer singled out nothing but buildings designed by Cumberland and his partners, all of which had been built in the previous five years.

By 1853 Cumberland was well established in the city, in three areas of endeavour. He was best known as an architect (and this would be true of the 1850s generally), but his career as a railway manager was already well under way. And he had not abandoned his early training in engineering, either. In 1853, for instance, he prepared an ambitious design for an esplanade along the Toronto waterfront (fig. 2.2).[34] He also did engineering work in Port Hope, although not much is known about his efforts there.

Cumberland had also become active in professional organizations. In 1849 he was a founding member of the Canadian Institute, and in 1851 served as recording secretary for the Provincial Industrial Commission sent to the Great Exhibition in London. He also joined fraternal organizations such as the Freemasons.[35] The insights that can be gleaned from studying his affiliations with these organizations are so extensive and so crucial to an understanding of what motivated his actions that they will form the basis of the next chapter.

CHAPTER THREE

Cumberland and the Canadian Interpretation of the Victorian Concept of Progress

Cumberland joined wholeheartedly in that peculiarly mid-Victorian brand of optimism that was a curious blend of science and spirituality.[1] The mid-Victorians believed that discoveries in natural science would gradually lead to a revelation of the workings of the Divine Plan. British writers compared Canada favourably with the mother country, noting with dismay the noxious conditions of Britain's industrial cities. Canada, with its vast spaces and equally vast potential, seemed morally as well as physically a New World. Such thinking helps explain why the first scientific studies undertaken in Canada were eminently practical – particularly in geology. Sir William Logan (1798–1875), the first director of the Geological Survey of Canada (founded in 1842), conducted arduous field research that demonstrated the value of Canada's varied natural resources. Like Logan, many other Canadian scientists conducted field research in the physical sciences as a way of exploring the frontiers of their disciplines. These men included the redoubtable consulting geologist Henry Youle Hind (1823–1908), and the inventor, engineer, and railway surveyor Sir Sandford Fleming (1827–1915). Cumberland knew and worked with both Hind and Fleming.

These and other Victorian scientists believed that all men should attend lectures and undertake disciplined reading.[2] Among the most effective vehicles for the dissemination of scholarly information to public audiences were the mechanics' institutes. Founded in England during the 1820s to encourage the skilled

workingman – the mechanic – to raise himself out of his working-class origins to the status of an educated person, by the 1830s they had expanded into Canada, where they attracted a wide membership and sponsored lively lectures.[3] In Toronto the Mechanics' Institute included as members Hind, Fleming, Cumberland, and many others interested in applied science and engineering. The significance of the mechanics' institutes to an understanding of the forces that shaped Cumberland's life and work cannot be overestimated, for it was in the lectures and debates of those institutions that mid-Victorian ideals of progress were most vigorously propounded.

Cumberland joined the Toronto Mechanics' Institute almost as soon as he arrived in the city. He was a life member by January 1848, and he may have attended lectures there even earlier.[4] He served as president in 1852–3, and again in the mid-sixties. Cumberland & Storm designed the building for the Mechanics' Institute, which was constructed from 1853 to 1859, without charging for their services.[5] The building later formed the nucleus of the Toronto Public Library.

Cumberland was also active in the Mechanics' Institute of nearby Hamilton, where he and Ridout were doing architectural work in the late 1840s. In December 1849 Cumberland delivered the Hamilton institute's closing lecture of the season.[6] Entitled 'On Science and Art, and the influence Which They Exercise on the Wealth and Character of Nations,' it ran to thirty-two closely written pages, and is the only known example of a work by Cumberland that addressed philosophical issues.

Cumberland set himself an ambitious goal in his lecture: to explain how the arts and sciences both depended on the success of commerce. Implicit in the lecture was the belief that the then-current capitalist values that he described represented the culmination of a long evolutionary process. Cumberland devoted more than two-thirds of the lecture to a historical survey of Western civilization, in which he emphasized the relationship between material progress and developments in the history of technology and commerce. The histories of Egypt, Phoenicia, Greece, and Rome were offered in support of his argument. Commenting favourably on the trading empires of the Middle Ages and Renaissance, especially Venice, Pisa, and the Baltic states, he strode rapidly across the terrain of European history, tracing a continuous line of technological innovation from early times to the modern age. His next stop was Britain, and the scientific breakthroughs of the Industrial Revolution – the cotton gin, the development of mass-produced cast-iron as a building material, and the modern factory – manufacturing – were paraded triumphantly as the consummation of an intricate process of historical development stretching back to antiquity.

But why, Cumberland asked, did all of the earlier societies he mentioned pass away – even those whose trade and commerce were so dynamic? The answer was religious superstition, poorly balanced social structures, and despotic rulers. In Cumberland's view, democracy was the only system that had allowed people free rein in their salutary desire to compete, and thus to improve themselves and their societies. According to him, nineteenth-century capitalist society represented the culmination of the human endeavours of all previous ages – not only technically but socially. Only under capitalism had universal enfranchisement and widespread education created a society whose material well-being was based on individual initiative, not tyranny or coercion.

The arts and sciences, he continued, would not have been possible without the driving force of commerce. And the engine of commerce, Cumberland believed, was fuelled by the laudable desire of men to compete and better themselves:

Science and the Arts are indissolubly blended with Commerce, each dependent on the other for the impulse which gives it life and for its full development; for if on the one hand Commerce did not offer the temptation of reward, men would be content to recline in slothful inactivity; so on the other, trade & commerce could not exist except as a means of exchanging the productions of individuals or communities.[7]

Societies reached such a state of healthful competitiveness through an evolutionary process; the rudeness and indolence of primitive peoples yield to the values of liberal capitalism, and 'thus the apathy and langour that exist in a rude state of society invariably give place to activity and enterprise according as man is rendered familiar by commerce with new objects, and is inspired, as will always follow, with a desire to possess them.'[8]

Because men are governed by self-interest and desire for material gain, they will respond favourably if it can be shown that science and art bring them material benefits:

If we can show men that by adopting a particular course they will gain, whilst by neglecting it they will forfeit, we shall surely have done something toward tempting them to the path we desire them to pursue: and altho' I fear the enthusiast and the pedant may charge me with taking the low ground in adopting an economical and political standard, a standard of material fruition, I am not sure but that the great majority of men are more open to such persuasions than to such as are yielded by the contemplation of the more ethereal unpalpable and unselfish rewards which satisfy the yearnings and constitute the happiness of the pure.[9]

Cumberland believed that the material world reveals the workings of the Divine Mind, but argued that people need more than this realization to motivate them:

It has been well said that the world may be accepted as a partial index of the mind of God, and that in discovering the laws by which Nature is governed we read the purposes and power of Infinite Wisdom. But as though such an object were too pure to excite our energetic research – as though it had been foreseen that such a purpose was too exalted to attract the efforts of the human mind, naturally sensual, the contemplation of palpable reward has been held, and that which should be induced as a grateful task, the pure yearning of a wise ambition, has (in indulgence to our frailty) been rendered necessary to our support, a fruitful source of daily comfort and of present happiness.[10]

Drawing on the biblical story of the expulsion from Eden and the condemnation of humanity to an existence of unremitting labour, Cumberland argued that ambition and the desire to work are perhaps natural to humanity: 'Here, then, in a word, is the impulse which governs all the world; for the object of labor, as everybody knows, is to procure the means of happiness: and as it follows that the greater the productiveness of labor, the greater are the means of happiness resulting from it, the first aim of mental energy is so to direct that labor that it shall be rewarded by the highest success of which it is capable.'[11] Labour results in material improvements to the world, in a manner akin to the transformation to raw materials into useful objects: 'Nature provides us with the elements, but it is man's labor which in changing their forms or place, gives them their value. Labor says Adam Smith was the first price, the original purchase money that was paid for all things. It was not by gold or silver, but by labor, that all the wealth of the world was originally purchased.'[12] Cumberland illustrated this argument with an example relevant to his Canadian audience – the value of real estate in a new country:

Some amongst us who may be large possessors of wild lands, may be startled on first contemplating that those lands, which perhaps represent all our capital, are really *in themselves* of no value whatever. The truth being that we have purchased the right to make them valuable, or to sell them to others who

desire to expend labor upon them. We have speculated upon a thing out of which we believe some one will be desirous of making a profit: but so long as it is unoccupied and unworked, so long in fact as it remains in the hands of the idle speculator, it has no other value whatever than is due to the prospect of future industry by others, and the probable advantage with which that industry may be applied towards production. Were it otherwise all land of equal natural excellence would be of equal value without reference to position, to the *time* or *manner* of its use.[13]

The rest of the lecture was devoted to statistics concerning English industrial production and to an appeal for education in the sciences and technical fields to become more common in universities and lower-level schools. Cumberland exhorted his audience to strive to meet the challenges of inevitable change, by fully using such resources as the mechanics' institutes:

So with men, new necessities are arising every day: new paths are opening, inciting new hopes & new ambitions; and I trust there are none amongst us who are so dull of soul as to be satisfied with the knowledge we possess, and, content to incur further risks or multiply past mistakes, recline in slothful inactivity, or yearn not to occupy our present sphere with more usefulness, or a higher one with more honor.[14]

Cumberland's argument, despite its far-ranging historical references and apparently idiosyncratic thesis, was not original. It proceeded in a straight line from the theories of well-known English and Scottish political thinkers, the most frequently cited by Cumberland in his lecture being the economist John Ramsey McCulloch (1789–1864).[15] McCulloch stood on the foundation established by Adam Smith (whom Cumberland also cited), as well as by utilitarian writers such as Jeremy Bentham and John Stuart Mill. Cumberland's central premise – that the ultimate source of wealth is labour, not commodities – can be traced to Smith, and beyond him to John Locke and even Thomas Hobbes. Cumberland, for instance, offered up the same example of the relative worthlessness of uncultivated land that was given by McCulloch in his 1838 edition of Smith's *Wealth of Nations*.[16] Cumberland's argument was thus firmly couched within the tradition of English and Scottish political economy.

There is no point in criticizing Cumberland for synthesizing other men's arguments for the purposes of a public lecture. Rather, the lecture ought to be mined for evidence of Cumberland's attitudes toward progress. Foremost among them was Cumberland's optimistic belief that his society was an improvement on all others that had come before, and that improvement continued to take place. The lecture was a paean to progress, a testament to the spirit of the age and to Cumberland's fervent belief that his own actions, and those of like-minded active individuals, were necessary and desirable for the further development of their society.[17] When analysing Cumberland's assessment of his own role in his society, and when trying to understand why he strove to excel in several fields of endeavour, it is therefore useful to keep the sonorous phrases of his lecture in mind: they reveal that Cumberland saw himself as a participant in an evolutionary process that rewarded people who knew how to unlock the mysteries of technical development and had the necessary drive and ambition to see change effected.

In addition to the Mechanics' Institute, there were other organizations in Toronto that offered public lectures, but their membership was restricted to practitioners of the applied sciences. Principal among these was the Canadian Institute, founded in 1849,[18] whose members were engineers and men in related fields such as surveying. The Canadian Institute's activities were similar to those of the Mechanics' Institute, except that the former's lectures were more technical. The Canadian Institute also produced an excellent periodical, the *Canadian Institute Journal*, in which many of the lectures were published. The Institute's first president was Sir William Logan, director of the Geological Survey of Canada, and its first vice-president Captain John Henry Lefroy, director of the Magnetical Observatory of Canada. Other men of similar stature filled out the executive, and the junior members included such future giants

of science and the arts in Canada as Sandford Fleming and Professor Daniel Wilson of the University of Toronto. The men who attended the Institute's lectures were experts in one or more technical fields, but also considered themselves intelligent generalists. They believed it was the duty of the educated man to have some knowledge of the arts and sciences outside his area of specialization. At the Institute botanists attended lectures by geologists, physicians attended lectures by architects, and everyone attended lectures by experts in natural history. During the 1850s it was still possible to believe in the well-rounded generalist, and for educated men to aspire to that ideal; the age of technical specialization, of narrow professionalism, of the inability of specialists in different disciplines to communicate with one another, had not yet arrived. That the Institute's members were assumed to share a wide knowledge of natural history is demonstrated by the following excerpt from a survey published in its *Journal* in 1852:

1. What is the most northern and what is the most eastern township in Western Canada, in which the cactus is found?
2. What are the limits of the Black Walnut (Jiglans nigra) and sweet or Spanish Chestnut (Castanea vesca)?
3. What is the botanic name of the tree which furnishes the white wood of Western Canada, and in what districts is it found?[19]

An earnest optimism and nationalism underlay such a precise awareness of one's country, and spoke volumes about the men who were expected to command such knowledge.

Cumberland was a charter member of the Canadian Institute and was actively involved in it in a number of ways.[20] He attended its inaugural meeting in September 1849 and assisted in organizing its debates.[21] He acted as the *Journal*'s corresponding secretary and in 1852 was elected the Institute's second vice-president. In 1856 he and Alfred Brunel comprised the editorial committee for the *Journal*'s articles on architecture and engineering.[22] Cumberland delivered at least two lectures before the Institute. In May 1851 he spoke 'On the works at

Portsmouth Dock Yards,' and in April 1852 'On Concrete, as applied in Foundations underwater.'

Cumberland & Storm designed an unexecuted building for the Canadian Institute. Cumberland's design showed an impressive series of spaces, including a gallery and lecture halls. That the design lay beyond the financial means of the Institute to execute does not change the fact that Cumberland was devoted to the future of the organization.

The Canadian Institute and the mechanics' institutes must be considered some of the most important cultural institutions in Victorian Canada. Cumberland participated energetically in their operations and shared their goals. On a more practical level, his participation enabled him to socialize with the important men who were responsible for handing out architectural commissions.

The members of the Canadian Institute and the mechanics' institutes were convinced that no other country but Canada provided as many, and as varied, opportunities for the future. Rather than feeling nostalgia for the past, and for the countries that most of them had so recently left, they often stated how glad they were to have come to Canada. It was Canada's status as a new country that excited their hopes for the future.

The story of Cumberland's changing attitudes toward Britain is an excellent case in point. In 1851, with his architectural practice thriving, he returned to England as a Canadian delegate to the Great Exhibition.[23] Cumberland was officially the delegation's recording secretary,[24] a position that enabled him to associate with key members of the Canadian society. His letters to Wilmot conveyed some of his sense of excitement at being in London for this epochal event. They also showed that in five short years he had effectively become a Canadian in spirit, and had left behind his British past. While his 1848 Mechanics' Institute lecture revealed that he had already begun to identify with his new country, by 1851 he was thoroughly Canadian.

Britain still represented for him the acme of material progress. However wondrous Britain's achievements as represented at the Great Exhi-

bition were, and however much Cumberland admired the technical prowess underlying the Crystal Palace, he felt a stranger in the country where he had so recently been a resident. In a letter to Wilmot he remarked that he was proud that Canada had won twenty-three medals at the Exhibition, but 'to tell truth I feel like a foreigner in England & certainly have no desire to stop here.'[25] He discussed the possibility that other members of his family might emigrate, and concluded that he and his wife could easily put people up for a year or more, as 'an extra knife & fork in Canada makes no difference.'[26]

His unease about England manifested itself in a variety of ways. For instance, he made it clear to Wilmot that he was unsympathetic to the rigid stratification of English life. His sentiments were markedly anti-English and pro-Canadian. In one letter to Wilmot he described a trip to Canterbury and drew an ironic contrast between the beauty of the countryside and the rigidity and cupidity of English society:

the country present[ed] no marked peculiarity – excepting perhaps the absence of wood – and yet abound[ed] in a very sweet variety of hill & dale, studded with picturesque villages and blessed with a stream insignificant in volume but not the less beautiful. Every village has its church & every Church has its Parson & in these days of clerical wealth every Parson has a devilish good house. Again every Parish has its Patron & the Patron of course enjoys all the blessings of a Country family Mansion, a home park, a pet experimental farm & perhaps a pretty dog kennel. Search further & you will find a Magistrate in every Parish with a lock up house a pond & a set of stocks all complete. In this way one might dish up any Parish in England on paper, filling up the scene with Village or Market Town ad lib taking care in the latter case to set apart the largest house for the rascally lawyer and the next in sise [sic] to the quack Physician – some M.D. of Baden Baden.[27]

Back in London, Cumberland observed that he scarcely understood English society, and could only do so 'were I an Englishman instead of a Canadian.' But London alarmed him. A mob that he saw there he called 'undoubtedly the most blackguardly of all assemblages ... a combination which no other arsenal of vice than London could present. This combination we saw in perfection and it further satisfied my mind that Canada enjoys that happy medium which unclogged by the pride of an indolent insolent & luxurious class on the one hand is free also on the other of that brutal & debased ignorant vicious & starving swarm which curses older richer & more aristocratic countries. Bah! I see plenty to admire & plenty to detest in "this remote region."'[28]

Outside of the city he found little to please him either. He visited the Chatham dockyard, where his former associates 'clung round me as Prisoners in Newgate to a fresh arrival, & it seemed to me that as I strutted freely through the gate they looked wistfully after me and sighed as their fetters galled them. But fetters were made for slaves so let them wear them, any other badge would be a lie.'[29]

In his letters from England he made frequent heavy-handed jokes whose butt was the stodgy old mother country. Commenting on a boring sermon, during which he nodded off, he wrote, 'Such tricks are pardonable when as in this case the parson is very fat and the clerk fattest. N.B.: keep them lean in Canada if you want good sermons.' He also told how an acquaintance from Port Hope, Elias Smith, had travelled all over Europe, 'has kissed the Blarney Stone at Killarney, the Pope's toe at Rome, he has studied absolute monarchy in Naples and Red Republicanism in Paris, art in the Louvre and in Hollowell Street Strand – in fact he has seen everything in Europe & yet nothing in Europe equal to anything in Canada so far as regards the comfort of life – & so say I. Of course Smith & I talked Canadian all the evening. Greek evidently to the rest of the company so far at any rate as politics were concerned.' In the same letter he related having met some fellow Torontonians who were 'quite delighted to see a Toronto face. Such miserable people as Canadi-

ans are in London, they do their best to enjoy the place but love of country keeps them panting to get home again. I don't think this feeling is so strongly developed in any other people. As to me I have a constant knawing [sic] at the core and wouldn't live here again on any consideration reasonably within my reach'[30] Indeed, he seems to have gone to considerable pains to demonstrate his Canadianness – including wearing a robe and gauntlets made of buffalo hide to show off to London friends.

In another letter he told Wilmot about a visit to an insurance company during which he had to handle some well-meaning but ignorant questions. The company directors 'smirked a bit asked me whether the climate of Canada agreed with me [and] looked incredulous when I said it was better than that which they lived in – and I believed felt piously sorry when they heard I was about to return to a country the chief characteristics of which are in their minds scalping knives tomahawks and grissly [sic] bears!'[31] A few days later Cumberland commented that more of the English middle class should emigrate to 'our glorious Canada.'[32] Such remarks provide ample evidence of Cumberland's belief that Canada was a promised land where the promise had been fulfilled.

The 1851 trip to England convinced him more than ever that his destiny lay in Canada. In Canada an ambitious and capable man could prosper. It must have been a marvellously optimistic time for members of the English middle class, who had been effectively shut out in England but who saw reason to rejoice in Canada. New Canadians of British origin, such as Cumberland, subscribed to the Victorian commonplace that material progress and the forward march of human society were inexorably linked. And Cumberland was not disappointed in his expectations: he worked hard, contributed to Canadian intellectual life, and prospered.

CHAPTER FOUR

Midcareer, Full Stride:
The 1850s

By the mid-1850s Cumberland had succeeded to such an extent that he could hardly revise his ambitions fast enough to coincide with his achievements. In a letter to Wilmot written in July 1854 – she was then in England for a holiday – Cumberland allowed himself to boast unreservedly of his political aspirations and his business dealings. 'When I scrawled my last,' he wrote, 'Mrs. Street was with us and I had been put to see Joe Morrison [a business associate] with reference to the annual meeting of the Northern Railway, preparations for which had kept me in a whirl of excitement and hard work. As usual I had to write everybody else's report as well as my own, Joe being too indifferent to do that duty for the Directors, and Sladden too stupid & too impolitic to be trusted with a financial statement.'[1] He mocked Morrison for agreeing to run in a local election, but left little doubt that his own interests lay in that direction also: 'How little we know ourselves, and what an ass *he* is to leave his business for public life for which he is so totally unfit. I laugh at the idea and condemn him to his face. However if he cannot curb his ambition & measure his strength – or rather his weakness – he must take the consequences. Nous verrons – by the time he has tumbled down the ladder I shall be thinking of laying hold of it and I will promise to eat all my old hats if I am not a better climber than he.' A discussion of business came next: 'As to business and the prospects. You need not be uneasy. My bridge contract altho' in consequence of the rise in prices not so profitable as [I] might have expected will go far with its profits to build my

house, and another heavy contract in which I am a partner, but about taking which I did not alarm you, will give a splendid yield if all goes well from £4–5,000 profit returnable about July 1855. One year!' These were the details of his finances:

I see a good time coming ... We have no bills anywhere except [one] and we have fully £2,500 debts on our books three-fifths of which give me £1,500 in hand. Now add all this together and include $10,000 – or £2,500 which – secret & confidential – I am to receive as a gift from U.C. Story & Co. for saving their contract from ruin two years ago – and which I only knew from Zimmerman when last at Quebec – & what it amounts to:

Humber Bridge	£1,500
Private contract	£4,000

say

Gift	£2,500
Debts due	£1,500

Shares in companies

	say £250
And from other sources of speculation this year	£500

	£10,250

The above is reliable, and will be exceeded – without reference at all to Railway salary – or works now in hand – and as all my debts do not amount to £450 including Caroline's and your Mama's – I believe firmly that on the 1st January 1855 I shall if I live be worth £10,000. Besides if I sold my three acres at Spadina I could get £3,000 for as Baldwin is refusing to sell the adjoining land to that which I bought for £500, for £1,000 whilst the lot I purchased in the Avenue has also risen in value very much & neither of these are included in the foregoing – then as to work. I have plenty to keep us going without trenching on property – and the Parliament Buildings will yet be good. Again in a conversation I had with the chancellor this morning we determined to go on with the University at once. So that is another source of income – and moreover I am importing Steam Machinery to manufacture 'compressed white bricks' which I am confident will yield a small fortune – Heroosh![2] Why repine or get nervous – give me four more years I will give you a butler and an estate: and we will gang merrily in independent comfort with M.P.P. stuck to our tails! I like your prudence however & think you are quite justified in enquiring how things stand. I shall send you £50 stg on the 10th of next month which you will receive about the 22nd and if you remain until October of course you will want more – & wanting will have of which however you must give me fair and frank notice so that you be not delayed for want of cash when ready to start.

He concluded the letter with an affectionate salutation: '*I am as true to you as steel* in thought & deed and altho I now & then repine a little am nevertheless delighted you went as I expect you to return my own jolly rosey Will of Derby day brightness.'

The sudden influx of such large amounts of money enabled Cumberland and Wilmot to plan seriously to build their own house. The Cumberland family kept growing during the 1850s and more room was needed. A daughter Julia was born on 30 November 1850, Helen (known as Nell) on 5 April 1853, Florence Harriet on 16 July 1857, and Constance Mary, the last child, on 24 December 1862.[3] The site Cumberland and Wilmot chose for their house was located at the western end of town, just beside the university that Cumberland had obtained the commission to design. By 1854 they had decided on a name for their new house, Pendarves. In a letter of June 1854, for instance, Cumberland related that 'at five in the evening I drove Harris, Storm, and Crawford to Pendarves and there made arrangements for fencing in *the estate*.'[4]

Cumberland's letters of this period confirm that he had lost none of his earlier formidable appetite for work. In the two letters of 1854 cited above, Cumberland discussed a number of current projects. In the June letter, which related the details of an unpleasant trip he had taken to Montreal to convince government officials there to accept his designs for the new Parliament Buildings,[5] he mentioned that the day of his government meeting had included a visit to the McGill University senate and a railway board meeting. The following morning he breakfasted with George Allan, 'to walk over his building schemes which I have taken in hand for him. Gzowski is here, and we have been talking over house building. He has purchased five acres close to Cayley's and has enclosed and fenced two acres intending to sell the remainder – probably to MacPherson. He Gzowski estimates his expenditures including planting and furniture at £8,000.' The day also included negotiations with the government on two subjects: an increased subsidy for the Northern Railway and Cumberland's designs for Parliament Buildings. He felt sufficiently optimistic about future prospects that he asked Wilmot to encourage her brother Tom to emigrate and promised to support him for a year.

From the letters one gets the impression of a man obsessed. Cumberland even felt obliged to apologize to Wilmot for his overweening ambition, remarking that 'instead of cosseting you I get smothered in ambitious or money grubbing pursuits.'[6] He certainly wasn't a miser, though, remarking, '"Where's the use" of working unless we get some gratification for the money?'[7]

Parliamentary elections were held in Canada in the summer of 1854 and the outcome did little to ensure the safe passage of Cumberland's project: 'The Elections are all over and the Ministry ensured a large majority. The house meets on the 5th of September – but I fear I shall have to be in Quebec next week, with Morrison & Cartwright to raise more money – £120,000 – to finish my road, as we have expended our last farthing & are running deeply into debt!'[8]

Although Cumberland counted on further government commissions, it appeared that certain avenues were gradually being closed to him: he was becoming too much involved in other business ventures that some saw as conflicting with potential government work. In June 1855, for instance, Thomas Ridout Sr wrote to his wife Matilda that Cumberland's numerous business interests were hurting Cumberland's chances of obtaining government work: 'I am afraid from what he [Sir Allan MacNab] says that Cumberland will not be employed again on the Public Works. That partnership with Worthington prevents it.'[9]

Cumberland found the task of asking government officials for money an unpleasant one, as he explained to Wilmot in a letter of August 1854:

We went as I told you in my last to Quebec whither Morrison and Cartwright had preceded me. My mission was a begging & therefore an unpleasant one, our wants inducing us to ask for a further grant of £150,000 and that in the face of an ungenerous and indeed violent opposition on the part of the Grand Trunk people who want to swallow up our road and with whom therefore we are just now engaged in an active warfare of the pen. Like the Kilkenny cats I fear we shall eat one another up before we are at peace. At any rate I am keeping them pretty busy & plying them with the heaviest artillery I can bring to bear. I remained in Quebec from Tuesday morning until Friday afternoon – literally writing all the time in the Hotel whilst Morrison & Cartwright did the diplomatic talking. Hincks *is* a *hyena*! and bit us all one after another becoming at length so savage that John Ross, Killaly, Morrison, Cartwright and myself absolutely ran away to avoid his violence. He quarreled with each of us in turn & not content with his personal exhibitions plied us with telegraphs & letters after we had absconded. I was the only one of the lot who dare go back so after spending Saturday Sunday & part of Monday in visiting the Grand Trunk works on the Richmond and Trois Pistoles Railways I bearded him again.[10]

In his final letter to Wilmot of the summer of 1854, Cumberland took her to task for her doubts about his faithfulness: '[I] must get you to teach me how to *double a superlative*: having *all* my love already how can I double it?' He then made one of the many sentimental and loving remarks that are found in these letters: 'Even my *ambition*, of which you are always jealous as occupying too much of my mind, has foundered in your absence because I can concentrate my thoughts on nothing of which you are not the centre.'[11]

Although many of Cumberland's letters to Wilmot reveal him to be an acerbic and astute critic of their social circle, others reveal an unexpected tenderness and kindness, even to strangers. In a letter describing his May 1854 trip to Quebec, he related how touched he had been at the sight of a forlorn young woman:

I was addressed by a very pretty Irish woman, who having taken a ticket for New York by an emigrant train had just been informed that it did not proceed further until 7 o'clock in the evening – she was neatly dressed & well spoken and as she was crying & had white ribbands in her bonnet I asked her if she was going down to be married whereupon she told me that she was on her way to meet her husband who had arrived some days since from Ireland & she was afraid that the delay would result in their passing each other on the road. Now thought I to myself I shall be here in 4 or 5 months on my way to meet my wife & how miserable if detained like this woman. So I slipped off, exchanged her ticket for one by the express, popped her into the train & left her crying for joy whom I had found in bitter tears. Jolly, wasn't it? I told her I was thinking of you & she quickly understood it all.[12]

A few weeks later, in early June, Cumberland went again to Quebec. After recounting to Wilmot the difficulties he enduring in getting there – the boat was first delayed, then ran aground – he movingly described the sufferings of the immigrant passengers:

I think absences & separations quicken one's sympathies. These poor immigrants suffer very sad trials: I was a fellow passenger with 1,500 of them from Quebec where they were huddled aboard like sheep, and so closely packed on deck that once established in a position there was no escape from it for sixteen hours; so that when we arrived in Montreal the poor creatures, young mothers with large families, were perched up on the same boxes and in exactly the same positions & postures as we had seen them the night before at Quebec. During the whole of Sunday many of them remained upon the wharf, which they openly left to suffer new & similar packing on the River boat. Accordingly when we got on board the *Magnet* at Kingston there they were, and a more pitiable wayward set it would be difficult to conceive. Moreover three poor creatures gave birth to as many babes upon the way – and altho' I do not pretend to more tenderness than my fellows I confess to a journey utterly miserable in its associations and the more so as *wish* your best you are powerless to do any the slightest good. Bah! If instead of the national Societies issuing 'bunkum' reports, parading in processions and giving anniversary dinners with very long speeches, they would buy a few gallons of milk, a few loaves of bread and a little brandy for the sick, & administer it to these poor voyagers – I would hesitate to cut their connection which I shall assuredly do at the end of the official year.[13]

Such tenderness was seemingly reserved for people such as these indigent strangers and for his family: to most others he was merciless. In this same letter, for instance, he called one woman 'a poetess of the intense and spasmodic school.' And later in the summer he had this to say about the wife of a Toronto client: 'Mrs. Widder is vulgar enough to annoy me professionally every time we meet & goes whispering round the room that she has been fortunate enough to engage my services for her drawing room! For the future I shall send her my clerks. I dread being trotted out at her first Ball as the author of her four walls.'[14]

In 1854 Wilmot began to keep a diary of her activities and Cumberland's.[15] Although the entries are usually confined to describing where she and Cumberland went, and who they saw socially and professionally, perusing the entries helps us piece together the minutiae of Cumberland's busy personal and professional life. In the 1850s most of his nights were spent out. He went frequently to the Masonic Lodge, the St George's Society (where he served twice as president), and the Canadian Institute. Somehow he found time to act as a school trustee for St David's ward. He played chess and whist. As a couple, the Cumberlands spent many nights with the Ridouts at the Bank, where they usually played bridge.

The Cumberlands entertained frequently during these years. In 1856, Wilmot recorded, she received forty-six New Year's Day visits, and Cumberland paid seventy-six. A few weeks later they attended a ball at the governor general's residence and did not get home until three. Their dinner companions included some of the cream of Toronto society: the governor general and his wife, the George Allans, the John Rosses, the William Robinsons, the Gzowskis, and, of course, many members of the Ridout clan. One gets the impression of a pleasing yet exhausting whirl of social obligations and activities.

The diary also provides additional evidence of Cumberland's insatiable appetite for work. On 10 March 1854, for instance, Wilmot recorded that he was at the university senate until past midnight, and on 13 March until 2:00 a.m. On 5, 6, 7, and 22 December 1854 he was in his office until midnight, and on one memorable night, 23 September 1856, until 3:00 a.m.

Because of the diary's style, it is difficult to construct a portrait of Wilmot as a living, breathing person, all the more so because her sphere of activity was circumscribed by the larger orb of her bustling, bumptious husband. The diaries do tell us, however, that she was active in charitable work. And the poignancy of her diary entries when she lost some of her infant children makes it possible to reach her through the common human bond of suffering and grief. But to us she is mostly a shadowy figure, existing in the half-light of the constricted world of a wife and mother in nineteenth-century Ontario.

It was a rare year when Wilmot or Cumberland, or both, did not spend a considerable part of the year away from Toronto, in England and elsewhere. Cumberland travelled more often than Wilmot, but for the most part his trips were briefer. His usual destinations were North American – Quebec, Montreal, Boston – whereas Wilmot's travels took her to England. In 1854, for instance, she left Toronto for England on 9 May and did not return until 24 October. But Cumberland also went to England, in 1856 for three months on university business and in 1859 for two months on Northern Railway business. Later he would spend even more time there on railway business – at least a trip a year, on average.

One of the most significant of Cumberland's trips from the point of view of a biographer is the 1856 journey to England. This was undertaken to see buildings recently erected in the United Kingdom and on the Continent whose design might be helpful in planning University College. Eight meaty letters to Wilmot have survived from this trip.[16] Cumberland was away from Toronto from 23 February to 30 May.[17] He sailed via Boston on the slow but seaworthy *Canada*, and followed an exhausting itinerary that saw him travel to London, Manchester, Dublin, Cork, Belfast, Edinburgh, Oxford, Cambridge, and Paris.

In a letter to Wilmot in March, written while he was staying at Morley's Hotel in London,[18] he mentioned having met with Lord Elgin and having received a message from Sir Edmund Head and Egerton Ryerson, who were helping to arrange the professional contacts for his trip.[19] He also reported that he had become even more estranged from English society. He confided to Wilmot that 'Englishmen are non-committal, distant & non-communicative. I have not spoken to anybody here yet but the servants, who are kind enough to take notice of me now & then.'[20] In a subsequent letter, he remarked that he had 'delighted in snubbing a Baronet's son & daughter of whom they were making grins & lofty lions.'[21] He planned to visit operating theatres and natural history museums, and his friend, the architect Fred Porter, had shown him the University of London.

The London letters are full of clever characterizations and jokes relating to natural history. Cumberland had gone to see the famous Swedish soprano Jenny Lind in a performance of music by Handel, and he provided a delicious description of her for Wilmot:

Jenny has a very interesting bunch of a nose closely approaching the form of a turnip radish – & possessing a combination, charming to behold, of the traits peculiar to the red & white species of that spicy vegetable – gray eyes – hair of [an] indescribably medium color ... carefully rolled round ... mysterious horsetail puffs pattern of which dangle in every

Barber's window & induce more speculative theories as to their uses than have arisen in any other Department of Natural History.

... Her mouth may be represented thus [he drew a wide narrow slit with serif terminations] two long thin horizontal lines terminated by two short thin vertical lines, very much like the geometrical slit in a post office letter box – except – if you will forgive the pun – that instead of *letters* going into it *words* come out of it. She was dressed in black – a very straight up & down arrangement as if measured off with a pair of compasses & accurately drawn with a parallel ruler. O'er her shoulders she wore a white silk shawl, drawn tightly round her throat & neck with the peculiar grace common amongst English women in adjusting that item of costume. The ensemble was so very delightful that of course I was overpowered and felt inclined to fall down & worship the musical image the cocknies have set up, and acting on the old regulation – established I think by the Philosophic Chesterfield – that when you go to Turkey you must do as turkeys do – I applauded enthusiastically with the extreme tips of my fingers & yawned out in the patronizing fashionable drawl Bra—vo! Bravo! At the same time I confess I am ignorant enough not exactly to comprehend why or by what rule of British eloquence or of English Grammar certain pronouns are given with an elongated shake & certain adjectives are invariably rendered in a scream! I imagine it must be one of those dreadful modern innovations of those mischievous Puseyites,[22] who, exchanging the plain commonplace straightforward reading of the scriptures, have put up a female Jesuit to decorate Bible texts as they bedaub and bedizen their churches! The chorus was very magnificent too men & women all screaming together deliciously assisted by an 80 horse organ and an extensive collection of double basses and trombones – one old dowager seemed to like it very much. But I could see what *her* taste was for she carried a trumpet in her ear. On the other hand however I was disgusted by a horrible country bumpkin who grinningly declared that having paid a guinea for this affair he thought he should do the economical tomorrow by going to the zoological gardens for a shilling. I enjoyed the termination of the entertainment vastly. In the twinkling of an eye all the girls put their heads into party colored cabbage nets with a multitude of cotton bobbins dangling amorously about their *buzzems* and all the 'gents' popped something very flat & black upon their heads – which I took to be – I suppose erroneously – Berlin Iron platters – and then they all lingered round the door – that they might be seen waiting for their 'carriage' manufacturing meaningless smiles at nothing & chattering about *less* in a languid lisping carry-on-home sort of painfully got up aristocratic drawl – eventually vanishing into dirty hackney cabs smelling fearfully strong of bad tobacco and stable straw![23]

Returning finally to his bed at his hotel, he had 'put out the light & embraced a very cold pair of sheets with a very solitary result magnanimously informed myself that "this is a Great Country" & fell asleep to dream of screech owls, hair puffs & fashionable quackery.' These sorts of asides provide more evidence, if that were necessary, of Cumberland's clever if somewhat heavily drawn character sketches.

The same letter also recorded that he had met with Sir Charles Barry, who had 'kindly promised to prepare a programme for my Continental trip which will be a great advantage. He has also given me an introduction to Sir Thomas Deane [architect of the Oxford Museum of 1855–68, probably the most significant Ruskinian building up to that time] – I am regularly run off my legs and in such a state of nervous excitement that I scarcely know how to write] – it will be quite a rest to get into a Railway carriage.' He then confided to Wilmot, 'I hope I shall complete my mission satisfactorily – but the time is short [and] I am very anxious lest I should fail.'

The next letter came from Dublin. Cumberland had been to visit relatives; their stuffiness and pretensions evoked his quick wit and sharp tongue. One female relative '*will always insist* upon introducing me with an emphasis – as an Architect who has built a Cathedral & done all sorts of other fine things & the result is my systematic martyrdom to the Shop. I wonder whether she presents a Surgeon as "a gentleman who can successfully cut for the stone."'[24]

There then followed an exhausting tour of Manchester, after which he returned to Dublin with a Toronto member of the Ridout clan who was also in Europe, twenty-year-old Charles. There they learned that a ball was to be held at Dublin Castle, and quite an adventure ensued to enable their attendance at the event, which required 'full court dress,' as he reported humorously, and at length, to Wilmot.[25] Some selections from his very long letter will have to suffice:

Of course we said we should be very happy [to attend the ball] – but quoth I to Howard – 'What is the etiquette as to dress?' 'You must attend in full court dress' said he. I looked around expecting to see Charlie go off in vapour or shrink down into the depths of his new Wellingtons but said I to myself 'in for a penny in for a pound' & a happy thought struck me – 'We are both militia men' said I. 'That will do capitally' said Howard. 'Of course you have your uniforms with you'? 'Yes,' said I – under a desperate determination to see it out – then said he 'Be in the Presence Chamber at half past 9. Bring two cards – one for the orderly, the other for the Chamberlain – as you must be presented before the Ball.'

... So we went up one street & down another looking for 'Fancy Dress. Masquerade Outfitters.' *There*! cries Charlie at last. There's the place. '*Court dressers but on hire.*' but alas they only had common civilian fellows' toggery & we couldn't condescend to that – so we went back to Gresham took the Porter into our confidence informed him that we were travelling & unfortunately had left our uniforms behind that we must go to the Castle tonight – & must get a rig and by hook or by crook – 'Be Jabers Sur, I know the very place – go to 2 Abbey street and you'll git all you want' ... By quarter past nine were complete & then didn't the Chambermaids look smirkingly at the officers as we passed down the passages, and didn't our swords give out sweet music as we came down stairs clanging against every step and didn't the Porter throw open both flaps of the folding door – and cry out 'A cab for Captain Cumberland!' and didn't the men, women and little ragamuffins make a land for us across the path – and didn't we nearly smash our epaulettes getting in – forgetting that our new breadth of beam was too much for the door of a cab?

... And then – but Lord I *can't* describe it – Beef Eaters – dragoons – horse artillery & servants in State Liveries – in two lines from the door – up the big staircase to the Presence Chamber. How we got up there Heaven only knows. Eyed all the way by everybody & not knowing what the devil to do with our caps with the silver lace upon them – very

4.1 Frederic Cumberland. Pendarves book-plate

troublesome to hold but so expensive to lose – and then we got out our cards & gave one to *the gentleman in a sergeant's uniform* – and then we passed down a dreadfully long corridor again between two lines of dragoons & horse artillery – and coming to the door of the Presence Chamber in our turn gave our cards to the first aide de Camp – a Life guardsman – who handed it another & so on straight through a line of at least twenty until it came to the Chamberlain who presented 'Captain Cumberland 3rd Battalion Toronto Militia.' Lord Carlisle stopped me, saying 'I am much pleased to have the opportunity of welcoming you to Dublin Castle.'

Soon they were caught in the crush of 1100 people in St Patrick's Hall, where the dancing began. They stayed until after one. Back at the hotel, ready to relax, they ordered hot punch – only to encounter two *real* militia men, also returned from the ball, anxious for conversation! They managed this as well as any other event,

however, 'evidently pursuading [*sic*] the men that they were green horns & that I was an authority!'

Amid the whirl of social events and architectural visits, Cumberland found time to visit old friends in Portsmouth, where, he related, 'I went everywhere saw everybody still alive amongst my friends – fought over many old battles – laughed a great deal at tricks good enough in their day & generation but rather unworthy of Historical account & found what I suppose is grateful to everybody – a most unanimous and cordial welcome from all who had known me of old ... I find my affairs pretty well known in Portsmouth. My eccentric & restless friend Rolph having told all my doings in Canada with such frightful exaggeration that I am regarded as a Millionaire & little less than President of the United States!'[26]

By this time he judged that he had seen enough buildings to be able to make some sort of original design of his own: 'I don't fear but I shall satisfy "public expectation" for I now feel thoroughly master of the subject & only want quiet to give it form. At present my brain is crammed – very much like a lump of yarn which requires to be spun out from the rude mass before it is worth much.'[27]

Still to follow, however, was a trip to Paris. This left him unimpressed, as he recorded for Wilmot in a letter written from London just a few days before he left for Toronto.[28] On returning from France, he reported, he and his English travelling companion had taken a night train, and 'at 3 in the morning [we] again found the Calais gendarmes rapturously examining the color of my eyes, the noble outline of my nasal promontory and the commanding stature of my person.' The letter continued with some spikily anti-French comments, as well as an account of the outrageously bad berth he had crossing the Channel. His ship's cabins, he joked, had been 'so delightfully cozey ... so nice & small that as you lie on the sofas you find your neighbour's toes intruding between your teeth, and the ceilings so deliciously low that when you prefer taking your own feet to those of another man you are sure to get up a little counter irritation at your upper end!' And the train to London was no better:

I had a most interesting journey from Dover to London – and *instructive* withal for having obtained the centre seat, the others being occupied by four lively & intelligent Englishmen. My attention was not diverted by the scenery from their animated snoring. They were evidently of different ranks in Society – the tone of the snore varying from the delicate contralto referable to Champagne through the regular gradations of Madeira & Bass's India Ale down to the deep base [*sic*] – the gurgling grunt – of Barclay & Perkins London stout! I look upon this as an important discovery in *Museological Physiology*! and shall probably read a paper upon it before the Institute. I am strongly of opinion that I can establish a theory settling the question that it is just as difficult to produce a polished snore on London Porter as it is to get Indian silk out of a sow's ear.

He concluded the letter with a discussion of Canadian politics, including the vexed question of whether his design for the Parliament Buildings would be approved.

Cumberland was back in Toronto on 30 May. Already by 2 June he was attending a meeting of the university senate.[29] Presumably all went well, for a short time later construction began on University College, the most important architectural commission of his career.

Meanwhile, work on Pendarves progressed. On 6 June 1857 Wilmot recorded in her diary that 'I ... went to Pendarves where Fred joined me on horseback.' In July they 'commenced hay-making and setting out the house. The digging commenced at Pendarves.' In early November 1857 Wilmot and Cumberland went to Pendarves to see the flag hoisted on the chimney. A housekeeper for Pendarves was engaged in the summer of 1859, and that year closed with the Cumberlands installed in their new mansion.[30]

In many respects the 1850s marked the apex of Cumberland's personal and professional life. As if to commemorate his many successes, he had a book-plate designed for himself, with the Latin motto 'Constantiâ Insequor,' which can be translated as 'I follow with steadfastness of purpose' (fig. 4.1). By this time, Cumberland & Storm was ranked among the leading architectural firms in the city.

The pinnacle of Cumberland's architectural career was reached during the heyday of such mid-Victorian organizations as the mechanics' institutes and the Canadian Institute, whose activities were examined in the previous chapter. During the 1850s, Canada's future seemed a magnificent tapestry whose intricacies would be fashioned by men who subscribed to the Victorian ideals we have traced, and architecture provided the symbolism that would reinforce the Victorian value of material progress. Cumberland was commissioned to design precisely those buildings that provided Canadian society with an architectural framework for its social ideals: courthouses, post offices, the Toronto Normal School, a university (with its laboratories and natural history museum), and churches. That Cumberland prospered was in a sense a fulfilment of the Victorian dream of material progress married to the larger Victorian dream of social progress, for the Victorians thought the best art should be well rewarded.

And yet the optimism of the mid-Victorian period was short-lived. Nor could it have been otherwise. One key premise of mid-Victorian thought – that informed generalists would unlock a finite world of knowledge – could not survive the evidence of science itself, which was characterized by increasingly specialized professionalism. The era of optimistic generalism epitomized by the program of the Canadian Institute lasted only a short time, and so too did Cumberland's early optimism regarding Canada. He gradually came to realize that the architect could not be an integral part of creating a new and positive society less fettered than Britain's. Surely it is no coincidence that, just as the optimistic Victorian attitude to progress did not last long, and soon gave way to the intellectual consequences of increased specialization, so too was Cumberland's architectural career brief. Perhaps he abandoned architecture not only because he wanted to concentrate on railway business, but also because architecture no longer provided opportunities to design important new buildings. Cumberland's last significant gesture as an architect came in 1861, when he went to the small town of Lindsay, Ontario, to present a design proposal for the Victorian County Courthouse. This was not the action of a man uninterested in architecture. But the Lindsay courthouse can be seen as the exception that proves the rule, for Cumberland's main architectural work was done by the end of the 1850s.

To ask why Cumberland 'abandoned' architecture, however, reveals a lack of understanding about the nineteenth century, for it implies that Cumberland left one distinct profession, architecture, for two others, railway management and politics. A change of careers was typical of many of Cumberland's contemporaries. Witness, for example, Sir Sandford Fleming, who started his working life as a surveyor and as a draftsman for Cumberland and others, and retired as a distinguished scientist. William Logan, Samuel Keefer, and several others among Cumberland's professional contemporaries followed multiple career paths. The 1850s were years of great social fluidity, when someone such as Cumberland could rise both socially and professionally as far as his ambitions would lift him. He abandoned architecture, but did so for the lucrative attractions of railway work and for the more alluring and socially prestigious activities that engaged him during the 1860s – politics, militia service, and service as the governor general's aide-de-camp, which very nearly brought him knighthood.

Thus Cumberland's career can best be understood as consisting of two phases. The first, inspired by a belief in the Victorian virtues of progress and national development, came gradually to an end during the later 1850s, and definitely with his inability to win the competition for the design of the Parliament Buildings in 1859–60. The second saw a more pragmatic devotion to railway affairs and, increasingly, to political life, which are the subjects of the next two chapters.

CHAPTER FIVE

Life on the Railway

Railways were a conspicuous manifestation of nineteenth-century progress in Canada West as elsewhere, and they attracted many capable men.[1] Although the railway came relatively late to Canada – largely because of the protracted completion of a canal system during the 1840s – an explosion of railway building in Canada rapidly made up for the slow start: from 1852 to 1859 more than 1,400 miles of railways were built in Canada West.[2] By 1857 there were 1,402 miles of railways in Canada East and Canada West, operated by eleven different companies. The Great Western operated 279 miles of roads, and the Grand Trunk 685. As Thomas C. Keefer remarked in *Eighty Years' Progress of British North America* (1864), 'The years 1852 to 1857 will ever be remembered as those of financial plenty, and the saturnalia of nearly all classes connected with railway.'[3] To compare the Canadian scene with other countries, by the end of 1858 there were 1,612 miles of railways in Canada – more than in Scotland or Ireland.[4]

Cumberland recognized the railway's potential very early. In a November 1851 letter to Wilmot – the first railway into Toronto had not yet been completed but the excitement over its arrival was mounting – Cumberland, then in England for the Great Exhibition, observed:

You seem to be all going Railway mad just now. I should like to be in the thick of it and to throw out a bait or two to see whether something in that line is not to be caught. So you *really* think Capreol a rascal!

Most other people arrived at that conclusion long ago and at any rate even were he *not* a rascal his vanity is so awfully rapacious that no man of business or common sense could condescend to attempt to satisfy it and so amongst such folk he must always be dubbed a bore & a humbug.[5]

Frederic Chase Capreol (1803–86) was among the first Toronto railway promoters, a shrewd talker but no man of business.[6] He floated schemes as if they were balloons and seemed not to mind when they flew away. Cumberland prided himself on his sound business sense, and seeing someone of Capreol's ilk flourish goaded Cumberland into becoming active in railways.

Given that the story of the Northern Railway of Canada, Cumberland's main concern, has been told in some detail elsewhere, this chapter will offer only an overview of its operations and development, which will make it possible to concentrate more on assessing Cumberland's contribution to its operations.[7] The railway was originally incorporated in August 1849 as the Toronto, Simcoe and Lake Huron Union Railroad Company; its charter permitted it to build a railway between Toronto and Lake Huron. But initially nothing came of this. A year later, in August 1850, the name of the railway was changed to the Ontario, Simcoe and Huron Railroad Union Company, the name by which it was known until the mid-fifties, when people began to refer to it as the Northern. In 1858 the name was officially changed to the Northern Railway, and it will be referred to as such throughout this

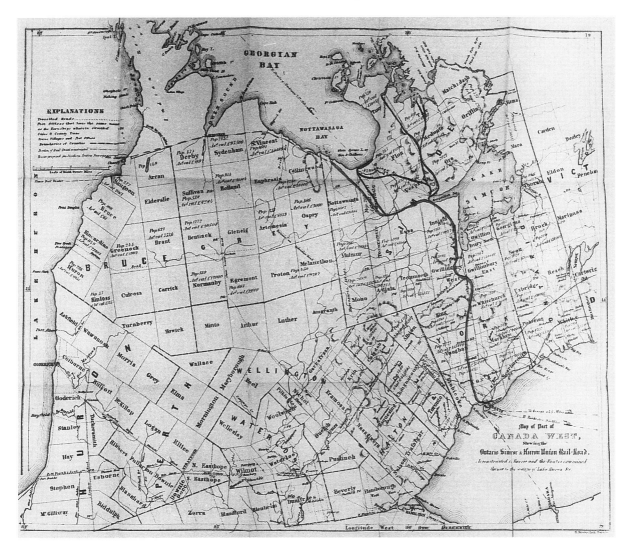

5.1 Map showing routes of the Ontario, Simcoe and Huron Railroad Union Company (predecessor to the Northern Railway of Canada). AO, Pamphlet Collection 1853, no. 3

chapter. From 1853 to 1855 the Northern constructed its principal lines, ninety-five miles of track between Toronto and Collingwood on Georgian Bay. With the exception of a later addition to Gravenhurst, this initial stretch represented the extent of the Northern's dominion (fig. 5.1).

In July 1852 Cumberland became the railway's chief engineer, and was responsible for all of its engineering improvements from 1853 to 1855. During his stint as chief engineer, Cumberland did much of the practical engineering work, which involved route selection, bridge design, and the like. He probably also designed some of the company's more significant buildings, including the Toronto offices and the main terminal at Collingwood.[8] After 1855, when Sandford Fleming assumed the position of chief engineer and Cumberland became more active in the railway's business operations, Cumberland appears to have designed few, if any, of the buildings for the railway. He delegated this responsibility to his employees and associates such as Sandford Fleming, Alfred

5.2 William G. Storm. Northern Railway of Canada offices, Front Street and Brock Street (now Spadina Avenue), Toronto, 1861–2. Photograph, c. 1862. City of Toronto Archives, SC 347, no. 5

Brunel, Clarence W. Moberly, and William Storm. For example, in 1861 he delegated to Storm the design work for the railway's new Toronto offices, a four-square dichromatic brick structure (fig. 5.2). With a profitable architectural business keeping him busy, he could not afford the time to do architectural work for the railway. The fact that he kept his architectural and railway activities separate suggests that he may have viewed architectural work as superior to simple engineering. Engineering work he happily delegated to others (although he doubtless kept abreast of the details); architecture he kept apart, to be tastefully executed through the application of his talents and those of his part-

ner Storm. By 1858, however, when Cumberland became the company's managing director (a position he held until his death), he had moved entirely into management and had left engineering and architecture behind.

The Northern Railway was absorbed into a much larger network of rail lines over a century ago, so it is difficult to recapture how it functioned during its heyday. Cumberland conceived of the Northern as part of a coordinated transportation system in which rails and shipping would permit access to the vast U.S. market as well as the growing western Canadian market. A map published by the railway in 1853 demonstrates that at an early date Cumberland

5.3 Map of 'Northern Railway of Canada and Connections,' n.d. AO, Railway Pamphlets, box 21f

and the company's directors sought to create a giant web of rail and steam lines extending from one end of the continent to the other, which would embrace Great Lakes shipping lines and a string of luxury hotels. This was a visionary plan, for the railway had not even completed its line to Collingwood! The map also helps explain why the company believed that a railhead at Collingwood was a good choice. Georgian Bay opens out into Lake Huron, which would, it was anticipated, provide ready access to all the American ports on the Great Lakes, while also being the gateway to the Canadian west via Lake Superior.

A later map gives an even clearer idea of the Northern's perhaps exaggerated view of its own centrality in North America. It is grandly titled 'Northern Railway of Canada and Connections – Great Collingwood Thro' Route Between Manitoba, Minnesota, Chicago & Milwaukee, and Collingwood, Toronto, Montreal, Ogdensburg, New England, New York, and all Eastern points in Canada & United States' (fig. 5.3). Still another shows the Northern's routes marked with thick black lines, visually emphasizing the claim that

the Northern provided the preferred route from Toronto to Lake Superior. Crosslake traffic was so essential to the Northern's long-term strategy that the railway formed the Toronto and Lake Superior Navigation Company to supply the necessary shipping links. The Northern's concept of an integrated network of rail lines, shipping links, and luxury hotels was typical of many railway companies during this period.

If the idea of linking rail and water travel was good in theory, it was less good – and far less profitable – in practice. The Northern never enjoyed financial success with the vessels it operated, and it seemed to make no difference whether the company owned or merely leased them. The Northern eventually owned three steamers: the *Algoma*, the *Cumberland*, and the *Chicora*.[9] The *Algoma* was built probably during the mid-1850s. Originally called the *City of Toronto*, it was renamed the *Racine* after being rebuilt in Detroit in 1863. After another rebuild the next year it was rechristened the *Algoma* because of its links with the District of Algoma (present-day Northern Ontario). The *Algoma* operated on the Great Lakes until 1872, when it

5.4 The Northern Railway of Canada steamer *Cumberland*. Photograph, n.d. AO, CFP, Photographs, misc. E-1, box 40

was taken out of commission – chugging out of the dock for one final trip, however, on the occasion of the visit of Lord Dufferin to Collingwood in July 1874. The *Cumberland*, a 750-ton vessel named for the subject of this book, was launched in 1871 and travelled the route from Collingwood to Lake Superior (fig. 5.4). In July 1877 it ran aground on Isle Royal during a storm and was lost. As for the *Chicora*, this colourful vessel was originally built as a Confederate blockage runner, and was known as the *Let-Her-Be*. It was brought to Toronto in 1877 to sail Lake Ontario for the Niagara Navigation Company, of which Barlow Cumberland was part owner. The company also operated its own hotels, the most luxurious of which was probably the Lake Couchiching Hotel, whose architect was Northern Railway employee Clarence W. Moberly (fig. 5.5).[10] The company's publicity engravings showed the multi-storey structure in an alluring light, with landscaped grounds, airy

canvas tents, and gazebos, and paddle-wheelers plying the waters of the bay in front of the hotel.

Why did the Northern fail to achieve the promise that its beginnings had presaged? And can its failure be attributed to its first managers – who overestimated the potential of Collingwood as a railhead and shipping centre – or more properly to Cumberland's later management? Perhaps both possibilities deserve consideration. In most works on Canadian railways of the period, Cumberland is considered a particularly successful manager. A typical view is that of Myles Pennington, who wrote in 1894 that 'the late lamented Col. F. Cumberland will long be remembered as one of the early railway pioneers of Canada, and the able manager of the Northern Railway for a quarter of a century.'[11] More recently, such unreserved admiration for Cumberland has been called into question. The historian Peter Baskerville has taken the lead in pressing for a re-evaluation.[12]

COUCHICHING.

LAKE COUCHICHING HOTEL.

5.5 The Northern Railway of Canada's Lake Couchiching Hotel. Exterior view, n.d. AO, Railway Pamphlets, box 21f

In particular, he has shown conclusively that Cumberland, who is widely held to have solved the problem of sloppy construction on the Northern when he took over as chief engineer in 1852, not only permitted slipshod work to continue, but also accepted a bribe of some $10,000 from the original contractors to permit them to be rehired on favourable terms.[13] Baskerville has also claimed that Cumberland's domineering personality got in the way of efficient management – that is, that he could not effectively delegate responsibility, but had to be involved in every aspect of day-to-day business. He has further argued that Cumberland was misguided when it came to defending through-freight traffic at the expense of local traffic.

When Cumberland became managing director of the railway in 1858, he had to give significant concessions to the government to obtain financial support for the reconstituted railway. Baskerville has analysed just what concessions the Northern had to grant. He has shown that the Northern was placed under virtually complete government control following a near-bankruptcy in 1858. Although Cumberland had control over daily operations, the government, through A.T. Galt, retained the right of final approval. In addition to the company giving English bondholders a vote for the first time,

'Any aid to steamboats required government approval; all repairs were to be overseen by a government official; and, most significantly, the road's capital account could not be augmented without both parliamentary and shareholder sanction.'[14] This suggests that Cumberland's managerial autonomy was much more circumscribed than has previously been believed. Still, even if Baskerville is correct that Cumberland's reputation as a railway manager has been exaggerated, a full reassessment of Cumberland's contribution will have to await studies offering more detail on the activities of his railway contemporaries.

There is none the less one aspect of the Northern's activities for which Cumberland deserves credit: his success at raising funds among English investors. The Northern Railway had a complicated financial structure, with both an English and a Canadian board of directors. The Canadian board was responsible for day-to-day operations. The English board, which comprised representatives of major bondholders, was, in principle, responsible for approving major decisions. Cumberland was the sole go-between, and his recommendations to both boards were nearly always accepted. Much went on behind the scenes, and only becomes apparent through documentary sources unavailable to earlier writers. Wilmot's diary, for instance, shows that year after year Cumberland was away in England for weeks or even months at a time. His reports to Wilmot on his English railway dealings are full of accounts of feathers unruffled, worries soothed, and financing obtained. Although it has not proved possible thus far to sort out the various financial players on the English board, it appears that the ones we know about depended on Cumberland as their principal source of informed judgment. Some idea of how Cumberland regarded the English investors can be gained from a letter to Wilmot written in 1866:

I went to the Wheelers to dinner & talk Canada and Railroads with the old gentleman – we have had two Board meetings – rather slow solemn & stupid for they don't travel fast enough for me altho nothing can exceed their kindness. Cutbill [perhaps the chief member of the London Board] is still in delicate health & staying at Bournemouth as he cannot stand the London fogs. I go down to him on Saturday & shall spend Sunday and Monday with him, as I find he is really the influential & governing mind amongst all people here. I shall probably call at Portsmouth for a day on my way up to town again.[15]

Sometimes board members rebelled against Cumberland's management style, but he was usually able to handle such opposition without difficulty, as is apparent from a letter to Wilmot written a few years later:

Between ourselves & the wall Reekie [a Montreal Board member] has been doing a lot of mischief here against me in consequence of losing his seat at the board, and has formed a part of 'opposition' to put out the Toronto Board and myself. He has sent private circulars to the Bondholders and is trying to get enough Proxies to carry the election, but of course he will not succeed. Yet it is irritating and gives us considerable trouble as it wd not do to be indifferent. I am obliged to go all the way into North Wales to see a large Bondholder whom he has poisoned and I am bothered every day with interviews in wh. I have to take the defensive! After all that I have done for them! However it is *only* an *annoyance* causing additional work and delay here,

but is of no real importance. Let Fred see this *but no one else is to know it.* The financial business here has been an *unusual* success. They *ought* to be very pleased in Toronto, but in Railways there is deuced little gratitude & I suppose that is the reason why as a general rule railway men take care of themselves![16]

The degree to which Cumberland regarded the Northern's English activities as his exclusive domain can be judged from the following comment to Wilmot: 'I had a hard day doing Bear leader to some Railway Dons from New York, taking them round and giving them a luncheon at the Club. They want to take all my new Bonds at a far better price than we can get for them in London which is most gratifying to me, as my London people after all my hard work and great success seem disposed to drive hard bargains and leave me in the lurch.'[17]

But in 1876, when Cumberland was called before a commission struck to examine the Northern's business practices,[18] the whole carefully balanced edifice of investment in the railway threatened to fall apart. In comparison with the Pacific Scandal of 1873, which brought down a government, Cumberland's own peccadilloes – namely, his responsibility for the Northern's questionable business dealings – were relatively insignificant, although the effect on Cumberland's professional life (and more particularly on his political career) was severe. For his long years of public service Cumberland might reasonably have expected a sinecure from the Conservatives. Instead, the door was shut in his face.

In his statements before the 1876 commission Cumberland attempted to justify the Northern's financial dealings, but his testimony was considered inconclusive. In 1877 Parliament therefore authorized a second inquiry to delve into the Northern's business dealings. Cumberland was called to testify on 16 March, the first day of hearings,[19] and among other questions was asked to explain why he had authorized a contribution of $2500 toward the parliamentary expenses of Sir John A. Macdonald during a dinner held in his honour in 1871, and then later ordered the amount entered on the books as a payment to a Northern board member, D.L.

Macpherson. An able line of questioning quickly established that Cumberland had made an improper political donation and then had attempted to conceal it. The questions also established that Cumberland had run the Northern as a personal fiefdom:

Q: If you had their [the other board members'] sanction why did you not bring it before them formally at a Board meeting?
A: Well, the administration of the company really was at that time largely personal.
Q: Personal to whom?
A: Personal to myself.
Q: What do you mean by yourself?
A: I mean to say that there was no 'stockholding' or 'stock' representations at this time.
Q: You were then, in fact, not only Manager, but you fulfilled the duties usually devolving on boards of Directors?
A: I should not like to say that I used the power of boards of Directors.
Q: I should like to know what you mean by saying the management was largely personal.
A: I will illustrate it. You will know better what I mean if I illustrate my position by the position of Mr. Broughton on the Great Western Railway, and the position Mr. Brydges held for many years on the Grand Trunk Railway.[20] These are systems of personal government beyond all question, and that is what I mean by the expression.
Q: I do not know what their position is with reference to local powers. Do you mean to say, in fact, that the local directors were merely figure heads? Do you mean to say that the real power was in your hands?
A: I mean to say that the local directors at that time did not charge themselves with the details of the work.
Q: What do you call the details? Was the payment of $2,500 for such a purpose a detail, a mere trifle? This is not an ordinary payment as you are aware. I want to know what you mean when you say that the board did not charge itself with mere details and because of that you did not bring this before them. What are details?
A: I call details, for instance, the passing of subordinate departmental accounts and that sort of thing. This is undoubtedly one of them; there is no use of mincing any matters about it. It was personal government at that time to a large extent, and the

board, until a somewhat recent date, did not charge itself with the details.
Q: The Board charges itself now, to a greater extent, with the control?
A: Yes, I should say so; I get more assistance now in the details than I ever did.
Q: How often did the Board meet in those days?
A: Irregularly. Sometimes once a month; and sometimes not so frequently. Not, however, in the average, more often than once in three weeks or a month.
Q: Who managed the affairs of the Company in the intervals between meetings?
A: I did.
Q: Entirely?
A: Yes, though sometimes there was consultation with the directors. They would from time to time drop in, and I would talk over matters with them.[21]

This line of questioning left no doubt about who was really responsible for the Northern's management: Cumberland, and Cumberland alone. And however much Cumberland attempted to defend his practices, the testimony spoke for itself:

Q: I find an entry in the Cash Book of 12 November 1869, 'Parliamentary Expenses, paid J.A. Macdonald's draft of 8 November, $500.' I also find in the Cash Book under date 29 November 1869, another entry, 'Parliamentary Expenses, paid draft of J.A. Macdonald of 10 November, $500.' What were these drafts for?
A: They were for $500 each.
Q: Yes, but what was the purpose?
A: I presume that they were in promotion of elections. These drafts, the effect of them, or anything related to them, has entirely escaped my memory. It was only since I returned to Toronto this last time, that I was made acquainted of them. My mind with regard to them, before that, was a perfect blank.[22]

Such a statement from a man who prided himself on being able to reel off reams of statistics defies belief.

Little support came from Toronto. The *Globe* published a sarcastic article on 28 March 1877 reporting that the inquiry was looking into allegations that the company had paid $380 for a presentation of silver to the managing director. Cumberland hotly contested this allegation, but the unsupportive tone of the *Globe* article is an example of how he could not count on backing even on his home turf. Cumberland was wounded deeply by the failure of his supposed friends in Toronto to come to his aid, and he expressed his feelings in a bitter letter to Wilmot written in November 1876:

You have known enough of all my present anxieties & how much they have absorbed all my time & thoughts & strength that you will not have been surprised at but will have forgiven my long silence. Now that in great measure they may be said to be over I thought I wd just write a short note as a sort of Herald of our comings for I am happy to say we purpose [*sic*] sailing from New York next Saturday the 11th by 'Britannic' and may hope to meet about the 20th. Judy and Mabel have had everything packed for the last three weeks or more – but the event has proved that I was right in remaining here until all was settled & now we shall start cheerfully instead of in the dumps – and in better health – for I have been far from well & am still suffering from a bad cough wh. however [Dr] Hodder assures me the sea air will drive away in a couple of days ... I suppose they have told you that my hair is very nearly *white*. I hope you won't object to an old worn out husband![23]

He had regained some of his composure by the following April, partly because he could sense a resolution drawing near, as he told Wilmot on the 11th of that month:

Just a line to say that we think that we begin to see daylight, as the Committee seems to be getting fatigued & to shew signs of a conclusion of the enquiry.

... I shd not be surprised if I leave here on Friday night for good & unless something untoward happens in the interval I shall return with my colors still flying altho perhaps a little soiled & torn as to what they might have been had men been faithful & true. I wonder whether I shall then be allowed rest?

... You can't tell how I yearn for quiet possession of Pen[darves].[24]

The inquiry submitted its evidence to Parlia-

ment ten days later. The report stated that the Northern Railway, under Cumberland's supervision, had indeed committed several offences.[25] At the heart of the matter was the railway's failure to pay interest on government loans dating back to 1853, although it had issued dividends to its stockholders. Instance after instance of creative financial diversions had come to light. In 1869, the inquiry found, Cumberland had diverted $1000 of the Northern's revenues to pay the campaign expenses of Sir Francis Hincks in his re-election bid in North Renfrew. Cumberland had instructed the bookkeeper to record this under 'Parliamentary Expenses.' The $2500 to Sir John A. Macdonald was also mentioned in the report. Another time, the railway had paid for stock in the Toronto *Mail* printing company, but again had entered the amount under 'Parliamentary Expenses.' Cumberland had overdrawn his personal account with the railway by more than $2000 to pay for his own re-election campaign, and then had simply written a cheque to cover the amount. In 1873 he had debited the company for more than $6000 to buy shares in the steamer *Chicora*, and, for good measure, for more than $4000 to cover election expenses. And in a feat of juggling remarkable even for the Northern's adept bookkeepers, the Northern had used the books of a subsidiary road, the Northern Extension Company, to hide the true assets of the Lake Couchiching Hotel Company (whose stockholders were mostly Northern directors). Thus when the Northern Railway took over the Northern Extension Company in June 1875, the Extension Company was 'owed' $45,235 by the Hotel Company (an amount written off on the Extension Company's books as a loss). When the hotel had burned down in 1876, the stockholders had collected $31,720.63 in insurance money. None of this had been registered on the Northern's books. Cumberland had hidden a valuable asset – the hotel – from the railway's government overseers, and done the same with the insurance money.

On 26 April 1877 the House of Commons, having received the inquiry's report, ruled that the Northern Railway should pay the government a fine of £45,000 within one year and a further $27,480.87 as repayment for sums improperly diverted from the company's books, and assign to the government the mortgage on the 180-acre site of the former Couchiching Hotel. It is difficult to know how badly these sanctions stung the Northern. Given that the company had avoided payments on its loans for so long, the penalties do not seem severe, and were probably treated as amounts simply to be written off by another exercise in bookkeeping legerdemain. The very next year the government subscribed $15,000 for mortgage bonds issued by the Northern, enabling the railway to take a lease on the North Simcoe Railway Company.[26] And although the Northern Scandal seems to have played a large role in preventing Cumberland from being awarded a sinecure by the Conservatives, he continued to operate with what appears to have been the same management style. Indeed, after 1877 the Northern was able to present respectable balance sheets, and in 1879 Cumberland engineered a takeover of the Hamilton and North Western Railway Co.

Perhaps his contemporaries should have the last word on his strengths and weaknesses as a railway man. In its obituary on Cumberland the Toronto *Mail* commented that he had been 'feared but respected by rival railway men,' and then gave good evidence of why he had commanded both fear and respect:

He struck out right and left in the most fearless manner in the interests of the road, and was always ready at a moment's notice to grapple with, and choke off, any opposition which raised its head in any quarter against the road. When the *personnel* of his board did not suit him he was always prepared with a hatful of proxies to decapitate any obnoxious member at his pleasure, and he used his power in this direction in the most fearless and uncompromising manner possible. As a natural consequence, enemies arose on all sides, and intrigues were freely set on foot for the purpose of getting rid of the managing director. Here again he was equal to the occasion, and as the English board stood to him through evil and through good report, the Canadian board had simply to do his bidding.[27]

With the same frankness the obituary then discussed some of Cumberland's machinations to ensure that the Northern would maintain its competitive advantage over rival roads:

He always kept ahead of the times, and lost no opportunity of originating feeders to the main line, With this object in view the Barrie and Orillia line was started by Col. Cumberland, who put forward other men as his agents, and by his superior talents he assisted the provisional board of directors in securing bonuses along the line of the road, until finally it was driven well into the Muskoka district, and then, when the road was ready to be operated, Col. Cumberland induced the directors to lease it to the Northern Railway Company, which now virtually owns the concern. Other feeders were projected in the same way, and Col. Cumberland soon had the satisfaction of seeing the resources of the country pouring over the main line to Toronto. Ever alive to the interests of his charge, he was up in arms against the narrow gauge roads when they were projected by Mr. Laidlaw [a rival manager], and he denounced the tramways, as he was pleased to term them, as inadequate to the requirements of the country. His foresight in this respect has been fully proved by the fact that the Toronto, Grey, and Bruce and the Toronto and Nipissing companies find themselves compelled to assimilate the gauge of their roads to that of the main lines. When Mr. Adam Brown and other enterprising Hamilton men began the agitation in favour of cutting into the traffic enjoyed by the Northern Railway, by the construction of the Hamilton and Northwestern road, with a terminus at Barrie, Col. Cumberland fought them inch by inch; but finally, when the Hamilton men won the day, and succeeded in constructing their line into Barrie, he accepted the situation, and showed his wisdom by inducing his former opponents to allow him to become managing director and to work the road, as the next best thing to be done when he could not prevent its construction.[28]

This obituary painted Cumberland as a capable strategist and a ruthless opponent, but also as a highly pragmatic businessman. When all of the evidence presented in this chapter is taken together, it makes a strong case for the argument that Cumberland not only controlled all aspects of the Northern, but that he managed his railway as well as or better than any of his contemporaries managed theirs.

CHAPTER SIX

Political Career

Cumberland entered politics for three reasons: to further the interests of the Northern Railway; because of loyalty to and affection for Sir John A. Macdonald and the Conservative Party; and because serving as a politician facilitated his access to the highest echelons of Canadian society. But the Northern's interests were foremost in his mind. This helps to explain, for instance, why he opted for the remote northern riding of Algoma instead of one in the Toronto region. The Northern's routes ran through the District of Algoma and he considered that it would be advantageous to represent one of the principal areas in which the railway needed good friends.

The first Ontario general election after confederation was held in August and September 1867.[1] Cumberland secured a seat for the Conservative Party in the new District of Algoma and served from December 1867 to February 1871. The next general election was held in March 1871, and Cumberland was again victorious.[2]

Speeches in the Ontario legislature during this period were usually lengthy and delivered in an affected and stilted manner. 'The gallant knight from Frontenac' was one typical stylistic circumlocution. Cumberland's speeches were in keeping with the general tenor of the House – they were often as much style as substance.[3] They typically focused on the parochial interests of his riding, even when ostensibly addressing a different topic. This was the case on 31 December 1867, when, the *Globe* reported, Cumberland delivered his maiden speech. 'Every lover of British institutions,' he observed,

must cordially unite in the adoption of the first clause of the Address [from the Throne]. Congratulations might very well be exchanged on such a happy occasion. To his mind it was a very happy event, that on the first exercise of their local authority, Her Majesty's representative who addressed them from the throne, should be an old and gallant soldier and a distinguished servant of the empire. It marked a most graceful and happy transition from the past to the present. He ... desired also to add his congratulations to the Speaker himself. In that gentleman the house recognized an exponent of those principles of moderation with which the revered name of Baldwin had always been connected. Nothing could be more happy than that the choice of the house should have fallen on such a man. The member for Algoma next proceeded to defend the Premier [the Reformer John Sandfield Macdonald], who, it had been alleged, had damaged the Reform party by the establishment of that government over which he presided. But he (Mr. Cumberland) believed that if Mr. Baldwin, the leader of the great Reform party, were alive, he would tread precisely in the same steps taken by the present leader of the Government ... Mr. Cumberland believed in party government, and believed it would quickly arise in the house, but it was not for hon. gentlemen to try and force it on before its time. As to his own position, he would take leave to say that he would not be pledged, then or at any other time, to a blind party adhesion. He had a bitter, unmeasured contempt for such a course. Mr. Cumberland, in commenting on the Address, regretted exceedingly that there had been no mention in it of dual representation [that is, of legislators sitting simultaneously in Parliament and in a provincial legislature]. That was a subject on which he was sure the house was unanimous; and hon. gentlemen occupying seats in both houses would be forced to elect at an early date for one or the other Legislature ... The hon. gentleman next alluded to the great importance of a good system of Crown land management – something the Province had not enjoyed – but would he hoped before long. It was said that free grants of agricultural lands were to be made to actual settlers. It would, he thought, be a great mistake if government hesitated to adopt the same liberal policy with respect to the mineral lands of the Province. He sketched the bad results of the Crown land policy in leaving the best mineral wealth of the North shore [of Lake Superior] untouched; while the United States had long since developed the Southern shore. He thought, too, that the Government should at once establish municipal institutions in the great region of Algoma; and the omission of any reference to the matter in the Speech was, he considered, a very grave one.[4]

Cumberland's other speeches in the House were likewise focused on the interests of his riding and were expressed in a similarly artificial style. In early January 1868 he addressed the House concerning the procedures of the standing committees on railways and private bills. A few days later he rose to respond to charges that the District of Algoma stood to receive more support from the government than it would have received by electing a representative of another party. His speech poked fun at those, such as his accuser, whose ambitions extended to federal politics, while cleverly evading his accuser's main point: 'Mr. Cumberland said he rose at some disadvantage, to make some observations on the course taken by his honourable friend from Bruce, inasmuch as his honourable friend enjoyed more than a Provincial reputation and had the benefits of a parliamentary experience of six weeks at Ottawa.'[5]

During his time in the legislature Cumberland introduced several bills. As might be expected, most of them were directed to the special inter-

ests of his northern riding: a bill to authorize and regulate the use of tractor engines on highways; a bill to incorporate the Rama Timber Corporation;[6] a bill to establish municipal institutions in Algoma. He was opposed to narrow-gauge railways.

Not all of the issues addressed by Cumberland were connected with the interests of his riding or of the Northern. In January 1868 he spoke, for instance, in favour of greater government support for suffering Nova Scotia fishermen. Still, most of his speeches were limited to his riding's concerns. Thus on the day that he spoke on the plight of the fishermen, he also made a lengthy statement calling for reform of mineral rights legislation affecting the Algoma region. Two days later he asked the government whether it planned to introduce a system of municipal government to Algoma. Such speeches paint him as the perfect small-riding politician.

He did, however, speak out on issues of a more general kind, as in 1871, when he supported his old friend Egerton Ryerson's bitterly contested Common School Improvement Bill. In keeping with Ryerson's long-standing interest in public education, an interest that Cumberland shared, the bill envisioned free public schools, compulsory attendance, standardized qualifications for both teachers and school inspectors, and municipal grants for secondary as well as primary schools. Cumberland said, 'If there are any two measures or two names that shed lustre over the country they were Baldwin's Municipal Bill [of 1849] and Ryerson's education bill.'[7] Politics thus finally gave Cumberland the opportunity to voice in an important public forum his support for the civic initiatives that he had championed in his speeches to the mechanics' institutes during the early 1850s.[8]

In 1868 Cumberland was asked to stand for election in the federal riding of Niagara, but he told Wilmot that he would resist the temptation:

Some Niagara people came over to offer me that seat in the House of Commons. Angus Morrison is to be collector of Customs here & so vacates his seat, and John A. insists upon my taking it. My present intention is not to do anything of the kind so don't be alarmed: but the position is very embarrassing & I am in absolute dread of being forced into the service if they can find no other man who can secure it which I have insisted upon their trying to do. Please don't talk about this – and don't get into a perspiration – I shall avoid the thing & fight against it to the last.[9]

Nothing apparently came of attempts to enlist Cumberland for federal office until 1871. Despite his earlier objections to dual representation, when the member for the federal riding of Algoma, Wemyss Mackenzie Simpson, was appointed Indian commissioner for the North-West Territories, Cumberland ran unopposed as a Conservative in the June by-election for Simpson's seat, and entered Parliament in April of the next year.[10] The prime minister had had a direct hand in assisting Cumberland to obtain the Conservative nomination in Algoma, and Cumberland expressed his appreciation as follows:

My dear Sir John:
I have to thank you very warmly and sincerely for the assistance you so kindly rendered in clearing my way in Algoma. I really feel deeply satisfied & indebted by the zealous aid so cordially given to me by so many kind friends and as chief amongst them especially to yourself. I was elected by acclamation & may now think myself as strong in possession.[11]

Cumberland did little to distinguish himself in the House of Commons itself. He does not appear in the index to the record of Commons proceedings for the period that he served.[12] Nevertheless, by June 1872, when a new law required him, as a provincial legislator, to resign his seat in Parliament, Cumberland had won a number of important friends. It has been written that in 1871, following the admission of British Columbia into Confederation, Sir John called on Cumberland for his advice concerning the establishment of the Pacific Railway – a claim that has not been documented, but which seems reasonable enough.[13] And even if this one instance cannot be verified, it is clear that Cumberland became a trusted confidant of the prime minister. Numerous letters between the two men have survived, and show that

Cumberland both gave advice to Sir John and received it from him.

Sir John relied on Cumberland for advice on railway matters and helped promote the cause of the Northern.[14] The two men had conducted negotiations concerning government support for the Northern well before Cumberland was elected to federal office. In 1868, for instance, Cumberland pressed Sir John to support a bill providing for new capital for the railway.[15] Sir John, in turn, helped ensure passage of the bill. In thanking Sir John for his help, Cumberland wrote:

Let me express my sincere and grateful acknowledgments for the support you so generously gave to in relation to the 'Northern' Bill just passed.
... I believe the Act to be a thoroughly sound and good one in the Public interests; and its ... acceptance by Parliament would seem to warrant that view. Many a better measure however has been lost for want of a friend – this one has been carried because it found one in yourself.[16]

Cumberland occasionally made demands on Sir John, some related to personal matters, others connected with the Northern. He succeeded, for instance, in having Wilmot's brother, Tom Bramley, appointed as a bookkeeper in the receiver-general's office.[17]

Sir John expected favours in return. In 1869 he asked Cumberland to go to Sault Ste Marie to help in the establishment of a militia company there.[18] In January 1871 he asked that a Conservative member of Parliament from Toronto, Angus Morrison, be added to the Northern's board. The prime minister told Cumberland that 'You will find him of very considerable value and he will be very grateful and so will I.'[19] Morrison was duly elected to the board. Three months later he presented a petition to Parliament in favour of the Northern. By early in the following year, however, it appears that he may have been asked to cede his place on the board to another man, for in a letter of February 1872 Sir John urged Cumberland to keep Morrison on the board, observing:

The next session of Parliament at Ottawa will be a

Railway Session in which all Railway interests will be discussed, including the extension westward to the Sault as well as along the North Shore of the Lakes to Fort Garry & the Pacific. The various rival projects will be fought out on the floor of the House and the weakest will go to the wall. I look upon it therefore as of the first importance that the Northern should be well represented in the House of Commons ...

... With you and Angus both in the House, there will not be much danger of Northern Road interests being neglected or set aside.[20]

Whether Morrison remained on the board is unknown.

As noted above, Cumberland was forced to resign his federal seat in June 1872, although he retained his provincial seat until 1874.[21] It appears that he acutely regretted leaving federal politics and fully expected to re-enter the federal arena when an appropriate opportunity arose. In 1873 he wrote two letters to Sir John concerning the prospect of re-entering politics via the by-election for the safe seat of West Toronto, where the sitting Conservative member, John Crawford, had died. In the first letter, written in August, he feigned indifference:

My dear Sir John:
In anticipation of a possible vacancy in West Toronto I am being appealed to as an available man. The constituency is not a difficult one: there are several men who wd make perfectly safe candidates assuming that the orange and green [Irish factions] can be brought together & personal jealousies avoided; so that I am not *a necessity* – i.e., the seat can be secured without me.

... I am told however that both colors would be quite satisfied with this child.

... You need not reply to this because I am not *seeking* a seat, & West Toronto is not in danger, so that you are entirely free both on personal & political grounds.[22]

Cumberland's apparent indifference to the prospect of a federal seat was belied by the obvious regret he expressed in his next letter to Sir John, in October, after learning that another man had been chosen to represent West Toronto for the Conservatives. His desire to run again for federal office was unmistakable, as was his belief that political life would confer on him a social status otherwise unobtainable. Also palpable was his admiration for Sir John:

The disappointment by which I am oppressed in regard to West Toronto is simply *crushing*. I suppose it is the last chance I shall ever have of joining again in public life or of making a name – and added to the *selfish* regrets is another scarcely less, that I am deprived of joining in supporting you through a struggle in which I should have [joined] with all my heart. That it will eventuate in success for you I hope does not admit of a doubt. For a doubt about it implies such black ingratitude that he will be a bold man who thereafter wd care to serve the Country. I shall look most anxiously for news – & be what it may – whether it lifts you, as I believe it will, to higher Eminence & greater power, or releases you from what in such a case would be a hateful service, you have & will have no more faithful and attached friend.[23]

Of Cumberland's attachment there can be doubt. But what about Sir John's? Was he cannily distancing himself from Cumberland? The Northern Railway scandal was about to break, and perhaps Sir John foresaw a time when association with Cumberland would be a liability. That Cumberland never received any sinecure from Sir John would appear to support the supposition that the prime minister was making an effort to distance himself. As it happened, an old acquaintance of Cumberland's, John Beverley Robinson, ran as the Conservative candidate for West Toronto in the 1874 election – and lost. T. Moss, a Liberal, won the previously safe Conservative seat.[24]

Although Cumberland entered politics to forward the interests of the Northern Railway, he came to believe in Sir John as a man and as a politician, although this did not prevent him from continuing to further the interests of the Northern. But his political aspirations were never realized on the scale that he had dreamed of, and when the prime minister's favour went elsewhere, Cumberland decided that political life was not worth the effort, and the railway reclaimed his full attention.

CHAPTER SEVEN

Later Personal Life

The two previous chapters treated the railway and politics and ranged widely across Cumberland's professional life during the 1860s and later. This chapter is devoted to considering aspects of Cumberland's personal and social life during the same period. After 1860 Cumberland enjoyed increasing social status and came to occupy a number of prestigious positions in Toronto society. In the 1860s militia companies were formed in Toronto and elsewhere because of a justifiable concern with the Fenians, those Irish-American nationalists who invaded Canadian territory on several occasions. Prominent Canadians such as the Toronto engineer and financier Casimir Gzowski took the lead in financing the formation of militia companies. Cumberland did likewise when he presided in December 1861 over a meeting held at the Mechanics' Institute, at which the formation of a local regiment from the mechanics of the city was enthusiastically approved. This regiment was initially known as the 10th Battalion Volunteer Militia Rifles, Canada. In January Cumberland became the regiment's commanding officer, with the rank of lieutenant-colonel, a position he retained until 1864, when he was made honorary colonel.[1] In April 1863 the regiment was renamed the 10th Royal Regiment of Toronto Volunteers, although later it was known more familiarly as the 10th Royal Grenadiers of Toronto or simply the 10th Royals.[2]

The volunteer regiments soon assumed a prominent place in the life of Toronto, where they drilled in the public squares, their colours swirling around them. In July 1863 Wilmot recorded in her diary that 'I presented two flags to the 10th Royals. Fred Commanding. Col. Robertson reviewed the troops. In the evening about 200 people came. Dancing on the lawn.'[3] The officers – Cumberland among them – were photographed wearing handsome uniforms. Cumberland even had himself photographed in a winter uniform that would have been suitable for a temperature of thirty below.

The militia companies did more than provide an impressive spectacle in the city's public squares. They fully expected to be called on to defend their country. Wilmot's diary is full of references to Cumberland and others preparing for battle. Eventually, during the Fenian invasion of June 1866, Cumberland was called to active duty at Fort Erie, a development that alarmed Wilmot considerably. Fortunately he never saw action.

After June 1866, the militia companies played more of a symbolic and ceremonial than a defensive role. It would be wrong, however, to downplay the social significance of the militia companies just because they never again engaged in battle. In fact their existence was an important demonstration of social cohesiveness.

It is also noteworthy that by the early 1860s Cumberland had enough prestige to sponsor his own militia company – evidence of his remarkable ascent of the Toronto social ladder. The number of prominent men who became involved in the militia during the 1860s testifies to the fluidity of mid-Victorian Canadian society.

7.1 Photograph of Frederic Cumberland, 1860s.
MTL/BR, Picture Collection T-13,682

The implied promise to middle-class immigrants – that they could rise as far as their talents and ambitions would carry them – was realized for Cumberland, Gzowski, Fleming, and many others. Seen in this light, Cumberland's move 'away' from architecture should probably be regarded rather as a move toward increasing social prestige and widespread respect in Toronto. Cumberland revelled in the prestige of his rank. It is revealing that Cumberland never relinquished his honorary colonelcy, for his rank was tangible evidence that he had been right to emigrate, right to chance the unknown in Canada. Had he stayed in England, he would likely never have been more than a drafting room supervisor. In Canada he mounted the social ladder to such a height that he was able to assume roles that in England would have been restricted to the gentry and aristocracy.

Even after the Fenian crisis had passed, Cumberland not only retained his military title but also often wore his military dress. He seemed to grow into his uniform, developing a statesmanlike yet dashing bearing. It was widely conceded that he cut a fine figure (Fig. 7.1). Fraternal societies and politicians alike found him an attractive person and actively courted his support. A gregarious and sociable person, he had never abandoned his earlier interests in the mechanics' institutes and other cultural bodies. In 1865–6 he served again as president of the Toronto Mechanics' Institute. He also filled a number of honorary positions for charitable organizations, including the St George's Society (a charitable organization). He was a member of the synod of the Anglican Church in Toronto, and in September 1866 even allowed his house to be used for voting for a new bishop. He served on several corporate boards[4] and was regarded as an excellent speaker. During a public meeting following a fire at the Gooderham & Worts distillery in 1869, for instance, he gave a speech of 'great eloquence.'[5]

Cumberland was particularly active as a Freemason, which provided another outlet for his enthusiasm for rituals and fraternal association. Such an interest was in no way unusual, for the Masonic lodges were places where business and fellowship merged imperceptibly. Most Toronto architects were Freemasons, as were many businessmen. Cumberland joined St Andrew's Lodge No. 16 in 1853 and rapidly ascended the Masonic hierarchy.[6] After serving as a warden for several years, he was installed as a worshipful master in 1857 and elected district deputy grand master in 1858. Later he was also a member of the St John's Chapter of Royal Arch Masons and of the Geoffrey de St Aldemar Preceptory of Knights Templar.[7] By 1878 he had become master of St Andrews Lodge and deputy master of the Toronto District. Such evocative titles hint at the degree of ceremony and ritual that filled the Masonic lodges.

On the professional front Cumberland did not entirely abandon his interest in architecture and engineering. Although his partnership with Storm had effectively come to an end by 1862,[8] in May of that year Cumberland attended the inaugural meeting of the Association of Surveyors, Civil Engineers, and Architects held at the Montreal Mechanics' Institute. He was elected to the Engineers' Division council and board of examiners (but not to any positions within the Architects' Division).[9]

During the 1860s Cumberland was at the peak of his public reputation and received some gratifying public tributes, for instance in December 1866 while in London on Northern Railway business, when he stayed with his old friend the architect Fred Porter and found himself having to give an impromptu speech. It was very well received, as he related in a letter to Wilmot:

I have breakfasted with Fred Porter who is as good a fellow as ever. He delivered an invitation for me to dine with the Clothworkers Company last night & a most sumptuous & magnificent affair it was – 'truly' regal. There were some great Dons there & the service & music exquisite. I enclose the programmes. The loving cup that was sent round was the gift of Sam Pepys in 1670 & the work of Benvenuto Cellini. Judge of my horror when after the Toast of the Army Navy & Volunteers the Toastmaster's stentorian voice exclaimed 'Gentlemen I crave silence for Colonel Cumberland in reply.' So I was in for it & made my maiden speech in the City of London & being in good voice & pluck I managed to bring down the house. The celebrated Mr. Justice – Sir James – Willes; Alderman Rose; Major of the City Volunteers; Sir Jno Musgrove and a lot more came to me in the drawing room afterwards & showered all sorts of compliments & kindnesses upon me & my poor speech has put me down for many dinners. When Sir James Willes came up to me he said, 'I have come to introduce myself to you as a volunteer & private in the Devil's own – for I want to thank you for the excellent speech you made for us.' So Fred Porter was delighted & I came home with a peacock's feather in my hat.[10]

During the 1860s and 1870s the Cumberlands continued to enjoy an active social life shoehorned into the times between Cumberland's frequent business trips and Wilmot's increasingly numerous trips to England. Their four daughters were growing up and starting to entertain suitors and travel on their own. In the summers Wilmot frequently vacationed at Beach House near Boston, where Cumberland joined her when he could. In 1863 they sent Barlow to school in England, where he studied at Cheltenham College, a private school run by Sir Charles Barry's son Alfred. Barlow returned to Toronto the following year and enrolled at Osgoode Hall, passing the initial course.[11]

Letters written during the summer of 1864 provide an idea of the nature of Cumberland and Wilmot's relationship at this time. The first letter was written by Cumberland in Toronto to Wilmot at Beach House. In it he said he had been to a picnic at Aurora at which 1500 people were present; there had been a thunderstorm; he had a rash; he had played croquet and drunk iced lemonade; there was no news from Barlow. He remonstrated with her for complaining that desultory if newsy letters of this kind were less enjoyable than love letters and that he had missed her birthday. He argued that true love is transformed by time into affection. The letter was peculiarly truculent but also touching in its reference to a birthday present of a prayer book, so many years before:

What do you mean by 'a real nice letter' a long one – full of news – or a soft one full of love, which is no news? News is worth telling because it is novel and won't keep, for it changes every day. Love is scarcely worth talking about, for, if it be true, there is not change or novelty about it and the older it gets the less it will change & the less need for its recital. To ask for an assurance of love is to doubt it. To give an assurance of it is to acknowledge a fear that it is not believed or appreciated. I think affection worth a dozen Loves – the first misses the absent companion, pleasant hours dimmed by separation, thoughts with no one to share them, mutual comforts withdrawn, the habits of quiet enjoyment broken & displaced, the system of life disturbed & … want & yearning weighing depressing changing & overcrowding everything & restlessness only left – the latter is a mere excitement in which impulse is always – sensuality very often – an element; it is erratic & unquiet & unsettled, selfish ever & ready to smack its lips over the honey of whatever pretty flower it lights upon. Affection may be likened to the steady sober settled & stable faith of the Church of England and love to the bawling braying sensational excitable & changeable system of the Plymouth saints or Mormon Sinners. Affection can live in its clothes, but Love would die if it didn't sometimes go naked.

Which do you yearn for? 'A little of both' I fancy, and so we'll compromise by adopting affection in its night shirt! Just think of it. Is not affection *Love refined*, with all its good intensified, and all its evil weakened – Love is *all-absorbing* it has one object & that one, concentrates all its aims & all its power, & I have no objection to the devotion *for a time*. But fortunately it doesn't *last* – new duties develop themselves, selfish efforts become essential – the wants of others supersede the thoughts of our own & to supply those wants new ambitions are opened out & he who was a lovesick idler *only* becomes something more & something better – his energies take new channels & higher force, and his heart settles down upon its old object with the higher more temperate more real & lasting sentiment & much more comfortable & satisfying habits of affection. We cease to swear by the apple of our wives [*sic*] eyes, to be excited by her pretty ankle & to lisp sensuous nothings into her ear. We walk & talk with her as our rational companion & ever & anon but not always we draw her to our natured reason & go roving back with her into the early extacies [*sic*] of Love's embrace. She is our daily comfort and our *periodical luxury*! But we cannot lie all day at her feet, all night in her luscious lap, as we dreamed of when we first loved her. And if we could she would soon tire of us in *both positions*. I wonder which you would choose were the choice available – my taxing ... insatiate thoughtless Love as it was of old, or old Lover – that *attractive* (!) dashing daredevil scapegrace that wooed & won you – or the matured ambitious businessman Paterfamilias who is just as fond of you as ever he was but has ceased writing sonnets to your eyes and turned some of his thoughts to daily duty & the Almighty Dollar. Write me a 'real nice letter' & say whether you yearn for your young Lover or your old husband – the first with all his *merits* & the last with all his faults. But remember – if you elect to put one back 18 years you must take the consequences which are awful to contemplate. I will ... and present you with a prayerbook on your birthday! ... As to the real nice letter I will get one ready & bring it with me – we will then celebrate your birthday & you make a new start in life with a prayerbook given not by a stripling of a young Lover – but by your loving husband.[12]

During the later 1860s an ever darker cloud

formed over their personal life. Wilmot seemed to be tired of hearing about Cumberland's endless business deals. She chided him for spending so much time away from home. He found this exasperating: 'I never go there [to Ottawa] unless I have something to do, and I shall always go there whenever I have anything to do which is worth doing & cannot be done elsewhere – objections therefore are only irritating & can have no effect with a man who thinks – as I do – that I know my own business best.'[13] The imperious tone of this letter hints at a rift between them. While in London in 1866 he criticized her for not having written, and she him for having left all the family finances in the hands of Barlow, who apparently was unnecessarily tight with money. In December he responded to a letter from her that was full of recriminations about financial matters and Cumberland's flirting with women. Cumberland complained, 'What a dreadful thing it is that no girl can mix in the same society with myself but at the expense of being attacked by you as tho' she were immoral or immodest. However let it pass as a hopeless monomania as miserable as it is false.'[14]

Relations between them deteriorated further, to such an extent that in September 1869 Cumberland even asked Wilmot's brother Tom to arrange for Wilmot to return to her family:

I have borne for some years and with what patience I could a system of treatment which few men of any mind or spirit would have permitted. I shall bear it no longer. I am entitled to the rest and comforts of a home, I work hard & successfully and the only place where I am not permitted to be happy – where I am vilified and slandered and irritated & disgraced [–] is in my own house, and the only living person who slanders and disgraces me is my own wife!

... I am not afraid of the verdict of our relatives, for I know that I have been an object of sympathy and commiseration to most of them for many a long day – *I* am therefore quite prepared for the (it seems) inevitable solution, and I commit Wilmot's interests to your brotherly care, prepared to do for & towards her all that can be fairly asked of me in this miserable conclusion for which I am not responsible.[15]

Had they always been an unaffectionate

couple, we might simply regard this letter as evidence of the inevitable drifting apart of two untethered ships. But they were romantic lovers in their early married life. What had happened? The documentary record is incomplete: none of Wilmot's letters survive and her diary is laconic and unhelpful. The sources of tension between them that we hear about are her allegedly fierce jealousy, her allegedly dilatory correspondence when he was away, and his belief that she was irresponsible with money. Wilmot was a dilatory correspondent, but Cumberland expected too much. She had five children at home and was busy enough with her charges. Moreover, Cumberland was such a gifted and voluminous correspondent – twenty-page letters were not unusual – that he might have been disappointed with anyone. The charge that Wilmot was irresponsible with money had substance; there are several instances where she apparently borrowed small amounts from one of the Northern's London board members but did not repay them. Nothing suggests that there were grounds for Wilmot's jealousy. There is no evidence of Cumberland having had extramarital affairs, and I doubt that he did.

What, then, underlay Cumberland's vehemence and his statement that he had suffered for a long time? And what about the suggestive phrase 'disgraced ... in my own house'? This can only refer to a private (and disgraceful) activity such as drinking.[16] No other possibility fits the evidence so well. But given that we have only Cumberland's point of view, it is probably best to be circumspect in asserting this.

By the mid-1870s Cumberland and Wilmot had evolved almost separate lives. They had begun to find the big house a burden, and apparently shut it down for long periods of time. Wilmot lived at the Rossin Hotel in Toronto for months on end,[17] and snippets from letters suggest that Cumberland was spending much of his time at his club.[18] Evidently, however, Wilmot did not leave Cumberland. The couple even seem to have regained their former mutual regard. By 1875, when Wilmot went abroad with their daughters Connie and Florrie, the letters were once again cordial and newsy.

The strained relations between Cumberland

and Wilmot during the 1860s might help explain why Cumberland looked outside the home for friendship and personal fulfilment. But there was a more important reason for this. We have seen that Canadian society during these years was extraordinarily fluid. A man such as Cumberland could rise from modest origins to a titled position, and he charted his trajectory well. His role as honorary colonel of the 10th Royals, and his earlier close acquaintance with Governor General Head during the 1850s (see chapter 11) made him admirably suited for service on ceremonial occasions involving visiting dignitaries. Even while immersed in party politics Cumberland served in October and November 1868 as aide-de-camp to Lord Monck, then governor general. As such, Cumberland arranged itineraries and ensured that the governor general's tours and meetings progressed smoothly. From 1872 to 1878 he served on several occasions as an aide-de-camp to Lord and Lady Dufferin.[19] He apparently performed his duties very ably, for there are frequent and flattering references to Cumberland in Lady Dufferin's journal. The governor general and his wife regarded him as a witty dinner companion and a capable organizer. Clearly he enjoyed their confidence. The evidence even permits us to say that he was a close friend.

At first glance, it is mysterious why Cumberland should have wished to attach himself to the symbolic representatives of Britain's political ties to Canada. As we saw earlier, his letters of the 1850s were full of anti-British snubs. He considered himself a Canadian; he was glad to be free of England, with its class distinctions and limited possibilities for advancement. On the other hand, there had been a substantial change since the 1850s both in his personal circumstances and in Canadian public opinion toward the British connection. Canadians no longer saw themselves as inhabitants of a neglected colony, but as the proud citizens of a great empire. Cumberland himself came to regard the governor general as the representative of an essentially *Canadian* political institution. Then, too, Cumberland was now one of Canada's elite, and as he saw his contemporaries honoured by the sovereign, he came to believe that his own career could be crowned with a knighthood as well.

It must be admitted, however, that the documentary evidence is somewhat confusing on the subject of a knighthood. Lady Dufferin recorded in 1876 that Cumberland declined the honour when Lord Dufferin asked him whether he would like to be recommended for a knighthood. Why he did this is difficult to determine. Perhaps it was a case of false modesty that misfired. Some of Cumberland's contemporaries, such as Sir Daniel Wilson, also refused knighthoods; Wilson only accepted his because it was thrust on him.[20] Perhaps it was customary to demur until pressed, and Dufferin took Cumberland's refusal too seriously. If this was so, Cumberland quickly came to regret his decision, and sought new opportunities for a knighthood.

By 1877 Cumberland was planning to resign as aide-de-camp. He was still running a business; he was getting older; his health was becoming shaky. He submitted his letter of resignation in November. Lady Dufferin recorded in her journal that the governor general was not willing to accede to this request immediately, and that he deferred consideration of the matter until December, when he hoped to be in Toronto and could speak to Cumberland about the appropriateness of his plan:

Taken by surprise, Lord Dufferin replied asking that the subject be not mentioned until further communication. Early in December, while in Toronto, he attempted to see Mr. Cumberland personally. The latter was in Hamilton on business, but had left some verses, marking the end of their lengthy association and their common interest in poetry. The following note was received at the Cumberland home:

My Dear Cumberland:

I cannot tell you how pleased I am. They are excellent, and I want to show them to Lady Dufferin. Won't you let me take them with me, or at all events you will send them after me to Ottawa?

I am so vexed at missing you. I heard that you had been away, or I should have asked myself last night to dinner. Tonight, I dine at the Lieutenant Gover-

nor's. I wonder whether they will have the happy inspiration to have asked you.

I will not say goodbye, as I trust we will meet yet. Yours Ever, D.[21]

They were able to meet after all. Wilmot's diary for 10 December records, 'Fred dined at Government House to meet Lord Dufferin.' Lady Dufferin noted that 'While there more poetry was personally presented and the matter of Cumberland's resignation agreed upon.'[22]

Although Cumberland had fully intended to resign his position in 1877, when the Marquis of Lorne became governor general in 1878 he sought to continue as aide-de-camp and asked for Sir John A. Macdonald's help in that regard:

My dear Sir John:

For twenty years I have served and followed you *in* and *out* of Parliament – and during the last five I have suffered more severely for my fidelity than any other member of your party. Looking back over that long period, whilst I remember many acts of kindness to the interests I serve, I think I am right in saying that I have *never once* appealed to you upon any matter *personal* to *myself.*

I may therefore perhaps venture with more boldness to say that when, as very soon, you are consulted as to Honorary appointments to His Excellency's staff I should be much obliged if you would promote my appointment to it.

You will readily understand that with me this is very much a matter of sentiment, and knowing all the circumstances as you do, you will I am sure cordially sympathize with my feeling, and will admit that I have a strong and peculiar claim to your good offices. I enclose for your perusal several – and of very many – letters received from my old chief [Lord Dufferin],[23] in order that you may understand my *personal* relations, and the better appreciate the ... political fears to which he and I were both for a time victims: for he subsequently seized every public occasion for personally distinguishing me – *even* on his recent arrival here, sending *the mayor* to request that during his sojourn here I would 'serve upon his staff' – which I did.

Cumberland then related some of the suffering

he had experienced in the political arena during the 1860s and 1870s:

It is indisputably true that all the assaults made upon *me* were aimed at *you* and at the *party* for political effect, and gauging my position by the example of *others from my class* I never doubted – indeed *I knew* – that I could have purchased personal immunity by treachery to my friends.

But they measured me wrong. I fought the battle out and if I signally failed it is against each of us – altho' my company was robbed – and *now* I confidently ask you to do me a favour and a *justice* in a matter to which *on all other grounds also* I have a leading title: by actual service as a militia man, and by the confidential favour of every governor general from Lord Elgin's time until today.

Pray read the enclosed letters and return them to me as I value them.[24]

If Cumberland had a distant knighthood in his sights, he may also have had a more immediate goal – the rehabilitation of his political reputation. Cumberland may have thought that if Sir John recommended him to the governor general, the world would see that Sir John still regarded him as one of the party faithful. A renewal of his prestigious appointment would be adequate compensation for his suffering in the political arena. The ardour with which Cumberland sought some sort of continuing recognition was reflected in the anguish of his letters. But Sir John may have sensed Cumberland's hidden motivations, and he decided against awarding him an honorary appointment of any kind. Perhaps Sir John associated Cumberland too closely with past embarrassment and scandal.

To Cumberland's credit, he retained his affectionate respect for Sir John, and even regained some of his old composure and self-confidence in his letters to the prime minister. This is shown by a letter to Sir John of March 1879, in which Cumberland, then in London looking after Northern Railway business, provided as acute an analysis of financial affairs as anything he wrote during the early years of their acquaintance:

Financially things look very hopeless here except in relation to government securities. As to Canadian Railways, every one wants to get *out* and no one wants to go *in* & my impression is that no more money is to be had. The multiplication of lines under subsidies of the Provincial Governments – and the utter absence of any protection to investments – have created much disgust and distrust & *now* the cool proposition to create a permanent Railway Commission above the Law and from whose dicta there shall be no appeal named seem to indicate – were such a proposal listened to – that the general law and special legislation offered no security for investments made under them. However I tell my people that in your hands we are safe & that things will come round all right with a little patience.

I am glad to tell you – if you are not already advised – that Brydges [a fellow railway man] is well and comfortably shelved – Land Commissioner of Hudson's Bay Co. – for which he largely thanks you. Lucky fellow. I wish someone would kick me upstairs, but I have good influence here & I expect to get the appointment of Master to the Shoreditch Workhouse, which *to me* will be peace and promotion.

Many thanks for yr note wh it was very kind of you to write. I am much too fond of you, & too much appreciate your difficulties, to add to the number of 'seekers' or *suckers* by whom you are oppressed.[25]

The reference to Brydges can possibly be read as another oblique appeal for an appointment, but if so it was couched in terms that Sir John could ignore if he wished. Which is what he did.

There is an ironic postscript to Cumberland's attempts to obtain an honorary position from Sir John. In 1879 Sir John did appoint an aide-de-camp to the governor general, but it was Cumberland's former client and subsequent business rival Casimir Gzowski, who was knighted that same year.[26] Cumberland, it seems, paid a heavy price for his involvement in the Northern scandal.

The last year of Fred Cumberland's life, 1881, opened auspiciously. Wilmot recorded in her diary on 12 January that 'We had a large dance in the evening about 200 were present we retired about 2 a.m.'[27] Cumberland was president of the Toronto Cricket Club that year, and he helped organize the Ontario Jockey Association. He still enjoyed a game of billiards when he was home.

His business pace remained as hectic as ever. On 31 January, Wilmot recorded, 'Fred went to Barrie & slept there.' On 2 February 'Fred left by early train up the line and returned at noon. He dined in the evening with the R.C. Archbishop of Toronto.' On 10 February 'Fred [came] home to dinner and returned to his office afterwards until 10 p.m.'

Let us recapture the rest of the year principally by recourse to Wilmot's diary:

17 February Fred dined with the Speaker at the House of Parliament.
18 Fred home to dinner busy writing in the evening.
19 Fred went to Hamilton and returned by 11 p.m. train, which was delayed until 3:30 a.m.
22 [Cumberland left for Ottawa by 7 p.m. train.]
25 [Cumberland returned from Ottawa.]
 1 March [Cumberland left for Ottawa.]
 9 Telegraph from Fred in Ottawa saying his bill had passed.
13 [Cumberland returned from Ottawa.]
16 Fred not very well & remained at home in the morning. He left by 7 p.m. train for Ottawa.
17 Telegraph from Fred in Ottawa that his bill had passed the Senate.
18 Fred returns from Ottawa.
 7 April [Cumberland left for New York to board the *Adriatic* en route for England.] [T]he girls went to the station to see him off ... We sent in the evening birthday cards to meet Fred on his birthday on the 10th on board ship.

Early in February Wilmot remarked that Cumberland was suffering from what was initially diagnosed as indigestion. All that spring he fought bronchitis and heart disease, and he left for England despite still feeing ill.[28] Although he sent a telegram on 26 May saying that he was well again, Wilmot was not convinced:

I have been very fidgetty [*sic*] about *you*[;] your letters quite alarmed me, & when I found you had not sent a cable message on business that week, I made sure you were confined to the house still and so I cabled, and my mind was relieved the day *after*,

[when I received] your cable. I saw in the paper you were present at the Canada Club dinner ... I hope you will be all right, and that you will be careful of your stomach & not *dine* too much. I must not let you go off to England again without *me* as you always have an attack of illness. You were ill each time, but with Julia or when we were there you were *not* ill. So prepare yourself for a companion next time.[29]

In the same letter she related some positive news: a theatrical that she had been involved in had been a success, and afterwards there had been a cheerful dinner for sixteen that did not finish till two; the garden was in splendid order; she had bought a new carpet. All seemed to be going well. She also mentioned that she had gone to see the 10th Royals troop the colours. That experience evoked mixed feelings:

We all walked over to the Park & saw the 10th troop the Colors. They looked very well & did wonderfully considering Dawson very fussy wheeling them about but Graset lay quiet & soldierly. The Band good & all very promising. I felt quite glad to see the old colors again, and yet I felt very sad to think of bygone days when I presented them & to think now of the old woman standing in the crowd of dirty children looking on in past glories unknown to anyone.

It would be easy to read this letter as a sign of worse things to come. Its contents lend themselves to the inference that the Cumberlands had slipped into the dismal desuetude of advancing age. What makes such an interpretation untrue is that Cumberland was still an effective and dynamic man of business, though he was seriously ill. By the time he returned to Toronto on 25 June he was terminally ill. Wilmot reported that 'Fred arrived from England at 4:30 p.m. Very poorly with asthma & bronchitis.' The next day was a Sunday, with 'Fred at home and a little better.' On Monday he was 'very poorly all day.'

Five days later, on 2 July, Dr Machell, the family doctor, called. By then, Cumberland could no longer maintain the pretence of being well:

 2 July Dr. Machell came to see Fred who was not as well.
 3 Fred very poorly.

4   Dr. Machell came & again in the evening. Fred very poorly all day – did not come down until 6 p.m.

5   Fred very poorly suffering all day ... Fred had his bed moved into the library.

On 6 July Wilmot sat up with him all night. He slept fitfully. Over the following days a disturbing rhythm established itself: hopes for recovery were entertained every morning, and dashed every evening, when his suffering intensified:

9   July Fred very weak all day & did nothing.

10   Fred had a very bad night. Sent to Dr. Machell at 3 a.m.

11   [B]etter in some respects but *very* weak.

During the following week he appeared to rally. On Sunday the 17th he even managed to sit on the veranda for a time and to see two friends. And on the 20th he seemed much stronger:

21 July Fred much better. In the afternoon I drove him to the Yacht Club Wharf & he went to the Island House returning at 6:15 to dinner.

22   Fred, Connie, Miss Whitehead, Phina & baby & I went by *Chicora* to Niagara and returned at night. Dr. Machell did not come.

24   Fred dined in the library by himself.

25   Fred had a very bad night of spasms which continued all day.

26   Fred a little easier though only kept under by opiates and injected morphia.

27   Fred very weak all day no change.

28   Fred very bad. Drs. Temple & Machell came twice.

29   Fred very ill all day. Dr. Machell came in the morning and injected morphine. He came again at 2 p.m. accompanied by Dr. Temple & Dr. H.H. Wright. Machell came again in the evening & injected morphine. Poor dear Fred a great sufferer.

On 30 July Wilmot admitted to her diary for the first time that this might be a terminal illness:

30 July Fred very ill all day. Very little hope. Dr.

Machell came twice.

31   All very anxious ... We moved Fred into my bedroom.

She went to Grace Church and prayed.

1 August Just the same ... Caroline came but was not allowed to see him.

2   Temple came at 11. Machell came twice. A very slight improvement. Mr. Lewis prayed with him. Caroline came in the morning & saw Fred in the afternoon. Matilda came from Keswick to stay here. Fred worse towards night. Barlow, Allen & Geo Ridout sat up.

3   No improvement in dear Fred. Dr. Temple came. Machell twice. Matilda here staying. Trevy [Ridout, a nephew], Archie & Barlow sat up.

It was hot, and he was slipping away from them:

4 August The end approaching. He took leave of us all in the afternoon. Mr. Lewis prayed with him on enquiring of him if he was putting all his trust in Jesus he said '*I Am.*' These were his last words. He became unconscious soon after.

On the morning of 5 August, Wilmot Cumberland lost her husband of thirty-six years:

5 August My dear son Barlow's birthday. 35 years old. My dear Husband died at 8:00 a.m. Old Joe Ridout & Fred Churchill sat up.

The numbing details of funeral preparations occupied Wilmot's time for the next two days:

6 August All preparations being made for the funeral tomorrow. Telegrams & letters of condolence and lovely flowers coming all day.

7   My dear Husband was buried between 3 & 4 p.m. A most beautiful coffin. He looked so handsome & young. Wreaths of flowers & crosses in profusion. The Freemasons & the 10th Regiment there, the Band playing. There were 3,000 people at the grave, all the employees came to see him in the drawing room where he was. Mr. Lewis performed the ceremony. There were 129 carriages in attendance.

Nothing could salve such suffering, but Wilmot may have taken some solace from the affectionate tributes that streamed in after her husband's death. Many newspapers published obituaries,[30] of which the *Globe*'s was typical: 'He was a man of strong individuality, and in the positions which he occupied [he] necessarily excited a good deal of antagonism, but in the family circle and the wider sphere of friendly social intercourse his good traits of kindness and generosity will long be remembered, and his loss deplored.'[31]

The funeral was held on a Sunday. The *Mail* reported the event in detail:

The remains of the late Lieutenant-Colonel Cumberland were buried yesterday afternoon with full Masonic honours. The greatest interest was taken in the sad event, and representatives were present from all parts of the line of the Northern railway and its branches, as well as from the Hamilton and North-Western and other roads. A special train consisting of sixteen cars, draped in mourning, arrived about noon from the north, with six hundred employees of the road. The train came through from Meaford, and at Allandale it picked up those coming from Orillia and Hamilton and intervening points; and upon reaching the station here luncheon was served to the deputation. Mr. Kerr, passenger and traffic superintendent, then took the party to the house of mourning, in University park, where they had the melancholy satisfaction of looking for the last time upon the placid features of their chief, who, during his lifetime, was exceedingly popular with the employees of the road, from the most prominent officer to the most humble labourer.

Long before the hour appointed for the *cortège* to start, thousands of persons had assembled in the neighbourhood of the family residence, and along the route leading to and through the Queen's park, along which it was supposed the funeral procession would pass. A considerable length of time was occupied by the vast multitude who paid their respects to the dead by looking on his remains.[32]

Leading the funeral procession to St James's Cemetery was the band of the 10th Royals, followed by the garrison artillery, the Masons, the St George's Society, employees of the Northern and Northwestern Railways, the officiating clergyman Mr Lewis, the hearse and pallbearers, the mourners' coaches, the Northern Railway directors' carriages, private carriages, and citizens on foot. The procession inched its way to St James's Cemetery, where Cumberland was buried in Lot 60, Hillside B. After referring to the solemn ritual with which Cumberland was buried, the *Mail* remarked that this had been one of the most widely attended funerals within memory: 'Only a very vague idea could be conceived of the vast number of persons who thronged the entire route of the procession, but it was admitted that the sad event attracted as large a concourse of citizens as ever assembled in Toronto on any similar occasion; but the procession, it may be stated, occupied half an hour in passing a given point.'

The funeral gives some idea of the size of Cumberland's social circle and the great respect accorded him by his fellow citizens. There were laudatory parchments from the city fathers and the Toronto Cricket Club, and tributes from the Masons, the Northern Railway, and many others. It will suffice to cite only one of these, from long-time Northern Railway architect and engineer Clarence W. Moberly:

Upon my return to Collingwood yesterday I was deeply grieved to hear of the death of Mr. Cumberland, my oldest and truest friend. During our connection, extending over more than twenty-two years, our friendship remained firm and unbroken – in fact his actions toward me were more as father to son than as an employee to a subordinate. If I had taken his far-seeing & sound judgment years ago I could have had any position in my profession in Canada I might have wished for.

Mr. Cumberland, as I well know, made himself beloved & respected by his employees on account of his firm and impartial discipline, and what was best of all he individualized himself with the interests of every man employed under him. I can never forget his unswerving friendship to myself.[33]

Cumberland was so well regarded by the men in his employ that they commissioned a bust of him by the sculptor A.B. Dunbar. It was unveiled at the Allandale station yard in December 1881.[34]

Cumberland's will shows that he devoted considerable attention to providing for his family.[35] He left Barlow all the professional books in his library, as well as silver and family portraits, including a large one of Cumberland in dress uniform. He also left an annuity to his invalid brother, Thomas James. At the time of his death Cumberland had considerable assets: $11,000 in household goods and furniture, $2500 in book debts and promissory notes, $3200 in bank shares and other stocks, $265 in cash on hand, and $20,000 in other property. Cumberland also left a separate trust account, the main provision of which was to provide an annuity of $1600 to Wilmot, the same to Barlow, and half that to his daughters. The trust fund included real estate in Toronto, Gravenhurst, and elsewhere, a part ownership interest in the *Chicora*, as well as stocks and insurance.[36] With real estate alone worth more than $24,000, exclusive of that named in the will, Cumberland left his family well provided for.

Wilmot's diary was quiet for most of the rest of 1881. Then, at the end of December, she recorded that the loss of her husband had not been the full extent of her suffering during that black year. Her final diary entry for 1881, on what was likely a very lonely New Year's Eve, was one of the longest entries she ever wrote:

All at home in the evening and thus ends the most miserable year of my life. May it please God to spare me another year to be with my children.

Flo's illness commenced in April. Poor Fred left us [for England] in bad health on the 10th. I was anxious about Flo for weeks [,] uneasy about Fred all the time he was away in England. [He] returned very ill in July died on the 5 Aug. My son-in-law Archie Campbell died on 26th Sept. and on the 23rd October my dear sister Matilda Ridout died. On the 6th Dec. my dear Constance was taken ill but happily recovered. My heart troubles me a good deal. 'Thy will be done.' Amen.

In the year's memoranda, she noted that Dr Machell came to see Cumberland fifty-two times from 6 February to 4 August, and another three times to see Flo. Dr Temple came eighteen times for Cumberland, twenty-two times for Flo, and once for her.

Wilmot eventually found Pendarves too large to live in. The house passed into other hands and today it serves as the University of Toronto's International Student Centre, but is gutted and without its original architectural character except for the silhouette.

Wilmot did not live to see the new century. She died on 9 May 1899 and was buried beside her husband and those children who predeceased her. The Cumberland family plot lies on a gently sloping site on the east side of St James's Cemetery, far from the chapel, its modest stone markers now cracked by time and barely legible.[37]

If the memory of Fred Cumberland the man has faded into obscurity, Fred Cumberland the architect still commands our interest – much more so, perhaps, than do his achievements in politics and railways. Part Two will consider in detail the buildings he designed during an architectural career as remarkable short as it was extraordinarily productive.

PART TWO: ARCHITECTURAL CASE STUDIES

CHAPTER EIGHT

Assessing the English Heritage

Although Cumberland was only twenty-seven when he emigrated to Canada, he had already gained considerable experience in several aspects of architecture and civil engineering. Four sources of information can be tapped for insight into Cumberland's English training and career: letters written by employers and colleagues;[1] the surviving contents of his professional library; the visual evidence, namely the sketch-books and drawings that he brought with him when he emigrated; and finally, his letters to Wilmot.

Following his apprenticeship with William Tress, and before joining the British Admiralty, Cumberland worked briefly for several less well-known architects and engineers and as an assistant engineer for various railway companies. In 1852 he stated that he had worked on the London and Birmingham Railway, the Blackwall, the North Midland, and the Derby Junction. There is nothing to connect him with the famous British engineer Isambard Kingdom Brunel, even though later Canadian studies have claimed such a connection.[2]

He seems to have created a favourable impression on his English employers. For instance, Captain Mould, RE, stated in September 1844 that 'I have found him zealous, intelligent, and extremely attentive to duty; and that the drawings prepared by him from time to time, for the guidance of the contractors and their workmen, have displayed an accurate knowledge of the principles and details of Engineering and Architectural construction.'

The noted architect Sir Charles Barry also wrote a letter of recommendation for Cumberland. Cumberland may have worked in a minor capacity on Barry's works at Westminster Palace, and Barry later became a friend and supporter.[3] Writing in 1851, Barry stated, 'Having known Mr. Cumberland for many years, and being well-acquainted with his professional engagements during that time, I have great pleasure in stating with confidence that, as an Architect and a Gentleman, I have the highest opinion of his qualifications and character.' But when one attempts to go beyond the superlatives, the testimonials prove to be all too general. They do not describe the work he did, but simply list job titles, for instance 'Assistant Engineer,' which could have meant anything from designer to site supervisor. To broaden the picture we need to turn to the other sources of information from the English period, the letters and the sketch-books. Because the sketch-books predate the letters they will be considered first.

The visual evidence concerning Cumberland's English career is scanty, consisting of two student sketch-books and a packet of drawings. Chapter 1 looked briefly at the sketch-books, which probably date from 1838, when Cumberland was eighteen years old. He had been apprenticed to William Tress for two years. It is not known whether Tress advised his pupil to begin the sketch-books or whether Cumberland started them on his own initiative. By 1838 he would have gained at least some understanding of architectural office practices, but he probably

8.1 Frederic Cumberland, c. 1838. Page from student sketch-book. Details of string courses in medieval buildings. Horwood Add. 5, box 8

had no formal training in architectural history. His sketch-book exercises, with their focus on historical buildings, were obviously intended to supplement the practical experience he had gained.

The sketch-book drawings show Cumberland learning a stylistic language based on the study of façades. The architectural orders were studied by preparing careful drawings of volutes, bases, and entablatures. Gradually he began to draw more complex parts of classical buildings as well as copies of sketches of Gothic mouldings and details. Eventually he produced a few drawings of identifiable nineteenth-century buildings. The sketch-books, therefore, can be seen as evidence that Cumberland was pursuing a self-study course in architectural history.

The drawings were, without exception, executed in a fine link line. Many show shadows created by fine hatch lines; only a few use an ink wash to convey depth. The drawings are rendered exactly as one would find them in a historical treatise, with a general view of a frieze shown alongside its cross-section. In keeping with this essentially stylistic conception of architecture, plans of whole buildings are rarely included; only details are dimensioned. For instance, one sheet shows details of buttresses, including those of Magdalen College and St Peter's Church in Oxford. In a sheet headed 'String Courses,' Cumberland copied details of ornamental friezes from the churches of St Nicholas and St Ouen in Rouen and from the cathedral of Notre Dame in Bayeux (fig. 8.1). Another drawing shows the doorway on the north side of the cloisters of the cathedral of Notre Dame in Rouen.

These drawings, with their emphasis on

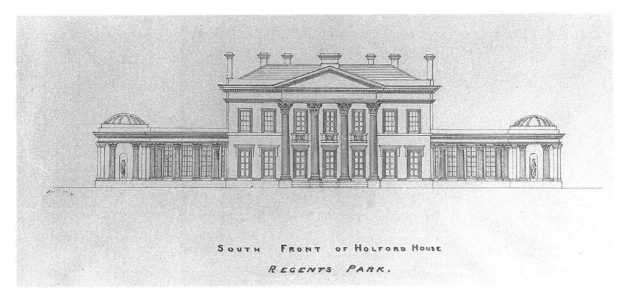

8.2 Frederic Cumberland, c. 1838. Page from student sketch-book. South front elevation of Holford House, Regent's Park, London, England. Horwood Add. 5, box 8

façades and details, were consistent with the architectural texts of the time, such as Thomas Rickman's *Attempt to Discriminate the Styles of English Architecture, from the Conquest to the Reformation* (1817), or Robert Willis's *Remarks on the Architecture of the Middle Ages, Especially of Italy* (1835). Among the most influential were the works of Sir William Chambers (1723–96), particularly his *Treatise on Civil Architecture* (1759), which ran into several editions, including Joseph Gwilt's of 1825.[4] Cumberland owned Gwilt's edition, and some handwritten notations on the plates suggest he may have copied drawings from it.[5]

Another of Chambers's works, reissued in 1834 when Cumberland was a young man, demonstrates by its encyclopedic title the evolutionary approach to architecture that Cumberland and others would have been exposed to: *A Theoretical and Practical Treatise on the Five Orders of Architecture; Containing the Most Plain and Simple Rules for Executing Them in the Purest Style; with the Opinion of Sir William Chambers, and Other Eminent Architects, Both Ancient and Modern, Exhibiting the Most Approved Modes of Applying Each in Practice, with Directions for the Design and Execution of Various Kinds of Buildings, Both Useful and Ornamental, and Suitable for the Climate of Great Britain. Including an Historical Description of Gothic Architecture, Shewing Its Origin, and also a Comparison of the Gothic Architecture of England, Germany, France, Spain, and Italy.* This book proceeds in exactly the same manner as Cumberland's sketchbooks, from detailed drawings showing how to delineate the bases and capitals of the architectural orders, and then to more complex designs.[6]

Chambers and most other architectural authors of the time organized their material according to a methodology borrowed from the natural sciences, specifically the Linnaean system of species classification.[7] Because Cumberland depended on authors who employed this methodology, he would have formed an essentially stylistic conception of architecture based on a recognizable visual vocabulary. This helps explain why Cumberland copied decorative mouldings from a variety of English and French Gothic churches. He learned from the parts, not the whole. Such a conception of architecture can be compared to the French system, where Beaux-Arts training encouraged students to learn about a building's organizing principles, its *parti* (although it must be admitted that the French system also emphasized, in its first years, copy-drawing from casts and engravings

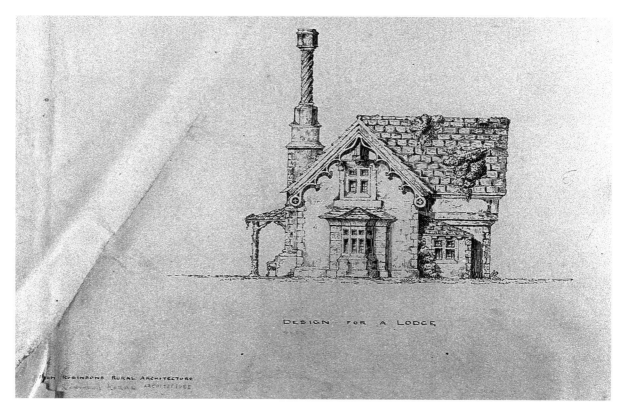

8.3 Frederic Cumberland, c. 1838. Page from student sketch-book. Drawing of a rural lodge copied from Peter Frederick Robinson, *Rural Architecture; or, a Series of Designs for Ornamental Cottages* (London: Rodwell 1823). Horwood Add. 5, box 8

of historical ornament). By contrast, very few of the Cumberland sketches shows a plan. Indeed, the drawings are so simple that it is doubtful that Cumberland yet had the skill to render complex spatial relationships.

Only one drawing of a building contemporary with Cumberland can be identified in the sketch-books. This is an elevation drawing of the south front of Holford House, an extravagant London mansion then valued at some £6000 (fig. 8.2). It was built in 1832 in the recently opened Regent's Park for a wine merchant, James Holford, to the designs of Decimus Burton. In the sketch-book it sits on an imaginary ground line, but no horizon line or landscape elements are included. The meticulously rendered ink delineates every fine line of the windows and doors. The drawing is disembodied and abstract, an effect heightened by relentless frontality. It is possible that the drawing is a copy of an engraving from some unknown publication, though it does not seem very likely that the building would have been engraved so soon after its construction. If Cumberland did copy an engraving, this would explain the lack of perspective, but not why he failed to also execute a perspective view showing the building in its setting. Surely he could have done so by paying the building a visit. That he did not reinforces the impression that he learned about architecture by studying frontal images and parts of buildings, rather than their spatial qualities. In fact there is only one perspective view in the sketch-books, and it was copied from a book. The absence of perspective drawings strongly suggests that Cumberland had, in 1838, an essentially two-dimensional conception of a three-dimensional art form.

Some of the sheets depict variant styles side by side on the same drawing. This is the case in

8.4 Wolverton Station, London and Birmingham Railway, England. Elevation, 1847 or earlier. Drawing by Frederic Cumberland(?). AO, Horwood (63)1

the 'Design for a Double Detached Villa in the Tuscan Style,' which also includes a rendering of the villa in the Ionic style. The lettering is meticulous and imitates several typefaces, including italic. Another drawing shows that Cumberland was learning about the differences between so-called High architecture and the more rustic and picturesque genres. This is seen in a laboured ink perspective drawing of a rural lodge that is reminiscent of John Nash's *Cottages at Blaise Hamlet* (1811). Cumberland identifies it as having come from Robinson's *Rural Architecture* (1823) (fig. 8.3).[8] The heavy stone-walled lodge is L-planned, picturesque, and irregular in profile, featuring bay windows and an inglenook. Details include an elaborate barge-board, a porch supported by rough logs, a huge spiral chimney block, and an artificially aged roof. This last detail is somewhat ludicrously and heavily rendered, making it appear as if the building is suddenly mouldering. This is a copyist's conception of the picturesque.

That virtually all these drawings were copied from books is nearly certain. Precisely which

books is unknown, except for two identified in the sketch-books, namely Chambers's *Treatise* and Robinson's *Rural Architecture*. Even though it has not been possible to identify the other works Cumberland drew on, we can reasonably surmise that his conception of architecture was derived from printed sources.

The few surviving Cumberland drawings from the English period that postdate the sketch-books show a considerable evolution in his command of architectural rendering. In a word, they seem to be the products of a practitioner, not a student. So however superficial Cumberland's knowledge of architectural history and practice may have been during the 1830s, by the mid-forties he had developed a very good working knowledge of the practical side of architecture, as well as a working knowledge of English architectural history.

The later drawings included plans for industrial structures and civil engineering projects, and also a façade drawing of Wolverton Station on the London and Birmingham Railway line, as well as related railway cottages on this same line

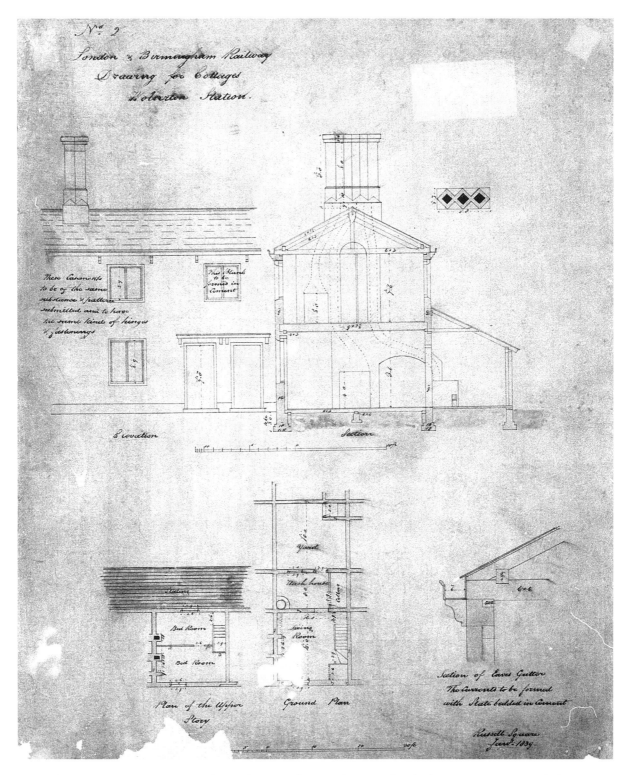

8.5 Wolverton Station cottages, London and Birmingham Railway, England. Elevation, sections, and plans, January 1839. Drawing by Frederic Cumberland(?). Horwood (50)2

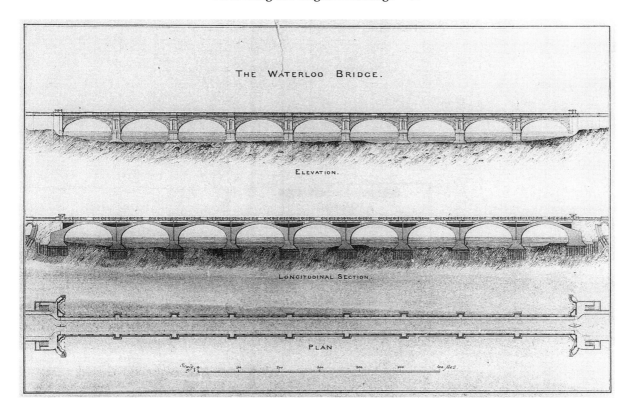

8.6 Waterloo Bridge, London, England. Elevation, longitudinal section, and plan, 1847 or earlier. Drawing by Frederic Cumberland(?). Horwood (61)1

(figs. 8.4–5).[9] Cumberland also brought with him a drawing showing an elevation, longitudinal section, and plan of Waterloo Bridge (fig. 8.6), and a drawing showing a section of a coffer-dam and river-wall for the new Houses of Parliament. This last, incidentally, provides the only evidence that he worked on Barry's Westminster Palace, likely employed in a minor capacity as draftsman.

Although there is no other documentary evidence to prove that Cumberland designed Wolverton Station and the railway cottages on the London and Birmingham line, the fact that he brought the drawings with him when he emigrated strongly suggests that he was responsible for their design. Moreover, the drawing for Wolverton Station is so stylistically consistent with Cumberland's slightly later Canadian work that an attribution to him seems reasonable.

Wolverton Station is designed in a simple yet dignified Italianate style, with a roundheaded arcade running along both sides of a simple projecting portico faced with Doric pilasters. As for the style of the drawing itself, there is still a sense of the copyist's linearity found in the sketch-books, but this drawing is more accomplished and shows an easier grasp of perspective. Cumberland has also used an ochre-hued watercolour wash that, by showing the arcade in a slightly darker tone than the rest of the building, succeeds in creating an illusion of three-dimensionality.

The drawings of the railway cottages for the London and Birmingham Railway, however, are dimensioned working drawings. They show a section of the heating system and other details, as well as a plan of the cottages. Taken together, the Wolverton Station drawing and those for the railway cottages demonstrate that Cumberland had a good working knowledge of the classical idiom and also enough practical knowledge to execute detailed working drawings.

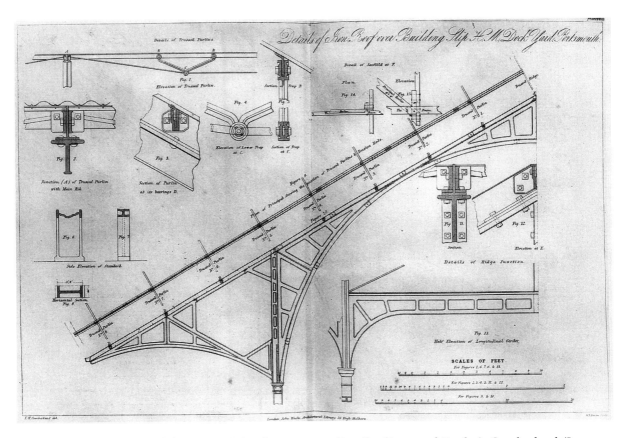

8.7 Frederic Cumberland, delineator. B.R. Davies, engraver. Details of iron roof. Frederic Cumberland, 'Iron Roofs Erected over Building Slips, Nos. 3 and 4, in Her Majesty's Dockyard, Portsmouth,' *Papers on Subjects Connected with the Duties of the Corps of Royal Engineers* 9 (1847), plate 17

Similarly practical are drawings of industrial roof structures that Cumberland executed while working in the Portsmouth dockyard from 1844 to 1847. These show construction details of various iron roof trusses, which Cumberland described in an article in the *Papers on Subjects Connected with the Duties of the Corps of Royal Engineers* in 1847 (figs. 8.7–8).[10] In this instance it seems less likely that Cumberland was chiefly responsible for preparing the designs. As part of a large dockyard architectural team, he would have worked on aspects of the project, and perhaps have supervised their construction. But what is more important than attributing specific design credit to him is seeing these drawings as evidence of the extensive architectural and engineering experience he had accumulated before emigrating. He was familiar with the practical engineering side of architectural

design – heating and ventilation as well as structure – and with the stylistic conventions of the time.

We turn now to the letters to Wilmot that discuss Cumberland's architectural work and tastes. The first is from August 1843 and in it Cumberland revealed a somewhat parochial attitude toward the use of foreign craftsmen for English work. He had recently visited Squire Bentley, whose house had been built by Sir Francis Head, grandfather of the former lieutenant governor of Upper Canada. Cumberland gave Wilmot a description of the house, and then remarked: '"Italian artists were employed by Sir Francis Head," said Mrs. Bentley. "Sorry to hear it Madam," said I to myself.'[11] In a letter of the same week he included a detailed definition and a quick sketch of the coved ceiling in Bentley's 'grand room,' which measured 130

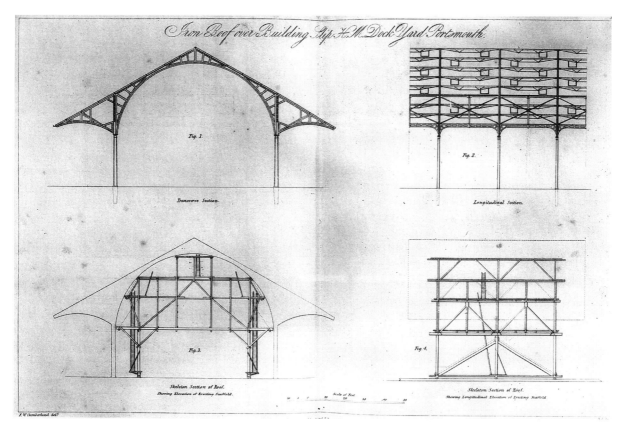

8.8 Frederic Cumberland, delineator. B.R. Davies, engraver. Sections of iron roof. Frederic Cumberland, 'Iron Roofs Erected over Building Slips, Nos. 3 and 4, in Her Majesty's Dockyard, Portsmouth,' *Papers on Subjects Connected with the Duties of the Corps of Royal Engineers* 9 (1847), plate 16

feet by 28 feet.[12] In December he related that on one Sunday he had gone to three church services, partly for the services themselves, partly to enjoy the architecture. He also mentioned that he intended to visit Sir Charles Barry's famous Reform Club and Travellers' Club, which were widely admired examples of Barry's London work: 'I shall greatly enjoy a visit to the Reform & Traveller's [sic] Clubs & it is very considerate of you to Lionise with me along my professional path.'[13] Cumberland had embarked on a serious course of professional self-study and improvement, one that included examination of notable English buildings recently completed.

A letter from April 1844 shows that Wilmot and Cumberland had been discussing current architectural theory. It reveals that he was knowledgeable about English church architecture and also knew enough about the so-called High Church reform movement to criticize its architectural pronouncements:

With regard to your question as to what would be called in Barracks 'the regulation position' of the reading desk [in a church] I must confess a doubt as to my opinion which is not formed – as it ought to be – upon the writings of the Camden Society, who enter into detail into all the proprieties of Church furniture their peculiar positions forms and uses – which are henceforth not to be matters of taste & judgments but implicit obedience to fixed laws.

... We [English architects generally?] invariably place the Altar Eastward but with this exception we have hitherto had no determined positions – I can quote cathedral precedents for facing to each quarter in the performance of one position of the service. In Rochester the Reader fronts to the North in Canterbury to the south in the Temple Northward, Dr. Dodsworth's southwards & so on.[14]

Such evidence convincingly demonstrates that Cumberland was a serious and committed student of architecture before he left England.

Nor did he cease to be interested in English architecture once he had emigrated to Canada. His letters written from England when he attended the Great Exhibition as a member of the Canadian delegation in 1851 reveal that he had a good understanding of the architectural principles of Joseph Paxton's Crystal Palace and that he was still very interested in ecclesiastical architecture. During his stay he travelled down from London to the south coast of England, visiting many churches along the way. His comments in an October letter show that he had a discriminating awareness of the stylistic evolution of English Gothic churches: 'On Sunday morning we went to service at the Parish Church a very quaint & most interesting Early English Building of original character ... The roof of the Church is as pure an Early English roof as I have ever met & should we have a wet day I shall sketch it & other bits worth remembering.'[15] While touring the area surrounding Canterbury he visited 'a sweet little Early English Church ... the 2nd church in England in which Christianity was preached.' After a good lunch he and some companions went over to the cathedral for afternoon service. He found the music memorable, the tour less so: 'Happily I know it all well for had it been otherwise I should have learned little seeing that we were hurried through at a gallop & that our conductress seemed to think that we cared about nothing but looking at the Tombs of all the ancient Knights who had had two wives and all the ancient ladies who had married two husbands. English History saith nothing of it but I verily believe that the ancient Britons kept seraglios.'

In the same letter he described further visits to towns on the south coast. He had gone to Brighton and visited a paper mill; the letter includes a learned discussion of the manufacturing process. He also told Wilmot that he felt his Canadian church commissions were unnecessarily restrictive:

Leaving the Mill, we discovered in the rear of it another example [the first being in Canterbury] of the small style of the Old Early English Church – in course of restoration. This we entered and enjoyed much. I find a marked improvement in the manner of these new restorations & evidence of great care in the faithful adherence to the original character of the structures. I would give my ears to be asked to build a *Small* Stone Church in Canada, but unfortunately with small resources they always will insist upon large accommodation and thus reduce us to the necessity of something very near a kin [*sic*] to four bare walls.

It would be idle for me to attempt to describe all the wonders of this church. I always *have* enjoyed it more than any other Cathedral that I know. It is in itself a complete history of Gothic architecture giving excellent examples of all the varieties of that fickle style, from the earliest to the latest eras. I am delighted to see that the Clerical rulers of this structure are an exception to their class & seem to understand that the responsibility of maintaining and restoring the building lies with them.

Cumberland also revealed that he was considerably interested in some local engineering works that involved relatively new techniques of concrete construction:

We afterwards made for home & luncheon subsequently walking on the pier where I left Nell to bask in the Sunshine whilst I went over the works of the New Harbour of Refuge. To my great surprise & pleasure I found them using blocks of concrete for their walling – a scheme proposed by Sir Wm. Denison whilst he was at Portsmo[uth]. The faces of the wall are of stone – the centre being filled in with the concrete, which is made in enormous blocks. The tide was at its highest & I had not the best opportunity of seeing the lower part of the wall so I intend to go again and if possible to get a peep at the drawings.[16]

The October 1851 letter alone would offer adequate proof of Cumberland's knowledge of and fascination with English church architecture and the architecture of industrial engineering, but there are others. In November 1851, for example, Cumberland related that he had visited an Old English church in the village of Broadwater, Sussex. He described it as 'a fine old Norman church somewhat mutilated and disfigured but capable of restoration & consequently in these days of seal [*sic* – zeal] very likely to be properly restored.'[17] In 1851 he also visited Southsea, where he noted a new church done 'in excellent taste' in the decorated style. This may have been T.E. Owen's church, St Jude's, built in 1850–1.[18] Owen was a Portsmouth architect who wrote a testimonial for Cumberland, although the exact nature of their working relationship is unclear. Cumberland reported that Owen had erected a large house in bad Gothic style – presumably Owen's own house, 'Dover Court,' of 1848–50 – as well as a parsonage (likely in better taste, since it elicited no negative comment). Cumberland also visited the Portsmouth dockyards: 'I went all over the works at the Dockyard which interested me vastly. I saw Captain Mould & all the rest & had long chats with everybody. I also went to see the new Portsea Barracks that we once worked so hard upon. They look very well as does the new Convict prison lately built in the same locality.'[19]

From late 1851 there is an important letter that shows that Cumberland had enjoyed a tour with Sir Charles Barry's son Edward, also an architect, of two of Sir Charles's buildings, Westminster Palace and the as yet unfinished Bridgewater House:

After my [last] letter was completed I rushed into town to keep my appointment with Edward Barry by whom I was most kindly piloted over the houses of Parliament. It would be folly of me to attempt any description of this amazing mass of building. The intricacy of the detail, the wonderful fertility and ingenuity of the composition & arrangement the high skill & extreme delicacy of the workmanship the beauty of the artistic embellishment in frescos – put criticism altogether at defiance or at least would in me make it impertinent. My observations then were confined to sage '*Hums*' & enthusiastic exclamations & I believe I said nothing that could be quoted against me & yet I hope said enough to evince my admiration. We spent some two hours in our journey Edward taking extreme pains to make me *acquainted* with all the beauties of the structure. From thence we made our way to Bridgewater House calling en

route in George Street to brush the Dust off and at Charles Barry's office to see him. He had grown very stout & full & looks bloated & unhealthy but was most cordial & friendly in his greetings to me indeed I am altogether at a loss to account for the very extreme kindliness by which my reception by the whole family has been marked – this, in the face of the vile calumny which emanated from Thomas's office has been highly gratifying & has relieved me from an anxiety which altho it was undeserved was most oppressive.[20] Charles, Edward & myself then went over [to] Bridgewater House which is still only in carcase as far as regards the interior being left for the present with one rough coat of plaster. The main feature of the structure is a magnificent central hall with open galleries all around on the first floor & lighted from the top by a lantern the glass of which being thick enough to admit cutting to the prismatic angle & consequently throwing all the vivid colours of the rainbow upon the interior. The Picture Gallery is a princely room – indeed all the apartments around the great Hall will form an unrivaled suite just suited to the *real noble* for whom they are constructing [it].[21]

As will be explained presently, it appears that Bridgewater House influenced Cumberland's work. Cumberland also toured Barry's Conservative Club, with a club member, not with the Barrys. Other letters related that he often talked shop with his friend, the architect Fred Porter, who was helping him find someone to execute perspective drawings of St James's Cathedral.[22]

The view that Cumberland had gradually developed a comprehensive knowledge of contemporary English architecture is reinforced when we consider the contents of his professional library. In it were books by and about the major English architects, including two books on Barry's designs: Barry's *The Travellers' Club House* (1839) and Henry T. Ryde's *Illustrations of the New Palace of Westminster* (1849). He also owned Augustus Charles Pugin's *Pugin's Gothic Ornaments* (1831), A.W.N. Pugin's *Glossary of Ecclesiastical Ornament and Costume* (1844), Raphael Brandon's *Parish Churches* (1851), and John Britton's *History and Antiquities of the Cathedral Church of Salisbury* (1814–15). It was a good working library, with books in three languages.

Cumberland kept his knowledge of architecture up to date after emigrating to Canada by buying recent architectural publications, for instance *Instrumenta Ecclesiastica* (1857–61), which introduced him to a new vocabulary of design. Touchingly, he used one of the plates from *Instrumenta Ecclesiastica*, a drawing of a gravestone, as a model for the gravestone of his son Walter, who died in 1850.

Given what has been said above, it is possible to draw certain conclusions about English influences in Cumberland's work. Cumberland developed a curious combination of bookish and practical architectural training – bookish with respect to 'high' architecture (public buildings and churches) and practical with respect to more utilitarian structures, such as those he worked on while in Portsmouth and Chatham. As for which buildings he may have actually designed, the drawings permit only a tentative attribution to him of the design for Wolverton Station and its cottages. But what about his comment to Wilmot (quoted in chapter 1), in which he mentioned having been able to supplement his dockyard income with money from private commissions? It has not been possible to turn up any information about those commissions; most likely they involved minor renovations.

Concerning engineering, it is possible to state with some confidence that Cumberland had sufficient training to design light industrial structures in concrete or iron. It is doubtful that he had the qualifications to design heavy industrial structures such as bridges, but presumably he knew enough about engineering to be able to understand the principles that governed their design. What he knew about railway engineering can only be inferred, for there are no drawings to show what he worked on, but we can assume that he would have undertaken a variety of duties.

With respect to architectural theory, Cumberland's letters to Wilmot show that he was well acquainted with the works of the principal figures in the reform movement in church architecture spearheaded by A.W.N. Pugin and the Ecclesiologists, a group of zealous Anglican and Roman Catholic reformers who called for a return to medieval forms of liturgy. In one letter he mentioned wanting to design a church of his own according to the principles laid down by the reformers, but his drawings show no particular talent in that direction.

Who among contemporary British architects did he especially admire? The only one he mentioned by name in his letters was Barry. He visited at least four buildings designed by Barry – Westminster Palace, the Reform Club, the Travellers' Club, and Bridgewater House. Now, every architect visiting London during the early 1850s would likely have made the effort to view Westminster Palace; there was nothing notable in that. But Cumberland had books by and about Barry in his library, and Barry was often mentioned in his letters.

Two qualities of Barry's work seem to have especially attracted Cumberland. Buildings designed by Barry evince a sort of sober dignity that Cumberland admired. Barry drew on styles from different periods, but mainly styles that embodied order and regularity, particularly those of the Italian cinquecento. The motifs that Barry used to modulate his façades were ones that Cumberland would later use: alternating triangular and segmental pediments, rusticated ground floors, decorative urns, and textured friezes. Inside Barry's buildings, stately arcuated colonnades provided a regular cadence. Admittedly, these were unexceptional hallmarks of the various classical styles that then held sway in England, and they can be found in the works of other architects working in the early 1830s and 1840s, particularly Sidney Smirke and Decimus Burton. Those architects were like Barry in that they effortlessly commanded a knowledge of different historical styles, which they combined to create an effect of sober grandeur and taste. But the design elements just mentioned were brought to their apogee in Barry's work.

In addition to the stately nature of Barry's buildings, and their apparently effortless command of a stylistic vocabulary drawn from the more restrained Italianate sources, there were other aspects of Barry's work that Cumberland seemed particularly drawn to, namely Barry's

frequent use of grand staircases to mediate between stories and his use of contrasting heights
in his buildings, especially in entrances and galleries. Bridgewater House, for instance, boasted
a magnificent square gallery supported by an
arcade. An imperial staircase (as the type featuring double arms is known) led to the gallery
above. Later, in Canada, Cumberland would use
just such a combination of square gallery and
grand staircase in Toronto's Osgoode Hall.
Whether he took this combination from Barry,
or from the Italian palazzi to which Osgoode
Hall has been compared, cannot be stated with
certainty. Even so, it would seem that Barry was
the single most important influence on the development of Cumberland's architecture.

Therefore, even if it has not proved possible to
determine with precision exactly which engineering and architectural works Cumberland
worked on while still in England, and still less
those designs for which he may have been solely
responsible, it is none the less possible to recon-
struct the main strands of Cumberland's English
career. Cumberland was a well-trained professional who was fully justified in describing himself as an architect-engineer. He had both a
theoretical and a practical knowledge of architecture and engineering. He knew much about
contemporary church architecture and was a
great admirer of Barry's work. That his training
was both theoretical and practical helps explain
why he was so quickly able to dominate the Toronto architectural community of the 1850s.
Had I been an architect working in Toronto in
1847, it would have given me some concern to
learn about the extensive training of a new competitor just then arriving from England.

'The Beautiful Medium' and Other Topics: Reconstructing Cumberland's Architectural Theory and Practice

Cumberland was a businessman-architect, the first of a new breed of Canadian professionals whose careers paralleled those of architects in mid-Victorian England, particularly George Edmund Street.[1] Like these architects, Cumberland strove for artistic expression, but regarded architecture first and foremost as a speculative venture from which he hoped to profit. He succeeded in architecture not only because of his talents as a designer (and his judgment in selecting partners), but also because of his ruthless and domineering personality – a personality that allowed him to regard the skills of his employees as expendable.

Subsequent chapters will discuss the projects designed by the Cumberland firms during the 1850s and 1860s, by looking in turn at various building types. This chapter will explore in some detail how Cumberland ran his architectural practice – first in government service, then on his own – and also examine how he shared responsibilities with his partners. It is also devoted to reconstructing Cumberland's theory of architecture, an art that he termed 'the beautiful medium.'

Cumberland coined the phase 'the beautiful medium' to distinguish his architecture from what he considered to be the equally bad options of American and French architecture. This was in 1856, when he visited France while researching the design for University College. In a letter to Wilmot he wrote that he had found little there to interest him, and that his opinion of American architecture was lower still: 'Direct the attention

of [Attorney General Lewis Thomas] Drummond[2] to "La belle France" and ask him if he would not choose the beautiful medium of Cumberland & Storm between the extravagances of Louis Legrand and Henri Quatre and the mean marble atrocities of Vermont republicans?'[3] 'The beautiful medium' might therefore be taken to represent Cumberland's attitudes toward architecture generally. By it he meant not only the ability to manipulate the elements of a particular style but also the ability to design buildings with ornament and styling appropriate to their function. Cumberland sought to vary the style to suit the purposes of his buildings – picturesque eclecticism, as this approach has been termed, although here we will use 'the beautiful medium' to describe Cumberland's work.

THE BUSINESS SIDE OF THE PRACTICE: AN IMPATIENT AUTOCRAT

While Cumberland's first significant jobs in Canada were for government bodies, it was just as well that he had his heart set on establishing himself in independent practice, for he was singularly ill-suited to working for others. Letters relating to his government work show that he was impatient with the glacial speed of approvals for his work and with the limits placed on his authority.[4] This is scarcely surprising, giving his scathing comments about his earlier employment with the British Admiralty. Perhaps Canadian institutional timidity and time-wasting were all too reminiscent of Her Majesty's dockyards and of the character of his sententious former supervisor, John Fincham. One Canadian Department of Public Works document in particular provides a good idea of why Cumberland experienced such difficulty working for the government. On 5 March 1850 Cumberland wrote to Thomas Begley, secretary of the Department of Public Works, explaining that for the new legislative buildings to be ready for occupancy by 15 April, £3706 was required.[5] But rather than wait for the requisite approvals, Cumberland acted on his own, as is apparent from a memorandum of 17 April, in which public works officials stated that Cumberland had subsequently taken £4000 from government coffers without having the authority to do so.[6] When new tenders were issued in mid-April, contractors were no longer to direct their bids to Cumberland but to the government directly.[7] What seems significant is the clear difference in style between Cumberland and the Department of Public Works. Cumberland was impatient with bureaucratic delay and took an assertive and energetic approach to getting the job done.

How did he operate his architectural office? A rare cache of his business records, now in private hands, makes it possible to answer this question in substantial detail. The papers include documents relating to draftsmen's hours of work, bookstore and gas company bills, receipts for tender calls published in local newspapers, and so on.[8] We even know how much the firm spent on drafting supplies.[9] Although the earliest papers are from 1853, and therefore do not offer a complete documentary picture of Cumberland's office operations, the fact that they were preserved at all is remarkable, perhaps even unique for architectural firms in mid-Victorian Canada West. Cumberland ran an extremely lean office, hiring staff only when necessary, and never delegating authority over important matters. Draftsmen, and even specification writers, were employed as needed. Most were hired for a specific job and paid by the job or by the hour. The papers also reveal that by 1853 the partnership of Cumberland & Storm owned real estate, on which it took out an insurance policy worth £250. The firm continued to speculate in real estate and profited greatly as a result.[10]

And what of Cumberland's relations with his two partners, Thomas Gibbs Ridout and William George Storm? Did he dominate his partners as ruthlessly as he ran his office? And did he claim credit for buildings designed by his partners? When he was in partnership with Ridout in 1851–2, Cumberland was responsible for all the major design and business decisions affecting the firm. All of the firm's surviving letters, for instance, are written in his own hand, even those whose writing would have been easy to assign to someone else.[11] When he did delegate responsibility, it was because he was unavoidably absent from the office, for example while he was in London in 1851. During that trip he apparently received a detailed report from Ridout, as is clear from remarks in a letter to Wilmot:

I am highly gratified by the tidings contained in Tom's letter – the very satisfactory tenders which were made for the Court House are positive proof of excellent management. By no other means could they have been so close in amount. The Normal School & Church too he says look well and give great satisfaction – but this pleasant intelligence although it relieves me of anxiety, has something of the effect of a trumpet on an old war-horse, I want to be at work again. He seems to keep a right sharp look out over the Contractors & there is nothing like it to ensure their good behaviour. We seem to have been fortunate in our choice of a Clerk of Works at Hamilton – indeed everything is just as it ought to be ... I am anxious about the Bank which I do hope will be finished to Mr. Ridout's satisfaction. Tell them not to spoil the place for want of a pennyworth of paint.[12]

Relations between Cumberland and Ridout were always cordial, and it is not clear why the partnership dissolved. It is possible that Cumberland no longer needed the social connections provided by the Ridout family. Then, too, he already had the promising young architect William George Storm waiting in the wings.[13] In 1853, the year after Ridout left the firm, Ridout Sr was instrumental in helping his son obtain the position of chief engineer of the Great West Railway.[14]

Storm became Cumberland's partner in February 1852. Cumberland was to receive three-fifths of the profits, and Storm the remainder, with the proviso that Storm would be paid £350 if the firm's annual profits did not reach that amount.[15] Cumberland dominated the business side of his new partnership with Storm as completely as he had with Ridout. He obtained all the firm's commissions, had most of the contact with clients, and in all the years when Cumberland and Storm were in partnership wrote all the firm's letters that have survived. To provide a trivial but telling example, in October 1855 Cumberland wrote out a receipt to one Dexter Baldwin for some $800 worth of marble, presumably for Casimir Gzowski's house, then under construction. Now, it is possible that Cumberland was alone in the office at the time, but it seems that this was yet another instance of his being unwilling to delegate responsibility for even the most trivial aspects of running the firm.

Cumberland was equally unwilling to delegate site supervision of the construction of important public buildings. This was certainly true of two of the courthouses that Cumberland and Storm designed – the Ontario County Courthouse in Whitby and the Victoria County Courthouse in Lindsay. Initially it seems that Cumberland handed site supervision for the Ontario County Courthouse to Storm, but when he visited the site in November 1853 and found that the work had been progressing unsatisfactorily he assumed personal direction. A letter from the county warden to the provincial authorities leaves no doubt that Cumberland made important decisions without having to consult his partner: 'Mr. Cumberland was here yesterday and is very much disappointed to find the County Buildings in so backward a state and talks of taking the Buildings out of the Contractors' hands. I have arranged with Mr. Cumberland to have a meeting of the building Commissioners in Toronto on Tuesday evening next.'[16] If this were the only example of unilateral decision making, it could hardly be taken as proof that Cumberland was unwilling to delegate important responsibilities. But it is not. A second and similar instance, concerning the Victoria County Courthouse, is all the more tell-ing because it comes from 1862, when he had all but abandoned architectural practice. In the case of the Victoria County Courthouse, a relatively minor commission in an out-of-the-way town, Cumberland was apparently unwilling to entrust Storm with the presentation of the plans to the county council, and so made the presentation himself.[17] After the commission was obtained, Storm became the project architect; there are frequent references to him in county council's minutes as the design progresses through the various stages of construction.[18] That Cumberland as late as 1862 should have reserved for himself the initial presentation of a relatively minor commission strongly suggests that he ran his architectural office as he ran the Northern: with nothing at all escaping his supervision.

No one can dispute, however, that Storm was a more gifted designer than Ridout. Nineteenth-century sources credit Cumberland exclusively with the design of the buildings built during their partnership. But many of the firm's drawings have Storm's signature on them. Is it possible that Cumberland took credit for his partner's contributions to the firm? The evidence from the drawings permits different interpretations. Determining the division of responsibility within nineteenth-century architectural firms is often a difficult exercise. One common method – analogous to the techniques used in analysing drawings and paintings in the fine arts – actually tends to muddy the waters rather than making them clearer. If an artist signs a drawing or painting we assume that he or she is also the one responsible for its conception. This is not always true in architecture. In large firms, the partner in charge might only execute a rough sketch, from which a draftsman or project architect prepares detailed working drawings. The draftsman signs the drawings but is in no way responsible for the design. Numerous instances of this may be cited. The English architect Sir John Soane, for example, frequently turned to J.M. Gandy for presentation perspectives. At the end of the nineteenth century, especially in large American offices, it was typical for a senior partner to only indicate in broad terms the conceptual nature of a sketch,

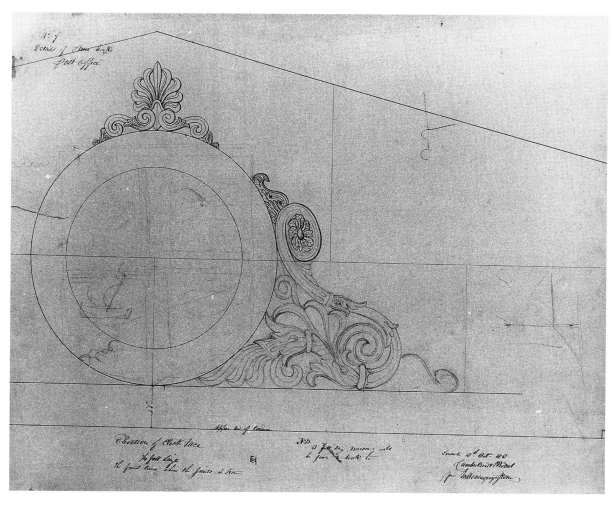

9.1 Cumberland & Ridout. Seventh Post Office, Toronto, 1851–3. Elevation of clock face. Drawing by William G. Storm, 18 October 1851. Horwood (76)6

and leave the mechanical execution to his staff. Certainly this was the case in the office of the American architect H.H. Richardson, whose capable staff included Stanford White, later renowned as a partner in the leading American firm of McKim, Mead & White.[19] Even architects such as Richard Morris Hunt, whose Beaux-Arts training gave them skill in delineation, called in outside delineators on at least some occasions. This was the case in 1893, when Hunt turned to E.L. Masqueray to delineate a drawing of The Breakers in Newport, Rhode Island.[20] Daniel H. Burnham and Edward H. Bennett commissioned draftsmen Jules Guérin and Fernand Janin to execute perspectives of the 1909 proposals for a new Civic Center Plaza for Chicago.[21] Even Frank Lloyd Wright – who had a beautiful drawing-hand of his own – turned from time to time to Marion Mahoney Griffith and other specialists in presentation perspective.

This background is relevant to the present discussion because Storm did all the presentation perspectives for Cumberland & Storm and also signed many of the firm's working drawings. Perhaps Storm sat on his office stool like some poor, overworked Bob Cratchit, cranking out master-designs and working drawings after his taskmaster boss, passing through the office on his way to a dinner with the governor general, vaguely described the particulars of the firm's latest commission. On the other hand, perhaps Cumberland designed everything himself and left only the mechanical execution to his staff. I favour a position between these extremes. The evidence already considered proves that Cumberland kept close tabs on all the work that came from the office. Moreover, whenever the records mention an architect in connection with the firm's designs, it is Cumberland, not Storm.

A specific example might help to illustrate this argument. One drawing signed by Storm exists for the Seventh Toronto Post Office (fig. 9.1). It is dated 18 October 1851, well before the beginning of the partnership between Cumberland and Storm, which suggests that Storm had been hired for his draftsman's skills. Storm signed the drawing 'Cumberland & Ridout per William George Storm.' Now, clearly this did not mean that Storm was responsible for the design of the project. He was only the draftsman. On the other hand, one can see from the fluidity of this drawing that Storm brought artistic verve to the future partnership as well as skill as a renderer of perspective. Cumberland's drawings of this period, by contrast, are plodding efforts. So it seems only reasonable to recognize that Storm's abilities as a draftsman far outshone those of his future partner. Cumberland and Storm complemented each other well: Cumberland was the capable manager who obtained commissions and developed the general conception of the designs, Storm was the able lieutenant who initially assumed the role of executant, but gradually undertook site supervision and design of details.

Yet Storm *was* crucial to the firm's success. Cumberland's drawings are not works of art: they are prosaic and informational, as befitted his training in engineering. Storm's, on the other hand, are graceful and evocative, filled with grace-notes such as foliage and staffage. Such work lay outside Cumberland's capabilities. But had Cumberland not obtained the commissions in the first place, Storm, who brought no business to the firm, would not have had the opportunity to execute his beautiful drawings. This, incidentally, might explain why

Storm worked so long with such an autocratic partner. Cumberland obtained lucrative commissions, and Storm was able not only to profit from his association with Cumberland but also to work on a great many buildings of immense importance.

To assume, therefore, that Storm was responsible for the overall conception of the firm's designs is not borne out by the evidence. Time and again, design details reveal Cumberland's tastes and his knowledge of the work of Sir Charles Barry and other English architects. Cumberland's interest in exploiting the architectonic potential of three-dimensional architectural space, as evidenced by his love of double-height courtyards and grand staircases – a love likely inspired by Barry's work – defined the essential character of Cumberland & Storm's accomplishments. And just as it lay beyond Cumberland's abilities to execute drawings as beautiful as Storm's, so too did it lie beyond Storm's abilities, for instance, to plan Osgoode Hall and create that building's dramatic spatial effects. Storm was the detail-man; Cumberland was the generator of ideas.

What about University College, the jewel in the firm's crown? The above argument holds true for it as well. Cumberland attached a great deal of importance to that commission. In 1856 he travelled widely through the United Kingdom and France looking at relevant precedents and conceived the general design while still in Europe. Storm went to Europe the following year, after the main design for the building was completed, presumably to see firsthand some of the buildings and details that Cumberland had previously looked at.[22] Storm then executed many hundreds of the drawings for the firm. Storm's view of his contribution is found in a letter written in 1890 after the building suffered a disastrous fire. 'My late partner W. Cumberland and myself designed the building from its inception to completion. Most of the work on the drawings and the principal portion of the details I designed, and what did not pass under my hand was done by clerks in the office under my personal supervision and received my approval before being handed to the mechanics for execution, and the construction generally was under my direct supervision.'[23] Perhaps this is why Storm eventually came to believe that he had been responsible for the design: having created so many of the drawings for it, and also perhaps for some of the building's details, he developed a proprietorial attitude. But unless my reading of the documents is wrong, it is Cumberland, not Storm, who should receive the credit for designing the main aspects of the building.

CHAPTER TEN

A Selection of Schools

With learning here you might store your mind,
Good schools throughout our land you'll find,
Then hasten on, pray don't delay,
Come graduate in Canada.[1]

This dreadful doggerel helps introduce issues central to this chapter, ones widely debated during the 1840s and 1850s. Should there be public schools? If so, who should pay for them, and what should their curricula be? Should institutions of higher learning have a religious foundation? As Canada grew in population and wealth, questions such as these had to be addressed and resolved. Cumberland, who designed several schools, entered the debates through his architecture.

Cumberland's design for University College is so important to his career and indeed to Canadian architecture generally that one tends to forget that he also designed four other educational institutions: the St James's Parochial School (which opened in 1851), the Toronto Normal School (1852), the Hamilton Central School (1853), and the Toronto Grammar School (1858).[2] Of these, the Hamilton Central School is the only one still extant. A fragment of the Toronto Normal School's centre bay and pediment was preserved and re-erected on the grounds of its successor institution, the Ryerson Polytechnic University. The four schools are none the less well worth analysing for the insights they provide into the evolution of his architecture. University College will receive its due in the next chapter; in the present chapter Cumberland's other schools will be considered. As will be seen, at least one of these, the Toronto Normal School, was a highly original and complex structure, significant on its own right. The complexity of the design for the Normal School also provided Cumberland with valuable experience when later designing University College. The Normal School was the first school Cumberland designed, and even though construction delays meant that the St James's Parochial School was finished nearly a year before it, the Normal School will be considered first.

THE NORMAL SCHOOL, TORONTO: 'THIS BEAUTIFUL PILE OF BUILDINGS'

The history of the Toronto Normal School is inextricably linked with Egerton Ryerson, a giant of nineteenth-century education who founded Ontario's publicly funded elementary school system.[3] It was the first state-supported public school in Canada West, and Ryerson regarded it as the principal vehicle for demonstrating the viability of his theories.[4] Thus the importance of the Normal School as a social institution needs to be recognized before its architectural character can be discussed.

After proposing the building of a Normal School for teacher training in 1845, it took Ryerson several more years to gather enough support before construction could begin. Meanwhile, a Normal School was fitted up temporarily in the ballroom of Old Government House, and then, when that building was required for

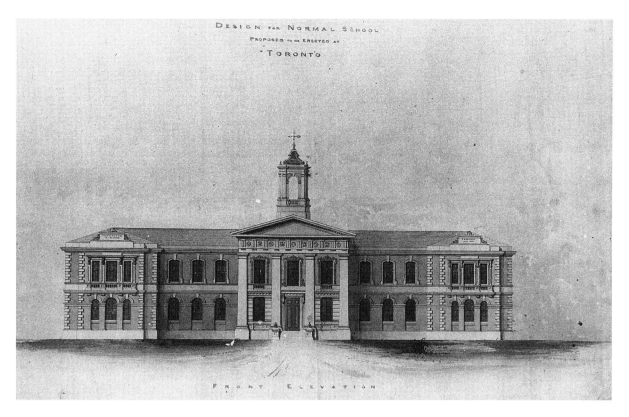

10.1 Cumberland & Ridout. Normal School, Toronto, 1850–2. Competition drawing of front (south) elevation, 1850. Horwood (79)3

official use following the transfer of the provincial government to Toronto, moved to the temperance hall in Temperance Lane, where it stayed for three more years. In 1850 the Council of Education for Upper Canada succeeded in obtaining an eight-acre building site, which was described as 'a very beautiful one, being considerably elevated above the business parts of the city, and commanding a fine view of the bay.'[5] It was bounded on the north by Gerrard Street, on the east by Church Street, on the south by Gould Street, and on the west by Victoria Street. (Portions of the original site are now occupied by St James's Square, located in the heart of downtown; the view of the bay has long been lost.) A competition for a new building was held. The designs were required to provide accommodation for the Education Department, the Normal School, and for two Model Schools – one for girls and one for boys – where student teachers would practise their skills (figs. 10.1–4).

The competition results were announced in October 1850.[6] First prize went to Cumberland & Ridout, the second to George Browne of Montreal, the third to William Thomas, the fourth to Thomas Young, and the fifth to John Tully.[7] The cornerstone was laid in July 1851, but the works were delayed because of a shortage of stone. The opening ceremonies took place on 26 November 1852 and were described at length in Ryerson's *Journal of Education for Upper Canada.*[8] According to the *Journal*, a throng of people attended, and only those with tickets were admitted. The dignitaries who addressed the crowd said a great deal about the theory of public schools and about the buildings as well (the architects themselves were not on the podium). Press reports were also generally favourable. One described the school as 'this beautiful pile of buildings' and went on to praise the buildings for their frugality as much as for their design, observing that 'they are an ornament to

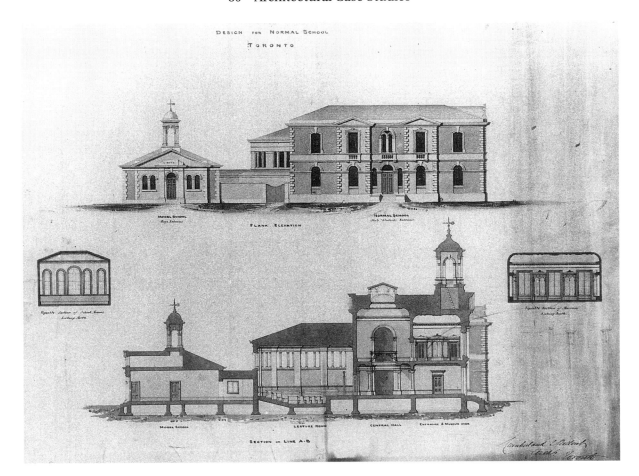

10.2 Cumberland & Ridout. Normal School, Toronto, 1850–2. Competition drawing of sections and flank elevation. Horwood (79)5

the city of Toronto, and will doubtless prove a blessing to the Province at large. They have been erected on the most approved plan, and at the same time in the most economical manner' (fig. 10.5).[9]

Chief Justice John Beverley Robinson delivered a highly complimentary speech. He remarked that

The larger portion of this audience are probably, like myself, not entitled to speak with confidence of the grace and propriety of architectural designs; but it is acknowledged that so far as may be consistent with strength and durability, what the art of the builder aims at is to please, – and to please not those only who can appreciate his difficulties but the greater multitude of observers who are ignorant of rules, and

who when they admire, they know not why, give a strong testimony that one great object of the artist has been attained. I believe I am expressing the general sentiment when I declare my admiration for the handsome edifice in which we are assembled. It would have been inconsistent with the circumstances of this yet new country to have expended much of the revenues necessary for the supply of so many pressing and growing wants, in decorating this structure with massive columns and elaborate carving which are required for creating an imposing grandeur of effect; but we have here provided in a style fairly in keeping with the country, and with the object, a large, substantial, and well-proportioned building – of durable materials, and yet of light appearance, and in its interior arrangements, I doubt not, perfectly well adapted to its purpose. I have

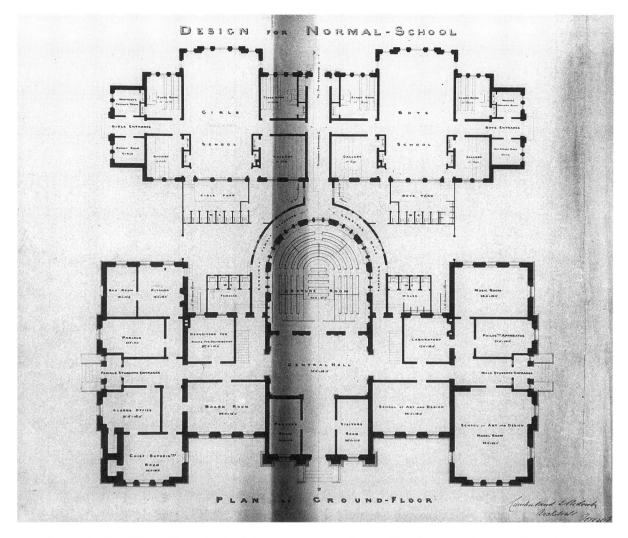

10.3 Cumberland & Ridout. Normal School, Toronto, 1850–2. Competition drawing of ground-floor plan. Horwood (79)6

heard of it generally spoken of as a striking ornament of the city in which it occupies a convenient and appropriate position, and by whose inhabitants I trust it will come to be regarded in successive generations with growing favour. In my own judgment it does great credit to the taste and talents of the architect, Mr. Cumberland, that the opinion came from a quarter which could give it value.[10]

The Rev. Dr John McCaul, president of the University of Toronto, then observed: 'The Building itself is an ornament to the City, and a credit to the Architect, and as we look around upon this

beautiful Theatre, – and bear in mind the admirable arrangements which have been made throughout every part of the Edifice, we cannot but feel satisfied that the remark has been justly made by the Inspector General [Francis Hincks, another Speaker], – that the appropriated funds have been most judiciously expended in the erection of this pile of Buildings, whose inauguration we are now celebrating.'[11]

Ryerson himself reported with some pride in his 1852 annual report that 'The Buildings are completed; the Grounds have been brought into a state of cultivation ... The Buildings and

10.4 Cumberland & Ridout. Normal School. Toronto, 1850–2. Competition drawing of rear (north) elevation, upper-floor plan, and sections. Horwood (79)4

Premises are by far the most commodious and elegant of the kind in North America; nor do I know of any one establishment of the kind in Europe which embraces all the conveniences and appendages connected with this. Yet the purchase of the ground ... preparation and first year's culture of it, and the erection and completion of the Buildings, have cost only about Twenty-five thousand pounds.'[12]

The press report quoted above mentioned that the building had been designed according to the 'most approved plan.' This may have been so, but attempts to connect the design of the Normal School to what we know about other

school designs of the period have proved fruitless.[13] In his work *The School House; Its Architecture, External and Internal Arrangements* (1857), J.G. Hodgins, the deputy superintendent of education for Upper Canada, offered a learned architectural description of the building: 'The front is in the Roman Doric order of Palladian character, having for its centre four pilasters of the full height of the building, with pediment surmounted by an open Doric cupola.'[14] But this description does not make it easier to link the design of the Normal School to those of other schools. Books such as Henry Barnard's *School Architecture; or Contributions to the Improve-*

10.5 Cumberland & Ridout. Normal School, Toronto, 1850–2. Exterior view, n.d. AO, Picture Collection, Toronto Normal School, L76

ment of School-Houses in the United States were often consulted by architects during this period, and Ryerson himself mentioned it.[15] But all the designs in that volume are too modest to serve as a comparison with the Normal School's. The same can be said of the designs in Hodgins's book, in which the Normal School itself is by far the largest building.

Ryerson was well aware of all the latest developments in institutions of public education. He had travelled throughout the Continent and the United Kingdom before deciding on a mandate for his own institution. It was not unusual at that time to see teacher-training schools with a quite elaborate program. Many included not only classrooms but also museums and art gal-

leries. The Normal School had, among other things, a theatre and a museum that held plaster copies of ancient busts, copies of oil paintings representing all the better-known European schools, scientific instruments, and agricultural tools.[16]

Ryerson provided these facilities partly as a response to current educational theory and partly because Toronto offered few cultural amenities. The Normal School had to provide far more facilities than might be found in a city with established public museums and art galleries. Ryerson believed it was essential to expose his unsophisticated teachers to high culture before he sent them out to preach the secular good word. One might say that the Normal School

10.6 Cumberland & Ridout. St James's Parochial School, Toronto, 1850–1. Front (west) elevation, Church Street, and flank (south) elevation, March 1851. Horwood (71)5

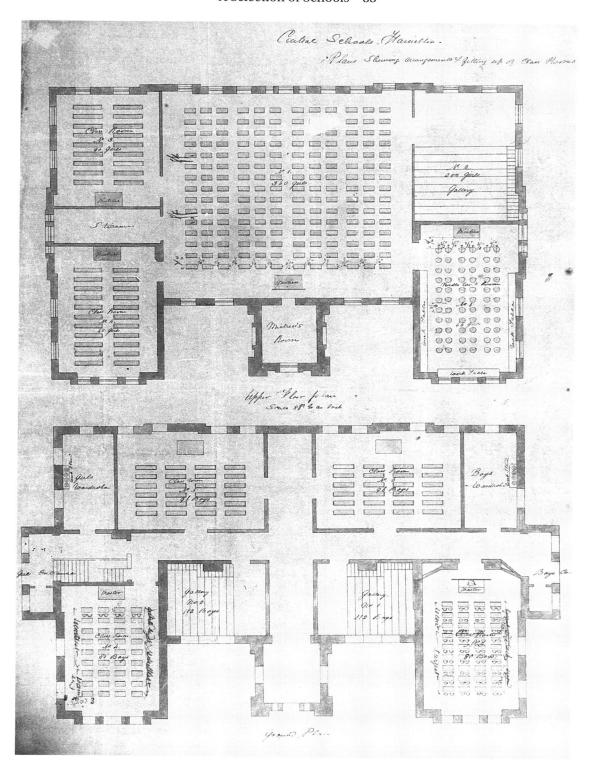

10.7 Cumberland & Ridout. Central School, Hamilton, 1851–3. Contract drawing of ground- and upper-floor plans, 8 April 1851. Horwood (70)3

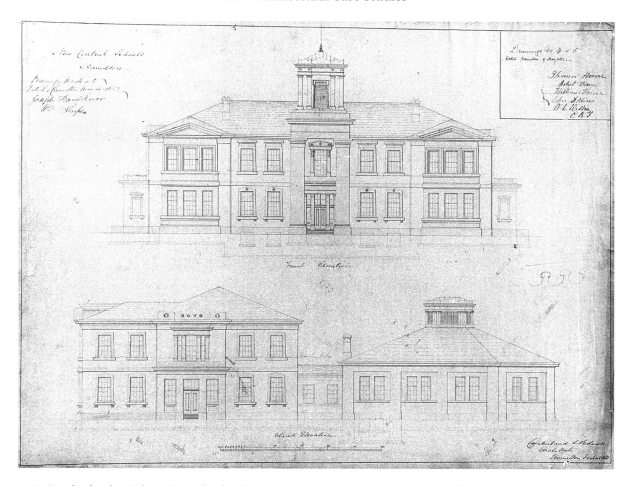

10.8 Cumberland & Ridout. Central School, Hamilton, 1851–3. Contract drawing of front and flank elevations, 8 April 1851. Horwood (70)9

was a social incubator, a place where the legacy of the Western cultural tradition was safeguarded and perpetuated.

If Ryerson established a mandate for the Normal School, Cumberland gave it its architectural articulation. The Normal School (the teaching centre) occupies the front part of the site in a very wide but symmetrical and axial plan. The principal elevation of the building faces south. Behind the Normal School, to the north, lies the two bilaterally symmetrical Model Schools, one for girls, the other for boys. The Model Schools are linked to the Normal School by a corridor leading from the auditorium. The system for managing traffic flow between the Model Schools and the Normal School is particularly effective.[17]

Stylistically, the building was a convincing essay in a classical vocabulary that was not indebted to an identifiable source. One senses echoes from Cumberland's earlier work, in particular the arcaded ground-floor that he designed for the Wolverton railway station. The pedimented entrance bay with Doric pilasters was a feature that Cumberland would use in the nearly contemporary design for the York County Courthouse.

The breadth of the Normal School's mandate has already been mentioned. On the ground floor were the offices of the chief superintendent (in the southwest corner), a school of art and design (including a room for plaster models), a music room, a book depository, a laboratory, and a room given over to what was grandly

10.9 Cumberland & Ridout. Central School, Hamilton, 1851–3. Photograph, 1903, showing the building after renovations by James Balfour in 1890: MTL/BR, Picture Collection, T-15,380

termed 'Philosophical Apparatus' – models of the constellations and the like. A second floor contained large classrooms located in the transverse length of both end bays. Adjacent to the classrooms were the library, the picture gallery, and the museum (museums were among the most important architectural types developed during the Victorian period, and they were excellent examples of that period's commitment to the principles of public education). These elements were carefully disposed to achieve maximum architectural effect and make the most of the available light. The gallery was located under the skylight behind the cupola, and the library and museum faced south, which was the best orientation for bringing in light.[18]

The landscaped grounds provided a living classroom for botany and agricultural lessons. A leading landscape architect, William Mundie, was hired to undertake the work.[19] Mundie levelled and drained the grounds, set aside a plot for a botanical garden and another for a fruit and vegetable garden, developed a small arboretum for foreign and domestic shrubs, and then prepared two acres for agricultural experiments.[20] When he and Cumberland were finished the entire eight-acre site had become a laboratory for learning.[21] Cumberland complemented Mundie's works by designing gas standards for the grounds that were graced with sinuous ornamental decorations.

Adjacent to the Department of Education offices on the ground floor was a private suite for Ryerson, the department head. One can easily imagine Ryerson working late in his office on a report, then taking a stroll around the halls, ab-

10.10 Cumberland & Storm. Model Grammar School, Toronto, 1857–8. Photograph, c. 1860. The Model Grammar School appears on the right. The Normal School is on the left. AO, Picture Collection, Toronto Normal School, L127

sently running his fingers over the sculpture busts and philosophical apparatus, thumbing through the books, and thinking up new tasks for himself and his able lieutenant J.G. Hodgins. One can also imagine him visiting the classrooms during the day, sometimes with distinguished visitors in tow, who at times quizzed the students to test the efficacy of Ryerson's theories.[22] The school not only embodied Ryerson's ideals but his character as well.

Ryerson's vision of public education outlived him, as did this building – but not forever. After Ryerson died the building underwent significant structural modifications. In 1888 alterations were made to the main elevation, and in 1896 a third storey was added, which necessitated the construction of a tower, shown in the frontispiece to an 1898 publication, *Toronto Normal School Jubilee Celebration.*[23] Some years later the building became the campus of Ryerson Polytechnic Institute. After having been occupied without interruption for more than a century, it was demolished in 1963, except for the central portico, which now sits incongruously in the middle of a square largely devoid of significant buildings. A physical-education complex designed by the Toronto firm of Lett/Smith Architects was added during the late 1980s. The original main entrance to the

Normal School now leads *down* to a sports facility, not *up* to a facility created for the purpose of public education.[24] The shift in usage says much about differences in values then and now.

Because the Normal School was substantially modified during the late nineteenth century, and eventually demolished, Cumberland's design has not received its full due in studies of his career. And yet the Normal School was not only significant as an example of mid-Victorian architecture, but an important precursor to University College. In University College, as in the Normal School, the schoolrooms were enriched by access to other facilities – a library and museums – that tended to make the building as close to a self-contained repository of general culture as possible. The Normal School ought to be granted more importance in Cumberland's career (and in the history of Ontario education) as a proving-ground for his ideas about making buildings social laboratories.

ST JAMES'S PAROCHIAL SCHOOL, TORONTO[25]

The St James's Parochial School was a more modest endeavour than the Toronto Normal School, both in its educational agenda and in the size of the structure (fig. 10.6). It was simply

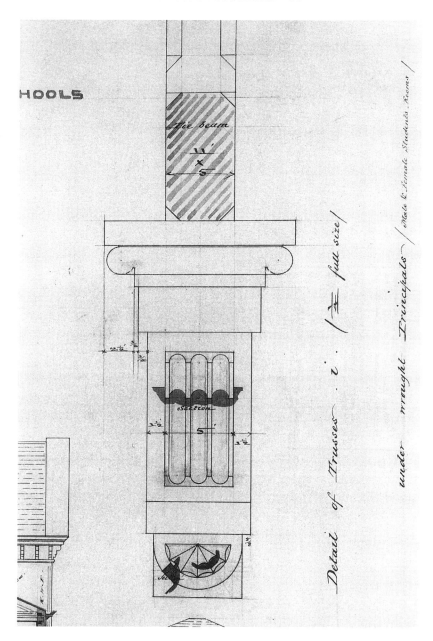

10.11 Cumberland & Storm. Model Grammar School, Toronto, 1857–8. Working drawing of detail of trusses. Horwood (100a)9, detail

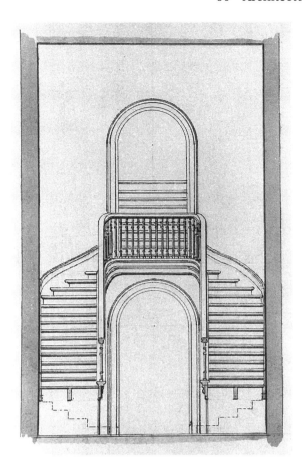

10.12 Cumberland & Storm. Model Grammar School, Toronto, 1857–8. Working drawing of staircase connecting Model Grammar School and Normal School. Horwood (100a)8, detail

a Sunday school for St James's Anglican Cathedral, which was a hundred feet or so to the north. The style was a chaste Gothic Revival, with handsome stone detailing and iron strapwork on the doors. As in the Normal School, the plan was symmetrical, with separate school rooms for girls and boys on the ground and second floors, respectively. In the newspaper of the Canadian Anglican Church an anonymous author remarked, 'every member of our branch society must rejoice at the completion ... of the Parochial School House. The building is of a most substantial character and is much admired for its architectural appearance which reflects great credit upon the accomplished author of the design, F.W. Cumberland Esq.'[26]

But G.P. Ure, writing in 1858, was less enthusiastic, commenting that the building was '[a]n ornament to the Street, but is somewhat disfigured by a very disproportionate bell-tower, of certainly antediluvian style.'[27] What is most interesting about this building for our purposes is the extent to which it demonstrates Cumberland's adeptness in designing in a Gothic Revival vocabulary. It was demolished in 1909.

CENTRAL SCHOOL, HAMILTON[28]

Two qualities distinguish the still-extant Hamilton Central School: its size and the Greek Revival style in which it was designed. This was a capacious box, designed to accommodate a thousand students. Cumberland received the commission because the newly established Board of Trustees of the provincial Department of Education visited the Toronto Normal School, liked what they saw, and asked Cumberland to design a building conceived on similar principles. When the Central School opened in May 1853 it was the only public school in Hamilton and the largest school in Canada West.

With respect to both the plan and the elevations, Cumberland borrowed much from the Normal School (figs. 10.7–8). As in the earlier design, the Central School featured a façade with projecting corner bays and a higher central element containing the main entrance. But inside there was none of the programmatic complexity of the Normal School, just one huge classroom after another, including one, with row on hypnotic row of desks, designed to accommodate 360 female students!

If the plan was a simplified version of the Normal School, the Greek Revival idiom in which the Central School was ornamented was most unusual for this period in Canadian architecture, and there can be no really adequate explanation for it.[29] Cumberland and Ridout had used a modified version of Greek Revival in their designs for the York County Courthouse and the Ontario County Courthouse in Whitby. The Normal School elevation had some elements – particularly the pilasters and certain window-surrounds – that belonged to the visual repertory of this style. In the Central School, however, the Greek Revival elements are particularly exaggerated. The Central School may have been a competent exercise in Greek Revival Style, but it made the building visually heavier than almost all of Cumberland's designs.

Like the Normal School, the Central School underwent substantial alterations. In 1890 a third storey was added, along with a new tower, gables to the elevation, new windows and doors, and a modified interior. At the same time the austere Greek Revival window-surrounds were altered to suit Victorian taste (fig. 10.9). So while the school survives, little of the original architectural character remains.

THE MODEL GRAMMAR SCHOOL, TORONTO[30]

In comparison with the showplace Toronto Normal School, which embodied Ryerson's gradually realized dreams concerning public education, or with the huge Hamilton Central School, a stylistic oddity, the short-lived Toronto Grammar School was modest in scale, only occasionally original in architectural conception, and a failure in terms of its intended use. The building, which stood immediately to the north of the Normal School, opened in 1858 and closed five years later (fig. 10.10). It was eventually demolished, although it is not clear when this took place. Its failure stemmed less from its architectural character than from its quixotic program. Grammar schools were essentially the equivalent of today's secondary schools. Although they provided a classical curriculum, they also offered vocational studies. A somewhat confused program resulted.[31] Apparently Ryerson believed that teachers who held a university degree would come to the Toronto Grammar School to perfect their teaching skills. But the school's five-year program attracted few candidates: 'The project was never a success. Few students attended, the opinion being that the holding of a university degree was sufficient evidence in itself of an ability to teach in a grammar school.'[32]

The Grammar School was not entirely devoid of architectural interest (figs. 10.11–12). The main elevation (which faced north, because the nearness of the Normal School constricted the site) featured a handsome façade distinguished by a second-storey Palladian window grouping flanked by pedimented windows. On the ground floor a linked arcade of roundheaded arches was used. Ornamental detail of a sawtooth Romanesque pattern enlivened the design. A spiral staircase linked the building to the Model Schools on its south side. For the Grammar School Cumberland drew heavily on the designs for his firm's other projects. The dignified elevation resembled the designs for public buildings, in particular the Toronto Mechanics' Institute, and much of the ornamental detail was reminiscent of his firm's residential commissions, although some of the more geometrical and robust ornament was taken from University College, the most complex and challenging architectural project that Cumberland ever undertook. It is now time to examine that remarkable building.

CHAPTER ELEVEN

University College

University College was the pride of Toronto (fig. 11.1). Erected in three short years from 1856 to 1859, with little concern for expense and every concern for rich visual effect, the building caused visitors to marvel at its elaborate detailing and dramatic picturesque effect.[1] Here, for instance, is the opinion of the noted English writer Anthony Trollope,[2] on a visit to North America in 1862, who found that University College was one of only two Toronto buildings worth singling out:

The two sights of Toronto are the Osgoode Hall [recently renovated and expanded in accordance with designs prepared by Cumberland] and the University ... [which is] the glory of Toronto. This is a gothic building and will take rank after, but next to the buildings at Ottawa. It will be the second piece of noble architecture in Canada, and as far as I know on the American continent. It is, I believe, intended to be purely Norman, though I doubt whether the received types of Norman architecture have not been departed from in many of the windows. Be this as it may the College is a manly, noble structure, free from false decoration, and infinitely creditable to those who projected it.[3]

Similar sentiments were expressed by Lord Dufferin, the governor general, who knew Cumberland's work well and considered University College his masterpiece. On a visit to Toronto in 1872 Lord Dufferin said:

Until I reached Toronto I confess I was not aware that so magnificent a specimen of architecture existed upon the American continent. I can only say that the citizens of Toronto, as well as the students of this University, have to be congratulated that, amongst the inhabitants of their own Province, there should have been found a gentleman so complete a master of his art, as to have been enabled to decorate this town with such a magnificent specimen of his skill.[4]

The building thus praised was a picturesque structure executed in a personal interpretation of the Norman-Romanesque style, U-shaped with the north side left open (fig. 11.2). With an asymmetrical plan and elevation, elaborately carved walls faced with stone, and a quadrangle and cloisters within, the building was felicitously sited amid landscaped grounds. Although the building's principal elevation was on the south side, where a massive stone tower dominated the centre of the composition, it could also be approached along a winding path from the east, whose aspect was as pleasingly informal as the one on the south was massive. A singular building in the history of Canadian university architecture, University College was easily the most complex building of any Cumberland ever designed. Like the earlier Normal School, it was an essay in stone, an embodiment of contemporary Canadian attitudes toward the value of a public education.

BACKGROUND[5]

University College's establishment as a secular

11.1 Cumberland & Storm. University College, Toronto, 1856–9. Perspective from the southeast, showing both south and east entrances. *Illustrated London News*, 5 November 1859, 454

institution of higher learning in the 1850s was the culmination of a long-standing controversy. In 1827 the churchman and educator John Strachan, bishop of Toronto from 1839, obtained a royal charter for an educational institution in York (Toronto) to be known as King's College. The college was to be financed by revenues from the Clergy Reserves, Upper Canadian lands set aside for the support of the Church of England. In 1842–3 the college trustees managed to construct a modest building, fully expecting that it would be enlarged later on. As the Province of Canada became more religiously diverse during the 1840s, however, many critics of the Clergy Reserves and of King's College raised their voices in protest against Anglican privilege. By the mid-forties a fierce controversy was raging over whether King's College should lose its religious charter and become a secular institution. In 1844 a pamphlet published by George Brown, editor of the *Globe*, who was strongly in favour of public schools and opposed to Strachan, stated that the religious charter of King's College was an affront to common sense, and that the arguments defending the existing charter were 'gross and anile.'[6]

Strachan, on the other hand, ardently believed a secular education was valueless without a religious foundation.[7] His goal was 'Sound learning and a religious education,' as he later said on the occasion of the opening of Trinity College,[8] the religious institution that he founded as a counterweight to godless University College.

Many people desired a nondenominational university in Upper Canada, but Strachan saw the idea as an imposition of impious and overarching forces arrayed against his Church. A Strachan biographer, writing in 1870, displayed a sounder knowledge than Strachan of Upper Canadian society in the 1840s when he wrote that 'In a colony, composed of people of all nations and all creeds, there will be an endless variety of opinions; and when the choice lies between no creed and all creeds, it would be wiser, perhaps, to select the former than the latter.'[9]

Cumberland, who designed St James's Anglican Cathedral, Strachan's episcopal seat, shared none of Strachan's convictions about education. Instead, Cumberland shared with his Methodist friend Ryerson a wholehearted belief in the value of secular public education, including secular university education. What Strachan

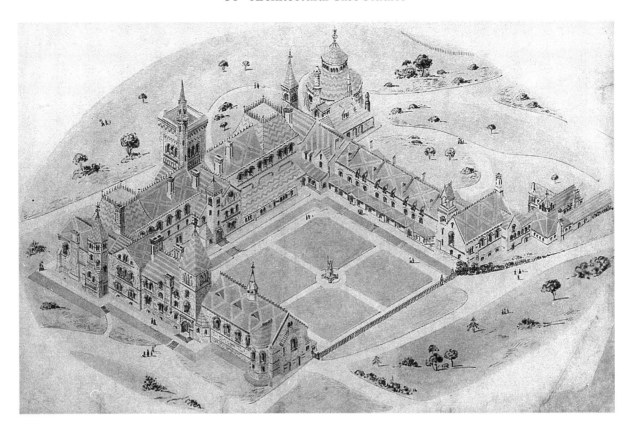

11.2 Cumberland & Storm. University College, Toronto, 1856–9. Bird's-eye perspective from the northeast. William G. Storm, delineator(?). Horwood (107a)

may have thought about his former architect – a devout parishioner – undertaking such an impious commission as University College is unknown, but it is perhaps revealing that there is no mention in Strachan's 1870 biography of the design and construction of St James's or of its architect.[10]

The critics of King's College eventually triumphed over Strachan and the advocates of a Church of England university. In 1850 King's College was secularized and replaced by the nondenominational University of Toronto,[11] with University College as its teaching arm. When the new university was founded, Sir John A. Macdonald is said to have recommended that its officials 'put the University endowment into a building – even a Methodist can't steal bricks and mortar.'[12] Perhaps the members of the university senate were inspired by that recommendation, for in contrast to the dilatory progress

that had marked the history of King's College, the new university was able to commission a building by 1856 and see it constructed in only three years.

OBTAINING THE COMMISSION

On 7 February 1856 the university senate – of which Cumberland himself was a member – appointed a building committee consisting of Chancellor Blake,[13] Chief Justice Draper,[14] and Vice-Chancellor John Langton. Cumberland was appointed architect.[15] Only two days later Cumberland toured the proposed University College site with John Langton to discuss what work would be necessary to prepare the grounds for the new building.[16] It might seem surprising that Cumberland was given the commission without a competition, but it must be remembered that he had done a great deal of architectural work in the Toronto area during the 1850s and knew most of the members of the university senate. In addition to supervising the university's grounds, he had designed the Royal Magnetical Observatory, prepared plans for a new legislature, and carried out extensive renovations on Upper Canada College, whose financial administration was then in the university's hands.[17]

A MOST VALUABLE TRIP

At a special meeting of the university senate held on 8 April 1856, Vice-Chancellor Langton moved that 'Mr. Cumberland be authorized to proceed to Europe to examine the Buildings which have lately been erected for the Queen's College and other educational establishments before deciding upon the plan of the University buildings, upon the payment by the University of his travelling expenses and that the Chancellor be requested to obtain for him letters of introduction as a member of this Senate and as the Architect employed by the University to such persons in Great Britain and Ireland as may be able to assist him in the object of his mission.'[18] On 15 April the senate approved Langton's motion and authorized Cumberland to go to Europe.[19] This course of action was consistent with Victorian architectural practice when new public buildings were being planned, which was to carefully study applicable building forms and adapt them to the requirements of the job at hand.[20]

Cumberland, in fact, had already left Toronto for Europe on 23 February. His letters to Wilmot show that his itinerary included the best recently erected educational buildings, museums, and art galleries in London, Manchester, Oxford, Cambridge, Edinburgh, Dublin, Galway, Cork, and Paris. To facilitate access to these buildings, Cumberland drew on his extensive network of English architect friends, particularly Sir Charles Barry, who furnished him with letters of introduction to, among others, Sir Thomas Deane, architect of the Oxford Museum. Barry also helped plan Cumberland's trip to the Continent. His carefully selected itinerary allowed him to develop an awareness of contem-

porary architecture based on firsthand knowledge of a wide range of buildings.

When Cumberland arrived in England he went first to London. The only reference to architecture in his first letter to Wilmot was when he said that a physician was going to take him to see 'good dissecting rooms & anatomical theatres.' This suggests that Cumberland was thinking of building something similar for the University of Toronto. He also reported that his friend, the London architect Fred Porter, had showed him the University of London, where they went 'all round over & under the building.' They then had visited other buildings in London, 'the Institute of British Architects to look over the Library & then under Fred's guidance to the Book shops – finishing off with the College of Chemistry & the School of Mines – I was utterly done up.'[22] They had spent some time in architectural bookstores, and Cumberland had gone to the reading room of the British Museum.

In the same letter Cumberland related that 'I called on Sir Charles Barry & am to dine with them on my return [from Ireland]. He has kindly promised to prepare a programme for my Continental trip which will be a great advantage. He has also given me an introduction to Sir Thos Deane – I am regularly run off my legs and in such a state of nervous excitement that I scarcely know how to write – it will be quite a rest to get into a Railway carriage.' The weight of his responsibilities was already pressing down on him: 'I hope I shall complete my mission satisfactorily – but the time is short I am very anxious lest I should fail.'

After a few days he went briefly to Manchester. He was dashing madly from city to city, arriving in Manchester, for instance, at 3:00 a.m. The morning of his arrival there he visited a number of buildings, accompanied by John Langton's brother. Cumberland's letter on this part of his trip mentioned a Congregationalist college, 'a good Gothic building over which we were conducted by the principal. Langton had an invitation for me to spend last Saturday and Sunday with Sir John Kay Shuttleworth – & I am to fulfill it on my way back. He afterwards took us to the Free Library – & all the chief buildings in the town – and I afterwards dined with him at his Club.'[23]

Taking the train to Liverpool with young Charles Ridout of Toronto, he visited the Collegiate Institution, 'a very large Gothic building where I found some hints – then to the Philharmonic Hall, Unitarian and R. Catholic Churches, St. George's Hall, Exchange Custom House and all the other buildings.'

The next stop was Dublin. That he went to Ireland so early in the trip testifies to the importance he accorded recent Irish designs as possible sources for University College. Since 1846 three large educational buildings had been erected in Ireland, in Belfast, Cork, and Galway. They were unflatteringly known as the 'Godless Colleges' because they admitted students of many religions.[24] Like the future University College, these Irish buildings combined educational facilities and student residences. The architect of Queen's College, Cork (now University College), which had been built in 1846–9, was Sir Thomas Deane. The architect of Queen's College, Belfast, which had been built in 1849, was Sir Charles Lanyon. It was a redbrick building with stone trim and a vaguely Elizabethan air. The architect of recently completed Galway College was Joseph B. Keane.

In Dublin he visited Deane & Woodward's Trinity College, with its beautiful Ruskinian polychrome mosaic interior, executed in 1853–7.[25] Armed with Barry's letter of introduction, Cumberland was able to see the building at his leisure. From his letters we can infer that this was an important visit for him, but unfortunately he said relatively little about the building. One wonders whether some letters from his European trip have gone astray. There are, for instance, no letters in which he discusses the architecture of the Oxford Museum, designed in 1854 by Deane & Woodward and constructed in 1855–68. Cumberland none the less seems to have been particularly obligated to Sir Thomas Deane. This can be seen from a letter he wrote to the university senate in which he requested that it 'would send by resolution Mr. Cumberland's indebtedness to Sir Thomas Deane of Dublin for his gracious and liberal aid.'[26]

After Dublin was Cork and its Queen's College, which featured carving on the façade in the manner favoured by Ruskin. This had probably been executed by the O'Shea brothers, who also worked on the Oxford Museum. The college was laid out with long wings enclosing a quadrangle, something that Cumberland was later to employ in Toronto. But Cumberland said nothing in his letters about this college, except that he found it and Queen's College, Belfast, to be very good buildings.

Belfast, which he reached on 10 April, was next. Here, his principal excursion was to Queen's College. He reported that 'we were most cordially received by Dr. Andrews the Vice President who gave us a couple of hours in shewing & explaining everything to us. I admire this college vastly hesitating in opinion of preference between it and Cork.' He examined the college's botanical gardens, which consisted of '17 acres of land with an Iron & glass Conservatory of small size but very pretty & perfect. The grounds are very beautifully planted & even at this season looked most refreshingly green, the laurels abounding.'[27]

In Galway his reception was not so warm as in Belfast:

We breakfasted and sallied out to the University where we were received by a very cool & courteous Scotch professor of Hebrew who seemed somewhat unwilling to accept us without other credentials than our own recommendations. He cross examined me on the constitution of our College & as Charlie declared afterwards was intent on flooring me if possible on the theological question. I swam through however & kept my head above water until he was mollified & graciously condescended to serve as our select guide to his own Class room & library then handing us over to the Bedel. The place was worth seeing for the sake of being able to say we had seen it & for the more important end of avoiding all that we had seen. The trial of the Dissecting Room was the worst we had encountered, the butchery being roughly & dirtily perpetrated with blunt tools – no ventilation & no smoking. We spent the rest of the afternoon exploring the town which has many fine public buildings & some good statuary. In the evening we mounted our cigars, strolled into the town & saw something of the character of the Galway population.[28]

The exhausting itinerary continued, with

plans to depart for Scotland on the 14th, reach Perth by noon, and get on to Edinburgh at eight. The 15th and 16th would be spent in Edinburgh. After that he would return to London, and then be off to the south of England by Sunday the 20th, do Oxford and Cambridge at the beginning of the following week, and then go to Paris.

Back in London he 'dined with the Porters & did a heavy stroke of business with him [Fred Porter] as he is preparing me drawings of the chief features of some of the buildings or their parts answering my purpose.' By 25 April he was feeling confident enough to tell Wilmot, 'I don't fear but I shall satisfy "public expectation" for I now feel thoroughly master of the subject & only want quiet to give it form. At present my brain is crammed – very much like a lump of yarn which requires to be spun out from the rude mass before it is worth much.'[29]

Although he had not yet visited the Continent, it seems virtually certain that his main architectural ideas for the university were already well developed. The buildings he later dutifully examined in France seemed only to confirm his antipathy to French design. In France he even found time to do a little sightseeing unconnected with his professional duties, in the company of a Mr Derbishere, who had been seven weeks in Paris and seen no more than the Louvre. Cumberland agreed to show him around the city, but his letter leaves little doubt about his condescending attitude to France and French architecture in particular:

We went to Notre Dame, the Morgue, and then on to the Jardin des Plants [sic] which is open free to the public. The Zoological collection is inferior to that of London – and to *my* taste the gardens are stiff & formal, the flower beds being in long lines of geometrical figures monotonously repeated and the flowers themselves set out in exact lines & at equal distances as though France – which is the gardener – has been a rigid starchey straight laced model moral old maid instead of – as she is – a free random thoughtless courtizan! After wandering amongst monkeys and camel leopards giraffes and gazelles, hippopotami & golden fish we entered the museum of Natural History, then out to another building, the Anatomical Museum, which contains everything from the eyetooth of a flea to the tusk of an elephant and the jawbone of a whale, subsequently visiting the library, and the Geological Museum which latter is by far the best & fullest I have seen. We went thence to the palace of the Luxembourg – where is a fine Gallery of Pictures, some of great beauty and not a few bad daubs of vulgar subjects atrociously treated. After spending a couple of hours here – Derbishere with an opera glass walking backwards with his head askance & one finger elevated to add to the expression of his arched eyebrow and compressed lip of criticism – we went all through the Chamber of Deputies, the Throne Room, Marie Antoinette's apartment and chapel &c &c the whole from beginning to end a mass of the richest carving entirely gilded except where color was introduced into the ceilings and bad cartoons in fresco painted in the panels. Decoration run extravagantly mad – ornamentation rioting in excess – architecture debased into a fantastic tasteless meaningless medley of gaudy enrichment prolific of vulgarity, indicative of kingly vanity & popular degradation and prophetic of national bankruptcy.[30]

This is the last mention of architecture in the 1856 letters; one is left wishing for more.

Can we tell which buildings Cumberland particularly admired during his journey? Fortunately, we can, thanks to some reference plans he commissioned in England.[31] He seems to have commissioned drawings of those buildings whose *programs* were complementary to that of the University of Toronto. For some of the buildings, for example the student quarters of Trinity College, Dublin, he only had parts copied. For University College, London, he had the whole building and its details copied. The buildings he admired were those, such as Queen's College, Galway, that provided spaces of several kinds: classrooms, museums, student and faculty housing (fig. 11.3). He also admired buildings that were graced with planned grounds. Interestingly, nowhere to be found were detail drawings of ornament and the like. Ornament, presumably, was only decided on after University College's plan was arranged. Furnished with his drawings, he returned to Toronto resolved to build a Canadian equivalent – but no mere copy – of the British buildings that had inspired him.

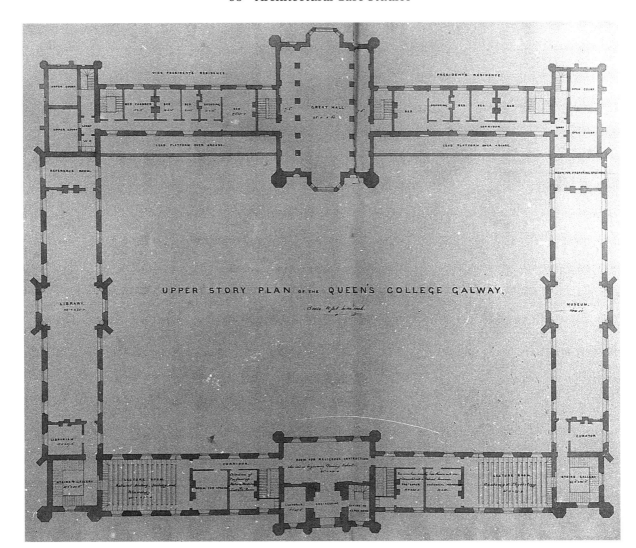

11.3 Queen's College, Galway, Ireland. Upper-floor plan, 1856. Draftsman Fred Porter(?). Horwood (1644)2

DEVELOPMENT OF THE DESIGN

Within just a few weeks of his return from Europe, Cumberland had prepared a working plan that bore the title 'Toronto University Buildings. First Study' (fig. 11.4). It clearly was based on the quadrangle plans he had seen in Europe. The plan showed a breathtakingly comprehensive building that included everything from a museum to residences for the students and for the university president. The quadrangles of Europe had encouraged him to conceive of the building as a series of four ranges. Although the cardinal

points were not indicated on the plan, one assumes that nineteenth-century mapping conventions applied and that north was at the top of the drawing. The main entrance was therefore to be on the south side. The south range was to contain separate facilities on the ground floor for the college and university administrations and on the upper floor for a library and convocation hall. The east range – which was to be interrupted in the middle to provide access to the quadrangle – would contain the university senate offices, the dean's offices, classrooms, and undifferentiated spaces. This

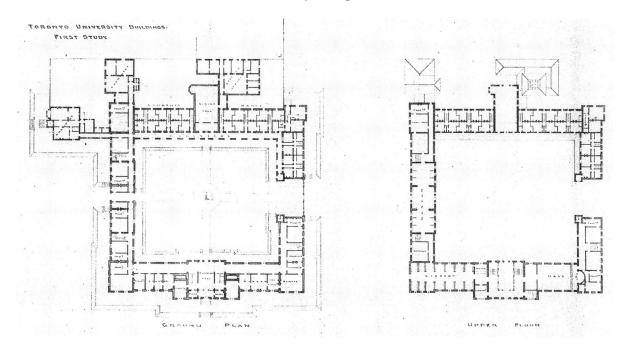

11.4 Cumberland & Storm. University College, Toronto, 1856–9. 'Toronto University Buildings. First Study,'
c. May–June 1856. Douglas Richardson, *A Not Unsightly Building: University College and Its History* ([Oakville,
Ont.]: Mosaic Press 1990), 55

proposed building was to be located on the same site as the building that was eventually constructed, and thus the east range would have faced meandering Taddle Creek. The view from the tower gives some idea of the degree to which the building stood as an isolated monument in a thickly forested site (fig. 11.5). The entrance on the east side of the building would have been most picturesque, in marked contrast to the more formal south range with its tower and stepped-forward entrance bay. On the west side was to be the teaching range, with classrooms running along the entire ground floor and terminating at the building's north end in a chemistry laboratory. On the second storey of the west range were to be a museum, a reading room, and classrooms. The north range would contain student residences and was thoughtfully provided with cloisters that would have enabled the students to walk from their residences into the dining hall and classrooms. In the centre of the north range was to be a two-storey dining hall, with a kitchen located asymmetrically to the north. The president's

residence and the dean's offices were to be located somewhat like book-ends on either end of the student residences.

The plan revealed subtleties and niceties that one would not expect in a preliminary design. For instance, the dining hall was designed asymmetrically to accommodate a head table standing three stairs above the level of the students' tables. All of the classrooms were to have tiered seating. The entrance hall was to feature a two-storey space with a gallery. The convocation hall would have a raised dais with an apsidal projection for seating the notables. Many of these features – with the exception of the entrance hall, a feature that Cumberland had used in earlier buildings – may well have been taken from the British universities that Cumberland saw. It is not known whether elevations accompanied the plan, although it has been suggested that during this phase of the design's development Cumberland was mulling over a Gothic style for the building.[32] The massing was deliberately asymmetrical and picturesque, with a number of details such as bay

11.5 Panoramic view from University College tower, Toronto, 1860. Photograph by William Notman. This was one of a series of four photographs by Notman providing panoramic views from the college. MTL/BR, Picture Collection, T-12,941

windows suggesting an affinity with English government or university buildings.

In terms of function, the proposed building represented a most interesting amalgam. As Douglas Richardson has observed, the plan synthesized design features of the medieval English residential colleges and of the newer colleges erected in England and Ireland.[33] The gatehouse, residences, library, and hall were features typical of Oxbridge; the convocation hall, museum, laboratory, president's house, and classrooms were typical of the newer Irish colleges.

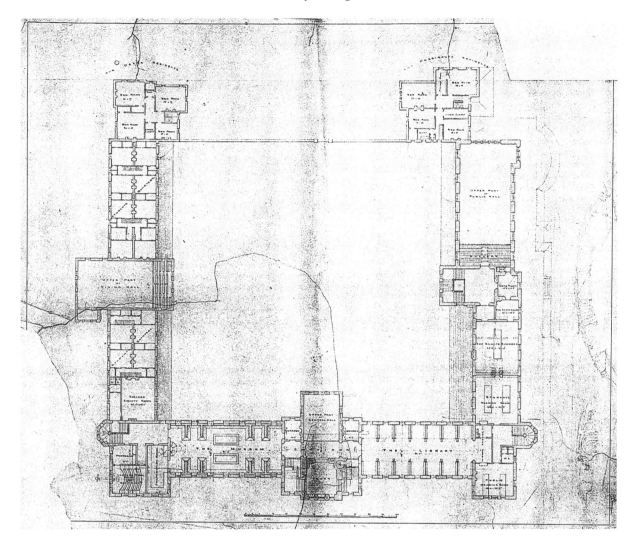

11.6 Cumberland & Storm. University College, Toronto, 1856–9. Study of upper-floor plan, c. July 1856. Douglas Richardson, *A Not Unsightly Building: University College and Its History* ([Oakville, Ont.]: Mosaic Press 1990), 59

It was not long before Cumberland and Storm developed a second plan that significantly improved on the first (fig. 11.6). The plan was now U-shaped, with the open side facing north. The spaces within the ranges were now more logically disposed than in the first scheme, with the east range given over to university functions and a public reading room, the south range to classrooms, and the west range to residences. The chemistry laboratory was moved to the southwest corner of the building. Residences for the dean and the university president were situated at the tips of the U. (The president's resi-

dence was eventually omitted.) Each of the ranges was thought through more carefully. The south range now combined the museum and the library. The new location of the chemistry laboratory was much more sensible than in the first scheme, where it had been tucked away on the north side of the building. Each range now had an obvious focal point: the towered entrance hall on the south side, the convocation hall on the east side, and the dining hall on the west side. By this point the design had coalesced; most of the significant design elements were carried over to the final version. The only

11.7 Cumberland & Storm. University College, Toronto, 1856–9. Study of south elevation, c. July 1856. Horwood (125)8

regrettable change occurred in the east range. Instead of being open to the morning sun and the picturesque view on that side, this range was now closed in, making its design less successful than in the first scheme.

With the fundamental principles of organization effectively established, Cumberland and Storm could turn to achieving a more dramatic silhouette. The essentially symmetrical south elevation was given a more subtle and asymmetrical organization, and the wall surfaces were enriched by stone patterning and carving (fig. 11.7). The design appears to have been substantially complete by October, although most of the ornamental details were designed as the building was constructed.

ANALYSING THE FINAL DESIGN

Although the complexity of the Normal School's program offered a precedent for University College, the design process was markedly different. In the Normal School Cumberland incorporated the different programmatic elements into the symmetrical silhouette of an essentially classicized building divided into five bays, with the central bay given the most elaborate treatment. At University College Cumber-

land abandoned classical symmetry and instead gave each of the programmatic elements a separate architectural expression. As a result the building was more varied in plan and elevation. One might call this approach picturesque, except that one would miss the crucial importance of the shift in thinking from the Normal School approach to the one followed at University College. The Normal School emphasized the unity of the *whole*; the building envelope was what counted. In University College the unity of the whole was still important, but it was achieved by combining distinct *parts*. These parts were taken from the best possible sources from several periods and recombined in a new synthesis.

These two approaches can be seen as summing up the differences between Early Victorian and High Victorian design. Cumberland's early buildings were connected most closely with Early Victorian architectural principles. When he came to design University College, everything changed. He went to England and Ireland, saw the newly built educational institutions, and realized that Britain's leading architects had developed a way of designing buildings that was different from the way in which he had been trained. Rather than looking mainly to

11.8 Cumberland & Storm. University College, Toronto, 1856–9. Detail of stonecarving on Croft Chapter House. Photo by the author

classical precedents, architects were now interested in the Middle Ages. The medieval university offered a number of important precedents for plans. In particular, the quadrangle – itself copied from monasteries – presented a way of fostering a sense of community by means of an architectural form. The university at Cork had a quadrangle, and so did other universities that Cumberland saw. The Oxford Museum based its chemistry laboratory on the abbot's kitchen at Glastonbury Abbey. This sort of selective combination of elements from the past, for formal and one might say symbolic reasons, is usually termed stylistic eclecticism. It has long been remarked that this approach helps explain Cumberland's choice of various elements.

Cumberland was well aware of stylistic eclecticism and of the mid-Victorian premise that architectural forms could evoke symbolic asso-

ciations, but really only the first approach has much bearing on the design of University College.[34] Cumberland was immediately drawn to stylistic eclecticism. He thought it worthwhile to use earlier forms. And he probably thought that certain forms were more appropriate than others. This would help explain why he – either in consultation with Governor General Head, or by himself – chose the Norman Romanesque style. Cumberland believed that its ruggedness was appropriate to Canada. But when it came to finding sources for the parts of the building, he looked to whatever sources provided the best possible form. Eclecticism could be a philosophy as well as a working method: one chose the best original source because it was the best.

Yet the stylistic eclecticism of the building does not explain every aspect of it. One additional element needs to be considered: Cumber-

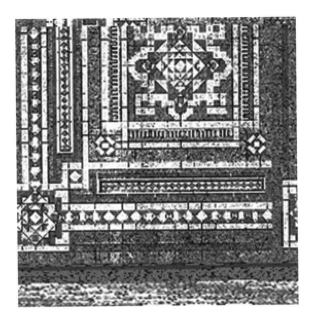

11.9 Floor tile from Maw & Co., Broseley, Shropshire, England, for University College and Osgoode Hall, Toronto. Maw & Co., catalogue of *Encaustic Tile, Geometrical Mosaic and Plain Tile Pavements*, item no. 226, late 1860s, in Douglas Richardson, *A Not Unsightly Building: University College and Its History* ([Oakville, Ont.]: Mosaic Press 1990), 91

11.10 Cumberland & Storm, University College, Toronto, 1856–9. Detail for stonecarving of stylized animal, c. 1858. Drawing by clerk of works John Morris(?). Horwood (119), recto

land's interest in craftsmanship and carving. University College was embellished with quite marvellous carvings executed by skilled German craftsmen (fig. 11.8). Inside, it was enlivened by polychromatic tiles from the Shropshire firm of Maw & Co. (fig. 11.9).[35] Such elements reflect the influence of Ruskin, who, rebelling against the crass materialism and shoddy manufactured goods of Victorian England, tried to assert the importance of craftsmanship.[36] At the Oxford Museum, which was designed with Ruskin's participation, craftsmanship was central. The carvings were executed by Ireland's O'Shea brothers, who, encouraged by Ruskin, introduced naturalistic motifs. Ruskin's goal was to assert the dignity of labour by making the labourers an integral part of the design process. Similar sentiments influenced the design of University College. The architects prepared hundreds of sheets of full-scale architectural details that the craftsmen then faithfully trans-

lated into stone (figs. 11.10–12). One memorable drawing actually shows the faint imprint of a real maple leaf that had been pinned up beside its drawn equivalent. The unique Canadian character of the building was thus proclaimed by a botanically correct carving of Canadian flora. The attention to detail extended literally from floor to ceiling: workers came from Maw & Co. to execute the distinctive tile pattern.

The whole, however, was greater than the sum of its parts. Even though specific elements of the building had recognizable medieval origins (such as the Glastonbury chapter house for the chemistry laboratory, and medieval monasteries and colleges for the cloisters) the synthesis made them new – just as the program for a comprehensive university was new. And the parts were expertly combined to create a memorable architectural and spatial experience defensible on technical as well as aesthetic grounds: the ample height of the chemistry

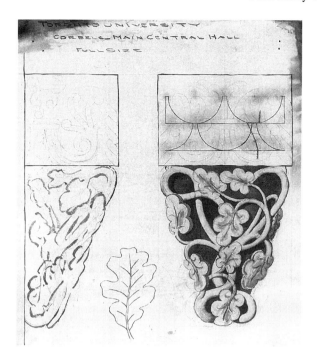

11.11 Cumberland & Storm. University College, Toronto, 1856–9. Detail for stonecarving of oak leaves on corbels in main central hall, c. 1858. Drawing by clerk of works John Morris(?). Horwood (118)

11.12 Cumberland & Storm. University College, Toronto, 1856–9. Detail for stonecarving of maple leaves on corbels in main central hall, c. 1858. Note stain indicating that an actual leaf was originally pinned to the drawing. Drawing by clerk of works John Morris(?). Horwood (118)

laboratory providing ventilation, but also a dramatic spatial experience; the cloisters providing not only protection from the elements, but also a close-up view of handsome woodwork – to say nothing of the cloister's role in fostering pleasing social encounters. Most of all, however, it was the interior of the building that must have evoked admiration. It is important to realize how painstakingly this building was crafted, and what a delightful experience it would have been to walk under the jagged archivolts of the main entrance, into the two-storey entrance foyer, and then into the classrooms, library, and other facilities. With its many beautifully carved features – the hundreds of wooden bosses, the exposed-truss ceiling in the convocation hall, the library shelves – the whole building would have provided a rich and marvellous experience for the undergraduates and instructors for whom it was intended. University College in fact dem-

onstrated Ruskin's tenet that the value of craftsmanship will make itself felt to the user. Perhaps this explains its perennial attractiveness as a building – the obvious attention to quality that reflects the serious yet joyous and liberating experience of higher education.

THE GEOLOGICAL MUSEUM AND LIBRARY

That University College included a museum is further evidence of its close links with other educational institutions of the time (figs 11.13–14). In Britain an act of 1850 had enabled towns to establish public museums and libraries. The resulting boom in museum and library construction gave rise to an extensive architectural literature. In 1853, for example, the brothers

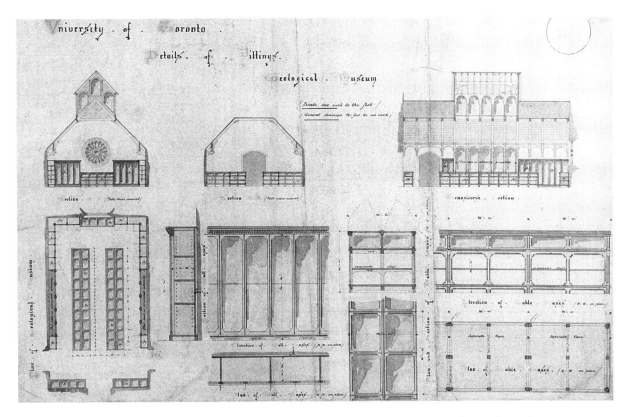

11.13 Cumberland & Storm. University College, Toronto, 1856–9. Details of fittings for geological museum, c. 1857–8. Horwood (107)1

John and Wyatt Papworth published a very sensible and thorough book entitled *Museums, Libraries, and Picture Galleries, Public and Private; Their Establishment, Formation, Arrangement, and Architectural Construction*,[37] which embraced a number of European and British models, including Rohault de Fleury's wing at the Musée Nationale d'Histoire Naturelle, and Labrouste's Bibliothèque Ste Geneviève, both in Paris, and the Munich Pinacoteca. All of these featured naturally lit interiors.

The college, as mentioned above, also had a library, whose wood fittings were beautifully decorated and carved (figs. 11.15–17).

THE ROLE OF GOVERNOR GENERAL HEAD AND SIR DANIEL WILSON[38]

When any success is brought into this world there are always many ready to claim that they were its midwives. In the case of University Col-

lege, two men, Governor General Head and Professor Daniel Wilson, have been credited with having made significant contributions to the building's design, Head with respect to the choice of style, and Wilson with respect to certain details of the south elevation. Much has been made of a comment by John Langton in a November 1856 letter to his brother:

The site being chosen Cumberland drew a first sketch of a Gothic building, but the Governor would not hear of Gothic and recommended Italian, shewing us an example of the style, a palazzo at Siena, which, if he were not Governor General and had written a book on art, I should have called one of the ugliest buildings I ever saw. However after a week's absence the Governor came back with a new idea, it was to be Byzantine; and between them they concocted a most hideous elevation.[39]

This has been interpreted to mean that the gov-

11.14 Cumberland & Storm. University College, Toronto, 1856–9. Perspective of geological museum interior, c. 1857–8. Horwood (107)2

11.15 Cumberland & Storm. University College, Toronto, 1856–9. Perspective of library interior, n.d.
William G. Storm, delineator(?). Horwood (747a)1

11.16 Cumberland & Storm. University College, Toronto, 1856–9. Details of library fittings, c. 1857–8. Horwood (119)2

11.17 Cumberland & Storm, University College, Toronto, 1856–9. Photograph of library interior, n.d. Horwood Add. 5, box 1, item no. 38

ernor general played a central role in the development of the design. Cumberland himself, during a speech at the topping-off ceremony on 4 October 1858, 'gave credit to His Excellency for having suggested the particular style of the building.'[40] Head was a cultivated man and a student of the arts who contributed frequently to art journals and was the author of *A Handbook of the History of the Spanish and French Schools of Painting* (1848), to which Langton was presumably referring.[41] It should be noted, however, apropos of Langton's remarks, that stylistic terminology was not as precise then as it is today. 'Gothic' – which today denotes a specific movement in western European architecture and art, from around 1100 to 1400 – was originally a pejorative term referring to anything

strange or barbaric. When Langton used the term Gothic, he might simply have meant, again in the words of the *OED* – 'belonging to the dark ages.'[42] Previous researchers have been assiduous in looking for a 'lost' Gothic sketch of University College, but such a sketch probably does not exist. The evidence suggests, in fact, that Cumberland completed the building *despite* the governor general's interference, not because of it. As W. Stewart Wallace wrote in 1927, 'the whole responsibility fell on the shoulders of Langton and Cumberland, subject to the spasmodic intervention of the governor general.'[43]

Professor Wilson later claimed some credit for the development of the design. According to Wilson's diary, 'Cumberland designed a Victorian Gothic building [note the looseness of stylistic designation], Sir Edmund Head wanted a round-arched Italian building, probably Renaissance. Cumberland compromised on the present style, which Lord Dufferin called "Norman-Gothic." Sir Daniel Wilson designed the large window on the front. This he told W.A.L. [William A. Langton] himself. Sir Daniel Wilson also added the four lumps at the top of the tower at the corners (see original sketch of elevation without them.')[44] There is no doubt that Wilson had an excellent knowledge of medieval buildings. While still in Edinburgh he had published *Memorials of Edinburgh in the Olden Time* (1847), a guide to the city's medieval and later architecture, which he also illustrated. He may therefore have been responsible for the 'lumps' in question. But was this really of any significance to the overall development of the design?

THE SYMBOLISM OF THE NORMAN-ROMANESQUE STYLE

If there is not much value in attempting to determine to what extent the governor general, Wilson, or others contributed to the development of the design (nor, it must be admitted, does there seem to be a reliable way to do so), the same cannot be said about examining the possible symbolic reasons for University College's Norman-Romanesque style. Mid-Victorian architects were motivated to look to the past not only for the formal language of earlier buildings, but also for the symbolic associations that resonated from earlier forms. This approach was motivated partly by architectural concerns, and partly by concerns lying far beyond the scope of architecture. Dissatisfaction with the materialism of the nineteenth century led architects to use earlier forms in an almost talismanic way – as if they could thereby regain some of the strength and veracity of simpler times. Certainly, this thinking underlines the work of one of the key theoretical writers of the period, A.W.N. Pugin, whose *Contrasts* (1836) mounted a plea for the rebirth of a religious architecture by arguing that the buildings of the past had had a sort of dignity that the present should emulate. But according to some commentators, Pugin engaged in an ethical fallacy when he argued that

one style is inherently better than another.[45] This perhaps helps us understand why the revival of earlier, particularly Gothic, forms took place first in ecclesiastical architecture, and then, only gradually, in public buildings.

The Victorians did not like employing a style without elaborating on its symbolic associations. Those who wrote about a particular style were at pains to explore its historical and literary associations. The Norman-Romanesque style – the terms Norman and Romanesque were used interchangeably – had precise but different associations in Britain and Canada. The British regarded the Norman-Romanesque style as evoking a time in English history when Christianity was undergoing a rebirth and democratic institutions were just being established. It therefore had pleasing political and religious connotations of purity and simplicity. These connotations were only marginally relevant to Canada, whose writers spoke more often about how appropriate the Norman-Romanesque style was to the new country. They pointed to the harshness of the Canadian climate and argued that the ruggedness of the Norman-Romanesque style was perfectly suited to the raw youthfulness of Canada. These ideas were put forward by Professor Wilson in his tribute to Cumberland during the 1858 topping-off ceremony:

[The governor general] has referred to its [University College's] admirable adaptedness to the purposes for which it is intended. More than this, it is peculiarly emblematic of this Province and the adaptations of our Institutions to it. It belongs to an old period, coeval with the laying of the foundations of British freedom, and is exhibited here with a wise adaptation to modern uses. The Architect has achieved the highest triumph an Architect can accomplish – he has finished a beautiful Structure, consistent in all respects with the style he has adopted, but in no one point sacrificed its wise and fitting adaptation to the modern purposes to which it is to be devoted.[46]

Wilson's speech provides an excellent example of how Victorian architectural symbolism resonated in the minds of educated Canadians of the time. The Norman-Romanesque style's associations were relevant to both Canada and England; yet it was not slavishly followed, but rather adapted to modern purposes. Indeed, appropriating a style for its symbolic connotations, and then adapting that style for modern purposes, is exactly what present-day universities do when they reproduce aspects of medieval education and combine them with a scientific curriculum.

One cannot be too literal, however, when interpreting architectural symbolism. Many of the justifications for the use of particular styles during the nineteenth century were inconsistent. The association of the Norman-Romanesque style with the birth of English democracy and the rise of English Christianity was problematic to say the least. The Norman Conquest in fact squelched indigenous English traditions, whether linguistic, legal, religious, or architectural. The Norman style in architecture was a foreign imposition; to gloss over this point is to misuse history.

Those few commentators who remarked on the Romanesque style's origins in the time of the Roman Republic also tied themselves up in inconsistencies. For instance, this is what Governor General Head said at the topping-off ceremony:

I congratulate the Architect upon having dealt with the structure in the successful manner he has done. So far as my knowledge extends, I am not aware of any other instance of the Norman, or Romanesque, style of Architecture on this Continent ... I believe that style is capable of the most useful results. To my own mind, it suggests a variety of analogies, some of them bearing particularly on the nature of the duties of the Members of the University here assembled. In the first place, I never see a Building in this style of architecture – whether it be ecclesiastical or civil – but I regard it as a type of modern civilization. It is the adaptation to modern purposes of forms which originated long ago, – it is the adaptation of Roman architecture to modern civilization. Where did you get these forms? Were did you get these ceremonies, under which Municipalities were formed, – those Municipalities, which, under different names, are creeping through the Continent of America carrying the principles of local self-government with them?

They are from Rome, from whence comes this kind of Romanesque Architecture, – they are the adaptation of Forms derived from Rome to the wants of modern society. Many things in modern Europe are precisely analogous to the style of the Building in which we are assembled. I say, moreover, that the style of the Architecture of this Building suggests some reflections upon the duties of the University itself, for it is the business of the University to give a sound Classical education to the youth of our Country and to impart to them that instruction and information which are essential to the discharge of their duties as Citizens, both in Public and private life, according to the wants and usages of modern society. I say, Sir, that we may take the Building in which we are assembled as the type of the duties standing before the University to discharge.[47]

Arguing that the Norman-Romanesque style was particularly appropriate in Canada because it was rugged and therefore well suited to a new and savage land was a little like Marie Antoinette dressing up as a milkmaid: an exercise in make-believe. The Norman-Romanesque style may have appeared rugged and simple, but the outward simplicity was only achieved through the application of a high degree of skill. The stonecarving was so complex that craftsmen from other countries had to be brought in to do the work. The commentators seized on only those stylistic connotations that they found palatable and ignored the others.

In the case of University College, the Norman-Romanesque style was considered particularly appropriate for a variety of reasons: because of its associations with Roman republicanism; because it recalled the dawn of English democracy; and because its apparent simplicity was appropriate for a new country. If there were some who were puzzled by the different texture of these veneered arguments, none ever commented on it. All accounts agree that the choice of the Norman-Romanesque style for University College was considered appropriate.

CONSTRUCTION

The construction of University College proceeded fairly smoothly for a building of its com-

11.18 University College, Toronto. Photograph, n.d., of south and east wings after the fire of 14 February 1890. MTL/BR, Picture Collection T-13,101

plexity. The chemistry laboratory was the first part to be completed, in the summer of 1858. There were rumours that the laboratory had been built first so that it would not be affected by threatened budget cutbacks. Construction costs had mounted even beyond the limits of a generous budget. The architects were eventually forced to scale down some of the college's more lavish features, such as the woodwork in the convocation hall, and the planned botanical gardens were scrapped. The architects watched with dismay as their out-of-pocket costs mounted, with no corresponding increase in their fee.

A TRIUMPHANT CEREMONY

On 4 October 1858 – two years to the day after the cornerstone was laid – an elaborate

ceremony was held to mark the laying of the tower's coping-stone.[48] Vice-Chancellor Langton toasted Governor General Head and, making an appropriate pun, remarked that 'At the very critical period, when the University was left without a head, His Excellency had afforded them his valuable assistance and advice.'[49] In reply, the governor general emphasized the importance of educational institutions in a new country, and then delivered the complimentary remarks about Cumberland already quoted. Professor Wilson then toasted the architect. His encomium read, in part:

Your Excellency has already anticipated what I might have desired to say in reference to this Toast, in the commendations you passed on this intellectual work of one of the Architects of the Province. Nor is it an unimportant thing that an Institution, where intel-

11.19 University College, Toronto. Photograph, n.d., of dragon newel recarved after the fire of 1890. Horwood Add. 5, box 1, item no. 36

11.20 University College, Toronto. Photograph, n.d., of woodwork recarved after the fire of 1890. Horwood Add. 5, box 1, item no. 44

lect is to be cultivated, the aesthetic faculty of the young minds of Canada should be specially nurtured by gazing, through every stage of such development, on works of gorgeous sculpture and beautiful architecture, showing the adaptation of intellect wrought in stone, for such purposes as this building is to be devoted to. All great Nations in past time have sought to establish memorials of their intellectual power in the architectural structures that they have handed down to other generations ... We look forward to a glorious future for this Institution, a noble destiny for this Building, upon which Your Excellency has laid that Crowning Stone, the evidence of the glory which, we trust, awaits us. I refer with sincere pleasure to the refined taste, the intellectual power, the true genius which our Architect has manifested in the erection of this magnificent Structure.[50]

These remarks proved prescient; for genera-

tions to come, University College, which admitted its first students exactly one year later, was the emblem of higher education in Canada.

THE FIRE

On 14 February 1890 Wilson recorded the following in his diary: 'A frightful calamity. Last evening I looked on while our beautiful university building was helplessly devoured by the flames. It is terrible. Thirty-three thousand carefully selected volumes have vanished. The work of a lifetime is swept away in a single night; a tray of lamps prepared for the microscopes at the Annual Conversazione upset, and in a few seconds the blaze defied every effort at its extinction.'[51] Thus Cumberland and Storm's University College fell victim to the most common scourge of architecture (fig. 11.18).

The college was rebuilt, however, and two

years after the diary entry just quoted, Wilson commented on the remarkable progress of the rebuilding, and even stated that it had resulted in some improvements: 'The anniversary of that calamitous day that two years since reduced our beautiful University building to a pile of smoking ruins ... We are on the whole gainers ... Even the beauty of the fine building has been increased by getting rid of the abominable engine-house and chimney-stalk [in the quad], as well as of a disfiguring afterthought of Cumberland's in an ugly chimney near the east end of the main front.'[52] Even the woodwork – including the magnificent newel in the shape of a dragon – had been carefully recarved (figs. 11.19–20).

But not all the changes were as favourable as these: the museum and library were never rebuilt, nor was the convocation hall. The loss of these spaces is particularly regrettable. The rebuilt college, although possessing the same dramatic silhouette of the earlier structure, lacked, in its interior, much of the programmatic complexity of the original. However, it may be that the fire only provided the impetus for changes that would have taken place anyway. By 1890 the college's original mid-Victorian premise, that a single building could be sufficient for all the needs of an institution of higher learning, had already become obsolete.

Since the 1890s University College has been continually remodelled and renovated. Although the silhouette of the building still resembles the original, two aspects of the building have been changed in ways that significantly influence visitors' perceptions. Sadly, the approach from the east, once informal and picturesque, is much changed: Taddle Creek has been rerouted underground, Hart House constructed in the former line of view of the college, and the entrance gates that once framed the view are long gone. A similar transformation of visitors' perceptions has resulted from the closing-in of the north arm of the building. The original col-

lege, it will be remembered, was U-shaped, with the north arm left open. In 1961 it was closed-in when the Laidlaw Library, designed by the firm of Mathers & Haldenby, was added. Although this addition is sympathetic in scale and handling to the original building – remarkably so for a building of its era – it tends to make University College more insular than it was.

Despite such changes, however, each generation of students discovers anew the history that still resonates in this place, the oldest university structure in Toronto. It is a fitting tribute to Cumberland that a copy of the Dunbar bust of the architect commissioned by the employees of the Northern Railway stands in the college's atrium.

REPUTATION

It is curious that a building whose character was so notably influenced by Ruskin should never have evoked any comment from him, so far as has been determined. And there has in fact been a distinct lack of scholarly appreciation of University College. Although nineteenth-century visitors – such as those cited at the outset of this chapter – were uniformly favourable in their comments, the college has never attracted much notice in international architectural circles as a building of outstanding character. For instance, the well-known historian of architecture, Henry-Russell Hitchcock, passes quickly over University College in his magisterial study of nineteenth- and twentieth-century architecture, observing only that 'its rich and rather bombastic Norman design is closer to English work of the earlier decades of the century than to the round-arched Ruskinian Gothic of the fifties.'[53] But even this rather brusque dismissal is more than what one finds in two specialized studies of Ruskin, in which University College is not even mentioned.[54] Perhaps future studies of mid-Victorian architecture will accord this building more prominence.

CHAPTER TWELVE

Steeples for the People: Church Designs

Ecclesiastical architecture during the nineteenth century attracted architectural theory the way a church steeple attracts lightning bolts. The Industrial Revolution had so undermined the spiritual basis of society that many people believed an architecture expressing true religious sentiment was no longer possible. In response, theorists of the 1830s and later argued vehemently for a return to architectural expressions with a spiritual basis. They thought the Middle Ages offered a model for a renewed Christian architecture. A.W.N. Pugin, for example, believed medieval society had been characterized by order and dignity, and that medieval buildings reflected this order and dignity through their honest use of natural materials and beautiful carving. He further believed his own society was chaotic and irreligious and that its architecture – particularly the 'Commissioners' Churches,' cheap boxes, the first of which appeared in 1819, that were covered with meretricious ornament – reflected the sad decline in spiritual life characteristic of the nineteenth century. He put forward these theories in a number of publications, including his *Contrasts, a study of the Parallel between the Noble Edifices of the Fourteenth and Fifteenth Centuries, and Similar Buildings of the Present Day: Shewing the Present Decay of Taste.* Despite being a Catholic in a country that despised popery, Pugin became pre-eminent among the many theorists who called for the creation of a religious architecture with a greater spiritual dimension.[1]

During the 1830s and 1840s, Anglican theorists connected with the universities of Oxford and Cambridge took up Pugin's theories and gave them an Anglican cast. They too called for a religious architecture capable of providing a setting in which a dignified form of worship could take place. Eventually the major theorists founded the Cambridge Camden Society, which from 1841 to 1868 published a journal known as the *Ecclesiologist.* The contributors to this journal favoured an architecture that expressed liturgical functions clearly. The chancel, the place where the most holy rituals of the church occurred, should, they argued, be expressed clearly as a separate architectural space. For this reason the *Ecclesiologist* looked with favour on such early-fourteenth-century churches as the Church of St Michael in the village of Long Stanton, near Cambridge. In this building each liturgically significant element was architecturally well defined. The long rectangular nave was clearly visible from the exterior, as were the chancel projecting from the east end and the side porch. By the beginning of the 1850s, a number of publications propagating similar views had been issued for the guidance of church building committees and their architects. To name but three influential works, churchman could refer to the Ecclesiologist's *A Few Words to Church Builders* (1844), Raphael Brandon's *Parish Churches: Being Perspective Views of English Ecclesiastical Structures* (1850),[2] and George Truefitt's *Designs for Country Churches* (also 1850).

The debates over whether to employ Gothic architecture in tandem with a renewed church ritual became relevant to churches in the British colonies became most were assisted financially by the Society for the Propagation of the Gospel in Foreign Parts and other organizations that depended heavily on the *Ecclesiologist* for guidance in church building. During the late 1840s several churches based on Ecclesiological principles were built in colonies such as Newfoundland and New Brunswick. The Cathedral Church of St John's, Newfoundland, designed in 1848 by Sir George Gilbert Scott (1811–78), was discussed in the April 1848 *Ecclesiologist*, which commented in particular on the difficulties created by trying to merge the functions of a cathedral and a parish church.[3] Christ Church Cathedral and the Chapel of St Anne, both in Fredericton, New Brunswick, were designed about the same time as the St John's church by the well-known English architect William Butterfield, later the architect of All Saints' Church, Margaret Street, London (1851–5), who was well aware of the Ecclesiologists' theories on church architecture.[4] Butterfield was assisted by the able Frank Wills, who was also familiar with the Ecclesiologists. In 1850 Wills published a book that illustrated Ecclesiological churches.[5]

Some architects working on Toronto churches during the 1840s were also interested in achieving a more exact version of the Gothic revival style than had been followed in the city up to that time.[6] William Thomas's St Michael's Cathedral of 1845–8 included a beautiful hammerbeam roof and a tall, graceful Gothic arcade.[7] Thomas, however, executed the main piers in wood that feigned stone, something that would have been frowned on by the Ecclesiologists. But by 1850 purer Ecclesiological views held sway. The designs by Frank Wills, Gervase Wheeler, and William Hay for the St. James's Cathedral competition were Ecclesiological, and William Thomas cited Pugin in the letter accompanying the plans for his entry.[8]

It is no wonder, then, that the four churches Cumberland designed all revealed an awareness of Ecclesiological principles. The first of these to be built was the Church of the Ascension in Hamilton. The others, all in Toronto, were the Cathedral Church of St James, the Queen Street Wesleyan Church, and the St James's Cemetery Chapel.[9] The cathedral is the best-known and was probably the earliest executed example in central Canada of a church that followed Ecclesiological design principles, and for this reason alone it is historically significant, apart from its merits as a design.[10]

Cumberland won the competition to design St James's in 1849, but the original plans were modified extensively the following year. In the meantime he designed the Church of the Ascension in Hamilton, which was built before St James's and thus was the earliest of his churches to be completed. For this reason, it will be considered first.

THE CHURCH OF THE ASCENSION, HAMILTON

Today the Church of the Ascension enjoys a favourable hillside site just north of Hamilton's downtown. With a prominently angled tower, and correct Gothic detail, it was a very early Canadian example of the picturesque asymmetry favoured by the Ecclesiologists (figs. 12.1–6). The plan was of a Latin cross with a generous nave and prominent transepts. The main entrance was at the west end, with secondary entrances in the transepts. The church was some eighty feet long from the west door to the wall at the east end of the sanctuary, and some sixty-seven feet long across the transepts. As was typical of church designs during this period, the pews were carefully counted: 502 people could be accommodated at one sitting.[11] The asymmetrical elevation was located at the north corner of the east side. The arrangement of the sanctuary was most unusual, being located beneath a tall grouping of three lancet windows. Two octagonal lecterns were placed behind a formal altar screen. The interior detailing included hood mouldings with label stops around the windows, and an ornate and carefully detailed wooden open-timber roof, all rendered in Gothic motifs. One gets the impression that this interior would have seemed broad and spacious, with a particularly generous allotment of light pouring in through the lancet windows.

12.1 Cumberland & Ridout. Church of the Ascension, Hamilton, 1850–1. North elevation. Horwood (73)4

12.2 Cumberland & Ridout. Church of the Ascension, Hamilton, 1850–1. Transverse section looking east. Horwood (73)1

WEST ELEVATION.

12.3 Cumberland & Ridout. Church of the Ascension, Hamilton, 1850–1. West elevation. Horwood (73)5

The elevations presented a carefully orchestrated variety of effects. Perhaps the most remarkable aspect of the building was the tall and delicately detailed corner spire. Located on the north corner of the east flank of the building, the spire effectively counterbalanced the rather broad transepts. The detailing on the exterior was original and yet also convincingly Gothic. The most elaborate detailing was reserved for the tower. It featured stepped buttresses and elaborate dormered windows surmounted by fleur-de-lys finials. The window groupings on the tower were varied and highly sculptural. On the ground floor, united under a stone frame with a pointed-arch profile, were two trefoil-headed windows with a separate trefoil above them. On the second storey was a most unusual cinquefoil window with a deep reveal; above this, on the third storey, was a larger version of the ground-floor window grouping. The Church of the Ascension's subdivided Gothic windows with roundels and trefoils are seen first in France's Rayonnant churches, for example in the nave of St Denis (1231–41), and then in English Decorated style Gothic churches, such as Hereford Cathedral and Westminster Abbey.

In comparison with the tower's elaborate detailing, the rest of the north flank was relatively plain, except for a most unusually detailed roundel at the gable end of the north transept. A perfect triangle of stone tracery spanned the rose, with trefoils inserted in the interstices and in the centre. The door at the north end sat beneath a pointed-arch gable and was enlivened by iron strapwork hinges. Stone window surrounds linked with a continuous belt-course completed the north elevation.

The west façade was dominated by the broad triangular form of the transepts, with a triple arch centred above the tall pointed-arch porch. Prominent buttresses, octagonal in plan, flanked the door. These featured tall stone watercourses and unusual lancet windows in the shape of a cross. The east elevation, where the tower was located, was notable for a group of three windows that was recessed into a large stone frame.

Although the church was not planned entirely felicitously – the east entrance must not have been used at all, for it led straight into the sanctuary – the building as a whole was quite beautifully detailed. Perhaps the most remarkable aspect of the external elevation was the way that Cumberland varied the ornamental effects, which were particularly lavish on the tower and at the west entrance, less so on the elevations. The springing of the arches and the continuous horizontal banding at the levels of the plinths were quite effective in unifying the building. The use of extra-large stone frames set back from the wall plane to form a huge triangle around the three-window group was a particularly original detail.

The cornerstone of the Church of the Ascension was laid on 9 May 1850, and the church opened its doors in June 1851. After undergoing considerable renovations of the interior during the 1860s and 1870s, the interior was destroyed by fire on 6 January 1887. Reconstruction started on 7 June of that year on the same plan but with a larger chancel, under the supervision of the capable Toronto architectural firm of Darling & Curry.[12]

How original a building was this? As Shirley Morriss has pointed out, a number of English churches designed during the 1840s featured correct Gothic detailing and asymmetrical corner towers.[13] These included R.C. Carpenter's St Paul's (Anglican) in Brighton of 1846–8, and A.W.N. Pugin's St Wilfred's (Roman Catholic) in Hulme, near Manchester, of 1849–52. Cumberland, however, was not striving to create a precise copy of an earlier building, but to synthesize the Gothic spirit in an original structure.

When the novelty in the Canadian context of this church's architectural features is considered – the correct Gothic detailing, the open-timber roof, the asymmetrical tower – it is mysterious that the church has not assumed a greater significance in discussions of Cumberland's work. Perhaps this is because it was a modest church built in a city now overshadowed by Toronto. Its reputation has simply been overpowered by that of St James's, the cathedral seat of the redoubtable Bishop of Toronto, despite the fact, as we will now see, that the design of St James's was compromised and incomplete.

12.4 Cumberland & Ridout. Church of the Ascension, Hamilton, 1850–1. East elevation.
Horwood (73)3

THE CATHEDRAL CHURCH OF ST JAMES, TORONTO[14]

Today the Cathedral Church of St James is a Toronto landmark; it is difficult to imagine King Street without this building. But the present church is actually the fourth to stand on the site, all of which were named for St James.[15] The second church burned down in 1839. The third St James's, designed by Thomas Young, perished in the fire that engulfed much of Toronto on 7 April 1849.[16] Members of the congregation, shaking their heads, walked among the ashes of the building and asked themselves how they could afford to build their fourth church since 1831. A sum of £4000 was still owing on the church that burned down. This debt weighed heavily on the minds of those charged with overseeing the rebuilding in 1849.

Winning the competition held later that year to design a new St James's helped establish Cumberland as one of the city's leading architects, but the building of the church was so protracted that Cumberland may well have asked himself why he ever entered the lists. There were three reasons why the commission to design St James's created difficulties: the congregation's unwillingness to confront its straitened financial circumstances; the lack of a clear building program (a problem exacerbated by insufficient funds and bitter arguments over possible sources of additional revenue); and interference by Bishop John Strachan, who wanted a church very different from the one his flock sought.

In retrospect, it seems that the congregation's financial situation was probably the principal reason for the unclear directions given to Cumberland. One faction of the congregation wanted to raise money by renting out portions of the King Street property on which the old church had stood, and to build the new church on Adelaide Street. Another faction considered this solution sacrilegious because it would disturb the old church's graveyard, and wanted to rebuild as close as possible to the old foundations. Some members wanted a church large enough to accommodate two thousand people, even though the still-indebted congregation was barely able to pay for a modest parish church. The £10,000 initially budgeted for the work was soon found insufficient to complete a major metropolitan church. This led to compromises, such as the decision to build in stages, the goal of the first stage being to bring the building to a point where divine services could be conducted; any embellishments, such as towers, would follow later. There was additional confusion with respect to whether the old foundations were structurally sound, whether the new church could build over the existing graveyard, and whether the former pewholders could be accommodated in the new building.

Initially the congregation moved with dispatch to replace the church. On 19 April, less than two weeks after the fire, a building committee was appointed. On 5 May, with Chief Justice John Beverley Robinson in the chair, it issued a preliminary report recommending that the new church should lie along an east-west line parallel with King Street, with its midpoint equidistant from the east and west boundaries of the site. The new church was to be large enough to seat 1800 to 2000 people. The materials were to be local white brick with stone trim. The style was to be Gothic, with the details left to the architect and the building committee. According to the committee, the ideal way to choose the design, time permitting, would be to send the architect to England to study the best churches recently erected. It was determined that £10,000 was needed to construct a building sufficient to accommodate public worship. Most of these recommendations appeared in the building committee's printed report of 5 May, which, however, contained a few additional details. The churchtower would have ten bells and face west. The style was now to be Early English, a variant of Gothic. The committee indicated that the church should seat 2000 people, for which purpose the church was to measure not less than 149 feet by 80 feet. For the competition the committee would require drawings of longitudinal and transverse sections, and plans of the main floor, gallery, roof, heating system, and basement. The design also called for a fireproof vault and both free and rental seating. The gallery would contain pews and an organ loft.

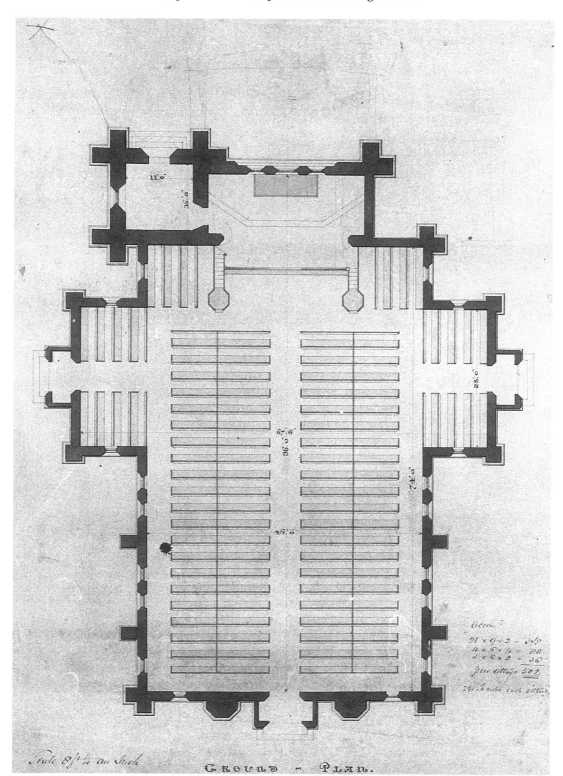

12.5 Cumberland & Ridout. Church of the Ascension, Hamilton, 1850–1. Ground plan. Horwood (73)2

The vestry adopted the report of its building committee on 12 May, and on 4 June issued a pamphlet entitled 'Conditions &c. of competition designs.' Advertisements were placed in various publications including the *Albion and New York Spectator*, the *Montreal Morning Courier*, and *The Church*. The competition's closing date was 14 August. Many architects submitted plans, including Frank Wills, George H. Smith, William Thomas, Kivas and John Tully, John Ostell, and the American Gervase Wheeler. Even at this early stage there were signs of delays to come. On 11 August both Ostell and Wheeler requested extensions to 1 September, which were granted. On 3 September all the plans were examined by the building committee, which then adjourned until the 6th. The next day, a subcommittee comprising Thomas Young, J.G. Howard, and John Johnston was struck to rule on the designs. As MacRae and Adamson have noted, this choice was peculiar, given that Young and Howard were enemies.[17] They may have been appointed, however, because both were architects and neither had entered the competition.

By this time some people were already predicting that cumberland's design would be chosen. *The Church*, Canada's official Anglican publication, assessed the entries in an article of 13 September, and remarked that 'On the whole we should not wonder if the choice of the committee were to rest with Mr. Cumberland.'[18] This prediction was presumably based on the knowledge that the subcommittee had, the day before, awarded its first-place premium of £75 to Cumberland, the second-place premium of £50 to Ostell, and the third-place premium of £25 to Kivas Tully. The committee indicated, however, that the premiums had been awarded without a decision on whose plans would actually be adopted for the construction of the church.

The announcement that Cumberland's design had been awarded the first-place premium excited considerable controversy. The Mechanics' Institute asked for permission to exhibit some of the plans, perhaps as a means of allowing the public to judge for themselves.[19] The controversy seems to have been brought on in large measure by the building committee's deci-

sion to consider a design submitted by George H. Smith of Montreal that was far more elaborate than the competition requirements called for. The committee – perhaps in deference to their bishop's desire for an impressive building rather than an economical one – entered Smith's design into the competition after the closing date. Those who defended Smith's scheme put forth sanguine but unreliable estimates as to its construction costs and projected unrealistically high revenues from its many pews.

Attacks were also mounted on other fronts. William Thomas had always believed Cumberland's design was inappropriate, and the move to consider Smith's design provided Thomas with an opportunity to make a new case for his own. Sometime in November he put forward a proposal to rebuild the church using the old foundations. He promoted this as an inexpensive option, apparently to appeal to those who did not want to rent out church land as a way of raising revenue, and to those who distrusted the extravagance of Smith's plan but did not wish to see Cumberland's scheme executed. Thomas's proposal was bruited about for some time, and it remained a dark horse, trotted out whenever Cumberland's opponents challenged the premises on which his design had been executed.

In December yet another new proposal was put forward. Kivas Tully published a pamphlet in which he argued that his design should be reconsidered.[20] Because his design, which as noted above had won the third-place premium, envisioned what was quite simply a modest parish church, it could, unlike the other designs, be built without exceeding the proposed budget and without disturbing the existing churchyard. Tully remarked that he too had considered Thomas's option of rebuilding on the old foundations, but that that would likely create a threat to the congregation's safety. After criticizing Cumberland and Smith for their profligacy, and Thomas for his inattention to danger, Tully included a new perspective drawing of his church for the vestry's consideration. His initiative, however, found no supporters.

In the meantime, someone else had started

12.6 Cumberland & Ridout. Church of the Ascension, Hamilton, 1850–1. Photograph, n.d. Hamilton Public Library, Special Collections

adding up the figures being tossed about so airily. 'Bramhill' sounded the alarm by taking it upon himself to show how credulous the church building committee was with respect to Smith's financial estimates, and criticized, too, the way that Smith's plan had been accepted into the competition.[21] Smith's champions claimed that the difference between the cost of executing his design and Cumberland's 'would not be great,' but 'Bramhill' pointed out that Smith's church would be nearly nine thousand square feet larger than Cumberland's, and thus much more expensive to build. 'Bramhill' considered sacrilegious the proposal of Smith's defenders to rent out church land that had been used for burials. Consecrated ground, he remarked, could hardly be unconsecrated for commercial purposes: 'If [consecration] is *not* a fiction ... then will no good Churchman wish or dare to alienate one inch of ground consecrated not alone by this service of the Church, but consecrated and endeared by the dust of those who died in the faith. Let all men be careful how they bring one service of the Church into contempt, lest the way being opened, doubt overshadow the remainder.' This was a powerful argument designed to appeal to the emotions of those involved in the church debate, and eventually gained popular support.

Yet there were still enough supporters of Smith's design to force Cumberland into a contest with Smith. The building committee paid for Smith to come to Toronto and explain his proposal, which he did on 27 October. The members then decided that they needed to compare Cumberland's and Smith's designs 'in or about the same size or scale. It was ordered that Mr. Cumberland shall, if he thinks proper, prepare a plan as large as that of Mr. Smith's.' Cumberland acquiesced, and on the day of the meeting with Smith, John Duggan, the committee's secretary, wrote that he 'saw Mr. Cumberland who says he will prepare enlarged plan and have it ready by Monday the 19th. inst.'

It took some time for Cumberland to prepare a new plan. He wrote to the Committee twice, on 10 and 17 November, stating that his drawings would be delayed. Smith's drawings were received on the 22nd. The committee saw Cumberland's revised plan on the 24th, but decided to wait a while before coming to a decision. A drawing exists that shows how Smith's and Cumberland's designs compared (fig. 12.7). Smith's church was significantly larger, with a long nave, very wide transepts, a narthex, and a polygonal apse. Cumberland's much more compact church had a square sanctuary and minimally projecting transepts. The long nave and very wide transepts of Smith's design resembled those of English cathedrals, but the polygonal apse reflected French influence. By contrast, Cumberland's compact church with its minimally projecting transepts was akin to French Gothic structures, although the square east end, where divine service would take place, was closer in spirit to the architecture of English cathedrals. Both designs, then, represented a compromise between the two main traditions – French and English – of Gothic architecture. Cumberland eventually abandoned the square design of the east end in favour of a polygonal plan, perhaps in deference to those who favoured Smith's design. Cumberland's design as constructed did have transepts of sorts, although these really did not project much beyond the aisles.

There is no mystery about who was forwarding Smith's case – Bishop Strachan. On 27 October Strachan attended his first building committee meeting to champion Smith's case. The vestry minutebook recorded that the bishop wanted a £15,000 cathedral with transepts, whereas the rector wanted a £10,000 square parish church (something like the previous church). The bishop was so eager for Smith's design that he offered to obtain a grant of £1000 from the Society for the Promotion of Christian Knowledge, but only if Smith's cathedral was built. His feelings were so strong that the next year, after the vestry had voted for Cumberland's design, he published a pamphlet entitled *Thoughts on the Rebuilding of the Cathedral Church of St. James*,[23] in which he stated that it was far better to build grand, in the hope that faith would overcome all obstacles, than small, according to one's purse. He also decried the claim that building over former gravesites would desecrate sanctified land. Finally, he

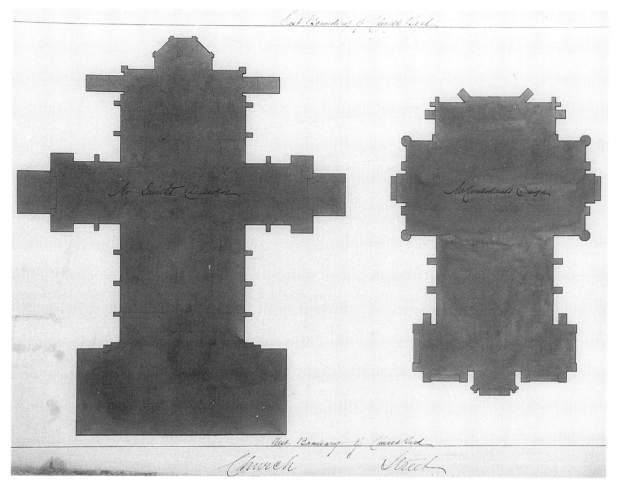

12.7 Frederic Cumberland. Cathedral Church of St James, Toronto, 1849–53. Outline of Cumberland's proposed design (right) and that of George H. Smith of Montreal, c. November 1849. Cumberland began work on the church in 1849 as a sole practitioner. He was later assisted by his partners Ridout and Storm. Horwood (55)19

stated that it would be appropriate to rent out churchyard land to raise funds.

The bishop's support for Smith's design was so forceful that he convinced the vestry to adopt it at a meeting on 1 December, despite the estimated cost of £15,000.[24] But the vestry soon reversed its decision and held a special meeting on the 14th during which a variety of proposals – none of them involving Smith – were discussed.[25] The meeting was held to examine the building committee's second report[26] and Thomas's proposal to rebuild on the old foundations. Given the financial burden the church had been obliged to assume when rebuilding the church that burned down in 1839, it was resolved that the vestry could not countenance going into debt in building a grand new one. Any option that avoided going into debt was to be favoured. William Wakefield, one of the vestrymen, supported Thomas's proposal, and said that he would move 'That, in the opinion of this vestry, a parish church of St. James is all that is required for the accommodation of the congregation; and that the new church to be erected be done so, on the walls of the old building, in accordance with the specification and estimate now produced, of William Thomas, Esq.'[27]

The crucial meeting was delayed to the 21st.

12.8 Frederic Cumberland. Cathedral Church of St James, Toronto, 1849–53. Site plans showing proposed east-west orientation of church and two arrangements for leasing of King Street frontage, 11 January 1850. The church as built was in fact oriented north-south and the frontage was never leased. Horwood (55)4

After a lengthy consideration of all the proposals, a vote was held to determine whether it would be appropriate to rent out church land. Twenty-three were for this idea, twenty-three against. The rector then cast the deciding vote in favour.[28] Next, a motion to approve Cumberland's plan was put forward: 'Resolved that the Original Plan of Mr. Cumberland be adopted by this Vestry as the one upon which the new church [be erected] provided that the amount be within £15,000.' Wakefield responded with an amendment on Thomas's behalf, 'That in the opinion of this Vestry a parish church of St. James is all that is required for the accommodation of the congre-

gation and that the new Church to be erected be done so on the walls of the old building in accordance with the specification and estimates ... of Wm. Thomas Esq., Architect – his being the only plan that can be used.'[29] Wakefield's amendment lost, and the original motion to go forward with Cumberland's design passed by a decisive majority of twenty-six to thirteen.

With the opponents of Cumberland's design seemingly defeated, it appeared as though it would proceed without further delays. On 9 January Cumberland was ordered to stake out the ground. The following day he sent two letters to the building committee, the first of which stated the conditions under which he would undertake the work, the second including a plan showing the seating arrangements of the old and new churches. The building committee discussed with Cumberland the possibility of increasing the length and width of the new building, but nothing was said about increasing the budget. On the 11th he submitted a drawing of that date shows the proposed building situated towards the Adelaide Street end of the site (fig. 12.8). The portion of the site along King Street was to be divided for leasing, with the exception of a nineteen-foot-wide corridor providing a sight-line and walkway to the south transept, which presumably was to be the secondary entrance, the principal entrance being from Church Street to the west. Cumberland later prepared two site plans, one showing the building only nineteen feet from Church Street, and the other set back forty-five feet.

In February Cumberland and churchwarden Thomas D. Harris went to New York to examine stone from various quarries. Cumberland was ordered to prepare alternative tenders for a stone church and a brick church. By 11 March he was engaged in the final preparation of the working plans and had prepared a ground plan showing the pews and the names of their owners. Then, suddenly, the vestry minutebook recorded that Cumberland was to suspend work until further notice, and the design debate was reopened. Inconclusive building committee meetings were held on the 25th and 26th, while Cumberland was in Hamilton working on the Church of the Ascension.[30]

On 6 April, with the bishop in England to see about funding for Trinity College, the Vestry considered Cumberland's plan and agreed that he would 'proceed at once and erect a Gothic Church upon the old site of St. James's Church or as near the old foundation walls as possible provided that the same does not exceed £10,000.' This was a roundabout way of avoiding the issue of renting out the King Street frontage: by locating the building at or near the centre of the site, with its chancel located to the north, the King Street frontage would be occupied by the new church, thus preventing future sale or subdivision of the land.

On the 9th Cumberland was instructed to prepare a new design for a church in the Early English Gothic style that could be erected on the old foundations, except at the north end. It would include a tower, but merely a truncated version of Cumberland's former structure. At the building committee meeting on the 16th, it was agreed that 'Mr. Cumberland is to furnish a new ground plan so as not to lose the two pews when the porch enters and to be ready with the same and the ground staked out on Tuesday the 23 inst. at 4 o'clock.'

Only a few more stumbles took place before the building actually got under way. On 23 April the committee met at Cumberland's office to assess the revised plan. Finding it satisfactory, the ground was finally staked out. Cumberland was asked to provide specifications, which he said he could not do before 1 June. It was not until 18 June, however, that the building committee, again meeting in Cumberland's office, examined and approved the final plans and bids from builders. The calls for bids, which were organized so that the work could, in keeping with the original intentions of the building committee, be executed in stages, were to be published in the *British Colonist*, *The Church*, and the *Patriot*. The closing date for bids was 15 July.

When Cumberland opened the tenders, however, he found that no builder was willing to construct the church for the sum allotted. On 15 July Cumberland gave the church officials the unwelcome news that the lowest bid was more than fifty per cent above the maximum amount budgeted. Metcalfe, Wilson, and Forbes were the lowest bidders, at £16,500; the highest were Garvey and Pollock, at £23,066.6.0. Bids for ancillary works followed. The proposed amounts were so much larger than what the building committee had expected that it could not issue a go-ahead for the works, although it optimistically asked builder John Ritchey to sign a document agreeing to keep his bid open for a month.

In July the building committee instructed Cumberland to modify his plan or prepare a new one whose cost would not exceed £10,000, the spire excluded. They confirmed the earlier decision to place the church in the middle of the

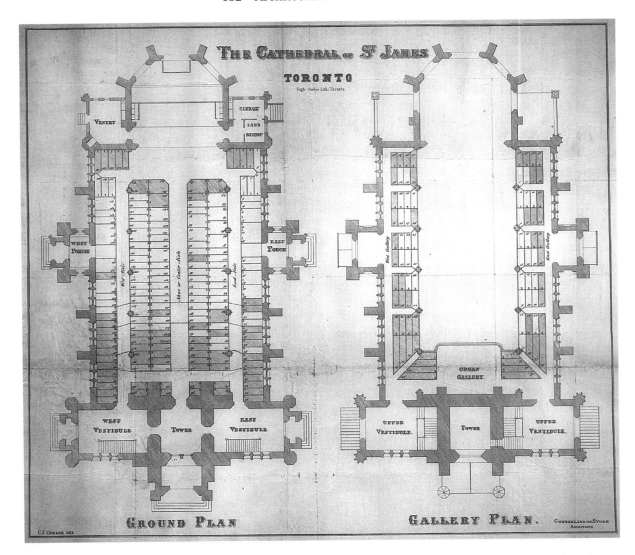

12.9 Cumberland & Storm. Cathedral Church of St James, Toronto, 1849–53. Lithograph by Hugh Scobie of ground plan and gallery plan showing arrangement of pews, c. September 1852. C.J. Crease, delineator. St James's Cathedral Archives

lot. Their published report of July contained the following sobering remarks: 'a church capable of containing the large congregation of 2,000 persons, could not be carried out, in a style that would be creditable, to the Metropolis of Canada, or the congregation of St. James's, for so small a sum, as that contemplated, by the Vestry, the church, however, can be rendered fit, and complete to public worship, restoring every person, to his pew, for the sum of £11,463.7, which amount it is believed, can be relied on.'

After further discussions concerning who had the right to appoint subcontractors, the work lurched to a start. In August Cumberland signed some drawings of leaf-motif bosses and other details of the stonework, which suggests that he was designing the building's final details even as it was being constructed. The contract drawings were not signed until 18 November. The corner-stone was laid two days later. The bland report of the ceremony in the *British Colonist* gave no hint of the struggles that lay behind the

12.10 Frederic Cumberland or Cumberland & Storm. Cathedral Church of St James, Toronto, 1849–53. Drawing of south elevation (transepts faintly visible in pencil) c. 1850. Horwood (55)21

12.11 Frederic Cumberland or Cumberland & Storm. Cathedral Church of St James, Toronto, 1849–53. Drawing of flank (west) elevation (transepts faintly visible in pencil), c. 1850. Horwood (55)18

12.12 Cumberland & Storm. Cathedral Church of St James, Toronto, 1849–53. Photograph by Octavius Thompson. This photograph shows the incomplete state in which the church existed for many years following its opening in 1853. MTL/BR, Picture Collection T-10,728; *Toronto in the Camera: A Series of Photographic Views of the Principal Buildings in the City of Toronto* (Toronto: O[ctavius] Thompson 1868), plate 6

approval of Cumberland's design. *The Church* published a long article on the ceremony and said that 'Everything, we are happy to say, passed off with the utmost regularity, and too much praise cannot be awarded to the gentlemen who were entrusted with the arrangements of the day.'[31] The bishop gave an inspiring sermon based on 2 Samuel 6:12, during which, it may be presumed, there was no reference to the discord that had so lately reigned where harmony now prevailed.[32]

Thereafter construction progressed smoothly. On 18 January 1851 Cumberland submitted a detailed progress report in which he stated that it was possible to have the roof in place by 20 November. The building committee voted on

22 January 'that the thanks of the Committee be tendered to the Architects Messrs. Cumberland & Ridout for the able and valuable report drawn up by them and that the same be recorded in the Minute Book.'

All went well during the rest of 1851 and into 1852. On 17 September 1852 the building committee authorized publication of five hundred lithograph copies of the ground plan and gallery plan (fig. 12.9). On 4 October the work was sufficiently advanced that Cumberland was able to recommend a forced-air heating system. During the winter of 1852 Metcalfe, Wilson, and Forbes went bankrupt, but after a flurry of negotiations another contractor was found. The church finally opened its doors on Sunday, 19 June 1853,

12.13 Cumberland & Storm. Cathedral Church of St James, Toronto, 1849–53. Photograph of interior by J.H. Noverre, n.d. This view shows the original galleries as well as the reading stand. MTL/BR, Picture Collection, T-10,740

12.14 Cumberland & Storm. Cathedral Church of St James, Toronto, 1849–53. Photograph of interior by Notman and Fraser, n.d., showing gallery. MTL/BR, Picture collection, T-10,739

but a circular dated 14 June was still asking for funds.

The final meeting of the building committee was held on 23 January 1854.[33] It was forced to release bad news to the congregation: the church had cost far more than the building committee could have imagined. In February it was revealed that the church had cost £18,803.17.7. St James's was left with a debt of £9,335.17.7. And this was for a barebones structure, without its planned five porches, its surrounding buttresses, its tower, or its finials.

This building was not Bishop Strachan's cathedral, in either form or function. It was not

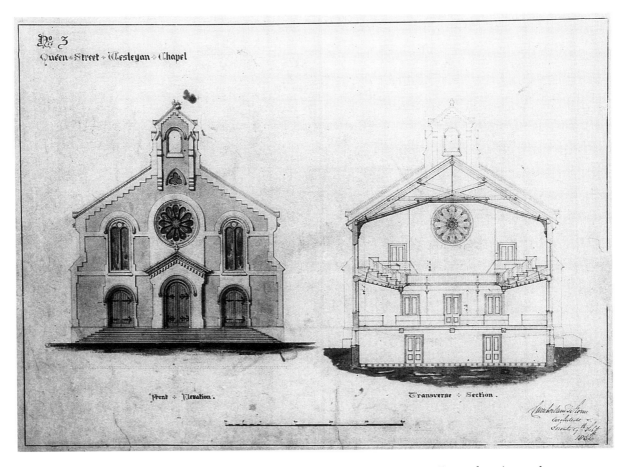

Nº 3
Queen · Street · Wesleyan · Chapel

Front · Elevation.

Transverse · Section.

12.15 Cumberland & Storm. Wesleyan Church, Queen Street, Toronto, 1856–7. Front elevation and transverse section, 9 February 1856. Horwood (101)4

grand enough to be a true cathedral. All it was was a parish church where a bishop had his seat. No chapter of dean and canons managed its affairs. The building, moreover, was hardly what Cumberland had set out to design, nor was it what the building committee had wanted.

It is somewhat difficult to piece together the various phases of the design's development. Cumberland and his partners prepared several different plans. In one pencil drawing, there were ghostlike transepts whose combined length was as great as the nave's (fig. 12.10). The transepts, presumably, were Cumberland's response to the demands of the pro-Smith camp. Both the transepts and the nave had aisles. One porch window had recessed trefoil, and in another spot there was a group of three porch windows. Trefoils were to be included on

the transepts as well, but these were eventually replaced by lancet windows in groups of three (fig. 12.11). Photographs of the completed building show that it was but a pale shadow of the beautifully detailed scheme that Cumberland initially proposed (fig. 12.12). For example, the only place where trefoils were included was in a window just below the roof line at the east end.

At this point it is useful to again consider Cumberland's approach to copying earlier buildings. We have seen that he made every effort to visit as many medieval churches as he could while working in England, so it should come as no surprise that he incorporated many medieval features into the design of St James's. According to the architectural historian Malcolm Thurlby, the exterior of the nave, with its three-window groups, was inspired by Salisbury Cathedral. Details of the south portal were similar to the north portal of the west front of Wells Cathedral. The polygonal apse, with its large traceried windows and stepped buttresses, was a smaller version of Lichfield Cathedral's Lady Chapel.[34] Thurlby also observes, however, that although 'Virtually every aspect of the design finds precedent in English Gothic cathedrals ... their combination is Cumberland's.'[35] As was pointed out in the previous chapter on University College, the Victorian design method involved *study* and *synthesis.* Cumberland was inspired by his sources but did not want to copy them literally. He would have disdained such an approach.

The initial design of St James's owed much to Early English Gothic, in particular the groups of tall lancet windows in the main elevation, which were similar to those of Salisbury Cathedral, and indeed can be found even earlier, in English Cistercian designs such as Rievaulx Abbey.[36] Also consistent with the Early English Gothic style were the mouldings, which were linear and simple and lacked the muscular three-dimensionality of Decorated English Gothic. However, the trefoil windows originally called for in the design, with their convex shape and deep profile, were in fact closer to Decorated English Gothic churches, especially Lichfield Cathedral.[37]

As for the final design of the interior of the church, it too was a compromise, although of a rather different sort (figs. 12.13–14). The vestrymen of St James's may have been willing to commission a church in the Gothic style, but they none the less wanted to retain some of the elements found in the buildings that had been destroyed by fire. Thomas Rogers's Georgian church of 1831 had been broadly proportioned and had had ample space for galleries. It clearly influenced the interior of Cumberland's church as he struggled to insert Georgian furniture into a Gothic shell. The same was true of Cumberland's pulpit and reading stand. The 1831 church had featured a tall octagonal pulpit mounted by a winding staircase and had stood well in front of the sanctuary as did the lower reading stand. Photographs show that Cum-

berland followed this pattern in his church, and approach hardly consistent with Ecclesiological practice, which would have called for all liturgical events to take place in the chancel. The chancel was where the Bishop's chair was to be located, which helps explain why the chancel was separated from the spaces devoted to regular worship. The church exhibited up-to-date external styling, which featured a clearly articulated nave, sanctuary, aisles, and transepts, curiously combined with an anachronistic placement of liturgical elements. The photographs also show that the church eventually set aside a row of free pews between the revenue-producing pews on the main floor.[38]

The building remained in an incomplete state for many years. It was not until 1863 that Storm prepared some drawings for proposed additions to the tower, and not until 1873 that the tower was completed by Henry Langley. The current building, with its handsome tower and porch, is much more elegant than it ever was during Cumberland's time.

It is fortunate that human memories are short, and that buildings can live a long time: looking at the church today one sees it as a statement of pride. This is as it should be, and the ridiculous and painful process of commissioning and constructing the building has become no more than an ironic historical footnote.

QUEEN STREET WESLEYAN CHURCH, TORONTO

In stylistic terms, this church, designed in 1856, stood between Cumberland's two churches of the early 1850s and the later St James's Cemetery Chapel (fig. 12.15). Storm, who came from a devout Methodist family, was the partner in charge of the design.[39] The building was constructed of red brick with white stone trim. The interior was simple, a broad gable-roofed space incorporating an undifferentiated preaching box with galleries on the second storey.

The most notable aspect of the building was the Norman-Romanesque style in which it was decorated, which represented a significant departure for the firm and which anticipated

12.16 Cumberland & Storm. St James's Cemetery Chapel, Toronto, 1857–61. Contract drawing of south elevation, c. 1857. Horwood (132)39

the firm's work on University College. The roundheaded arches of the main door, the wooden doors with vertical boards and ornamental ironwork, and the jagged mouldings on the main door's archivolts and cornice were the firm's first essays in this style. A huge rose window with wheel-spoke mullions dominated the front elevation, which, somewhat curiously, terminated in a bellcote without a bell. Notable too was the beautiful ornamented lettering on the drawings prepared for this building.

What inspired the firm to employ this style? One might be tempted to infer that its roots were in the firm's work on University College, but the firm had only just been given the university commission. The church drawings are dated 9 February 1856, only two days after Cumberland was appointed university archi-

tect. He had not yet gone to England. The firm, therefore, had already designed a building in the Norman-Romanesque style before it began work on University College. Should Storm be credited with the design? If so, he seems to have drawn only on published sources. (He would follow Cumberland to England, but not until 1857.) The Romanesque styling of the church, for instance, was somewhat unconvincing. In particular, the doorcase was almost generic, with alternating zigzagging and curving lines. Romanesque details were combined incongruously with features in other idioms, namely a Gothic trefoil window and Tuscan Gothic windows. Perhaps Cumberland and Storm were already discussing whether to use the Romanesque style for University College and were experimenting with it.

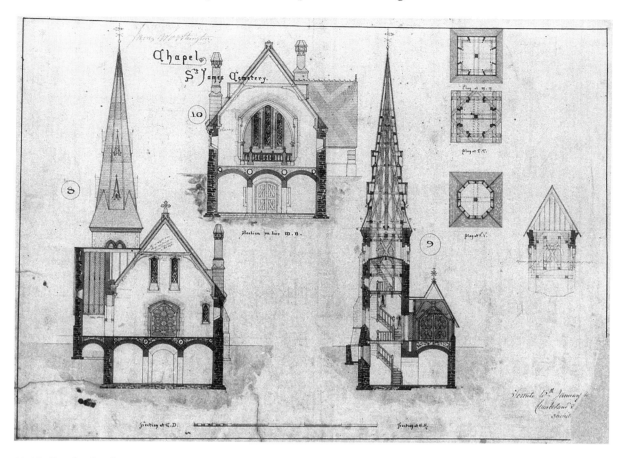

12.17 Cumberland & Storm. St James's Cemetery Chapel, Toronto, 1857–61. Contract drawing of sections and details, c. 1857. Horwood (132)42

One wonders whether the Methodists wanted to use this style to distinguish their church from those of the older denominations. The Queen Street design might be compared with the open and unencumbered church designs adopted in the thirteenth and fourteenth centuries by the new preaching orders such as the Dominicans and Franciscans, who wanted to develop a new architectural idiom to mirror their liturgical practices. Historians have shown how closely the Gothic Revival style was associated with the Anglican and Roman Catholic faiths in Canada. It is entirely consistent with what is known of architectural symbolism and religious architecture that the Methodists would have looked for an architectural style that was not associated with other denominations. In nineteenth-century Ontario the Presbyterians and the Method-

ists (and, later, the United Church) seem to have preferred Romanesque buildings to a greater extent than did either Anglicans or Catholics. But it cannot be determined whether the Queen Street Methodists suggested the style to Cumberland & Storm, or whether the firm recommended it to them.

ST JAMES'S CEMETERY CHAPEL, TORONTO[40]

This church was the closest Cumberland ever came to designing the '*Small* Stone Church' that he said he would give his ears to design (figs. 12.16–19).[41] Perhaps because it was the smallest and simplest of his church commissions, it was also the least compromised during construction. It is also the best-preserved of his churches. The chapel lies several kilometres

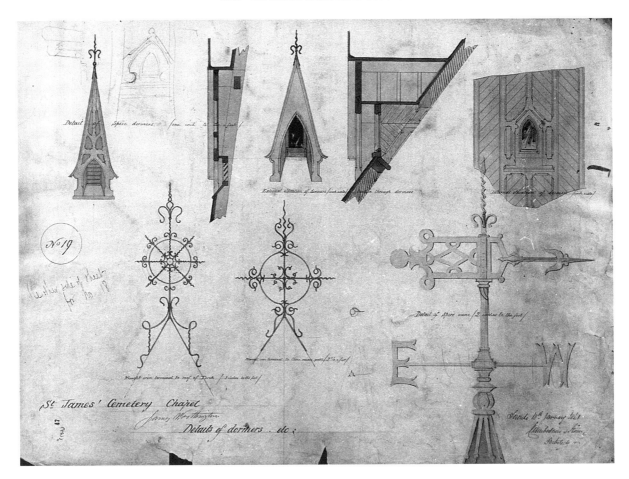

12.18 Cumberland & Storm. St James's Cemetery Chapel, Toronto, 1857–61. Contract drawing of details of dormers, weather-vane, and wrought-iron terminals, c. 1857. Horwood (132)47, verso

northeast of St James's Cathedral. Although today the site is bounded on the north by a major arterial road (the Bloor street viaduct), and on the east by Parliament Street, during the nineteenth century the area was rural and well beyond the city limits. The parish of St James bought sixty acres of gently sloping land in 1844 and commissioned John G. Howard to lay out grounds for use as a cemetery. The results were felicitous: the grounds were bucolic and picturesque. Bishop Strachan had the idea to build a chapel on this property and over many years he gradually took the steps necessary to construct it. The ground was consecrated on 5 June 1845, when the bishop, accompanied by members of the clergy and the congregation, led a procession to the property and then read the sonorous and powerful Forty-Ninth Psalm: 'But God will redeem my soul from the power of the grave: for he shall receive me.'

But nothing more was done for several years.[42] When the idea was resurrected, so to speak, in 1857, Cumberland was a member of St James's vestry, and one of those who gave the go-ahead for a chapel – evidence of his somewhat cozy relationship with the church authorities.[43] The vestry minutes suggest that Cumberland was given informal approval to prepare a design before he received formal approval, which was granted on 27 April. By 11 May a building committee was considering the design, and eight days later, at a meeting at which Cumberland served as secretary, the design was approved.[44]

The development of this design was as

12.19 Cumberland & Storm. St James's Cemetery Chapel, Toronto, 1857–61. Contract drawing
of details of tower, c. 1857. Horwood (132)32

12.20 Cumberland & Storm. St James's Cemetery Chapel, Toronto, 1857–61. View from southwest. Photo by the author

12.21 Cumberland & Storm. St James's Cemetery Chapel, Toronto, 1857–61. Perspective of interior (not as built), c. 1857. William G. Storm, delineator(?). Horwood (132)27

smooth as the earlier commission for St James's Cathedral had been rocky. For one thing, the site could not have been more favourable, being located on a slight rise just inside the gates. The chapel was oriented east-west, as St James's Cathedral would have been had the plans to rent out the land on King Street gone ahead. To make the best use of the natural advantages of the picturesque site, Cumberland devised a design with a tower located at the chapel's southwest corner (fig. 12.20). In doing this he looked back not only to his earlier design for the Church of the Ascension, but also perhaps to English churches included in Raphael and J. Arthur Brandon's *Parish Churches* (1851), such as Marston Church, Bedfordshire.[45] Marston Church, like St James's Cemetery Chapel, featured an asymmetrically located tower with massive corner buttresses abutting a simple nave. However, the nave at Marston Church was subdivided by piers, whereas the Toronto chapel was an undifferentiated space.

Cumberland prepared two designs for the chapel's interior (figs. 12.21–2). Presumably this was done to give the committee a choice of a less expensive and a more expensive option. One design showed rather pallid pointed-arch windows and an open-timber roof, without, however, any carving on the timbers. The other scheme was more sculptural in approach, with trefoil windows, and, for the roof, elaborate carving and hammer-beam timbers. Perhaps surprisingly, the committee chose the more expensive option. The extra expense was well worth it: the executed building was rich both inside and out. Even the drawings were beautiful, with bold colouring and lettering and picturesque treatment of the sculpted elements on the façade.

The chapel was initially intended to accommodate mourners in an undifferentiated space. The plan was correspondingly simple. The sloping site of the church enabled Cumberland to design an entrance for the hearses at the lower level at the back of the chapel. Coffins were raised to the floor of the nave, where funeral services were held. When services were completed, the coffins were lowered and taken out to the adjacent cemetery.

Materials were used in the chapel for both their structural and decorative effects, an approach that owes much to University College. The architect ably balanced many different elements: picturesque asymmetrical siting; thick, battered stone walls; forged iron; and carved wood. The chapel was constructed of stone left in a heavily rusticated state, which created a convincing Gothic feel. The building was richly ornamented from its base to the crest of its roof with wrought-iron work, elaborately carved wood, and richly hued stained glass. The roof was given a polychromatic treatment. Trefoil windows were set in deep reveals beneath heavy stone hoods with carved bosses. A particularly beautiful entrance porch flanked by a fence of wrought iron, of original design, led into a simple, dark interior that featured an open-timber ceiling. The rich treatment of the materials, and the desire to exploit their possibilities, differentiated this design from the Church of the Ascension. That is, even though the asymmetrical massing of the two structures was similar, the earlier church showed none of the interest in sculptural effects that characterized the later design. By the later 1850s, Cumberland was certainly not alone in Toronto in striving for such effects: other churches erected in Toronto at this time incorporated a very convincing treatment of Gothic motifs. One example was Thomas Fuller's 1858 design for St Stephen's-in-the-Fields, where Cumberland was later to worship.

The chapel opened in 1861. By the following year it was being used not only as a cemetery chapel but for divine service on Sundays. In 1863 Rev. Samuel J. Boddy was given pastoral charge of the chapel, where he was attempting to establish a regular congregation. How long the building was used for Sunday services is unclear. Apparently it fell into disuse early in this century.

In 1938 the 'near forgotten' chapel was rededicated for prayer,'[46] but today is no longer used for regular services. Occasionally, however, it still functions as a cemetery chapel. The building retains most of its original architectural details, including the striking entrance porch with its wrought-iron work. The grounds themselves

12.22 Cumberland & Storm. St James's Cemetery Chapel, Toronto, 1857–61. Perspective of interior (as built), c. 1857. William G. Storm, delineator(?). Shirley G. Morriss, 'The Nine-Year Odyssey of a High-Victorian Goth: Three Churches by Fred Cumberland,' *Journal of Canadian Art History* 2 (summer 1975), fig. 19

are still bucolic. On a sunny winter morning – a favourable time to visit the building, for it is unlikely that there will be another person in the place – wan light streams in through the south quatrefoil windows with their deep reveals and dark-toned stained glass. The shafts of coloured light are almost palpable as they spread across the dark-stained pews and make the nave glow. In no other building, perhaps, was Cumberland able to achieve such a harmonious balance of picturesque site and natural materials. Here the fragility of human life and the durability of stone are juxtaposed to particularly poignant effect.

CHAPTER THIRTEEN

Post Offices, Courthouses, and Other Public Buildings

If a strong case can be made that the Normal School has been the building most neglected by Cumberland scholars, an equally strong case can be made that his buildings designed for the general public represent the most significant building type neglected in previous discussions of his work. Cumberland designed two post offices for the Province of Canada, renovations and additions to Osgoode Hall, and the Toronto Mechanics' Institute. He also lavished attention on three unexecuted designs for a building to house the Canadian Institute. These will be the subjects of the following discussion.

POST OFFICES

Cumberland designed the Seventh Toronto Post Office and the Hamilton Post Office, which were completed in 1853 and 1856, respectively. The stone-covered Seventh Toronto Post Office, located on the west side of Toronto Street, was one of Cumberland's smallest and simplest buildings (figs. 13.1–2). It was austerely elegant, couched in a classical revival style of the utmost refinement. On the east side of the building, where the main entrance was located, four tall Ionic columns, placed between terminal Doric pilasters, set the tone for the rest of the building's classical detailing. The columns added a vertical unity to a two-storey façade that featured three bays. On the ground floor, doors were located symmetrically on either side of the centre bay, which had a window framed by smaller pilasters. On the second storey were

three windows with eared Greek Revival surrounds and battered sides. An entablature bearing the words 'Post Office' terminated the elevation, and a clock with elaborate volutes was originally planned for the centre of the elevation above the roof-line, although a carved coat of arms was substituted during construction. Of particular note inside were two subtly tapered Doric columns that sat widely spaced along an elevation whose every inch was covered with delicate linear detailing (fig. 13.3). A smaller version of the clock on the main elevation was centred between the two columns. Miniature framed doorcases flanked by elaborate pilasters sat below incised framed squares. The classical revival idiom in which the building was couched may have been unusual for Cumberland, but it was fairly common in the work of other architects, particularly those of the early nineteenth century. For example, Francis Goodwin's 1819 Old Town Hall, King Street, Manchester, had a similar Ionic colonnade centred between pilasters and set below a centralized sculptural motif.[1] Goodwin's and Cumberland's buildings were not exactly the same – the Old Town Hall was a larger and more complex structure – but overall the feel for classical detailing bore close comparison. On the other hand, the Post Office's stylish combination of various elements was typically Victorian in its eclecticism. The building, now converted to private offices, can still be appreciated today, being located on a street whose buildings are of a scale similar to what was there in the nineteenth century.

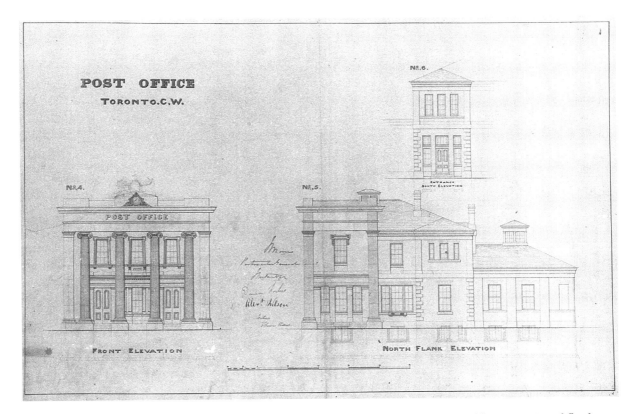

13.1 Cumberland & Storm. Seventh Post Office, Toronto, 1851–3. Contract drawing of front (west) and flank (north) elevations, 1851. Horwood (76)4

The Hamilton Post Office was a competent exercise in Italian palazzo massing – a tidy, four-square, two-and-a-half storey hipped-roof structure extended on each side by a bay set back from the street plane (figs. 13.4–5). The elevation was defined by three tall, round-headed openings, the main door being located in the central opening. On the second storey were three pedimented windows with Gibbs's surrounds. Above this storey was a simple attic level with three square windows set beneath a dentillated cornice. A liberal application of rustication on several parts of the building gave it a somewhat ponderous air. The rusticated elements included the ground-floor quoins and vermiculated voussoirs with bearded heads as the keystones. The building was similar to English urban structures of the same period, for example Sir Benjamin Heywood's Bank, St Ann Street, Manchester, designed in 1849 by John Edgar Gregan (fig.

13.6).[2] It also resembled the Kingston Post Office designed by the Montreal firm of Hopkins, Lawford & Nelson in 1856.[3] The Kingston Post Office had a two-storey elevation, with roundheaded openings strongly articulated by means of rusticated patterning and patterned voussoirs.

The Hamilton Post Office has been renovated many times since its construction. Nineteenth-century photographs show that the bays were eventually filled in. In 1888–9 the building served briefly as Hamilton's city hall. Ten years later it became the regional office of the Sun Life Assurance Company and was enlarged and substantially renovated. In 1926 it was renamed the Federal Building and now accommodates stores, offices, and apartments. The only original portions of the building still extant are the pedimented second-storey windows with their distinctive floral-motif surrounds and keystones.

13.2 Cumberland & Storm. Seventh Post Office, Toronto, 1851–3. Photograph by Octavius Thompson. MTL/BR, Picture Collection, T-12,067; *Toronto in the Camera: A Series of Photographic Views of the Principal Buildings in the City of Toronto* (Toronto: O[ctavius] Thompson 1868), plate 1

COUNTY COURTHOUSES[4]

As noted in an earlier chapter, the 1849 Municipal Act led to the establishment of county-based governance in Canada West. Building a number of new courthouses immediately became necessary. In 1850–2 Cumberland designed three courthouses, for the counties of Haldimand,

York, and Ontario; in 1861 he designed a fourth, for the county of Victoria.

Before turning to these, however, one unexecuted project for a combined courthouse and jail needs to be considered. From 1848 to 1853 Cumberland put forward several designs for a courthouse and jail in the Gore District. The final design, for which drawings exist, can be

13.3 Cumberland & Storm. Seventh Post Office, Toronto, 1851–3. Interior elevation showing details of joiners' work, c. 1851. Horwood (76)7

analysed for the insights it provides into his later executed courthouses (fig. 13.7).[5] This uninspired design incorporated a five-bay plan, with the main central bay given prominence by a pedimented elevation and a somewhat spindly tower to the rear. Roundheaded windows with prominent keystones and stone heads, and the quoining at the corners of the centre bay, constituted the only ornament on the building. The proposed jail was perhaps most notable for its plan. The compact layout would have made it easy for the guards to make their rounds. But although the design superficially resembled the Panoptic schemes popular at the time in prison architecture, there was no intention to place the guards at the centre of the jail, as would have been the case in a Panoptic structure.[6] The chained swags and fortress-like air of the main entrance were typical features of English jails constructed at this time: an expression in stone of the warning 'All hope abandon, ye who enter here!' of Dante's *Inferno*. To name only the most obvious example, chained swags and an exaggeratedly secure entrance were features of George Dance the Younger's Newgate Prison in London, built in 1770–85.

Cumberland's earliest executed courthouse was in Cayuga, the county seat of Haldimand County.[7] Today a tiny, picturesque community on the banks of the Grand River in southwestern

Ontario, during the early 1850s Cayuga dreamed of a great future for itself. The river's attractiveness as a conduit for American goods would, it was thought, guarantee prosperity, and the town had been made the county seat in 1849, after which the county officials wasted no time in calling for designs for a new fireproof courthouse. A competition was announced on 23 February 1850, and Cumberland & Ridout's design, submitted on 22 March, was immediately accepted.[8] Tenders were issued on 9 April and the building was completed by January 1851.[9]

The courthouse was situated on a promontory overlooking the river, on a large tract of land adjacent to the county agricultural grounds (fig. 13.8). A square brick box dressed up with stone facings and a modest cupola, it sat well back on its sloping site (fig. 13.9). The two-storey, stone-covered centre element, which was in the shape of a square, was flanked by brick wings one storey high. The front of the building featured Doric pilasters, the windows battered Greek Revival frames made of stone. The drum of the cupola stood on an open arcade of roundheaded columns. In addition to courtrooms, the building accommodated the offices of the county registrar, treasurer, clerk of the Surrogate Court, and clerk of the peace. There was also a jail linked to the courthouse by a party wall. As in the unexecuted design for the

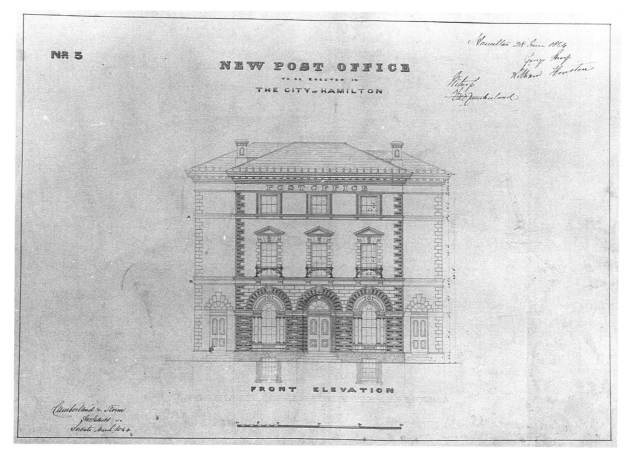

13.4 Cumberland & Storm. Post Office, 72 James Street North, Hamilton, 1854–6. Contract drawing of front elevation, March 1854. Horwood 91(13)

Gore District jail, Cumberland made the façade of the Haldimand County jail exaggeratedly secure, by employing rustication (particularly on the projecting centre bay), chained swags, and a doorcase and window frames that were heavy and battered. Quoining emphasized the already substantial quality of the jail's façade.

The building impressed visitors such as W.H. Smith, author of *Canada: Past, Present and Future*, who commented in 1852 that 'A handsome court house and jail have been erected, of stone, from the design of Messrs. Cumberland and Ridout. It is well situated, on a rising ground, with plenty of land attached, and has every convenience necessary for such a building. The village is now holding up its head, and looking forward to its ultimately arriving at the importance of a city.'[10] But such optimism was ill-founded. Although the addition of the courthouse did much to contribute to the character of the town, Cayuga's prosperity was short-lived. A writer observed in 1877 that 'This [courthouse] contributed greatly to the growth and advancement of the village, which for many years was a busy and prosperous place; but the building of railways diverted the trade from the river, and when the timber in the surrounding county was exhausted, Cayuga, in common with the other villages along the river, received a check in its progress from which it has not, even yet, fully recovered.'[11]

Today the village is even sleepier than in 1877. There is still a county courthouse on the site, but Cumberland & Ridout's building was destroyed by fire in 1922. The jail, however, still stands, although the interior has been transformed.

13.5 Cumberland & Storm. Post Office, 72 James Street North, Hamilton, 1854–6. Photograph, n.d. Hamilton Public Library, Special Collections

The next courthouse that Cumberland designed was in Toronto, which in 1850 had been made the seat of the newly constituted York County. Cumberland, as we have seen, was county engineer, and accordingly was well situated to offer his services when approval for a new courthouse came through in 1851.[12] This project was different from Haldimand County's in several respects. The Haldimand County Courthouse stood on a picturesque hillside, whereas the York County building stood on a densely built-up site on Adelaide Street in downtown Toronto (fig. 13.10). The construction of the Haldimand County building proceeded with alacrity; the construction of the

York County building was protracted. And even though Haldimand County's construction budget was modest, that project was constructed more or less as the architects had designed it. The design for the York County building, by contrast, was whittled away to the point where the original architectural conception was substantially compromised.[13]

The York County Courthouse was intended to accommodate both civil and criminal courts. Eventually the design was enlarged to include judicial facilities for the counties of Ontario and Peel, which amalgamated with York County in January 1852. Cumberland and Ridout seem to have found it a struggle to accommodate the

13.6 Sir Benjamin Heywood's Bank, St Ann Street, Manchester, England. Exterior view by architect John Edgar Gregan, 1849. Cecil Stewart, *The Stones of Manchester* (London: Edward Arnold 1956), 42

building's various functions, and they prepared several plans,[14] whose many ink and pencil alterations are a possible indication of the difficulties they faced in preparing an acceptable design. They finally decided to locate the courtrooms on the second storey. The largest courtroom, for criminal trials, was in the centre, and the other courtrooms in the east and west wings. Beneath the criminal court was the council chamber, called the Shire Hall.

The architects' drawings show a three-part façade in sober Greek Revival idiom (fig. 13.11). The centre bay was emphasized by means of a Doric colonnade and a sculpted coat of arms above the main elevation, while the side bays were emphasized only by slight projections and

recessions in the façade and by stone window-frames.

Cumberland was asked to modify the design several times (fig. 13.12).[15] The county commissioners met with him on 15 July 1851 and directed him to prepare sketches and plans for two different schemes, one including basement- and ground-floor offices to be rented out, the other including only spaces for the lawcourts, council chamber, and public offices. By the 28th, Cumberland had prepared the sketches, and at a meeting on that date the commissioners opted to forgo including rental spaces in the design. They also directed Cumberland to produce a less costly design and to consult with the judges and other officials

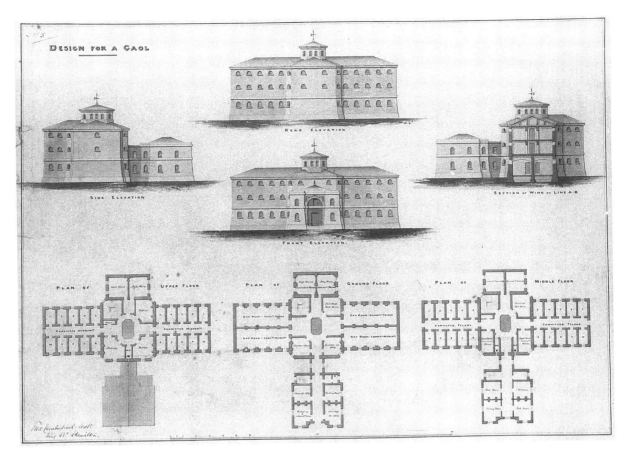

13.7 Frederic Cumberland. Proposed Gore District Courthouse and Jail, Hamilton, 1848–53. Presentation drawing of jail. Horwood (52)4

who would be using the building, including the chief justices of the Courts of Queen's Bench and Common Pleas and the judge of the County Court. A revised plan was submitted in August and was returned for further changes. Meanwhile, the proposal for rental spaces was resurrected, reconsidered, and turned down again. Finally, on 6 September, Cumberland was authorized to put the work out to tender. The lowest bid, that of John Ritchey for £6720, was the one chosen.

The final plan provided for a rabbit warren of different spaces. On the ground floor the centre bay enclosed an entrance hall forty-one feet long by thirty-six feet wide, and the Shire Hall, thirty-six feet long by thirty-four feet wide. The interior, photographs show, included a pair of startlingly severe baseless Doric columns.[16] Six

committee rooms filled out the rest of the centre bay. The wings were given over to offices for the County Court (two rooms and a vault), the county treasurer (two rooms and a vault), the clerk of the council (two rooms), the Division Court (two rooms), the clerk of the peace (two rooms and a vault), and the sheriff (two rooms and a vault).

Budget cutbacks eventually led to some intended architectural embellishments being abandoned. The original plan, for instance, showed a colonnade of free-standing columns; eventually this was replaced by pilasters. Problems in the delivery of stone from Ohio caused construction delays.[17] By 1853, however, the building was finished, and it was used until 1898–9, when the courts were moved to E.J. Lennox's new Municipal Building (now known

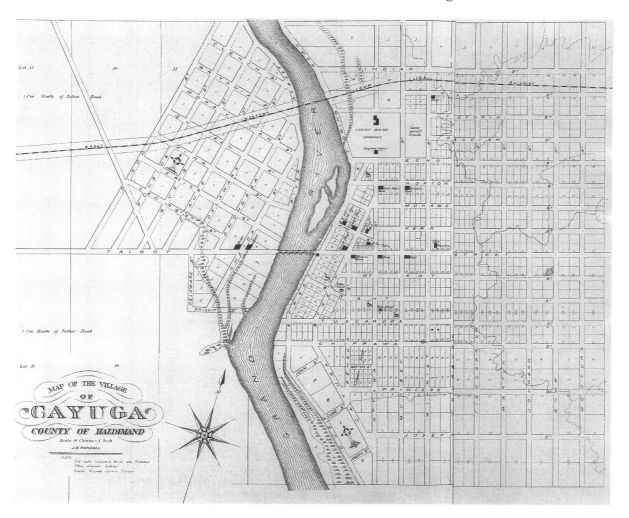

13.8 Map of the village of Cayuga, showing the site of the Haldimand County Courthouse, designed by Cumberland & Ridout in 1850–1 (near top of map, fronting the east bank of the Grand River). Not identified on the map is the adjoining jail, also designed by Cumberland & Ridout. *Illustrated Historical Atlas of the Counties of Haldimand and Norfolk* (Belleville, Ont.: Mika Publishing 1972 [1877]), 38–9

as Old City Hall). The central pediment of the building is still extant, and it still is surrounded by nineteenth-century buildings. The building which it fronts is now a theatre.

In many respects the third of Cumberland's courthouses – the Ontario County Courthouse in Whitby, begun in 1852 and completed two years later – was the most straightforward of his courthouses of the early 1850s (figs. 13.13–14). Not surprisingly, it was also the most artistically accomplished. The townspeople of Whitby, like those of Cayuga, wanted to use architecture to

express their sense of self-importance. Town officials provided Cumberland with a site that, while not as favourable as Cayuga's, was none the less more generous than Toronto's. As a result the building conveyed a feeling of spaciousness and was impressive to see. Cumberland had by now developed a formula for courthouse designs, which embraced an elaborate pedimented exterior crowned by a drum and dome; ground-floor wings flanking the centre element; and Greek Revival styling. Although this building was, like the Haldimand County Court-

COUNTY BUILDINGS, CAYUGA.

13.9 Cumberland & Ridout. Haldimand County Courthouse and Jail, Cayuga, 1850–1. Exterior view.
Illustrated Historical Atlas of the Counties of Haldimand and Norfolk (Belleville, Ont.: Mika Publishing 1972 [1877]), 27

house, constructed of brick with stone facing, it did not seem diminished by the use of brick instead of the more expensive stone. The scope of the Whitby design was much simpler than York County's, and as a result was clearer and more easily comprehensible. The two-storey volume behind the main pediment led through an entrance hall down some wide steps to a two-storey courtroom, which was lit by tall, roundheaded windows encased in elaborate frames. The judge's chambers were behind the courtroom. As in Cayuga, there was also a jail, but in this case separate from the courthouse (fig. 13.15). The principal elevation of the Whitby jail plagiarized the firm's Cayuga design: it had the same battered doorcase, the same chained swags, the same exaggerated rusti-

cation and quoining. The courthouse is still extant.

Cumberland designed one more courthouse, for the town of Lindsay, about a decade later. Lindsay, northeast of Toronto, was incorporated in 1857 when the Port Hope, Lindsay, and Beaverton Railway brought a rail-line there. In 1861, when Victoria County was created and Lindsay became the county seat, Cumberland & Storm submitted plans for a courthouse without being asked (figs. 13.16–17).[18] These so impressed the local officials that they awarded the commission to the firm. Storm superintended much of the construction, and it could also be that much of the design work fell on his shoulders as well.

The design of the Victoria County Courthouse

13.10 Cumberland & Storm. York County Courthouse, Toronto, 1851–3. Photograph of south side of Adelaide Street East, looking east from Toronto Street, c. 1860. The courthouse is the tripartite building on the left. MTL/BR, Picture Collection, T-12,418

was similar in its massing to the earlier courthouses. Like them it had a pedimented centre bay flanked by wings (in this case, two storeys high). But the stylistic idiom was markedly different. Gone was the colonnaded Greek Revival of the earlier buildings; in its place was an idiom more reflective of Ruskinian interests, one characterized by pointed-arch windows, heavy stone coursing, and a massive if somewhat denuded main entrance. Yet the design remained unresolved. For instance, there were several fenestration and arch motifs. The cupola featured rounded-arch elements, the projecting main bay pointed-arch ones. The window-surrounds on the wings combined a sort of Greek Revival eared design with a pointed head.

13.11 Cumberland & Storm. York County Courthouse, Toronto, 1851–3. Presentation perspective. William G. Storm, delineator(?). Private collection of Gordon deSaint Wotherspoon, Uxbridge, Ontario (photograph by John Glover)

The provision of a colonnade of Doric pilasters on the second floor of the main elevation was perplexing and unconvincing.

The building contained a square, two-storey courtroom space like that of the Ontario County Courthouse, but also spaces for other functions. The county council chambers were there, as were offices for the county warden and his clerks. The jail presented close stylistic links with Cumberland's earlier designs; once again there were the chained swags and heavy stone-trimmed window-frames. The main door featured iron strapwork that seemed to derive from the firm's designs for University College or perhaps St James's Cemetery Chapel.

Construction progressed smoothly. By the fall of 1862 the building committee was able to report to council that 'progress has been so remarkable as to exceed expectations, both of your architect and committee.' On 31 October it reported that 'the progress of our Buildings has been so marked as to exceed our most sanguine expectations.' Finally, on 16 January 1863, it

took 'extreme satisfaction of [sic] congratulating you [council] upon the near completion of your public buildings.'[19] The council first met in its new chambers on 15 May.

The design for the Victoria County Courthouse casts a somewhat unfavourable light on the abilities of Cumberland and Storm. Although the plan seems to have functioned well, the stylistic confusion of the elevation suggests that the firm was no longer able to design in a consistent idiom. Even if we were not already aware that Cumberland's heart was no longer in architecture by the early 1860s, the unconvincing resolution of this building's design would make such a conclusion difficult to avoid. Despite its stylistic flaws, the building still stands, and although much renovated, and without its cupola, continues to give visitors some idea of the original design.[20]

OSGOODE HALL, TORONTO[21]

Anthony Trollope's positive comments on Uni-

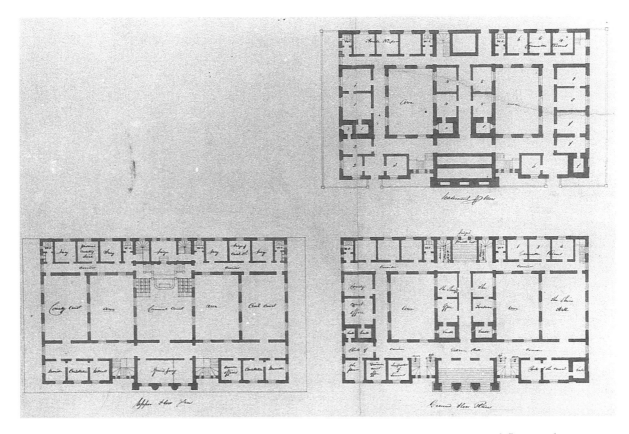

13.12 Cumberland & Storm. York County Courthouse, Toronto, 1851–3. Basement, ground-floor, and upper-floor plans, 1851. One of the several schemes prepared by the firm. Horwood (77)5

versity College have already been cited. His comments on Osgoode Hall were equally enthusiastic:

The Osgoode Hall is to Upper Canada what ... [Dublin's] Four Courts are to Ireland.[22] The Law courts are all held there. Exteriorly, little can be said for Osgoode Hall, whereas the exterior of the Four Courts in Dublin is very fine; but as an interior the temple of Themis at Toronto beats hollow that which the goddess owns in Dublin. In Dublin the Courts themselves are shabby, and the space under the dome is not so fine as the exterior seems to promise that it should be. In Toronto the Courts themselves are, I think, the most commodious that I ever saw, and the passages, vestibules, and hall are very handsome.[23]

The building he described did not begin with any architectural pretensions. The original building, designed by John Ewart as a home for the Law Society of Upper Canada, was completed in 1832. Originally a small brick box, it was eventually modified to accommodate the Courts of Chancery,[24] Queen's Bench, and Common Pleas, and has been added to intermittently ever since – fourteen times in all.[25] The renovations undertaken by Cumberland & Storm beginning in 1856 to provide much-needed additional room for the Courts of Queen's Bench and Common Pleas, however, conferred on it a formal unity that was as remarkable as it has been long-lasting (figs. 13.18–19). The problems faced by the architects were considerable. The Osgoode Hall that they were asked to redesign consisted of the nondescript block designed by Ewart, to which in 1844 Henry Bowyer Lane had added a new wing, porticos, and a connecting arcade crowned by a sickly and unconvincing dome. In 1856–60 Cumberland & Storm added a centre section that included additional spaces for the superior courts,

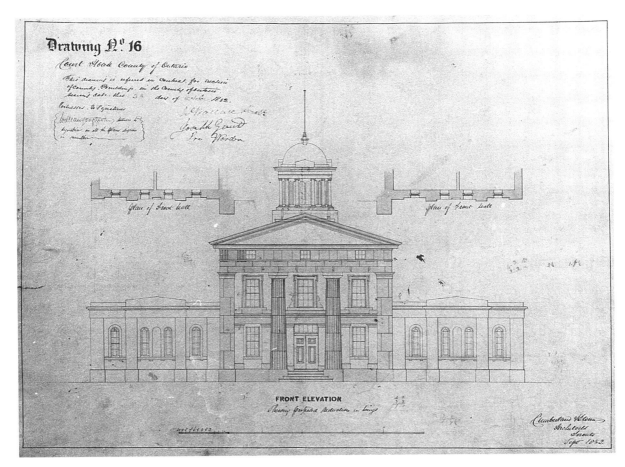

13.13 Cumberland & Storm. Ontario County Courthouse and Jail, Whitby, 1852–4. Contract drawing of front elevation of courthouse, September 1852. Horwood (82)21

room for a motions court, new rooms for the judges and court officials, and a library. The main formal element of the new plan was the centre block, a tall atrium space with courtrooms on the north, west, and east sides of the upper floors, and the library on the south side of the upper floors.

The architects retained Lane's tall arcaded pediments on the porticos and inserted their own pedimented version in the recessed centre bay. Theirs, however, was more lavishly ornamented and heavily rusticated, which left no doubt in visitors' minds about where the main entrance was located (fig. 13.20). The architects also faced their centre bay all in stone, which offered a contrast to the brick wings, which were merely trimmed with stone. They placed round-headed windows in the centre block, whereas the wings had squareheaded pedimented windows. A band of tall pilasters was added to the centre block. This disregard for the earlier building has been decried by at least one author,[26] but on closer examination one sees that in fact many of the main design features – the beltcourses and the cornice, for instance – do match up with the wings.

The exterior of the centre block has been compared with French architecture, in particular the garden front of Versailles.[27] Given what is known of Cumberland's methods and the architects he admired, it is unlikely that he would have wanted to adopt a French design. It is much more likely that he turned again to Sir Charles Barry's buildings. For instance, a

13.14 Cumberland & Storm. Ontario County Courthouse and Jail, Whitby, 1852–4. Photograph of courthouse, n.d. The top half of the jail is visible to the rear of the courthouse. Whitby Historical Society

number of Osgoode Hall's design motifs – spiked urns, vermiculated arcades, roof balustrade – are seen in Barry's work, such as Bridgewater House in London, which Barry designed for Lord Ellesmere and Cumberland visited in 1851 (fig. 13.21). One can also see the influence of Barry's third son, Edward (1830–80), whose extravagant Royal Opera House, Covent Garden (1857), with its Floral Hall (1857–8), shows precisely the same combination of rich yet controlled ornament that one finds in Osgoode Hall (fig. 13.22).

Another English building to which the exterior of Osgoode Hall has been compared is Sir William Chambers's Somerset House in London. Begun in 1776 and completed in 1786, it was one of the leading examples of English neoclassical public design, and must have provided a general model for Cumberland.[28] Certain formal devices that are found in Osgoode Hall, such

as the heavy, rusticated, roundheaded arches on the Hall's ground floor, are reminiscent of Somerset House. But as was pointed out above, the arches were a feature of the 1844 design. Another relevant building was the park front of the Treasury in Whitehall, designed by William Kent in 1733–7 (fig. 13.23). This was a dignified structure with a heavily rusticated basement and a pedimented centre bay. The sober and powerful phrasing of English neoclassicism was in favour during the 1850s, and was given additional richness by the architects of those years.[29]

The interior of Osgoode Hall, a magnificent, naturally lit two-storey space with a large double-arm staircase and a superbly designed library, has excited much praise (figs. 13.24–5). For instance, Eric Arthur, the well-known historian of Ontario architecture, wrote that the library was 'one of the finest [rooms] in Canada.'[30] Historians have suggested as possible sources

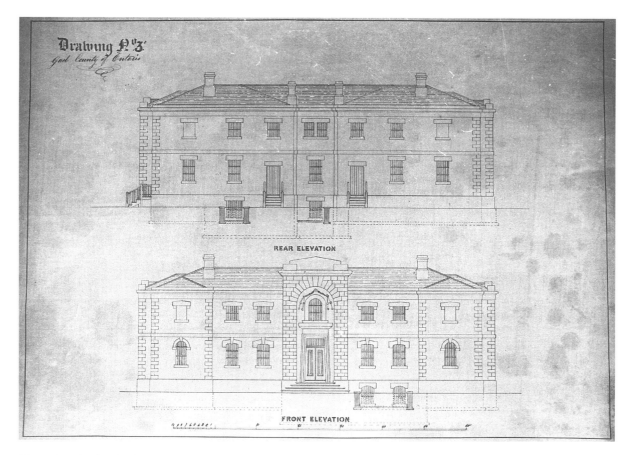

Drawing Nº 3.
Gaol County of Ontario

REAR ELEVATION

FRONT ELEVATION

13.15 Cumberland & Storm. Ontario County Courthouse and Jail, Whitby, 1852–4. Contract drawing of front and rear elevations of jail. Horwood (82)29

for the library, with its coffered domes and guilloche bandings, the work of Inigo Jones and John Nash, the Queen's House at Greenwich, and Buckingham Palace.[31] The square centre atrium has been compared to the Genoese Palazzo Tursi-Doria, designed by Rocco Lurago in 1564.[32] Several features of the interior elevation of the palazzo remind one of Osgoode Hall, including the two-storey superimposed arcade supporting a balustraded upper storey. The plan, however, was not so similar, for in the Italian building a grand staircase was located at the end of the court, whereas in Osgoode Hall the staircase was located transversally. There were differences, too, in the principal exterior elevation. The palazzo's arcades sprang from columns, whereas there were piers at Osgoode Hall. Also, the Italian building's spandrels were rusticated, Osgoode Hall's smooth.

Another possible source, closer in spirit to Cumberland's work, was the saloon of Bridgewater House (fig. 13.26). The second-floor picture gallery was completed by 1850, when Cumberland visited the building.[33] A feature of another of London's large town houses, erected shortly after Bridgewater House, may also be compared with the interior of Osgoode Hall. This was the grand staircase hall of Dorchester House, erected for R.S. Holford to the designs of Louis Villimany (fig. 13.27). It was planned in 1848 and completed in the 1850s.[34]

Architectural historian Angela Carr has proposed that Cumberland may have combined architectural features of the English private club with features drawn from public buildings, as a way of recognizing Osgoode Hall's role as both a private facility (headquarters of the Law Society) and a public facility (site of the superior courts).

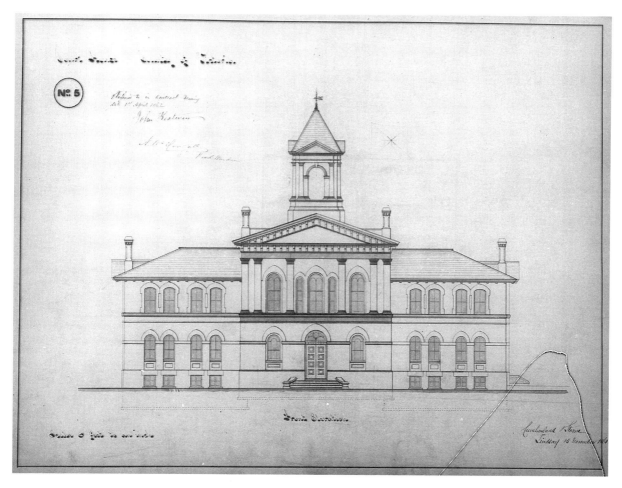

13.16 Cumberland & Storm. Victoria County Courthouse and Jail, Lindsay, 1861–3. Presentation drawing of front elevation of courthouse, 15 November 1861. Horwood (127)23

This is an ingenious and convincing proposition.[35] As with his other buildings, it is likely that Cumberland would have turned for inspiration to English rather than French sources. There was nothing unusual in taking features from English houses and using them, with modifications, for public buildings in Canada. For their private residences Victorian Canadians could not afford to build on the scale of the great houses of London, but they could afford to reproduce aspects of great-house design in public buildings.

But one should not forget that Osgoode Hall is also a very beautiful building. It is beautiful because of the coffee-and-cream tint of the expensive and lavishly applied Caen stone, a particularly fine-textured material that enabled the architects to create vermiculated arcades that are enhanced by contrasting light and shade;[36] because of the tallness and grace of the interior court, a space punctuated by a cadence of sturdy piers, above which float brightly hued skylights with delicate iron tracery; because of the dignity and drama that the double-armed staircase imparts to the building (figs. 13.28–9); and because of the serene, uplifting space of the library, with its generous height, magnificent plasterwork domes, and tall columns. To be sure, there are inconsistencies and incongruities. Some might find that the polychromatic and geometrically ordered tiles on the main floor – the same tiles supplied by Maw & Co. for University College – present an unfortunate

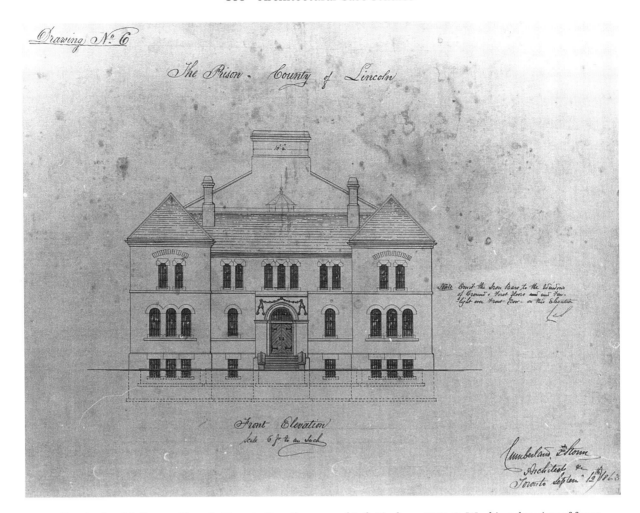

13.17 Cumberland & Storm. Victoria County Courthouse and Jail, Lindsay, 1861–3. Working drawing of front elevation of jail, 12 September 1863. Horwood (134)18

contrast with the more serene and delicate effects of the rest of the building, such as the delicate tracery on the skylights. It is generally considered a solecism (in architectural terms) to mix such different sensibilities as are found, on the one hand, in the rugged, angular design of the tiles, and on the other, in the graceful classicizing effects seen elsewhere in the building. And yet the contrast in sensibilities created by Maw & Co.'s quintessentially High Victorian tiles in a predominantly classical interior characterizes perfectly the confident eclecticism of the 1850s.

Osgoode Hall is also admirable – and perhaps beautiful – because of the subtlety with which

its architects responded to its complex operational demands. This was a building with as many programmatic quirks as the York County Court House. In the earlier judicial building, no space had been left unfilled. The result was a mean and cluttered interior. In Osgoode Hall, the complexity of the building's operational demands was effectively masked by the provision of large amounts of functionally useless space. The atrium with its deep space-well added nothing to the building from the point of view of cost-effectiveness, but everything from the point of view of architectural experience. For first-time visitors to Osgoode Hall, the building's exterior offered no clue to the drama of

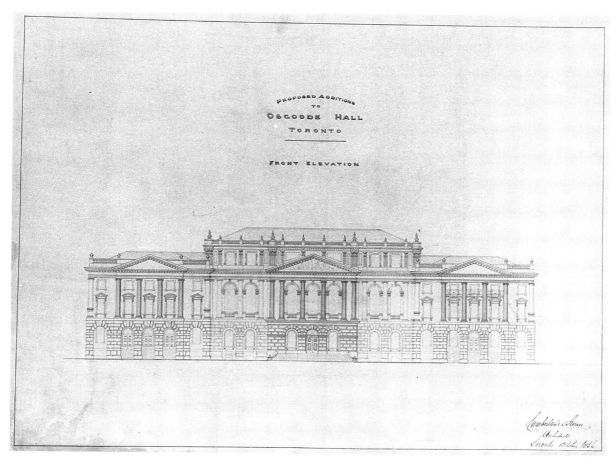

13.18 Cumberland & Storm. Centre Block of Osgoode Hall, Toronto, 1856–60. Presentation drawing of front elevation, October 1856. Horwood (102)10

what lay within. Nor, on passing through the front doors as a prelude to entering the courts or the Great Library, could they anticipate the dramatic sequence of movement – the procession through the atrium and the slow march up the grand staircase – that emphasized the dignity of the law. Of all of Osgoode Hall's spaces, the Great Library summed up the building's purpose best. As MacRae and Adamson have written, 'The designers of this great room were architects who valued daylight as the best illumination, and who saw the Great Library as much more than a repository of the printed word. They planned it to be a room whose lofty spaces might encourage the process of reasoned thought and the growth of the spirit.'[37] One would have to be blind to the power of architec-

ture not to see the Great Library as a tribute to the abstract concepts of knowledge, law, and justice.

Today, Osgoode Hall still sits on a spacious site that displays the building to great advantage. The tall and elaborate cast-iron fence surrounding the grounds, designed by Storm in 1866, also enhances the building's appearance especially well. All around one finds architectural reminders of Toronto's past. To the west is the neoclassical house of Chief Justice Sir William Campbell, constructed in 1822.[38] To the east, Osgoode Hall's High Victorian splendour is set against the backdrop of several generations of later buildings: the Richardsonian Romanesque Old City Hall (designed by E.J. Lennox in 1889–99); the International Modernist New City

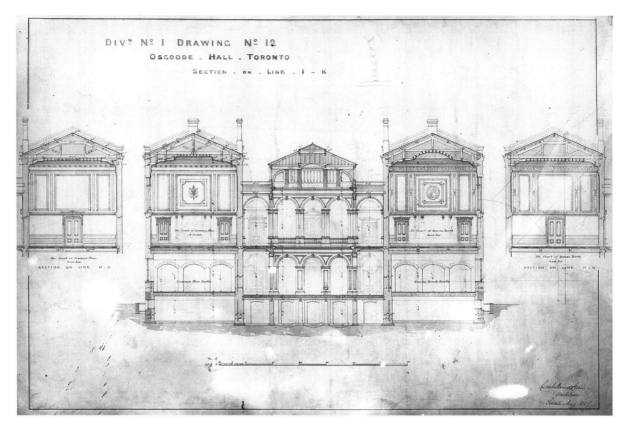

13.19 Cumberland & Storm. Centre Block of Osgoode Hall, Toronto, 1856–60. Working drawing of sections, May 1857. Horwood (102)25

Hall (designed Viljo Revell with John B. Parkin Associates and completed in 1965); and the commercial postmodernism of the Toronto Eaton Centre (designed by Bregman & Hamann and the Zeidler/Roberts Partnership and built in stages since 1975). In its form and in its symbolic power, Osgoode Hall more than holds its own among this architecturally distinguished group.

THE MECHANICS' INSTITUTE, TORONTO

As was pointed out in chapter 3, the mechanics' institutes were important social and cultural institutions in nineteenth-century Canada. Cumberland was a life member of the Toronto Mechanics' Institute and twice its president. In 1853, when Upper Canada College donated some land to the Mechanics' Institute that was then sold to raise funds for a new building,

Cumberland quickly volunteered his firm's architectural services at no charge.

Cumberland's Mechanics' Institute, which included a music hall, stood just north of St James's Parochial School, another of his designs, described in chapter 10. One never would have known from simply looking at the buildings that they had the same architect, however. The school was designed in a restrained Gothic idiom, whereas the Mechanics' Institute was a flamboyant Italianate structure (fig. 13.30). Essentially square in plan, with a hipped roof, the Mechanics' Institute was constructed of brick trimmed with Ohio stone. The ground floor featured roundheaded openings gathered together in a triplet in the centre, with a heavy dentillated frieze dividing the ground floor from those above. The two upper storeys were united vertically by the addition of colossal Composite pilasters. Squareheaded windows were set one

13.20 Cumberland & Storm. Osgoode Hall, Toronto, 1856–60. Detail of intrados of main entrance arcade. Photo by the author

above the other, with especially large ones in the centre bays. The elevation terminated with a heavy cornice, above which were a balustrade and a commemorative title panel emphasized by paired spiked urns above the centre bay. The music hall was entered from Adelaide Street, the other parts of the building from Church Street.

The construction of the building went smoothly enough at first, but costs soon mounted alarmingly. By mid-1855 a public appeal for funds had to be made.[39] Renting office space to the government of the Province of Canada enabled the Mechanics' Institute to raise some funds, and, after the government vacated the premises in 1861, the building was completed. Its design would have been familiar to the citizens of any British city. The square massing and predilection for heavy stone surrounds on the window-frames, for instance, were also features of John Gregan's Mechanics' Institute in Manchester's Princess Street, constructed in 1854.[40] Edward Walters's Manchester & Salford Bank of 1860 displayed the same rusticated ground storey, elaborately framed second-storey windows, and roof balustrade punctuated by spiked urns (fig. 13.31).[41] The Mechanics' Institute, an architectural and cultural landmark in downtown Toronto for decades, survived until 1949; condominiums now occupy the site.

THE CANADIAN INSTITUTE BUILDING, TORONTO

The commission to design new headquarters for the Canadian Institute must have been both exciting and frustrating for Cumberland, a faithful supporter of the organization. In 1855–6 he prepared no fewer than three designs (figs.

13.21 Sir Charles Barry. Bridgewater House, London England, 1845–54. Perspective.

13.32–4).[42] As with the Mechanics' Institute, the plans were supplied at no charge. On 14 November 1855 the cornerstone was laid at an elaborate ceremony presided over by Governor General Head.[43] The project stalled, probably because money was lacking. Tender calls were published in the *Globe* on 28 August 1857, but after that nothing more happened.

Although the drawings for the project are undated, an evolution in the design can be discerned. Cumberland first prepared some rough sketches of the plan,[44] presumably discussed these with the building committee, and then worked up the elevations and a modified plan,[45] a rich, substantial design that incorporated many elements seen in other examples of the firm's work of the mid-fifties. The modified design resembled Cumberland's designs for houses during this period, but with a sense of civic grandeur that the houses lacked. For the

Canadian Institute Cumberland proposed a stone façade more luxurious than any in his houses, indeed as luxurious as any ever created in Toronto, with carving and ornamental motifs from basement to cornice. The square, two-storey hipped-roof structure was to be divided into three bays, with the centre bay being particularly strongly emphasized by the use of a variety of motifs. Especially notable was the heavy rustication of the ground storey, achieved by a formal device that Cumberland had not until then used in his visual vocabulary, namely vermiculation on the stone courses, contrasted with patterned bands of ashlar. The main entrance featured a triple-arched arcade standing at the head of broad, low stairs. This entrance was designed to present a magnificent elaboration of the stonecarver's art, combining vermiculated stone courses with exaggerated anthropomorphic keystones, banded ashlar,

13.22 Edward M. Barry. Royal Opera House, Covent Garden, London, England, 1857–8. Exterior view. *The Builder*, 15 (1857), 611

and corbelled supports leading up to the second storey. The walls of the second storey were to be smooth-textured, as a contrast with the heavy stone courses below and also with the intricate second-storey windows, which were to be bracketed by huge and individually detailed Palladian frames. The centre bay featured a different window rhythm, a roundheaded triple-arched grouping such as Cumberland frequently used in his domestic commissions. Here, however, the windows were to be given added emphasis by scalloped lunettes and free-standing flanking columns. A heavy cornice capped the design. The centre bay was accentuated by a vertical extension consisting of yet another balustrade flanking an elaborate segmental pediment. The balustrade featured spiked urns on its corner stanchions and the face of the segmental pediment was to be carved. Cumberland added ex-

aggeratedly wide quoins on the upper storey, which he repeated on the centre bay. By having quoining on the centre bay, the architect achieved an effect of continuous verticality extending from the rusticated piers on the centre bay on the ground floor to the quoining on the second storey, and finally to the spiked urns that terminated the elevation. And yet a countervailing horizontal effect was created by the heavy balustrade dividing the two storeys and the equally heavy cornice. Overall, this would have been a most remarkable design – grandly civic, majestically ornamented, and proudly proclaiming its links with the great palazzi and town houses of earlier architectural traditions.

Given that the second, modified design was so accomplished, it is a mystery why a third design was prepared.[46] The third design called for a very simple subdivision of spaces, with a mu-

PARK FRONT OF THE TREASURY, WHITEHALL.——As Designed by William Kent.

13.23 William Kent. The Treasury, Whitehall, London, England, 1733–7. Exterior view. *The Builder*, 15 (1857), 419

seum occupying most of the ground floor and a meeting hall occupying the equivalent space on the upper floor. There was to be spiral banding on the window-surrounds, spiral columns on the main elevation, and pointed polychromatic window-heads of a Ruskinian kind. The windows, cleverly detailed inside their frames, had colonnettes from which sprang subsidiary roundheaded arches that did not extend vertically all the way to the top of a frame but left room for a roundel elaborated by more spiral banding. This was a Venetian motif.

Although Cumberland's designs were never executed, he was able to employ some of their formal elements in other buildings. The vermiculated triple-arched main entrance and spiked urns of the second design were used in Osgoode Hall. From the third design he borrowed, also for Osgoode Hall, the roundheaded Italianate windows divided in two by spiral banding.

That he prepared three designs, at least two of which were rendered in considerable detail, for a project that was never executed, must have been distressing to Cumberland. Only twice, with Osgoode Hall and University College, was Cumberland given the opportunity to fully display his talent for designing public buildings. These two designs were so rewarding that they induced him to try again and again to express public aspirations through architecture, but for the rest of his life that goal proved elusive.

13.24 Cumberland & Storm. Centre Block of Osgoode Hall, Toronto, 1856–60. Perspective of library interior. William G. Storm, delineator. Horwood (747)1

13.25 Cumberland & Storm. Centre Block of Osgoode Hall, Toronto, 1856–60. Perspective of library interior. William G. Storm, delineator. Horwood (747)3

13.26 Sir Charles Barry. Bridgewater House, London, England, 1845–54. Photograph of saloon. Christopher Simon Sykes, *Private Palaces: Life in the Great London Houses* (London: Chatto & Windus 1985), 289

13.27 Lewis Villimany. Dorchester House, London, England, c. 1848–55. Photograph of grand staircase hall.
Christopher Simon Sykes, *Private Palaces: Life in the Great London Houses* (London: Chatto & Windus 1985), 293

13.28 Cumberland & Storm. Osgoode Hall, Toronto, 1856–60. Skylight above main court. Photo by the author

13.29 Cumberland & Storm. Osgoode Hall, Toronto, 1856–60. Imperial staircase leading from ground floor to courts and library above. Photo by the author

13.30 Cumberland & Storm. Mechanics' Institute, Toronto, 1853–5. Photograph by Octavius Thompson. MTL/
BR, Picture Collection, T-11,999; *Toronto in the Camera: A Series of Photographic Views of the Principal Buildings
in the City of Toronto* (Toronto: O[ctavius] Thompson 1868), plate 7

13.31 Edward Walters. Manchester & Salford Bank, Manchester, England, 1860. Exterior view. Cecil Stewart, *The Stones of Manchester* (London: Edward Arnold 1956), 41

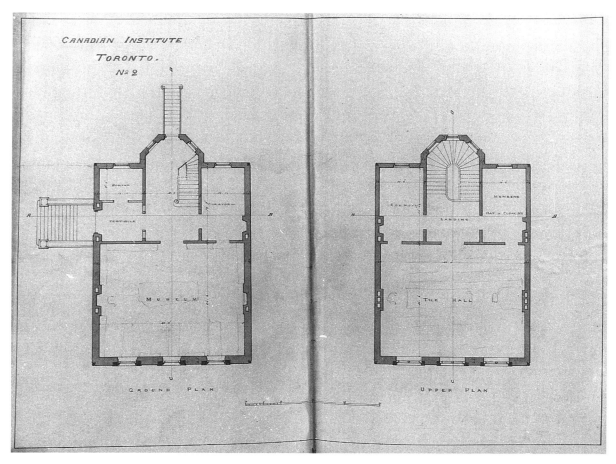

13.32 Cumberland & Storm. Proposed Canadian Institute Building, 1855–6. First scheme. Presentation drawing of ground- and upper-floor plans. Horwood (110)1

13.33 Cumberland & Storm. Proposed Canadian Institute Building, Toronto, 1855–6. Second scheme. Main(?) elevation. Horwood (110)4

13.34 Cumberland & Storm. Proposed Canadian Institute Building, Toronto, 1855–6. Second scheme. Details of stonework, windows, and cornice. Horwood (110)11

Private Commissions:
Houses and Commercial Buildings

HOUSES

Although Cumberland designed scarcely a dozen houses during his career, his clients included judges, politicians, merchants, and railway entrepreneurs – all leading figures in Toronto both financially and politically. Cumberland was able to obtain these commissions because of his connection with the Ridout family, which placed him on an equal social footing with a clientele that included both members of the old Toronto establishment and others who had risen to the top through business acumen alone.

As early as 1848–9 Cumberland undertook house renovations for Justice Robert Baldwin Sullivan (1802–53), who had served as Toronto's second mayor in 1835.[1] Cumberland's next residential project of note came early in 1851 when he undertook renovations for his brother-in-law Thomas Gibbs Ridout, who wanted to enlarge his residence and offices at the Bank of Upper Canada building on Adelaide Street East. In July 1852 Cumberland designed a house for Justice John Hawkins Hagarty (1816–1900), who served forty-one years on the bench and was later knighted.[2]

During the mid- to late 1850s Cumberland designed a number of increasingly lavish houses for an even more august group of men, including the fabulously wealthy George William Allan (1822–1901), merchant, philanthropist, and art collector. John Ross (1816–71), a railway entrepreneur active in public life, was also a client.[3]

So too was William Benjamin Robinson (1797–1873), a driven and talented man who involved himself in many aspects of Canadian politics and business.[4] Another client was William Hume Blake (1809–70), a brilliant but unstable and excessively ardent lawyer and politician.[5] Cumberland also designed a house for his old friend and supporter Egerton Ryerson.[6] For fellow engineer and railway rival Casimir Gzowski he produced, in 1854–6, a lavish design for one of the largest houses built in Toronto up to that time. In 1856–8 he designed nearly as large a house for Thomas Gibbs Ridout.[7] Another of Cumberland's mansions was Chestnut Park, built in 1855 for Gzowski's railway partner, the politician David Lewis Macpherson (1818–96).[8] Other clients included Toronto notables such as Canada Company director Frederick Widder and lawyer J. Lukin Robinson.[9]

Many of these clients were involved with Cumberland in civic and business ventures. Ross, for example, was a director of the Northern Railway from 1862 to 1869. Cumberland and Ross strongly supported Francis Hincks when he was premier of Canada. Blake was chancellor of the University of Toronto from 1853 to 1856, the crucial years when Cumberland was lobbying for the commission to design University College. Hagarty, like Cumberland, served as president of the Canadian Institute. On the other hand, some clients, such as Gzowski, who was closely associated with the Great Western Railway, were business rivals.

It is perhaps not surprising, given his social

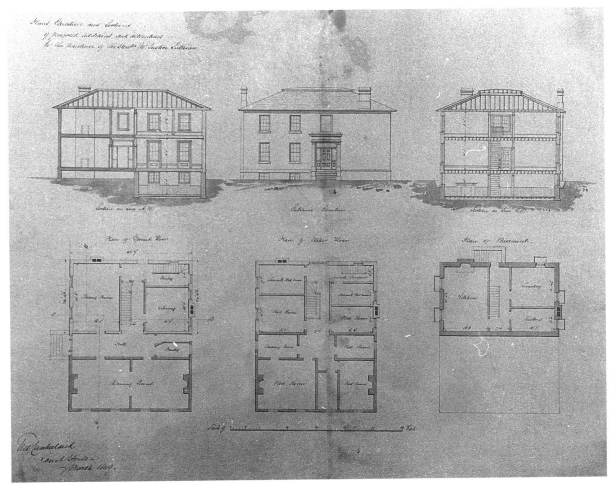

14.1 Frederic Cumberland. Additions and alterations to Robert Baldwin Sullivan House, Toronto, 1848–9. Contract drawing of plans, sections, and elevation, 7 March 1849. Horwood (53)1

milieu, that Cumberland designed relatively few modest houses. One modest structure that is still extant is his 1853 Trinity Parsonage House on King Street East. For the university he designed three small but remarkable residences, one for Professor George Templeman Kingston, director of the Royal Magnetical Observatory on the university grounds, and, adjacent to Kingston's house, a pair of cottages for the observatory staff.

The only Cumberland house built outside Toronto was George Moberly's unpretentious residence in Barrie. Cumberland may have taken this on because of Moberly's political connections in Collingwood, where he was mayor and

helped promote the interests of the Northern Railway. Two of Moberly's nephews were employed by Cumberland and it seems likely that they brought the commission into the office.

Cumberland's earliest known domestic commission, for Sullivan in 1848–9, was limited to creating new, suitably ornamented rooms for an existing residence (fig. 14.1). The modifications that Cumberland undertook for the Old Parliament Buildings were also restricted to interior work (fig. 14.2).

A dwelling that Justice Hagarty decided to build in 1852 was probably the earliest complete house that Cumberland (in partnership with Storm) designed (fig. 14.3). It was a compact,

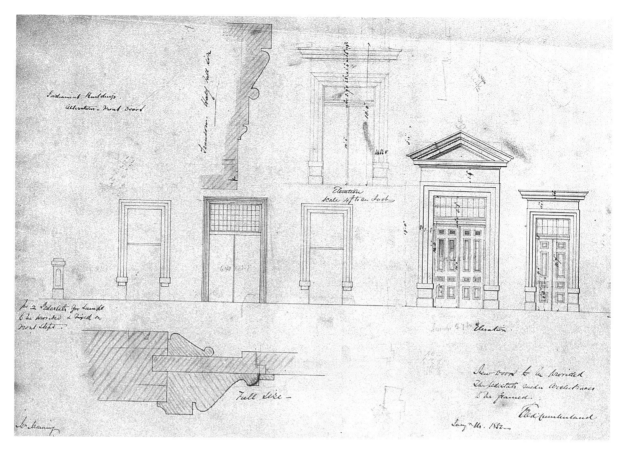

14.2 Cumberland & Ridout. Additions and alterations to Old Parliament Buildings, Toronto, 1849–50. Working drawing of details of interior woodwork, 16 January 1850. Horwood (54)17

comfortable, and unpretentious two-storey structure constructed of brick with stone quoins. The main entrance was on the west side, where a two-storey pedimented and projecting entrance bay was located and an imposing stone porch led up to an equally imposing tall door flanked by sidelights and topped with a transom. The south side featured a second entrance underneath a generous veranda supported on thin, graceful posts that extended the width of this flank. The veranda continued on the east side, where the kitchen door was located. Above the south door, on the second storey, was a large, multi-sided bay window.

The house defied easy stylistic characterization. Certainly the roundheaded windows gave it an Italianate air, but this was belied by the more casual and domestic character conferred by the flat-headed windows and bell-cast veranda. The nearly cubic massing and slightly eared surrounds on the windows had some affinities with Greek Revival idioms, but none of the ornament was Greek Revival. In fact, the ornament – particularly on the portico, but also on the veranda – did not conform to any identifiable style. The flat-headed, sash-hung windows and veranda were more consistent with the domestic architecture of 1820s than with that of mid-Victorian period.

Such a combination of disparate stylistic elements was characteristic of most of Cumberland's later houses, which, like the Sullivan house, incorporated several stylistic idioms, which were combined to achieve an effect both formal and informal. The later houses typically featured a nearly square silhouette crowned by

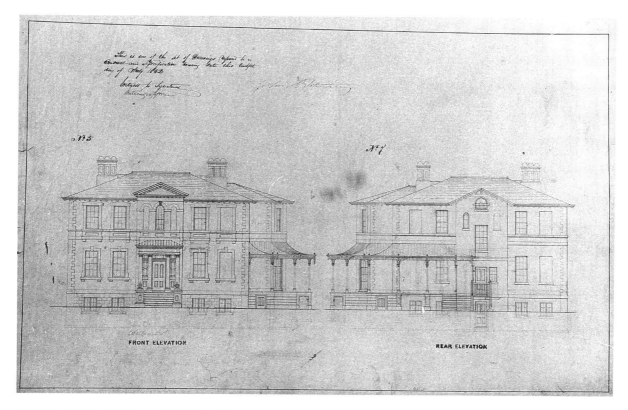

14.3 Cumberland & Storm. John Hawkins Hagarty House, Toronto, 1852. Contract drawing of front and rear elevations, 12 July 1852. Horwood (81)5, 6

a hipped roof above a formal entrance suitable for admitting distinguished visitors; a secondary entrance beneath a long veranda; and yet another entrance, usually to the kitchen, where the servants could enter. Cumberland seems to have been particularly fond of bell-cast verandas, which added a pleasant, informal touch to houses that might otherwise have seemed overly formal. And he became so fond of triplets of roundheads windows – a feature of what is often termed Tuscan Gothic – that they were seen in almost every house design after Sullivan's.[10] With respect to plan and organization of rooms, Cumberland favoured a divided organization, with formal rooms for entertaining located near the main entrance and staircases positioned transversely with respect to the entrance, away from the main hall. Clients who could afford it were provided with conservatories.

The Trinity Parsonage House was an example

of Cumberland working with essentially the same design principles as were seen in the Sullivan House, albeit in Gothic Revival style (fig. 14.4). The cubic form of the house was simplified so that the roof-line was broken only once, on the main (north) elevation, where (as in the Hagarty house of the year before) a two-storey bay provided a focus for the elevation. Trefoils replaced the squares of the Sullivan house. A Gothic finial crowned the main elevation. The windows featured unusual Gothicized mullions, elaborately scalloped surrounds, and slightly pointed heads (as did the heads of the doors). And yet there were also motifs taken from the Sullivan house, particularly the quoins, which here ran riot. A picturesque effect was achieved by placing the main door to the right of the centre of the entrance block.

Cumberland designed terraced houses on only one occasion, in April 1855, when he designed a six-house block of brick town houses

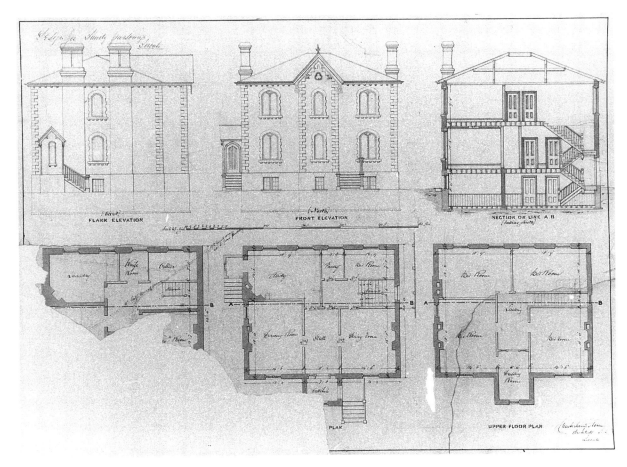

14.4 Cumberland & Storm. Trinity Parsonage House, Toronto, 1853. Working drawing of elevations, section, and plans, July 1853. Horwood (84)2

for J. Lukin Robinson[11] in a small square park halfway between Front and Wellington streets, near Bathurst Street (only two houses were built) (fig. 14.5). Three storeys high and constructed of brick with stone surrounds, these town houses did not depart from the general idiom of downtown Toronto residences of the period, although the siting was distinctive. It seems that Robinson had in mind a subdivision resembling a London square, which would have been quite unusual for Toronto, though the site was later spoiled by the expansion of nearby railway yards.[12]

Gzowski's house, erected in 1854–6, was the largest Cumberland ever designed (figs. 14.6–9). The main elevation was seventy-four feet wide and featured a giant terrace extending its whole length and continuing along an adjacent side. The portico alone was twenty-five feet wide. A large conservatory at the back was further evidence of Gzowski's ability to afford the best. An English basement provided ample light to the lower floor. The house featured all the amenities available at the time, including a water tank located beneath the main staircase.

Despite its gigantic dimensions, this house shared many features with Cumberland's earlier houses. Like them, it had a hipped roof and was nearly square in plan. The general stylistic idiom was Italianate, with prominent towers glazed to provide light into a central hall, and generous verandas along three sides. There was a glazed attic that formed a sort of third storey and was given over to bedrooms. A grandiose main

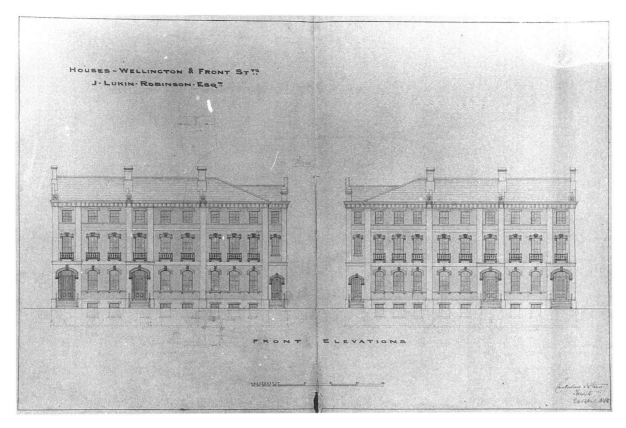

14.5 Cumberland & Storm. J. Lukin Robinson Town Houses, Toronto, 1855–6. Front elevations, March 1855. Horwood (94)2

façade with huge stone-framed paired windows on both storeys flanked a magnificent entrance bay that was gained by climbing a tall set of stone stairs whose railings swept up and out in a convex arc. The second storey featured a large square terrace projecting from a morning room accessible from the main bedrooms, which faced south.

The inside of the house displayed all the features typical of Cumberland's more expensive commissions. Ample spaces for entertaining guests were combined with cleverly de-emphasized private spaces. The ground floor featured a large oval salon twenty-seven feet long by twenty feet wide, which was entered via the wide entrance hall. The salon had a coved plasterwork ceiling, as did the adjacent dining room, which was twenty-five feet long. After dinner, guests could retire through the library to the drawing room, which was thirty-two feet

long and opened up onto the long (west) side of the terrace. The conservatory was located beyond the north end of the drawing room. As was typical of Cumberland's houses, the main staircase was positioned unobtrusively, in this case off the salon. When guests were not present, the Gzowskis could use two south-facing rooms that were otherwise closed off, namely the main-floor boudoir, from which one could enter the drawing room, and a breakfast room. Otherwise family life took place on the upper storeys, where the nursery and bedrooms were found. From the bedrooms in the attic one gained access to a monitor. This was a house that provided Gzowski with both intimacy and grandeur. He lived there for the rest of his life.

When attempting to assess the extent to which Cumberland's designs resembled other Toronto houses of the period, it is useful to compare the Gzowski house with the unexecuted

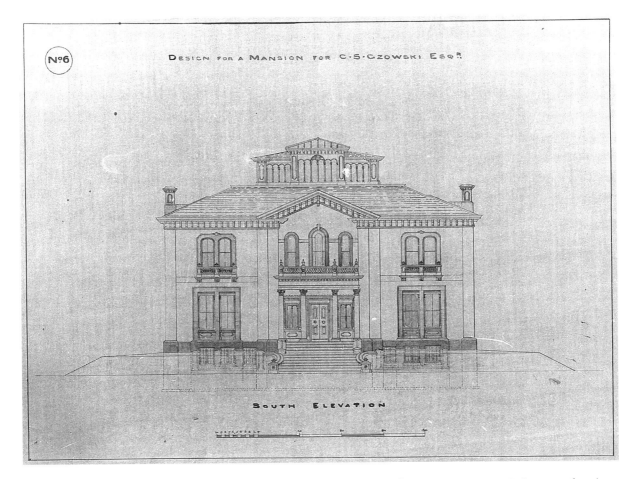

No 6

DESIGN FOR A MANSION FOR C·S·GZOWSKI ESQ.

SOUTH ELEVATION

14.6 Cumberland & Storm. Casimir Stanislaus Gzowski House (The Hall), Toronto, c. 1854–5. Contract drawing of south elevation. Horwood (638)

design prepared for Gzowski by Kivas Tully, the architect who in 1851 defeated Cumberland in the competition to design Trinity College. The drawings for Tully's design, dated 1 August 1854, are still extant and are found with Cumberland & Storm's Gzowski drawings, one of which (the only dated one) is dated 1855, which suggests that Gzowski considered Tully's design and then rejected it for the one by Cumberland & Storm (figs. 14.10–11). The two designs resemble one another, however, with respect to plan and massing. Both Cumberland and Tully included a glazed attic roof designed to admit some light into the interior. Both planned the same sequence of rooms on the west side, namely a boudoir leading into a drawing room and thence to a conservatory. Tully, however, posi-

tioned the dining room differently, adjacent to an oval hall and the main entrance. In Tully's scheme the library was to be on the east side of the house, between the main staircase and the kitchen. There was nothing wrong with the sequence of spaces proposed by Tully, which in fact may have resulted in a more dramatic spatial effect than the one achieved by Cumberland. But stylistic idiom differentiated the two, and probably to Tully's detriment. His design was more strictly Greek Revival, as was shown by the Ionic order on the portico and by the more symmetrical principal façade. As such, Tully's design lagged behind trends in domestic architecture at the time, which embraced designs of a more Italianate sort. Tully's drawings look washed out next to the more sophisticated

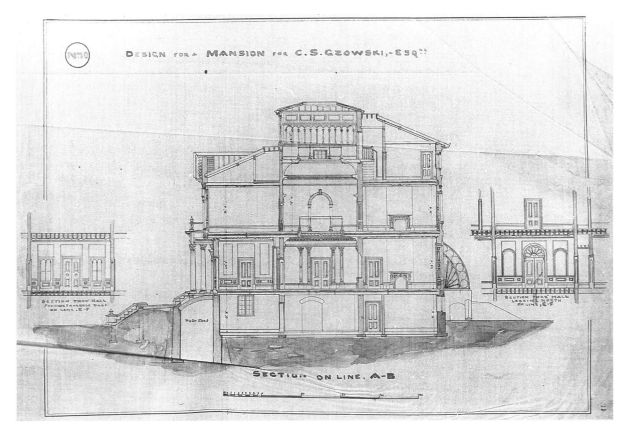

14.7 Cumberland & Storm. Casimir Stanislaus Gzowski House (The Hall), Toronto, c. 1854–5. Contract drawing of sections. Horwood (638)

portfolio produced by Cumberland & Storm. Whereas Tully drew up only a main-floor plan and a principal elevation, Cumberland & Storm prepared a complete set of elevations, plans of every floor, and even sections. Some of the sections actually showed subsidiary elevations, such as how the main door would have looked from inside the hall. Most people find architectural drawings difficult to read. Gzowski, an engineer, would have been an exception, and yet Cumberland & Storm did not rely on his ability to grasp technical material, but presented him with a suite of beautiful drawings that would have made it possible for him to easily envisage the finished building. It is little wonder that Tully lost out to Cumberland & Storm, whose presentation drawings may well have made all the difference.

In 1855–6 Cumberland designed a house for

William Hume Blake. It is interesting that the drawings provided variant designs for the front (south) elevation. One anticipated a two-storey square house with a hipped roof, the other a one-and-a-half storey structure with a cross-gable roof (fig. 14–12). Both designs, however, included Cumberland's trade mark bell-cast veranda.

In late July 1857 Cumberland undertook renovations to Frederick Widder's house, Lyndhurst, for which photographs of the interiors and porch survive (figs. 14.13–15). The interior columns were elaborately ornamented, with flaring capitals and impost blocks. Even the shafts were ornamented. As was mentioned in chapter 4, Cumberland himself did not think much of this project, and dreaded 'being trotted out at a ball as the author of [Mrs Widder's] four walls.' The porch posts, however, with their flaring

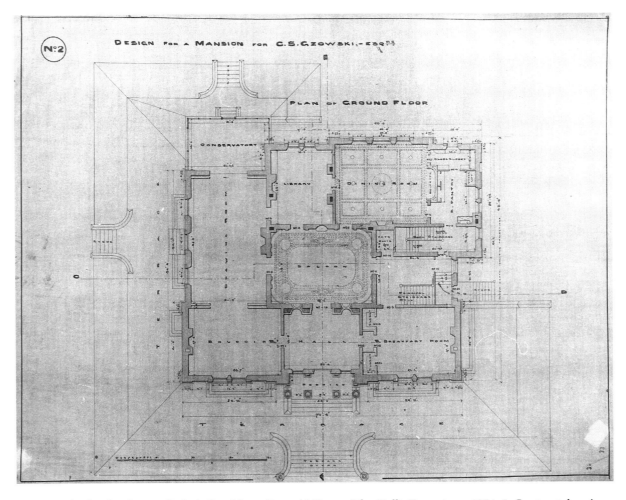

14.8 Cumberland & Storm. Casimir Stanislaus Gzowski House (The Hall), Toronto, c. 1854–5. Contract drawing of ground-floor plan. Horwood (638)

supports and pendant drops, were graceful and well proportioned.

Cumberland's own house, Pendarves, and Sherborne Villa, designed for Thomas Gibbs Ridout in 1856–8, bore many similarities to Gzowski's house. Pendarves was not markedly different from any of the other large Toronto houses of the period (fig. 14.16). Like them, it has a vaguely Italianate feel, created by pairs and triplets of roundheaded windows, a hipped roof, and stone window-surrounds, and combined formality with the informality of a long veranda. Sherborne Villa, which has been described as a 'Tuscan villa,' featured a relaxed L-shaped plan (figs. 14.17–21).[13] As in the Sullivan

and Gzowski houses, there was a graceful bell-cast veranda. The flat-headed windows found in the Hagarty house were replaced by round-headed windows or windows with segmental heads. On the principal elevation the windows were disposed in pairs, and, on the short arm of the L, in triplets. As in the Gzowski house, Cumberland lavished attention on designing ornament for the doorcase and other prominent parts of the building. Sherborne Villa's ornament was even more elaborate than that of Gzowski house, with vertical piping decorating the pilasters, and capitals alive with foliage.

Cumberland was capable of designing houses

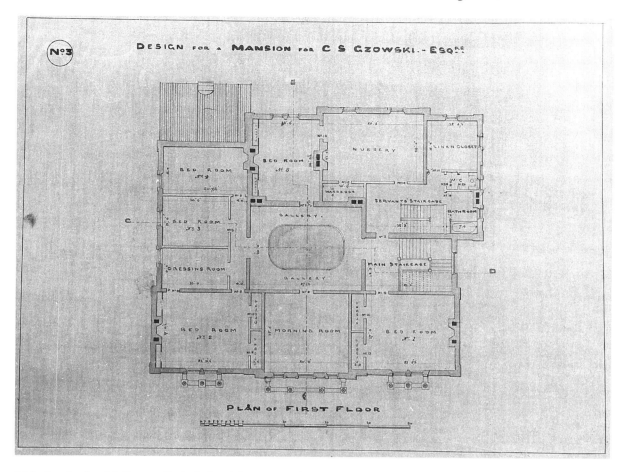

14.9 Cumberland & Storm. Casimir Stanislaus Gzowski House (The Hall), Toronto, c. 1854–5. Contract drawing of first-floor (i.e., second-floor) plan. Horwood (638)

in styles quite different from the relaxed Italianate he chose for Ridout, Gzowski, and himself. Chestnut Park, a house he designed in June 1855 for David Lewis Macpherson, appeared in Gothic Revival garb (figs. 14.22–4). Although the house has been demolished, photographs show that it was a sprawling complex consisting of a main L-shaped block linked with at least two other Gothic Revival structures.[14] The L-shaped plan gave prominence to the gable end, where a triplet of windows was decorated with prominent hood-mouldings that terminated in pronounced label-stops. It also featured decorated bargeboards and prominent finials and quoins. Inside the house, in the drawing room and dining room and on the main staircase, were large and very beautiful

floral bosses executed in plaster. The main bosses featured gothic ornament combined with natural motifs, in particular interlaced oak leaves and acorns. Bosses on the ceiling beams of the porch were embellished with stylized leaf ornament. Such motifs also abound at University College, which is generally thought to be the first building for which Cumberland adopted naturalistic ornament. That Cumberland employed such ornament in 1855, before his university-sponsored trip to England and the Continent in 1856, indicates that he was aware of the 1850s trend toward increasing naturalism. This house, therefore, is important as a demonstration of Cumberland's stylistic diversity during the mid-fifties.

Cumberland also designed several residences

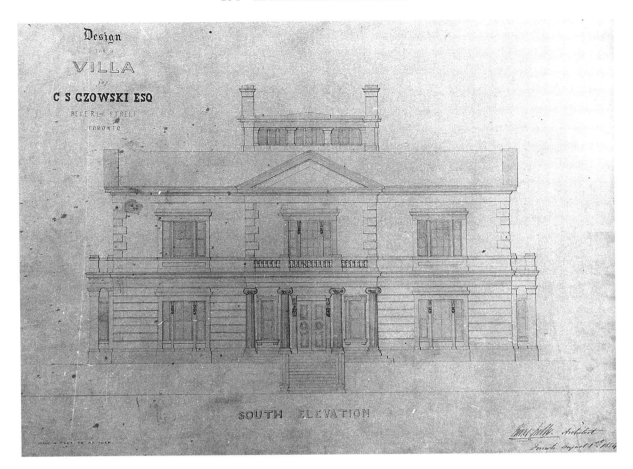

14.10 Kivas Tully. Proposed Casimir Stanislaus Gzowski House, Toronto, 1854. South elevation, 1 August 1854. Horwood (638)

for managers of the Bank of Upper Canada. This company, unlike some other Canadian banks of the period, usually preferred its offices and accommodations for resident managers to be in the same structure, not in separate buildings.[15] Accordingly, Cumberland's designs for Bank of Upper Canada buildings are, in appearance, simply large houses. Indeed, with their Italianate air and low-hung, bell-cast verandas, they were indistinguishable from the houses he designed. A discussion of them therefore belongs here, rather than in the discussion of commercial buildings. Cumberland presumably received his Bank of Upper Canada commissions on the recommendation of Thomas Gibbs Ridout, the bank's long-time Cashier. The Windsor bank was typical. Designed in July 1855, it featured the familiar combination of a two-sto-

rey, hipped-roof structure fronted by a bell-cast veranda (fig. 14.25). Attached to the house was a one-storey bank building, which closely resembled Cumberland's 1849 design for a registry office in Toronto. The residence dominated the small appended bank agency.[16] Other banks favoured palazzi in the manner of Barry's clubs. The Bank of Upper Canada building in Sarnia, built in 1857, was more in keeping with this approach (figs. 14.26–7). Bank and residence shared the same building, so that the massing of the structure was unified. The south side, where the manager entered his home, featured a veranda running along its length. On the east elevation, where clients entered the bank, the structure was more imposing, with a heavy accretion of ornament and an imposing door surrounded with exaggerated stone voussoirs. All

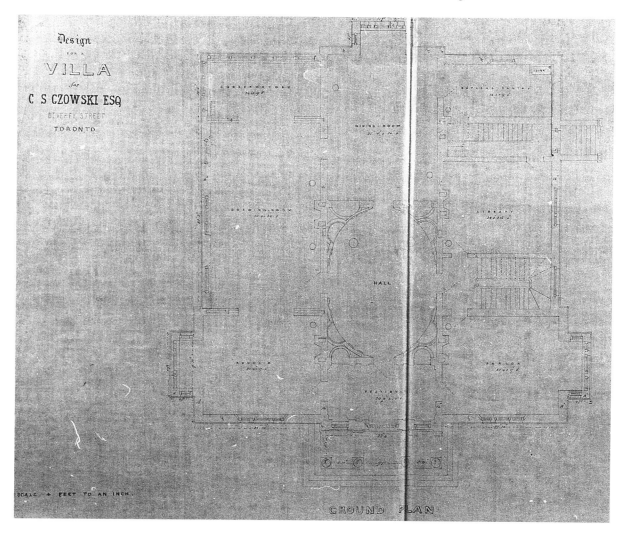

14.11 Kivas Tully. Proposed Casimir Stanislaus Gzowski House, Toronto, 1854. Ground-floor plan, 1 August 1854. Horwood (638)

the ground-storey windows on this side were topped with decorated pediments, and those on the second floor were provided with elaborate projecting porches and topped with even more highly decorated broken-apex pediments. For its Sarnia branch the Bank of Upper Canada was willing to spend more money than it usually did on a branch office, the intention being to create a building that would convey a message of financial solidity, though the bank would soon be forced to reveal that its financial position was far from secure.[17]

Certain aspects of Cumberland's house de-

signs were identical to the work of other Victorian architects. For example, his preference for rusticated bases with quoins, and for second-storey Palladian window-frames topped with segmental pediments, was shared by England's Samuel Hemming (fig. 14.28).[18] Cumberland's architecture was therefore couched in an idiom largely indistinguishable from that of others working in England at the same time.

After returning from Europe in 1856, Cumberland (and his partner Storm) designed a remarkable group of dwellings for Professor George Templeman Kingston, the director of the Royal

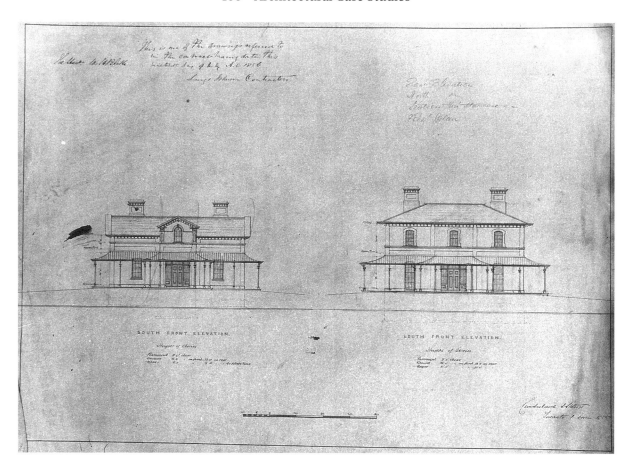

14.12 Cumberland & Storm. William Hume Blake House, Toronto, 1855–6. Contract drawing of variant designs for south front elevation, 1 June 1855. Horwood (100)8

Magnetical Observatory, and for his staff. These featured picturesque silhouettes, irregular massing, overhanging eaves, and pronounced wooden brackets. They are so similar to mid-Victorian designs in England that it seems virtually certain that Cumberland derived fresh inspiration from English houses while he was looking at public buildings with a view to designing University College.

The house that Cumberland & Storm designed for Kingston is a particularly fine example of mid-Victorian house design (figs. 14.29–31). Kingston was appointed director of the Royal Magnetical Observatory in May 1855 (Cumberland & Storm also designed the observatory). The house appears to have been designed late in the fall of 1858. At this time the firm was working on the St James's Cemetery

Chapel, and the techniques of graphic presentation employed for the ecclesiastical project clearly influenced the drawings for Kingston's house, particularly with respect to the title blocks, which were rendered in Gothic script and red and black ink. This sort of lettering was found in the Ecclesiologists' *Instrumenta Ecclesiastica*, published in 1847–56, which Cumberland owned and annotated.[19] The Kingston house drawings themselves were prepared using inks and washes of several colours, a practice first followed by the firm in its drawings for University College.

Kingston's modest house was constructed of white brick with stone window-hoods and mouldings and elaborately carved exposed wooded posts. The plan comprised two equally sized rectangular elements joined slightly off-

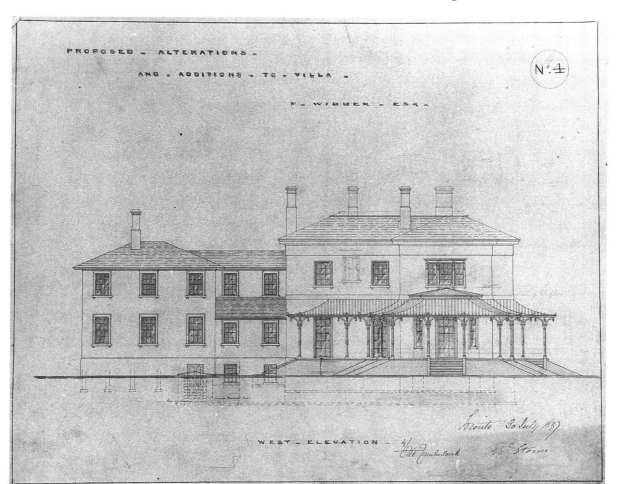

PROPOSED · ALTERATIONS ·

AND · ADDITIONS · TO · VILLA ·

F · WIDDER · ESQ ·

Nº 4

WEST · ELEVATION ·

14.13 Cumberland & Storm. Additions and alterations to Frederick Widder House (Lyndhurst), Toronto, 1857. Contract drawing of west elevation, 30 July 1857. Horwood (116)19

centre on their long sides. As in the firm's larger designs, the main staircase lay beyond the first cluster of rooms, where a small hall gave way to a back entrance. A simple cross-gable roof united these somewhat disparate elements. What was most remarkable about this house was its ornamental detail. There was clearly an interest on Cumberland's part in exploiting the decorative yet sculptural potential of his materials. Stone coping was applied to the chimney; relieving arches made of brick sat above flat-headed stone arches; heavily carved wooden brackets supported a multi-coloured slate roof. Nail-head patterning ran up the eaves and along the chimney, which was enlivened by a

corbelled brick arch that likewise featured nail-head ornament. The entrance porch consisted of a great hooded canopy replete with chamfered posts and an exaggerated corbelled profile that showed off to perfection a genuine king-post construction system. The door beneath this canopy featured wrought-iron strapwork hinges. Benches at the entrance were individually designed and equally well constructed. Even the roof was ornamented, with sawtooth cresting. This was a building ornamented in a way that Ruskin would have advocated, and it is doubtful that its like had been seen before in a Canadian domestic commission.

Many of these motifs, particularly those asso-

14.14 Cumberland & Storm. Additions and alterations to Frederick Widder House (Lyndhurst), Toronto, 1857. Photograph of porch posts, c. 1959. MTL/BR, Picture Collection, T-10,091

14.15 Cumberland & Storm. Additions and alterations to Frederick Widder House (Lyndhurst), Toronto, 1857. Photograph of drawing room, 1890s. MTL/BR, Picture Collection, T-11,346

ciated with the woodwork and ornament, had undoubtedly been taken from the firm's designs for University College. Other motifs – the strap-work hinges and dark-stained vertical-board doors – were used in St James's Cemetery Chapel. What is remarkable, however, is just how ably these features were adapted to this unassuming house.

The cottages built for the observatory staff were quite similar in character (figs. 14.32–4). Each presented a picturesque profile, with hooded dormers breaking a colour-banded slate roof. Finials, nail-head ornament, and brack-eted porches adding to the picturesqueness.[20] The architects achieved a dramatic sculptural effect simply by patterning the roof and by add-ing brick to the fascia, window-surrounds, and gables.

All these dwellings were demolished early in this century, shortly before the observatory was dismantled and moved to a different part of the university campus. Today the observatory serves as the headquarters of the university's student council and other institutional build-ings occupy the former site of the observatory residences. The observatory houses were the last dwellings that Cumberland was to design, and their significance in his career has until now been overlooked. They show that Cumberland was able to move beyond the Italianate style into a vigorous style eminently suited to the ar-chitectural polychromy of the 1850s.

COMMERCIAL BUILDINGS

In his few commercial buildings Cumberland

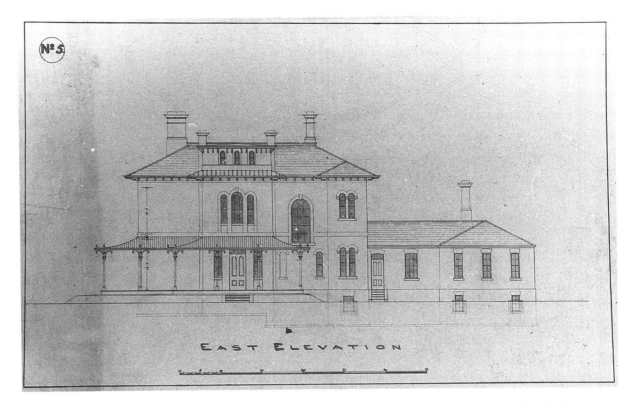

14.16 Cumberland & Storm. Frederick William Cumberland House (Pendarves), Toronto, c. 1856–60. East elevation, c. 1856. Horwood (133)19

strove, as in his houses, to create designs notable for their solidity and impressiveness. Most of these structures were utilitarian, and none are known to have survived. Those of the early 1850s were generally designed in an idiom characteristic of the Toronto architecture of the day and featured dignified ornament that conferred on the buildings an air of stately sobriety. His 1854 design for the Provincial Assurance Co. was typical (fig. 14.35).

Among his sober corporate buildings, however, one design stood out as forcefully as a melodramatic thespian among timid amateur players. This was the exceedingly elaborate 1858 design for the offices of the Edinburgh Life Assurance Company, which incorporated from basement to cornice the most expensive materials available (including marble of various colours), hand-carved details, and other attractive but unnecessary elements (figs. 14.36–9).[21] The design caught the attention of at least one

English journal. London's *Building News* remarked:

One of the most beautiful buildings which has yet been erected in Toronto is that for the Edinburgh Life Assurance Company, on Wellington-street, next to the Commercial Bank. This, when completed, will be a really handsome edifice, and one of the many admirable works which have formed the reputation of Messrs. Cumberland and Storm, whose architectural skill has been here displayed most advantageously. The style is somewhat peculiar, but nevertheless embraces some very interesting features – the Norman or Early English prevailing. The front is of pressed brick and cut white stone, interspersed with red Malone stone. The building covers an area of 90 by 32 feet, and will be four storeys high. The stonework is remarkably fine, and the columns, of turned Ohio stone, with the floral caps, are singularly effective, being as perfect in proportion as they are varied in design, giving a

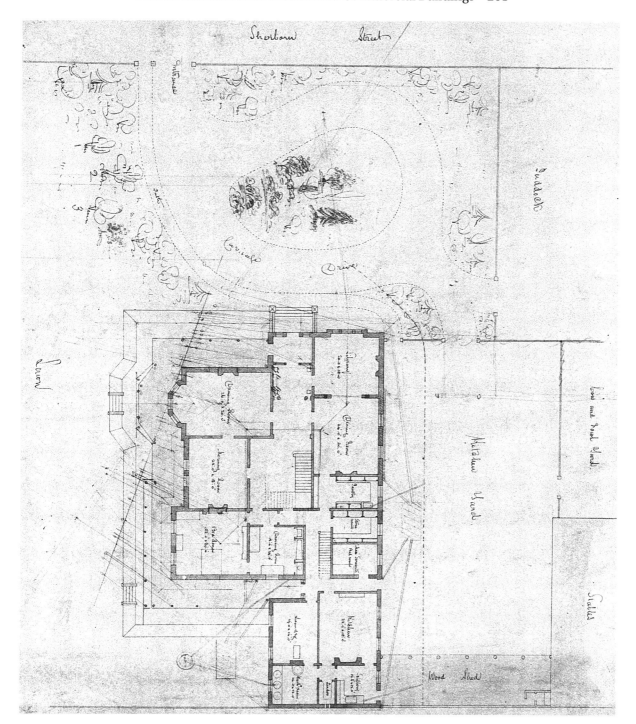

14.17 Cumberland & Storm. Thomas Gibbs Ridout House (Sherborne Villa), Toronto, 1856–8. Contract drawing of site plan, 8 November 1856. Horwood (633)

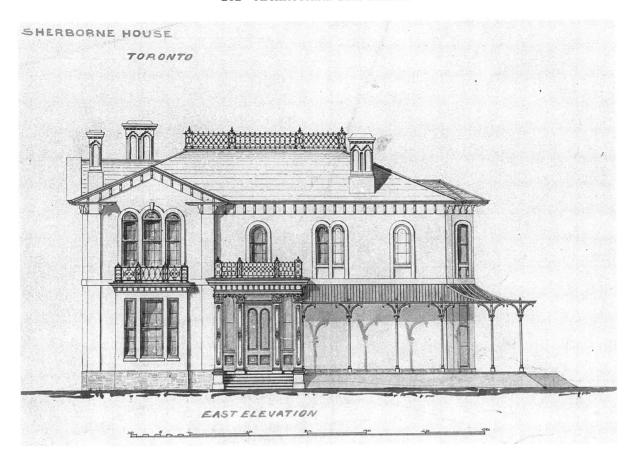

SHERBORNE HOUSE

TORONTO

EAST ELEVATION

14.18 Cumberland & Storm. Thomas Gibbs Ridout House (Sherborne Villa), Toronto, 1856–8. Contract drawing of east elevation, 8 November 1856. Horwood (633)

richness and variety to the front, which constitutes its chief beauty. The building is now only as high as the first storey, but already presents sufficient evidence that it will be an object of admiration when completed. The internal work will be in accordance with the exterior – rich and novel, and as the cost is likely to be near £5,000, we may expect something worthy of a more perfect description when the building is completed. Messrs. Worthington Bros. are the builders, and it is calculated that the work will be perfected by September.[22]

The building truly was remarkable, as an example of Cumberland and Storm's work and certainly regarding the stylistic idiom in which it was designed: pure John Ruskin. The hallmarks of this approach were the pointed arches above the windows and doors and the polychromatic banding of the stone. Such features were combined with an approach to design that was, for Cumberland, uncharacteristically unreserved. Take, for example, the proliferation of window-surrounds, particularly on the second storey, where a partial blind arcade was squeezed between three fully developed pointed-arch windows supported by free-standing columns whose bases broke forward heavily from the plane of the building's façade. Or take the magnificent but functionally useless third-storey balcony, which stood on heavy corbels, three of which extended downwards to intersect with the keystones of the arch, and thus emphasized the centre of each bay. Terminating the building was a heavy cornice consisting of a stepped-brick corbel table.

Inside, spiral columns held up a staircase. The

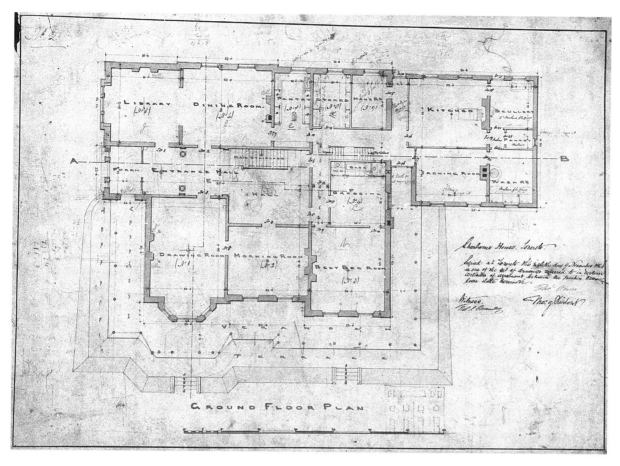

14.19 Cumberland & Storm. Thomas Gibbs Ridout House (Sherborne Villa), Toronto, 1856–8. Contract drawing of ground-floor plan, 8 November 1856. Horwood (633)

capitals featured highly original, spiky ornament that combined nail-head forms with stars and contrasting curvilinear forms. Cable mouldings surrounded every door, and even extended up around the transoms and sidelights.

An extravagant and indigestible design, it was one of only a handful of commercial buildings erected with Ruskin's tenets foremost in the architects' minds. Only two other architectural firms (both in England) are known to have designed similar commercial buildings. The firm of Deane & Woodward, which designed the Oxford Museum, that important source for University College, designed two London branch offices in a Ruskinian style for the Crown Life Assurance Agency, the first in 1857 in New Bridge Street, and the second in 1864–5 in Fleet Street.[23] In 1861, Alfred Waterhouse, later the architect of London's Natural History Museum (1878), designed the Ruskinian Royal Insurance Building in Manchester, which bore a close resemblance to Cumberland & Storm's Edinburgh Life building of three years earlier (fig. 14.40).

To assert that the Cumberland & Storm building was simply a derivative version of the two buildings by Deane & Woodward probably overstates the nature of the relationship. Rather, it seems that all three were inspired by Ruskin's rhetoric to design buildings wherein a generically Venetian vocabulary was employed liberally. It is slightly ironic that the commercial buildings mentioned above, including Waterhouse's, were commissioned by insurance companies, whose principals probably did not

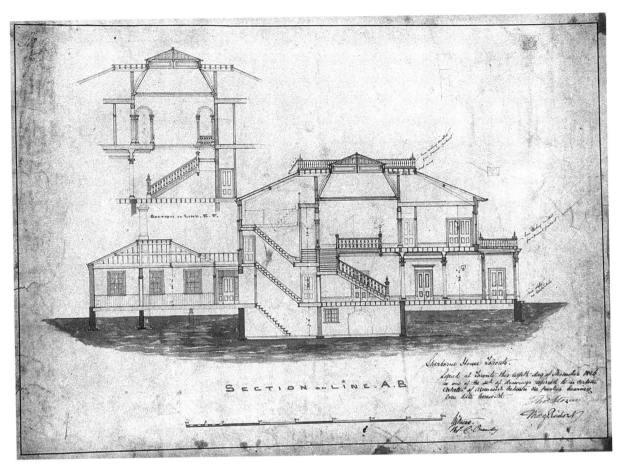

14.20 Cumberland & Storm. Thomas Gibbs Ridout House (Sherborne Villa), Toronto, 1856–8. Contract drawing of longitudinal section, 8 November 1856. Horwood (633)

subscribe to Ruskin's belief that hand-crafted buildings were most worthy of emulation. Perhaps they merely liked excess, and mistook that for taste. Whatever the truth may be, the Edinburgh Life building stands as a unique if gaudy monument to a passing taste in the development of architectural theory in the nineteenth-century English-speaking world.

14.21 Cumberland & Storm. Thomas Gibbs Ridout House (Sherborne Villa), Toronto, 1856–8. Contract drawing of details of porch, 8 November 1856. Horwood (633)

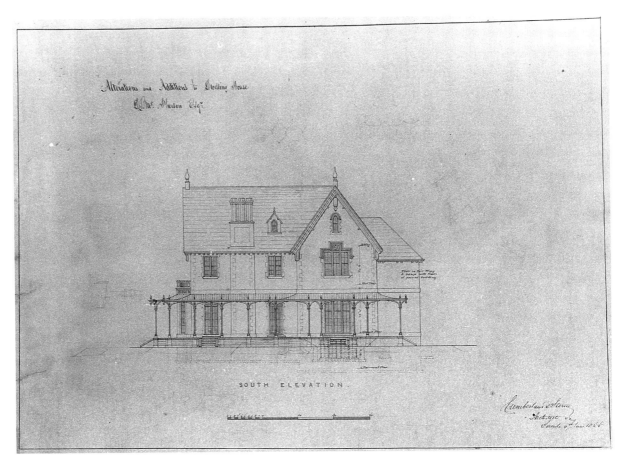

14.22 Cumberland & Storm. Additions and alterations to David Lewis Macpherson House (Chestnut Park), Yorkville, 1855. Contract drawing of south elevation, 6 June 1855. Horwood (92)2

14.23 Cumberland & Storm. Additions and alterations to David Lewis Macpherson House (Chestnut Park), Yorkville, 1855. Photograph, c. 1900(?). MTL/BR, Picture Collection, T-11,413

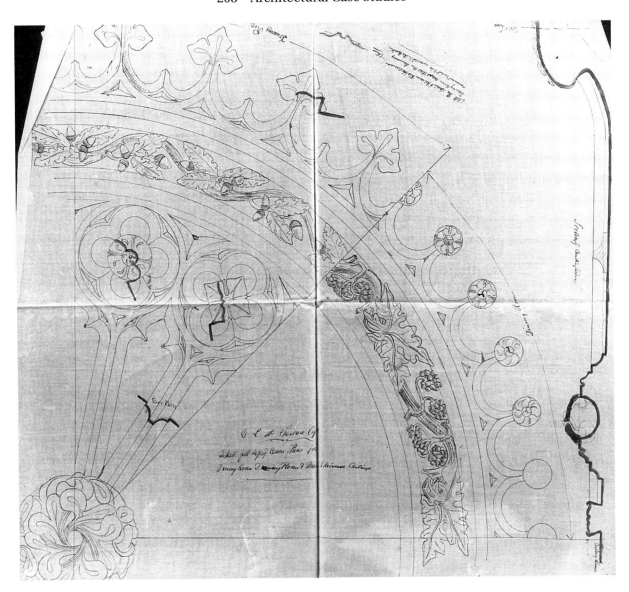

14.24 Cumberland & Storm. Additions and alterations to David Lewis Macpherson House (Chestnut Park), Yorkville, 1855. Details of plasterwork on ceiling showing naturalistic Gothic ornament, 6 June 1855. Horwood (92)

14.25 Cumberland & Storm. Bank of Upper Canada Building, Windsor, 1855. Contract drawing of front elevation, July 1855. Horwood (99)5

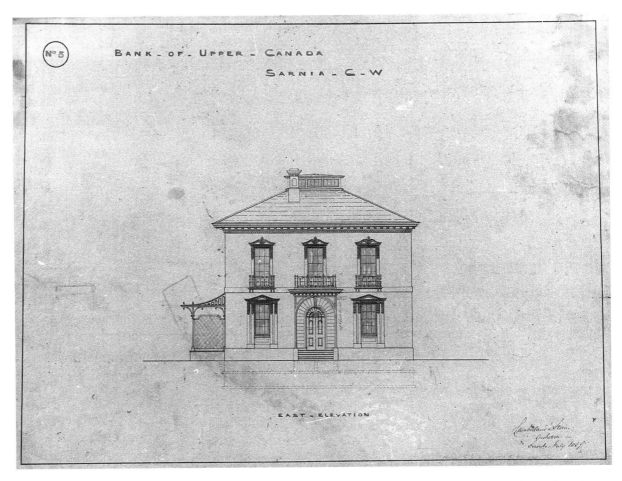

14.26 Cumberland & Storm. Bank of Upper Canada Building, Sarnia, 1857. Contract drawing of east elevation, July 1857. Horwood (112)5

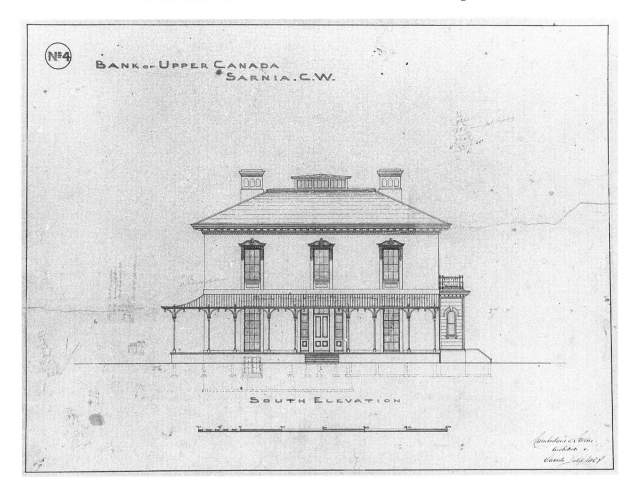

14.27 Cumberland & Storm. Bank of Upper Canada Building, Sarnia, 1857. Contract drawing of south elevation, July 1857. Horwood (112)4

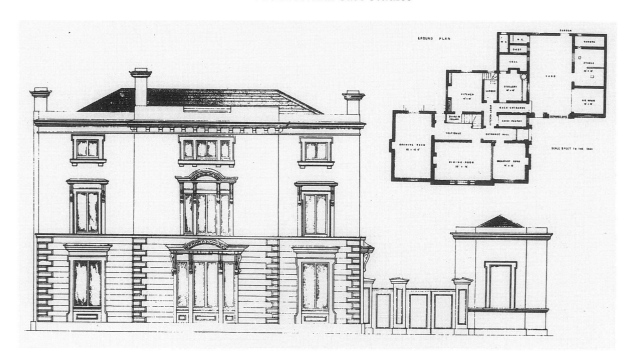

14.28 Samuel Hemming. Villa, London, England, c. 1855. Elevation and plan. Henry-Russell Hitchcock Jr, *Early Victorian Architecture in Britain*, vol. 2 (New Haven: Yale University Press 1954), plate XIII–2

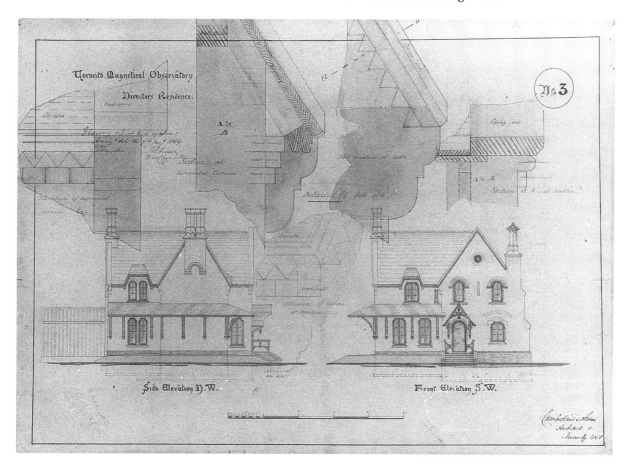

14.29 Cumberland & Storm. Director's House, Royal Magnetical Observatory, Toronto, 1858–60. Contract drawing of side and front elevations, November 1858. Horwood (120)18

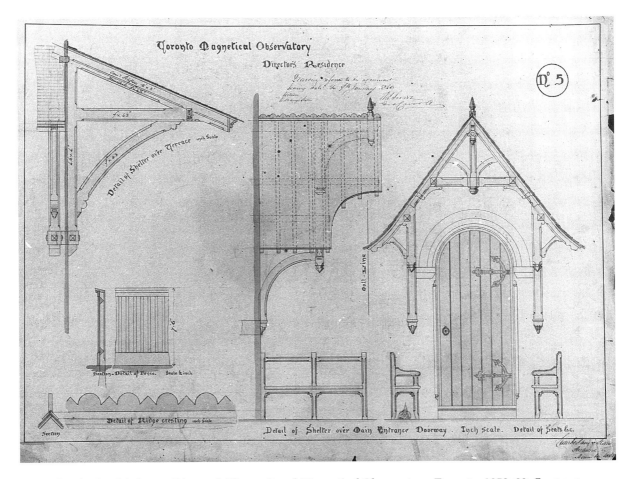

14.30 Cumberland & Storm. Director's House, Royal Magnetical Observatory, Toronto, 1858–60. Contract drawing of ornamental details, November 1858. Horwood (120)20

14.31 Cumberland & Storm. Director's House, Royal Magnetical Observatory, Toronto, 1858–60. Photograph by W.H. Ellis, c. 1888. MTL/BR, Picture Collection, T-11,375

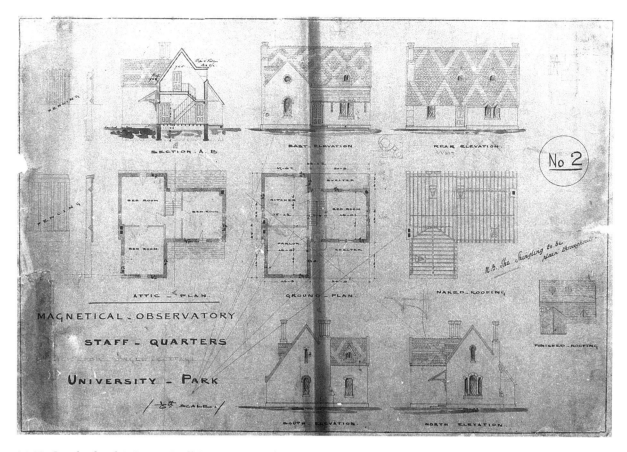

14.32 Cumberland & Storm. Staff Quarters, Royal Magnetical Observatory, Toronto, c. 1858–9. Contract drawing of section, elevations, and plans for single cottage. Horwood (120)

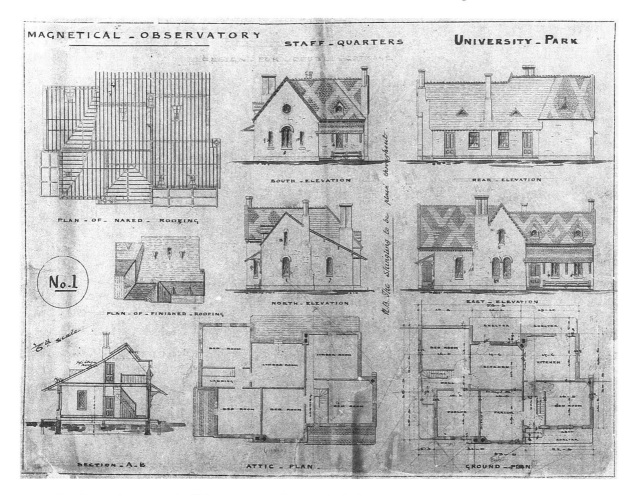

14.33 Cumberland & Storm. Staff Quarters, Royal Magnetical Observatory, Toronto, c. 1858–9. Contract drawing of section, elevations, and plans for double cottage. Horwood (120)

14.34 Cumberland & Storm. Staff Quarters, Royal Magnetical Observatory, Toronto, c. 1858–9. Photograph of south elevation of double cottage (labelled 'Gardener's Cottage'), 1890s. MTL/BR, Picture Collection, T-12,964

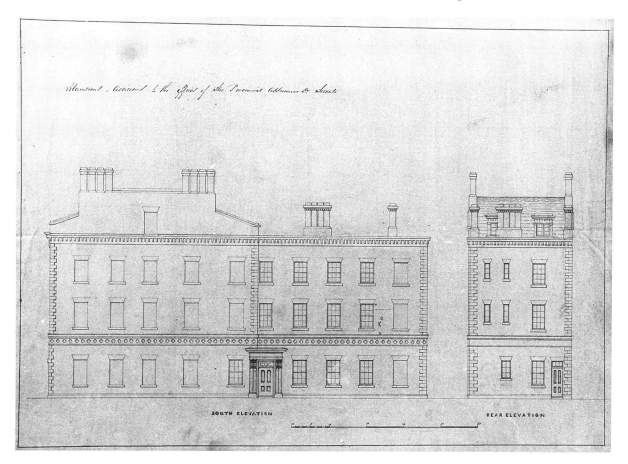

14.35 Cumberland & Storm. Additions and alterations to Provincial Assurance Co. Building, Toronto, 1854. South and rear elevations. Horwood (628)4

14.36 Cumberland & Storm. Edinburgh Life Assurance Company Building, Toronto, 1858. Front elevation. Horwood (90a), detail

14.37 Cumberland & Storm. Edinburgh Life Assurance Company Building, Toronto, 1858. Photograph by Octavius Thompson (second building from right). MTL/BR, Picture Collection, T-12,834; *Toronto in the Camera: A Series of Photographic Views of the Principal Buildings in the City of Toronto* (Toronto: O[ctavius] Thompson 1868), plate 23

14.38 Cumberland & Storm. Edinburgh Life Assurance Co. Building, Toronto, 1858. Details of staircase and landing. Horwood (90a)8

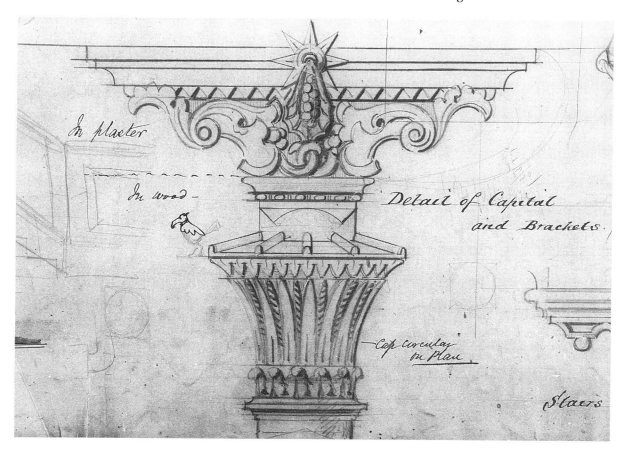

In plaster

In wood –

Detail of Capital
and Brackets.

Cap circular
in Plan

Stairs

14.39 Cumberland & Storm. Edinburgh Life Assurance Co. Building, Toronto, 1858. Detail of capital and brackets. Horwood (90a)8

14.40 Alfred Waterhouse. Royal Insurance Building, King Street, Manchester, England, 1861. Exterior view. Cecil Stewart, *The Stones of Manchester* (London: Edward Arnold 1956), 75

Proposals for Building a National Capital

In 1853 Cumberland & Storm submitted plans for a governor general's residence and a new legislative building in Toronto. This scheme was eventually rejected. Later, in 1859, two years after Ottawa was selected as the Canadian capital, the firm entered the competition to design a governor general's residence and Parliament Buildings for the new seat of government. Again, Cumberland's ambition to be the architect of grand government buildings was thwarted, but not before his design for a governor general's residence came close to realization. Other authors have claimed that Cumberland attached a great deal of importance to these projects and that losing them was in large measure responsible for his decision to abandon his architectural career. It is time to bring together all the evidence supporting this claim, to consider the political context, and to analyse the designs that Cumberland and his partner put forward.

After 1841 the Canadian government had no permanent seat but moved every four years.[1] This was an obviously inefficient system and in 1853 government officials decided to fix the seat of government at Toronto and commission designs for the necessary buildings. In 1849–50 Cumberland had been responsible for fitting up a motley collection of Toronto buildings for government use, and when the legislature approved an expenditure of £50,000 toward constructing new buildings, it seems that he was well situated to obtain the commission on the strength of his earlier governmental work (figs. 15.1–2).

The general nature of Cumberland's designs of 1853 can be reconstructed from building plans and two subdivision plans of 1854 (fig. 15.3).[2] The latter show that the new legislature would have been located at the north end of College Avenue (now University Avenue), in the centre of University Park (now Queen's Park). The building plans drawn up for the legislature reveal an essentially classical design (fig. 15.4).[3] The main rectangular block of the legislature, which would have been executed in a combination of brick and stone trim, was to have rooms for the Legislative Council and Legislative Assembly and to be set back from the main entrance, which would have featured an arcaded convex colonnade with curved wings. At the end of each wing were to be smaller square elements containing departmental offices. The public would have entered the building through a central portico, while legislators would have had their own entrances located on either side of the main block in the bend of the colonnade. Axiality and clarity were the plan's hallmarks. From the main entrance visitors would have seen a corridor leading straight to a library, to be entered via a picture gallery. The library was planned as a smaller rectangular block attached to the north side of the main block. A transverse corridor would have provided access to the symmetrically disposed legislative spaces.

In contrast to the axiality and monumentality of the proposed legislative buildings, the plan of the governor general's residence placed more emphasis on picturesqueness (fig. 15.5).[4] This building, which, like the legislature, was to be

15.1 Cumberland & Ridout. Additions and alterations to Old Parliament Buildings, Toronto, 1849–50. Photograph of renovated interior, c. 1895. AO, Picture Collection, S-1,347

constructed of white brick with stone trim, was to have two sorts of spaces, one sort devoted to private, domestic life, the other featuring a formal sequence of rooms suitable for state functions and the entertainment of guests. The plan envisioned that visitors would have entered the building after driving through landscaped grounds. Carriages would have pulled up at the terminus of Canada Drive, a cul-de-sac, and discharged their passengers underneath a *porte-cochère*. On descending from their carriages, visitors would have entered an oval vestibule featuring shallow sculpture niches. A barrel-vaulted corridor would have provided access to the spaces – dining room, audience chamber, and drawings rooms – set aside for official purposes. For guests who wanted to take a walk after meals, Cumberland provided a conservatory and a generous veranda facing south and west and overlooking University Park. Verandas were a feature of all of his domestic commissions, although this would have been by far the largest.

The governor general's morning room was to face south and east to take advantage of the morning sun. A magnificent room suitable for

15.2 Cumberland & Ridout. Additions and alterations to Old Parliament Buildings, Toronto, 1849–50. Photograph of renovated interior, c. 1895. AO, Picture Collection, S-1,355

public functions was to be fully two storeys high, and would have been lit from above by a clerestory roof, an invariable detail in Cumberland's domestic designs of this period. The servants' rooms and kitchen were to be discreetly situated on the north side of the building. Although the distance from the kitchen to the dining room would probably have resulted in cold food being brought to the table, one notes this same failing in the work of other Victorian architects.

The scheme called for landscaping the whole property. An interest in landscaping is one of the lesser-known aspects of Cumberland's work. For the Toronto Normal School project of 1851–2, as we have seen, Cumberland called on the services of landscape architect William Mundie, and he did so again for the governor general's residence.

Cumberland was far from satisfied with the proposed financial arrangements for his government designs. Letters between him and the Department of Works reveal that he was deeply indignant about the government's offer of a flat fee of £2000 for the work. Moreover, the government refused to specify exactly what sort of work would be involved, or when he was expected to start and finish his duties. Despite

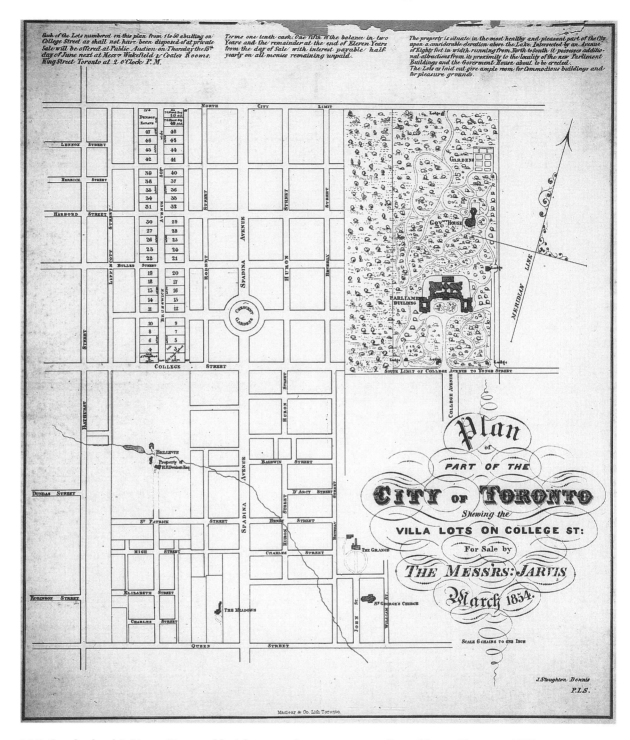

15.3 Cumberland & Storm. Proposed legislature and governor general's residence, Toronto, 1853–5.
J. Stoughton Dennis subdivision plan showing the location of Cumberland & Storm's proposed buildings
('Parliament Building' and 'Government House'), March 1854. Thomas Fisher Rare Book Library, University
of Toronto, RBSC map 3524 T625 1854 D4

15.4 Cumberland & Storm. Proposed legislature and governor general's residence, Toronto, 1853–5. Ground plan of proposed legislature. Horwood (54)1

such misgivings, Cumberland felt sufficiently confident about the outcome of the project that he boasted to Wilmot that 'On Wednesday morning I went to the Postmaster General & did business with him. He told me the Council had decided to entrust the whole Architectural business in Toronto to me without further competition, & were quite prepared to justify that course if any row was made.'[5] But this prediction was overly sanguine, and Wilmot correctly intuited that the government buildings project would not go ahead.

On 4 June 1854 Cumberland admitted that the situation had apparently reached a critical point. All his business matters were 'veiled in mysterious uncertainty and I am unable to approach any calculation of the results. I have no official reason for doubting that the works will be executed. Yet there are so many rumours to the contrary that I cannot help being anxious. The newspapers are attacking me with some violence but no justice. I told Caroline to send you a sample or two, but as you know how groundless these squibs are & how jolly thick my skin is getting you will not regard them as of any importance. The Governor & Hincks are still at Washington but will reach Quebec on Wednesday and then "To be or *not* to be"?'[6] Sensing how critical matters had become, he had gone to Quebec City to lobby for approval for his project. Someone in a high position (it is unclear who) encouraged him to remain hopeful. In early July Cumberland strove to reassure Wilmot that all would work out well: 'You seem to have a great dread about the Parliament buildings not going on. Now the truth is altho' they are suspended I shall build them next year if not in Toronto somewhere else: and in the mean time I am engaged on the University which is a very fine work and will be sufficiently profitable.'[7] It seems as if Cumberland was already rationalizing an expected defeat, and it

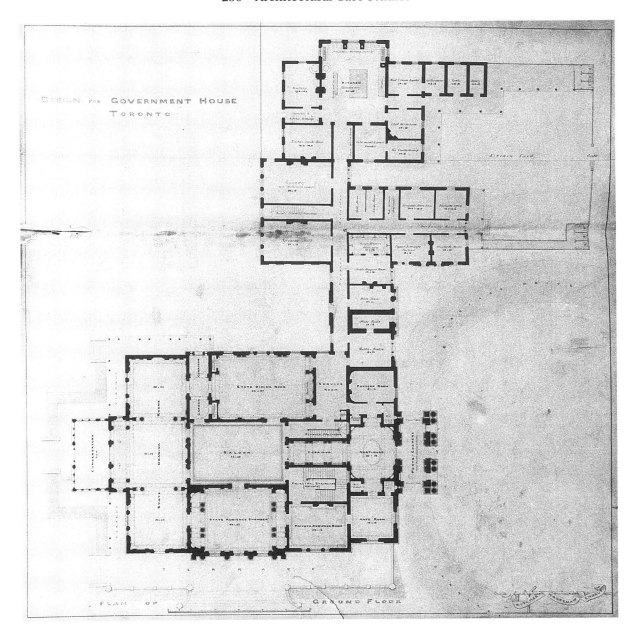

15.5 Cumberland & Storm. Proposed legislature and governor general's residence, Toronto, 1853–5. Ground-floor plan of proposed governor general's residence. Horwood (139)1

was just as well that he did, for when the Hincks-Morin government fell in September and was replaced by the MacNab-Morin government, the new ministry called a halt to the large building projects initiated by its predecessors.

By then it had become obvious that the £50,000 originally earmarked for the new

government buildings would have been inadequate. Cumberland & Storm prepared a revised estimate of £122,745. And even this was considered far too low by the government. In a letter of March 1856 to F.P. Rubidge, an assistant engineer with the Department of Public Works,[8] departmental secretary Thomas Begley remarked that Cumberland & Storm's estimate was 'not a safe guide, as, independent of strong objections raised to [the estimate] at the time with respect to security from fire not being sufficiently provided for, items of considerable importance and which would necessarily involve a large expenditure are wholly omitted – such as main sewerage, heating, lighting, fencing, road-making, barracks, lodges, &c., &c.'[9]

Early in the winter of 1856, the executive branch considered the problem anew, and asked the Department of Public Works for detailed cost estimates. An Executive Council committee report of March 1856 had stated that the government had not even made a final decision on which city would become the capital of the Province of Canada, let alone on who would design the new government buildings:

It having been declared by resolution of the House of Assembly that it was expedient to postpone the consideration of a permanent seat of Government, until a statement were furnished to the Legislature of the estimated expenditure for the erection of the necessary public buildings at the cities of Montreal, Quebec, Toronto, Kingston, and Ottawa.

The Committee respectfully recommend that the Commissioner of Public Works be instructed to produce with the least possible delay, the required estimates, and that for that purpose they do refer to the estimates already made for public buildings at Toronto or elsewhere, and establish the probable difference of cost of construction of similar buildings at Montreal, Quebec, Kingston, and Ottawa; and that they also be instructed to state in their report what are the grounds and buildings belonging to the Government, or about to be transferred to the Government, which may be made available in each of the cities above named for the accommodation of the Government and Legislature.[10]

In April Hamilton Killaly, the assistant commissioner of public works, submitted the requested financial estimates, which amounted to £203,163, excluding site work, which brought the total to £214,163.[11] And even this impressive sum was insufficient to build what was required. According to Killaly, additional costs would be incurred for fireproofing, site preparation and drainage, gas, water, heating, and ventilation, and also to establish a ten per cent contingency fund. The result was that it would in fact cost £301,579 to construct Cumberland & Storm's buildings – more than double the estimate provided by the architects, and more than six times the amount originally allocated. The sum was so large that the project was abandoned.

At about the same time, the politicians decided to settle the seat-of-government issue once and for all. Governor General Head, recognizing how difficult it would be to choose among the leading contenders, recommended a compromise choice – Ottawa, located at the confluence of the Gatineau, Ottawa, and Rideau rivers. The site itself, Nepean Hill, was particularly beautiful.[12] In May 1859 notices were sent to architects in Canada, the United States, and England announcing an open competition for the commissions to design Ottawa's Parliament Buildings and government offices and a governor general's residence.[13] The architects were asked to submit their plans under a pseudonym. At the governor general's request, Samuel Keefer and F.P. Rubidge of the Department of Public Works were put in charge of the competition. Keefer was the department's deputy commissioner and the senior of the two competition judges. In August he informed the governor general that thirty-three designs had been received from eighteen architects (one a New Yorker, the rest Canadian). Cumberland & Storm, using the pseudonym 'Odahwah,' entered designs for both the Parliament Buildings (figs. 15.6–10) and the governor general's residence. First place among those who provided designs for the Parliament Buildings was awarded to 'Semper Paratus' (the pseudonym for Fuller & Jones). Second place went to 'Stat nomen in umbra' (the pseudonym for Stent & Laver).[14] Both designs were described as being in the 'Civil Gothic Style,' a term meant to distinguish them from designs for religious buildings inspired by the Gothic Revival style. The same firms also topped the list of competitors seeking to design the government offices, although in this case Stent & Laver came first. Here again the designs were described as being in the Civil Gothic Style.

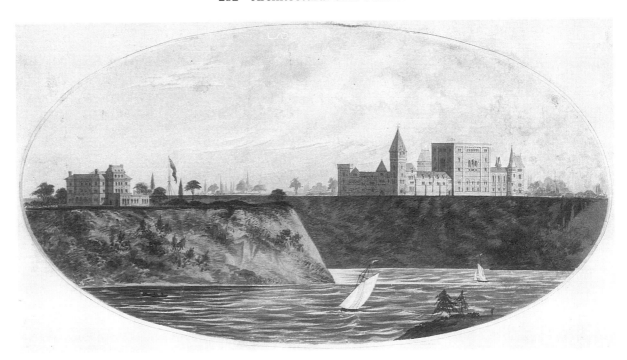

15.6 Cumberland & Storm. Proposed Parliament Buildings and governor general's residence, Ottawa, 1859–61. Perspective, 1859. William G. Storm, delineator(?). Horwood (122)2

Cumberland & Storm's Parliament Buildings entry did not fare well with Keefer and Rubidge. In a letter to Keefer of 23 August, Rubidge observed that '"Stat Nomen" shews a high claim for "beauty of design," and a medium one for interior arrangement; "Odahwah" is exactly the reverse of this.' The judges' comments on the Cumberland & Storm submission focused on two deficiencies: the lack of detailed cost estimates and the unattractiveness of the design. Their harshest comments were reserved for the design: 'To the undersigned [Rubidge], it appears that there are other grave objections to this design beside the question of cost. For, however much it might be adapted to the scenery, it possesses neither truth nor beauty – and the heavy castellated style in which it is conceived, renders it prison-like and defiant in its aspect, and therefore unsuited to become the seat from whence should emanate the laws of a free country.'[15]

The rational disposition of the elements in Cumberland & Storm's plan, and the effective management of traffic flow, were obviously indebted to Barry's Westminster Palace. The chambers for the Legislative Council and Legislative Assembly were located at opposite ends of a central corridor, as was the case for the House of Lords and House of Commons in London. The governor general's wing was appropriately located next to the Executive Council's chamber. A particularly striking feature would have been the grand staircase leading from the area in front of the governor general's entrance to the Legislative Council's chamber. But it was the library that overpowered the rest of the design. Square in plan, it did indeed make the design seem, as Rubidge said, 'prison-like,' and would have been not only fireproof but impervious to cannon as well. It compared most unfavourably with the more delicately rendered library designed by Fuller & Jones. The Cumberland & Storm library would have overpowered quite attractive elements in its vicinity, such as the octagonal hall with skylights that was to stand in front of it. Yet despite the monumentality of the library, the rest of the plan had a fragmented quality to it that resulted in architectural dishar-

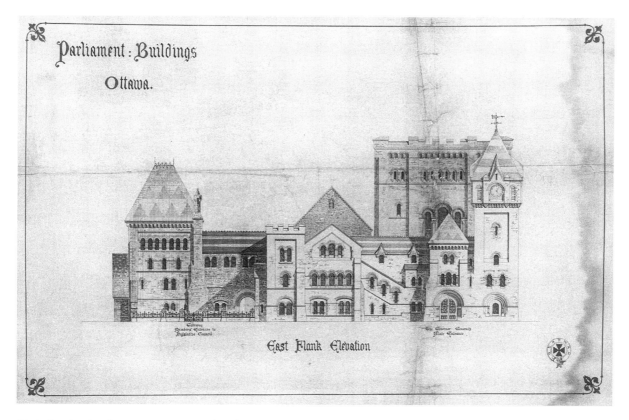

15.7 Cumberland & Storm. Proposed Parliament Buildings, Ottawa, 1859. Competition drawing of east flank elevation. Horwood (121)1

mony. This was true, for instance, of the forlorn library courtyard. A disagreeable massiveness was also a characteristic of some of the elevations, particularly the west, which, because it lacked modulation, such as was provided on the east side by the governor general's staircase, would have seemed overwhelming and out of scale. Despite having several pleasant courtyards, most of the building would probably have been dark and uninviting.

Architectural fashion also may have hindered Cumberland's chances in the competition. His Parliament Buildings would have been covered with Romanesque detailing – the judges called it Norman – reminiscent of University College. But by 1859 the Norman-Romanesque Revival had lost some of its popularity. Many architects now preferred the delicate tracery of Gothic Revival in combination with a sort of vigorous polychromy.

Cumberland's proposal for the governor general's residence was more stylistically up-to-date, and probably more successful as a design (figs. 15.11–12). The plan for the main (south) elevation shows that it would have been an imposing structure. As in his 1853 proposal, Cumberland separated the private from the official spaces, and this separation was expressed architecturally on the building's façade. The imposing block of rooms for official purposes was located on the west side of the south elevation. Also as in the 1853 proposal, there was to be a conservatory facing west. Gone, however, was the classical vocabulary of a colonnaded exterior. In its place was a curious combination of Second Empire and High Victorian Ruskinian Gothic. Second Empire elements included the mansarded pavilion roofs, a feature that Cumberland had employed in University College. But it was the boldness of the massing, the

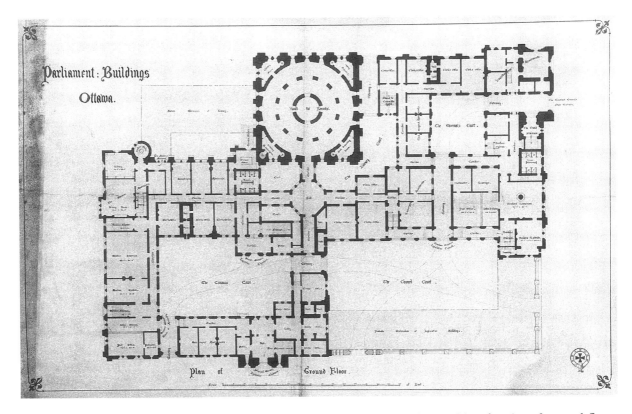

15.8 Cumberland & Storm. Proposed Parliament Buildings, Ottawa, 1859. Competition drawing of ground-floor plan. Horwood (121)2

generosity of the windows, the richness of the ornament and detailing, that marked this as a truly Second Empire design. The polychromatic pointed arches above the windows provided a Ruskinian contrast.

Inside, the building would have had the same axial staircases and naturally lit two-storey salons of the 1853 design, which would have given the building a feeling of grandeur. Another feature taken from the earlier design would have been the *porte-cochère* providing access through a vaulted staircase into a main hall. An imperial staircase on the north end provided access to the second storey. In 1856–7 Cumberland had designed for Osgoode Hall a naturally lit two-storey atrium whose vertical elements were mediated by an imperial staircase, and its grandiose elegance shows what he would have done with the governor general's residence.

The judges, however, did not like the design for the governor general's residence much bet-

ter than Cumberland & Storm's Parliament Buildings. Nor, in their eyes, was there much stylistic difference: both designs were classified as 'Norman.' In their report to the governor general, the judges stated:

For the Government House there are only two designs at all worthy of consideration, and neither of these, from obvious defects, would the undersigned recommend Your Excellency to adopt. The arrangement contemplated by 'Semper Paratus' [Fuller & Jones] of providing accommodation for the domestics in the basement is inadmissible, while it would appear that the skylight roofing of both of this and the plan submitted by 'Odahwah' is impossible in the way in which they are represented. They are, however, both handsome designs, and might be modified to suit Your Excellency's wishes: but it is not likely that either of them could be built at less than fifty per cent above the Architect's estimate of $25,000.[16]

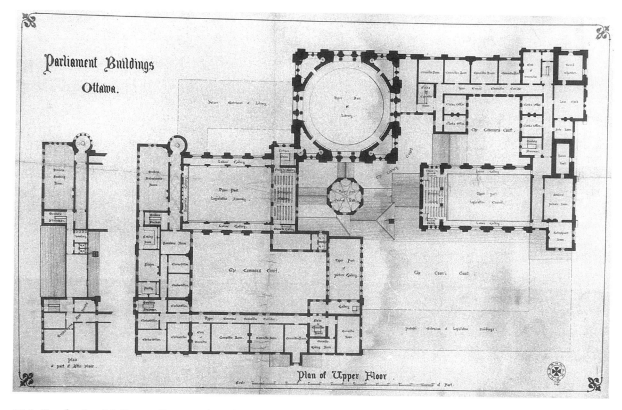

15.9 Cumberland & Storm. Proposed Parliament Buildings, Ottawa, 1859. Competition drawing of upper-floor plan. Horwood (121)3

The judges awarded first place in the competition to Fuller & Jones for their 'Grecian' entry and relegated Cumberland & Storm's design to second place.

Despite the second-place finish, Cumberland was invited to revise his firm's design (figs. 15.13–15). It is unclear why he was given this chance. Perhaps the reason was that the government did not consider Fuller & Jones capable of supervising two large projects (the Parliament Buildings and the governor general's residence) simultaneously. It is also possible that Governor General Head may have intervened on Cumberland's behalf, for, as has been shown, he had been closely involved in the planning of University College.

The new version got rid of some features but added others. The axial sequence of barrel-vaulted staircase from the south *porte-cochère* was maintained, but gone was the conservatory on the west side, which was replaced by a wrap-around veranda on the south, west, and north sides. Gone too was the clarity and simplicity of the first version. In place of the centralized elements on each elevation, particularly the north, that anchored the first proposal, the new version offered only a mean and unfocussed terrace with no grand entrance to the building.

The stylistic elements of the main elevation were not entirely unlike the first version, but it was as if the project had been pumped up from within, resulting in curvilinear towers. And as if to keep the convex towers company, roundel windows were added. In terms of style, there was no longer any trace of the Ruskin-inspired polychrome arches. Instead there was a grand and somewhat bloated idiom more closely resembling contemporary usages in central Europe, especially Vienna.

Cumberland undertook the preliminary work on these revisions in December 1859, following which he was asked to prepare contract draw-

15.10 Cumberland & Storm. Proposed Parliament Buildings, Ottawa, 1859. Competition perspective of interior of Legislative Assembly chamber. William G. Storm, delineator(?). Horwood

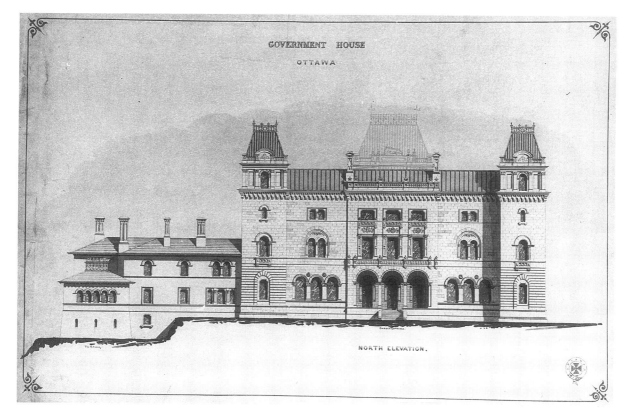

15.11 Cumberland & Storm. Proposed governor general's residence, Ottawa, 1859–61. Competition drawing of north elevation. 1859. Horwood (123)12

ings. Government records show that the plans were originally expected to be ready by 8 January 1860, but Cumberland petitioned for a ten-day extension. The secretary of the Department Public Works wrote back to 'convey ... the very great dissatisfaction felt by the Government at this delay.'[17] Some newspapers issued a sharp rebuke to Cumberland. In an article printed in mid-January, the *Quebec Morning Chronicle* remarked that a delay in the announced dates for the tenders had been blamed on the government, when really the blame was the architect's. The newspaper, apparently responding to some unnamed critics of the government, did not approve of any extensions for Cumberland, and used the occasion to criticize Cumberland's design:

The design selected for the Governor General's residence was certainly not that upon which our

choice would have fallen. It was not even second in our estimation; but, as we learn economy influenced the decision,[18] we have nothing further to say to the selection than, that the Toronto architect ought to consider himself a very lucky fellow. The designs, being long decided upon, it would be natural to suppose that the successful competitors would have been prompt with their plans and specifications for the contractors. In Mr. Cumberland's instance this has not been the case; for he communicates to the government that his plans will not be ready for inspection before the eighth of February, instead of the twenty-third of January, as originally advertised. This delay in the preparation of Mr. Cumberland's plans caused the necessity for the Commissioner's second advertisement. The crime, therefore – if there be any – of delay lies solely at Mr. Cumberland's door, and not at that of the Board of Works. If our parsimonious friends in the West think the extra expense of advertising ought to be borne by those

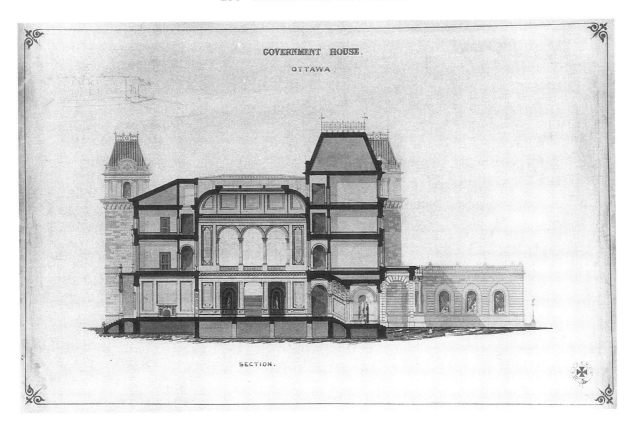

GOVERNMENT HOUSE.

OTTAWA

SECTION.

15.12 Cumberland & Storm. Proposed governor general's residence, Ottawa, 1859–61. Competition drawing of longitudinal section, 1859. Horwood (123)10

who caused it, we shall, certainly, not object to its being placed to the debit of the dilatory architect.[19]

Neither such negative press nor the government's prodding could make Cumberland move any faster. The delay took place because he was, in essence, preparing a new design. Cumberland & Storm worked feverishly throughout January to prepare the contract drawings for the governor general's residence, but in a letter of 3 February Cumberland had to admit that his firm could not complete the drawings in time, and petitioned for another extension, a request that prompted the Department of Public Works to respond that it was 'very much dissatisfied' with the firm's progress. The drawings were finally completed, and Cumberland & Storm quickly put the project out to tender. On 1 March the executive committee of the Department of Public Works authorized a payment to Cumberland & Storm of $1500 in recognition of the fact that the architects had produced plans that were more detailed than had been called for. By 8 March eighteen contractors had responded with bids for the governor general's residence, which ranged from a high of $209,000 (from Elliot L. Melville of Quebec) to a low of $93,900 (from Jones, Haycock & Co. of Ottawa). Most of the bids were in the $150,000 range. An executive committee report of 16 March recommended to the governor general that the lowest tender be accepted, and it was. An internal memorandum of 2 April, however, expressed some misgivings about the tender's accuracy. Cumberland & Storm was asked to develop a more detailed set of cost estimates, which the public works officials then subjected to intense scrutiny by comparing them to the cost of the works under way on the Parliament Buildings.

Months passed and still no construction took

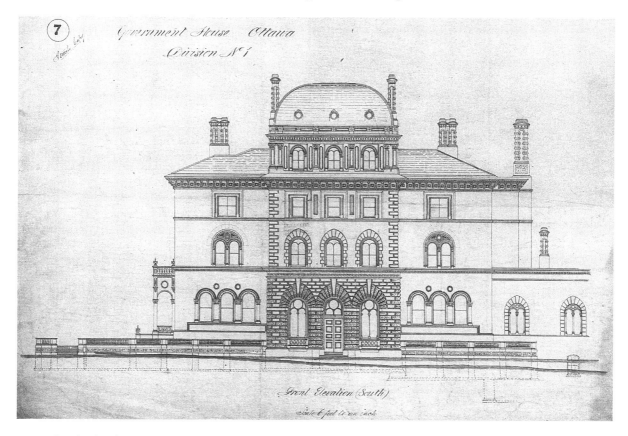

Front Elevation (South)

scale 6 feet to an inch

15.13 Cumberland & Storm. Proposed governor general's residence, Ottawa, 1859–61. Revised design. Contract drawing of front (south) elevation, c. 1860. Horwood (123)22

place. The delays were due principally to the contractors, who seem to have had second thoughts about doing the work for the very low price to which they had committed themselves, and offered a variety of excuses to justify their inaction. In January 1861 the Department of Public Works sent the contractors a letter stating that the deal would be cancelled unless a contract was signed by the 19th of that month. The contractors waited until 1 March before responding, and then merely remarked that they thought the contract had already been signed. Faced with such evasive behaviour, in May the department reviewed all of the tenders and found that it could not place confidence in any of them. The officials in charge of the residential project also had to confront the unwelcome news that all the money allotted to it had already been spent on the Parliament Buildings. More money was requested.

On 27 August Cumberland wrote to Samuel Keefer requesting payment for work done during the previous two years, and his letter revealed some of his frustration about the way events had unfolded:

Our work was done now nearly two years since & it involved besides our own labor, heavy office expenses and cash disbursements. The delays have in no way been attributable to us and it is not fair that we should be deprived of that portion of our Commission connected with the preparation of the contract drawings, specifications, &c which were far fuller & more complete than the others at Ottawa submitted & our work was adopted & acted upon by the Department upwards of 18 months since. I dislike *dunning* – but we are in *real necessity* for the money and shall *suffer most seriously* if we cannot get it immediately. It cannot be said that we have been impatient and I appeal alike to your official

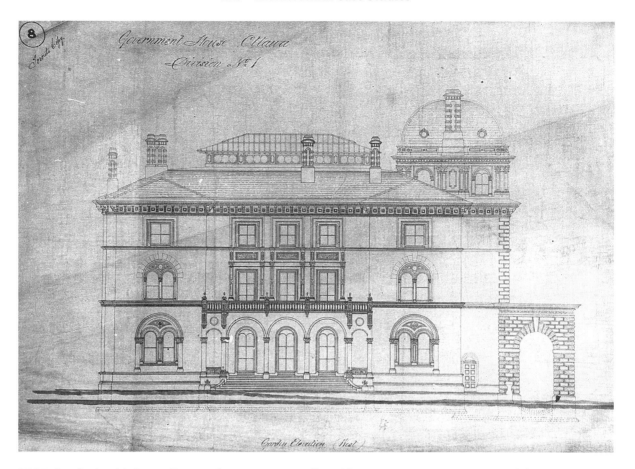

15.14 Cumberland & Storm. Proposed governor general's residence, Ottawa, 1859–61. Revised design. Contract drawing of garden (west) elevation, c. 1860. Horwood (123)23

sense of justice and to your personal consideration to promote our appeal to an early and favorable conclusion.[20]

This appeal gained the architects an additional $1000. The contractors, however, had shown themselves to be utterly unreliable, and in addition the work on the Parliament Buildings was already costing far more than expected. Any hopes that Cumberland might have had that the project would go ahead were dashed.

It was not until 1864 that the subject of the governor general's residence was again broached in official correspondence. This time, however, the government decided not to build a new residence but to lease and renovate Thomas MacKay's estate, Rideau Hall. Although Rideau Hall was not intended as a permanent

residence for the Queen's representatives, it of course still serves today as the official home of the governor general.[21]

What, finally, can be said about Cumberland's designs for a governor general's residence? Even though the visual evidence for the 1853 design is limited to plans, they suggest that it would have been a remarkable building, especially if the grounds had been landscaped as Cumberland and Mundie intended. The 1859–60 designs, more symmetrical in elevation and plan than the 1853 design and thus more monumental in character and effect, were graced with the typically Cumberlandian combination of grand staircases, formal double-height rooms for entertaining, and generous verandas. They were also more contemporary in their styling than the 1853 design. The first 1859–60 design fea-

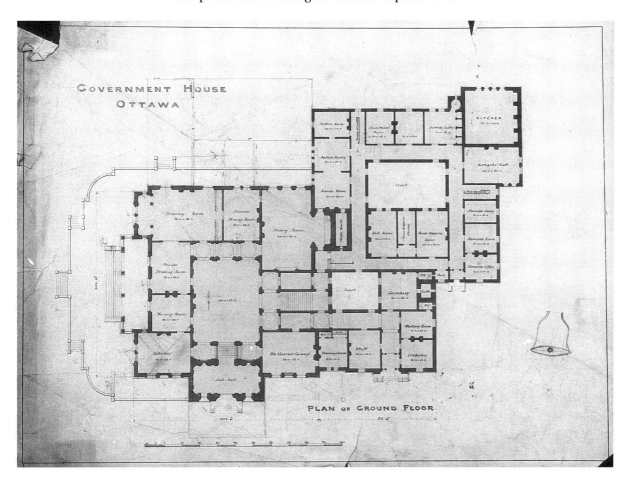

15.15 Cumberland & Storm. Proposed governor general's residence, Ottawa, 1859–61. Revised design. Ground-floor plan, c. 1860. Horwood (123)8

tured a fashionable Second Empire silhouette, and the second also adopted a Continental idiom. Either of the buildings contemplated in 1859–60 would have been a significant addition to the Ottawa skyline.

As for Cumberland's legislative designs, Canadian architecture is probably none the worse for their non-execution. The 1853 design for a legislature in Toronto would have resulted in a competent but stylistically outmoded building. Its classical character and regular plan were more akin to early Victorian buildings than to those expressing a mid-Victorian idiom. The

1859 design, the product of an imagination too much influenced by the rugged Norman-Romanesque style employed so ably at University College, was, quite simply, inferior to the winning entry. But is it possible that the massiveness of the 1859 design, interpreted then and since as an architectural blunder, was meant by Cumberland to symbolize the strength and sense of purpose of the Canadian people? If so, the attempt miscarried, for, despite the importance he attached to the commission, his architectural imagination was, in the final analysis, unequal to the task.

Cumberland's Legacy

The Canadian government's failure to execute Cumberland's designs for the governor general's residence, coming as it did on the heels of officialdom's rejection of his proposal for Ottawa's Parliament Buildings, was probably the last setback to his architectural career that he was prepared to tolerate. It was no doubt with mixed emotions that he watched from the sidelines as the cost of constructing his competitor's Parliament Buildings mushroomed to the point where the work was halted for two years while an official inquiry was held.[1] Although the firm of Cumberland & Storm continued to exist on paper until 1871, Cumberland's heart was no longer in architecture, which he abandoned for the more lucrative world of the railways. For the rest of his life he immersed himself so fully in non-architectural concerns that it seems as if he was running from thoughts of what might have been, of how an architect whose career began in a dreary clerk's office in the Chatham dockyard might have set his stamp on the capital of a new country. But the fairy tale ending was not to be.

When Cumberland died in 1881, the newspapers devoted little or no space to his architectural achievements. The *Mail*, for example, offered only one sentence on that aspect of his life, and was concerned primarily with his time as managing director of the Northern Railway.[2] This was one example of how, in the eyes of Canadians of 1881, Cumberland's earlier architectural accomplishments were of much less consequence than his colourful railway career. Several generations later, however, memory of the Northern Railway has faded almost to nothing, but much of the architecture remains, and it is a considerable legacy: University College, Osgoode Hall, St James's Cathedral, St James's Cemetery Chapel, and courthouses in Whitby and Lindsay. University College, for instance, despite the fire of 1890 and continual remodelling over the years, is still a remarkably cohesive and powerful building, the architectural and symbolic heart of the University of Toronto. Thousands of graduates have been photographed in front of the sharp-edged Norman profiles of the main door's archivolts, and thousands more have attended classes in the college or walked through its halls and quadrangle. To have designed buildings that have remained in use and touched the lives of thousands for more than a century: an architect can ask for little more.

PART THREE:
CATALOGUE RAISONNÉ OF CUMBERLAND'S WORKS

INTRODUCTION

This *catalogue raisonné* lists all known works, executed and unexecuted, by Fred Cumberland working alone and in association with his two partners. Where applicable, the partnership responsible for the work in question is listed, as are (if known) the name of the partner-in-charge and the names of the clients and contractors. Surviving specifications are also noted, as are tender calls. Because the latter were often published in several newspapers at once, for simplicity's sake only those from the Toronto *Globe* are given. This *catalogue raisonné* also cites the more important manuscript sources and magazine and newspaper articles connected with a work.[1] Some views of Cumberland's buildings from nineteenth-century atlases and maps are listed, as are certain early photographs. If a building was later altered or demolished, and the date when this occurred is known, it is provided.

The catalogue is divided into the following sections, each of which is organized chronologically and, for entries that bear the same date, in alphabetical order:

1. Drawings executed or possibly executed by Cumberland before emigrating to Canada.
2. Canadian projects (excluding Northern Railway projects and non-architectural works). Works attributed to Cumberland by others but rejected by the present author for lack of evidence are marked with an asterisk and found at the end of the section.
3. Northern Railway projects.
4. Non-architectural works (excluding those for the Northern Railway).
5. Reference drawings.

Some explanation of these categories is necessary. When Cumberland emigrated to Canada in 1847 he brought with him two student sketch-books and a package of drawings, presumably for demonstrating his architectural abilities to potential clients and employers. My research has also uncovered some drawings of his that appeared in a military engineering journal in 1847.

While the surviving material from Cumberland's English period is limited, the opposite is true of his Canadian career. Cumberland's drawings were preserved by successor firms and seem to have survived nearly intact. Every one of the several thousand known surviving drawings is listed here. Certain areas of Cumberland's practice are more fully represented than others. For many projects there are competition or presentation drawings as well as annotated working drawings. But the drawings for his railway buildings are scanty and uninformative, and no presentation or working drawings survive for those structures. The lack of presentation drawings is easily explained by the fact that there was no client to impress, only a board of directors prepared to follow Cumberland's lead. The lack of working drawings is more difficult to explain. Perhaps they were saved for a time, but then recycled or thrown away.

It is difficult to say how much of a hand

Cumberland had in designing the Northern Railway's buildings. Only the buildings authorized by him in July 1854, when he was chief engineer, are likely his work.[2] The evidence shows that he frequently delegated railway design work to his chief engineers, who included Sandford Fleming and Clarence Moberly and were capable designers in their own right. The design work for certain Northern Railway buildings in Toronto, notably the company's head office, was delegated to Storm. The few railway building drawings that are dated, are signed either by Storm, Fleming, or Moberly. It therefore seems unlikely that Cumberland designed many of the Northern's buildings. All the railway drawings that accompany Cumberland material are, however, listed here in the interests of completeness.

The case for Cumberland's authorship of some of the unsigned drawings relating to non-architectural works listed in section 4 of this *catalogue raisonné*, or at least for his oversight of the projects for which they were created, is stronger. Before he came to Canada Cumberland had already gained experience as an engineer of heavy-foundation works, but there seems to be no easy way to determine what projects of this sort he undertook in Canada. The surviving drawings are merely isolated sheets from what must have been extensive suites (most are connected with the building of foundations for the harbours at Port Hope and Pickering). As in the case of the railway drawings, items that cannot be definitely attributed to Cumberland but that are filed with Cumberland material are listed here.

The final category of this *catalogue raisonné* lists reference drawings found with Cumberland & Storm's drawings. All of these (with one exception) were purchased from other firms or made to order by outside draftsmen, not executed by Cumberland or his partners. Most are of museums and education buildings and seem to have been purchased when Cumberland was abroad in 1856 as preparation for designing University College. The significance of these drawings lies in the insights they provide into the sources the firm drew on for its University College work.

The majority of the drawings listed here are found in the J.C.B. and E.C. Horwood Collection at the Archives of Ontario. This vast collection, comprising thousands of sheets of architectural drawings and other related materials from seventy-two different firms, is perhaps the single largest collection of nineteenth- and early-twentieth-century Canadian drawings. Donated to the archives in 1978, the collection had been passed down from architect to architect since Cumberland's time. Unfortunately, many of the drawings had been carelessly stored and haphazardly organized. Conservation problems exacerbated the challenge of assigning each sheet an archival classification. It was ultimately decided to assign each sheet a new call number, grouping the sheets according to the firm that produced them, and, failing that, according to building type. In the rush to catalogue the huge collection it is scarcely surprising that a good number of drawings by Cumberland and his partners were not correctly classified, a fact that has created some problems in organizing this *catalogue raisonné*.

In the Horwood Collection each project is designated by a number in parentheses, and individual sheets by a subordinate number or number set. Thus 'Horwood (23)1–26' refers to project 23, for which there are twenty-six sheets in all. In the course of reattribution by archives staff some drawings have been assigned new numbers. Often these consist of a project designation followed by 'a' or 'b.' For instance, (78a)2 indicates the second sheet in redesignated project 78a. The existing system may be cumbersome and its numbering arbitrary, but its peculiarities can easily be mastered. Moreover, previous researchers have adhered to the system in their publications. Finally, it is possible to access the archival files that document the original bundle in which each drawing was found. For all of these reasons I have been content to rely on the Horwood numbering system.

As was mentioned above, this *catalogue raisonné* also lists the specifications prepared by Cumberland and his associates. These survive almost in their entirety, and their usefulness to the historian cannot be overemphasized. Often signed and dated by the contractor, client, and partner-in-charge, they contain detailed information about materials, dimensions, and other matters, such as, in the case of a specification for a common school in Toronto, an explanation as to why the client was offered both a Gothic and an Italianate elevation on the same plan. In many cases both the rough draft and the final version survive. Attached to many of the specifications are copies of contracts with clients and contractors.

Archives of Ontario staff have grouped the specifications by firm. Thus 'Specifications: Horwood (C & R) no. 1' denotes the first specification prepared by Cumberland & Ridout. C & S stands for Cumberland & Storm and FWC for Frederic William Cumberland working alone. The date of a specification may be assumed to be the same as that for the main project unless otherwise noted. However, when the date of a specification differs from that of the main project, or, as is often the case with larger projects, when the specification was created as part of a large project undertaken over several years, the date is given in parentheses. Undated specifications that cannot be assigned to a specific firm are designated 'misc.'

I have made a considerable effort to include references to sources of information regarding tenders. However, it must be remembered that just because a project was put out to tender, or successfully bid on by a contractor, does not mean that it went ahead or was completed. Moreover, for its evidence on tendering this *catalogue raisonné* relies heavily on the papers of one builder, William H. Pim, which are unusually extensive.[3] Pim constructed many of Cumberland's buildings, probably more than any other contractor, except, perhaps, John Worthington. His papers have proved invaluable, for his tenders supply evidence of works not mentioned elsewhere. Yet he was only one builder; if the papers of other builders had been preserved as thoroughly, we might have a more complete picture of Cumberland's activities.

Two sources have been especially helpful in determining what work Cumberland performed for the Province of Canada during the early 1850s. The first is a group of forty letters between Cumberland and the secretary of the Board of Public Works from the years 1850–3, held by the National Archives of Canada.[4] The second is an 1868 Department of Public Works survey of all government works undertaken before Confederation, which provides detailed information unavailable elsewhere concerning the names of architects and contractors, the dates during which works were undertaken, and the precise amounts of money paid out by the government.[5]

For Cumberland's public school designs, J. George Hodgins's twenty-nine-volume *Documentary History of Education in Upper Canada* is an important source.[6]

G.P. Ure's Toronto handbook of 1858 has often been cited by historians of mid-Victorian Toronto architecture.[7] However, it must be used with caution. Douglas Richardson has shown that the architectural portions may have been ghost-written by William Hay, a competitor of Cumberland's, who as a result tended to undervalue Cumberland's contribution to Toronto architecture in favour of his own.[8]

Catalogue of Works

1. DRAWINGS EXECUTED OR POSSIBLY EXECUTED BY CUMBERLAND BEFORE 1847

Drawings in Two Student Sketch-Books

Two brown sketch-books, each nine-and-a-half inches wide by fourteen-and-a-half inches long

F.W. Cumberland (signature on inside front cover of vol. 1)

DATE: Vol. 2, p. 4, bears the date 30 January 1838

LOCATION: Horwood Add. 5, box 8

Sketch-books, which date from Cumberland's time as an apprentice to William Tress, contain precise, academic drawings of various features of classical, medieval, and later buildings, from books and from actual observation. Two authorities are noted: Sir William Chambers's *Treatise on the Decorative Part of Civil Architecture* and Peter Frederick Robinson's *Rural Architecture.*

Wolverton Station Cottages, London and Birmingham Railway

Drawing by Frederic Cumberland (?)

DATE: 1839

DRAWING: Horwood (50)2, January 1839; elevation, sections, and plans

SEE ALSO: Thomas Roscoe, *The London and Birmingham Railway* ... (London: Charles Tilt [1839?]), 82–3, which describes Wolverton Station as among the most important on the line

Although the present attribution to Cumberland is uncertain, the cottages are included here on the grounds that Cumberland brought the drawing with him to Canada and that there are stylistic similarities between the cottages and his known works.

Portsmouth Dockyard (1)

Drawings by Frederic Cumberland (?)

DATE: sometime in 1843–7

DRAWINGS: Horwood (51)2–4, n.d.; details of ironwork, including roof and marine slip

As Cumberland worked at the dockyard for several years and must have produced dozens of drawings of this kind, these three sheets were presumably samples brought to Canada to demonstrate his ability to undertake projects related to industrial engineering.

Portsmouth Dockyard (2)

DATE: 1847. Two undated engineering drawings delineated by Cumberland, engraved by B.R. Davies, and published in Cumberland's article, 'Iron Roofs Erected over Building Slips, Nos. 3 and 4, in Her Majesty's Dockyard, Portsmouth,' *Papers on Subjects Connected with the Duties of the Corps of Royal Engineers* 9 (1847), 59–65, plates 16–17

DRAWING: Horwood (51)3 is the original pencil drawing (unsigned and undated) for plate 17

Cumberland also provided drawings for other engravings in the 1847 volume: see plates 22–25, 2[8]–30.

Houses of Parliament, London

Drawing by Frederic Cumberland (?)

DATE: 1847 or earlier

DRAWING: Horwood (65)1, n.d.; section of coffer-dam and river-wall

Wolverton Station, London and Birmingham Railway

Drawing by Frederic Cumberland (?)

DATE: 1847 or earlier

DRAWING: Horwood (63)1, n.d.; elevation

St Michael's Church, Tettenhall, Staffordshire

Drawing by Frederic Cumberland

DATE: 1847 or earlier; probably a student effort
DRAWING: Horwood (67a)1–4, n.d.; details, drawn to scale of one inch to one foot

Waterloo Bridge, London

Drawing by Frederic Cumberland (?)
DATE: 1847 or earlier
DRAWING: Horwood (61)1, n.d.; elevation, section, and plan

---

2. CANADIAN PROJECTS (EXCLUDING RAILWAY PROJECTS AND NON-ARCHITECTURAL WORKS)

Town Hall, St Catharines

Frederic Cumberland
DATE: 1848 (competition entry; not built)
DRAWINGS: Horwood (67)1–4, n.d.; sepias of plans and alternative elevations
SEE ALSO: AO, GS 2022, St Catharines Minute-books, 16 March 1848 (council approves building of market house and town hall); 6 April 1848 (council approves advertisement of design competition; competitors required to submit plans for market building, town hall, lockup house, civic offices, hook-and-ladder house, and engine house; winning design to receive £15); 19 June 1848 (Kivas Tully's design approved by a vote of 4 to 1, provided that its construction does not exceed £3000; clerk instructed to ask Tully and Thomas [sic] Cumberland to demonstrate that their designs can be constructed for this amount); 6 July 1848 (communications from Tully and Cumberland guaranteeing the erection of the buildings for £3000; Tully's design accepted). AO, MS 74, William Hamilton Merritt Papers, reel 8, Thomas Gibbs Ridout to Merritt, 10 June 1848 (introduces Cumberland and states that 'he takes with him the drawings that he has executed for [the competition] for the inspection of your Board of Police')

Home District Registry Office, Toronto

East side of Toronto Street, between Court and Adelaide streets
Frederic Cumberland
DATE: 1848–9; served as registry office from 1850 to 1875; demolished
DRAWINGS: Horwood (60)1–3, (68a)1, (72a)1; elevations, sections, plans, and details, dated 1849
TENDER: Toronto *Globe*, 14 February 1849, p. 3; closing date 26 February; for fireproofing of district registry office; alterations to and fireproof vaults for district courthouse; alterations to district jail
CONTRACTOR: A. Stewart
SEE ALSO: MTL/BR, Home District Minutes, 30 June 1848 (report stating that Cumberland, who was district surveyor, has prepared plans for the registry office and its fireproof vaults); 31 January 1849 (passage of by-law appointing commissioners to spend £700 towards building a registry office; detailed drawings and specifications not yet prepared); 15 June 1849 (report that registry office is complete and ready to be occupied)
EARLY VIEWS: MTL/BR, Picture Collection, T-12,085 (watercolour, c. 1913). Robertson, *Landmarks*, 1: 672–3

Robert Baldwin Sullivan House, Toronto

Yonge Street
Additions and alterations
Frederic Cumberland
DATE: 1848–9
DRAWINGS: Horwood (53)1–5; contract drawings. (53), 1–2, 4–5, are signed and dated Frederic Cumberland, 7 March 1849. 53(3) is signed and dated Frederic Cumberland, 10 February 1848.
SPECIFICATIONS: Horwood (FWC) no. 1, signed 4 April 1849
CONTRACTOR: Alex Manning (signs Horwood (53)5, 4 April 1849; also signs specifications)

Gore District Courthouse and Jail, Hamilton

Main Street East
Frederic Cumberland

DATE: 1848–53 (not built)

DRAWINGS: Horwood (52)1–4; plans and elevations. Drawing (52)3, signed and dated Robert Kerr, Gore District Surveyor, Hamilton, 15 January 1848, is a plan of the structure as it was on that date. The other drawings show Cumberland's proposed renovations and are undated.

TENDER: Toronto *Globe*, 24 January 1849, p. 3; closing date 6 February; for prison attached to courthouse and jail

SEE ALSO: AO, RG 21, Municipal Documents Collection, *Journal of the Proceedings of the Municipal Council of the United Counties of Westworth and Halton*, 1850–54, 29 October 1850 (committee struck to consider improvements to jail and courthouse, also the possibility of building a new courthouse); 2 December 1850 (council grants approval for a 'substantial story [*sic*] and a half building') (no mention of architect); 3 December 1850 (passage of by-law to pay for minor improvements); 9 November 1852 (diatribe by reeve on slow progress of jail construction); 1852 (by-law to raise £5000 for building of new jail next to courthouse; Cumberland's plans accepted; tenders to be received until 20 December 1853); 2 August 1853 (Cumberland's plans and estimates deemed unsatisfactory). New plans and estimates were later obtained from William Thomas and from Clark & Murray, both of Hamilton; the latter firm's design was eventually built. For a report on the desultory progress toward construction of a new building see Hamilton *Weekly Leader*, 26 December 1852, p. 2, col. 5. John Weaver, 'Crime, Public Order and Repression: The Gore District in Upheaval, 1832–1851,' *Ontario History* 78, no. 3 (September 1986), 175–208 (Horwood (52)4 illustrated on p. 200)

Elmsley Villa, Toronto

Northwest corner of Grosvenor and Bay streets

RENOVATIONS: new servant's hall, kitchen, bedrooms (three) with fittings, and coachhouse; alterations to stable and harnessroom; other interior work

Cumberland & Ridout

DATE: 1849–50. Built in 1840 for a son-in-law of the chief justice, Elmsley Villa was used intermittently as the governor general's residence by Lord Elgin in 1847–9 (when Elmsley House was occupied by the Normal School), and was the home of Knox College from 1855 to 1875. It was demolished in 1876.

SEE: NAC, RG 11, A1, DPW, vol. 14, item 10,996, FWC to Thomas A. Begley, secretary of the Board of Public Works, 5 March 1850 (explains extent of works authorized by previous public works commissioner); vol. 14, item 11,263, Cumberland & Ridout to Begley, 10 April 1850 ('the above works are entirely complete [except for the roadway].' *General Report of the Commissioner of Public Works for the Year Ending 30th June, 1867* (Ottawa: Hunter, Rose & Company 1868), 251–2. Robertson, *Landmarks*, 1: 297–8, 299. Hubbard, *Ample Mansions*, 113

EARLY VIEWS: MTL/BR, Picture Collection, T-11,393–96. NAC, Picture Collection, C-106,053. David B. Read, *The Lives of the Judges* ... (Toronto: Rowsell & Hutchison 1888), part 1, 48a

Old Government House (also Known as Elmsley House), Toronto

Site bounded by Wellington, John, King, and Simcoe streets

In 1849–50 the following works were undertaken: removal of fittings added for Normal School (which occupied the building from 1847 and 1849); division of rooms into offices; painting; papering; repairs to roofs; fitting of bells; construction of gates and road. Further additions and alterations were undertaken in 1855, including addition of stables and a conservatory. Work ceased in November 1855 by order of the commissioner of public works (MTL/BR, Pim Papers, Commissioner to Pim, box 2, 23 November 1855).

Cumberland & Ridout (1849–50); Cumberland & Storm (1855)

DATES: 1849–50, 1855. Elmsley House was built in 1798 and, on being acquired as a residence for the lieutenant-governor of Upper Canada in 1815, was renamed Government House. In 1850–1 it was the governor general's residence, until the provincial capital was transferred to Quebec. It was used again by the governor general when the legislature returned to Toronto in 1856. The building was destroyed by fire in 1862 and replaced by a building that was later demolished.

DRAWINGS: 1) Horwood (97)1–36, n.d.; plans, elevation, sections, and details. 2) Horwood (97a)2, n.d.; plans. 3) MTL/BR, Pim Papers, contractor's copies of drawings, signed and dated June 1855; four sheets on linen (plans, elevation, and section) and one sheet of full-size details

SPECIFICATIONS:

A) 1849–50: 1) Horwood misc. no. 27, n.d. (for first division); no. 21, n.d. (for second division); no. 10, n.d. (for third division)

B) 1855: 1) Horwood misc. no. 1, 1855; larder and dairy. 2) Horwood (C & S) no. 44, n.d.; larger, dairy, laundry, coalshed, and woodshed. 3) Horwood misc. no. 12, n.d., 'Spec. of works to be done & materials to be provided in altering the schoolhouse on King St. attached to the Old Government House – and adding thereto a Drive House, Stable & appurtenances.' 4) MTL/BR, Pim Papers, 1854–55; greenhouse

TENDERS: 1) Toronto *Globe*, 1 November 1849, p. 3; no closing date; for additions, alterations, and repairs to Government House and the Parliament Buildings, Toronto. 2) AO, MU 2321, Pim Papers, Notebooks 1854, 1 June 1854, for £2682. 3) (Possibly) Toronto *Globe*, 9 January 1855, p. 3; closing date 5 June; for additions to Government House. 4) Toronto *Leader*, 15 June 1854, p. 4; closing date 20 June; for stables, coach-houses, and other outbuildings. 5) (Possibly) Horwood (C & S) no. 29, n.d.; for stables

CONTRACTOR: William H. Pim (1855) (signs Horwood (97)3); other contractors probably also involved

SEE ALSO: NAC, RG 11, A1, DPW, vol. 14, items 10,610 and 10,996, Cumberland to Board of Public Works, 15 January, 5 March 1850; vol. 14, item 11,263, Cumberland & Ridout to Thomas A. Begley, secretary of the Board of Public Works, 10 April 1850 (Cumberland

states that 'the [Old Government House] works – except for the road – are complete'); vol. 18, items 18,072 and 18,233, Cumberland to Begley, 6(?), 16 October 1852 (requesting temporary use of apartments in Old Government House by the Canadian Institute). *General Report of the Commissioner of Public Works for the Year Ending 30th June, 1867* (Ottawa: Hunter, Rose & Company 1868), 257 (early history of building). Robertson, *Landmarks*, 1:304–6 (early history). Hubbard, *Ample Mansions*, 111 (Elmsley House described as 'a Regency Italianate villa with spreading eaves and tall corniced windows')

EARLY VIEWS: MTL/BR, Picture Collection, T-11,867–71

Old Parliament Buildings, Toronto

Simcoe Place (lot bounded by Front, John, Wellington, and Simcoe streets)
Additions and alterations
Cumberland & Ridout

DATE: 1849–50. The buildings, constructed in 1829–32, were used for legislative purposes until 1893 and were demolished in 1903

DRAWINGS: 1) Horwood (54)14–19 (sheet 17 is signed and dated Frederic Cumberland, 16 January 1850). 2) NAC, National Map Collection, 13/450, Toronto, 1865: interior plans of the Parliament Buildings drafted by James Grand and others; one sheet signed and dated 25 April 1865

SPECIFICATIONS: Horwood misc. no. 12, n.d., but watermarked 1848 (rough draft; contains rough draft of letter to commissioner of public works justifying works previously undertaken)

TENDER: Toronto *Globe*, 1 November 1849, p. 3; no closing date; for additions, alterations, and repairs to Government House and the Parliament Buildings, Toronto

SEE ALSO: NAC, RG 11, A1, DPW, vol. 14, item 11,263, Cumberland & Ridout to Thomas A. Begley, secretary of the Board of Public Works, 10 April 1850 (description of works undertaken; 'the above works [the Parliament Buildings] are yet incomplete,' but Cumberland expects they will be completed in a fortnight); vol. 14, item 11,309, FWC to

W.H. Merritt, 15 April 1850 (Cumberland objects to tender called for carpenters' work at the Parliament Buildings, which ought to be under his superintendence); vol. 15, item 11,644, FWC to Begley, 4 June 1850 (estimate of balances still payable to various parties for work on the Parliament Buildings; total £5853, including £330 to Cumberland & Ridout). *General Report of the Commissioner of Public Works for the Year ending 30th June, 1867* (Ottawa: Hunter, Rose & Company 1868), 251–2 (description of works undertaken by Cumberland). Sylvester, *Sketches of Toronto*, 21–3 (description of buildings). Robertson, *Landmarks*, 3: 317–22 (history of buildings and reproductions of plans adopted for 1857 government offices)

EARLY VIEWS: MTL/BR, Picture Collection (various). AO, Picture Collection (various). Robertson, *Landmarks*, 5:566ff. (eighteen interior and exterior pen-and-ink views) NAC, Picture Collection, C-11,369 and 11,370 (an interior and an exterior view from 1892)

Cathedral Church of St James, Toronto

King and Church streets
Cumberland; Cumberland & Ridout; Cumberland & Storm
DATE: 1849–53. After the third church on the site was destroyed in the Toronto fire of 7 April 1849, a design competition for a new church was held, the commission going to Cumberland. The cornerstone was laid on 20 November 1850, and by 1853 the new building was finished, except for the tower, spire, and pinnacles, which were constructed in 1867–74 based on designs prepared by Storm and Henry Langley. According to Elliot Grasett Strathy, *A Guide to the Cathedral Church of St. James* (Toronto: n.p. 1932), 13, 'originally galleries extended along the two sides and the south end, but in 1889 the side galleries were removed, the south gallery made much smaller and the choir, originally with the organ in the south gallery, was removed to the handsome stalls in the chancel. Since that time other extensive improvements have been made. In 1906 the organ was completely remodelled and an echo organ

installed in the organ loft. In 1914 the wooden floor was removed and replaced by a concrete floor with red tile in the nave and encaustic tile and marble in the chancel.'

CONTRACTORS: 1) Metcalfe, Wilson, and Forbes (main works). 2) Jacques and Hay (woodwork)

DRAWINGS:

A) St James's Cathedral Archives: 1) ten sheets dated 18 November 1850; plans, elevations, and sections. 2) seating plan, c. 1852. 3) Storm, 'Proposed addition to tower,' October 1863. 4) Henry Langley, 'Details of Transepts,' c. 1870. 5) plan of woodwork, n.d. 6) numerous twentieth-century drawings for additions and alterations.

B) Horwood: 1) 55(19); outline of Cumberland's proposed design and that of George H. Smith of Montreal, c. November 1849. 2) (55)1–8; plans of the church and its windows prepared by Cumberland, n.d. 3) (78)1–32; full-size masonry details by Cumberland & Ridout, 1852. 4) (81a); elevation and details by Cumberland & Storm, 1852. 5) (75a)1; sepia elevation, undated and unsigned. 6) (78) 55 (part 2), full-size masonry details, signed and dated by Cumberland, 26 August 1850. Note: drawings (75)1–3 are erroneously filed with the Cumberland material. (75)1, 'Proposed Addition to Tower,' is a linen, probably by Henry Langley. (75)2 and 3 are two unidentified pencil drawings of the tower

TENDERS: 1) Toronto *British Colonist*, 21 June 1850, p. 3 (Cumberland & Ridout); closing date 15 February. 2) Toronto *British Colonist*, 28 May 1852, p. 3 (Cumberland); closing date 10 June; for completion of carpentry and joiners' work

SEE ALSO:

A) St James's Cathedral Archives: three sources from the church archives provide a virtually complete picture of the rebuilding of the church. First among these is a folder containing letters from the entrants in the design competition, titled 'Rebuilding of St. James Cathedral, 1849–1854.' Then there are the building committee minutebooks of 1849–54, which provide detailed information about the progress of construction. Finally, one can turn to the vestry minutebook for 1842–1907, which bears the title 'A Church Journal' and includes information not found in the building committee minutebooks. Particularly important is its record of a crucial meeting of 21 December 1849, during which Cumberland's design was nearly abandoned in favour of George H. Smith's, which had originally been rejected by the vestry. The vestry minutebook also contains, pasted in at the front and back, printed reports by the building committee and other pamphlets, as follows: a) *Report of the Committee Appointed by the Vestry of St. James's Church to Report on the Rebuilding of the Church*, 5 May 1849; b) *Second Report of the Building Committee Appointed by the Vestry of St. James's Church to Report on the Rebuilding of the Church*, 4 December 1849 (copies also at the AO and MTL/MR); c) a pamphlet titled *Resolutions and Amendments, to Be Submitted to the Vestry of St. James's Church, at the Meeting to Be Held on Friday, December 14, 1849*; d) a broadsheet, signed 'F.R.S.' and dated 3 December 1849, reprinting a letter to the Toronto *Globe* criticizing the vestry's second report; e) a pamphlet by 'Bramhill' titled *To the Vestry-men of the Parish of St. James* and dated 17 December 1849, in defence of Cumberland and against the grander design submitted by Smith; f) a handwritten document comparing Cumberland's and Smith's designs to each other and to the dimensions of eighteen English cathedrals; g) [John Strachan], *Thoughts on the Rebuilding of the Cathedral Church of St. James* (Toronto: Diocesan Press 1850) (copies also at the AO and MTL/BR). The church archives also have several files of clippings from early newspapers; a notebook kept by Henry James Grasett (1808–82), rector of the church from 1839 until his death, which contains references to the 1849 fire, the design competition, and Cumberland, but adds nothing to what can be found in other sources; a biographical file on Cumberland, again not very helpful; and a file devoted to the building of Langley's tower and spire in 1872–4.

B) MTL/BR: Henry James Grasett scrapbook, containing sixty-five items on the rebuilding, including copies of most of the printed items mentioned above, as well as two slightly different versions of Kivas Tully's broadsheet titled *Memorandum for the Congregation of St. James' Church*, 12 December 1849

C) Other sources: *The Church*, 13 September 1849, 26, 'Rebuilding of St. James's Church, Toronto' (assesses the competition entries and records that the building committee found it difficult to choose a plan, though 'On the whole we should not wonder if the choice of the committee were to rest with Mr. Cumberland'). Toronto *Globe*, 9 August 1850, p. 23, col. 1 (brief notice of the blasting of the tower's remains). *The Church*, 21 November 1850, 132 (detailed description of corner-stone-laying ceremony; also reported in the Toronto *British Colonist*, 22 November 1850). *Anglo-American Magazine* 1 (July–December 1852), 362 (description of the new church reprinted from the *Montreal Herald*: 'This church, built of white brick, for which Toronto is famous, in the restored style of Church architecture, is decidedly the most beautiful and appropriate structure to be seen in Canada'). Sylvester, *Sketches of Toronto*, 11–13 (description of church). Toronto *Telegram*, 11 December 1886, p. 6 (description of church). Robertson, *Landmarks*, 1: 509–10; 3: 367–71; 4: 586–90. Strathy, *Guide*, especially 13. Morriss, 'The Church Architecture of Frederic William Cumberland' (thesis). Morriss, 'The Church Architecture of Frederic William Cumberland' (article). Morriss, 'The Nine-Year Odyssey of a High-Victorian Goth.' MacRae and Adamson, *Hallowed Walls*, 155–8. Dendy and Kilbourn, *Toronto Observed*, 56–9

EARLY VIEWS: Toronto *Globe*, 13 December 1856, p. 2. *Toronto in the Camera*, plate 6. St James's Cathedral Archives, photographic negatives of interior views, c. 1872. St James's Cathedral Archives, copies of photographs from the Notman Photographic Archives, McCord Museum, Montreal: No. 34, 455-Misc. I (looking west from St Lawrence Hall, 1868 [and thus before spire erected]); No. 34, 483-Misc. I (from King Street, n.d., before spire erected); MP 128/77 (from King Street, n.d., with spire); MP 129/77 (looking west from King Street, n.d., with spire). Toronto *Telegram*, 11 December 1886, p. 6. Robertson, *Landmarks*, 3: 368 (perspective drawings)

Haldimand County Courthouse and Jail, Cayuga

Munsee Street
Cumberland & Ridout
DATE: 1850. The courthouse was destroyed by fire in December 1922 and replaced in 1923 by a redbrick structure designed by Frank Barber & Associates; the jail is still standing.
DRAWINGS: 1) Horwood (74)1–10; plans, elevations, and sections, signed and dated 1 May 1850. 2) Horwood (74a)1; perspective sepia, n.d.
SPECIFICATIONS: Horwood misc. no. 26, n.d., jail
TENDER: Toronto *Globe*, 9 April 1850, p. 171, col. 3; closing date 10 May
CONTRACTORS: 1) John Worthington (main works). 2) William H. Pim (fence and grounds)
SEE ALSO: Haldimand County Council rough minutes at the County Museum, Cayuga (these appear to be the only surviving minutes). Simcoe County Local Architectural Conservation Advisory Committee, 'By-laws of the Provisional Council of the County of Haldimand,' no. 5, 1850, 'An Act to Determine on a Plan According to Which the County Buildings and Gaol Are to Be Erected; and for the Appointment and Payment of Architects to Superintend the Erection of the Same.' Haldimand County Museum, doc. X978.1122.16, Extract of Minutes of Council Meeting, 27 January 1851 ('On Aug. 9th the Council settled with Messrs. Worthington and Pim in full for their work in the construction of the County Buildings. Claims by them for extras were not considered. The sum of £110 was paid to Messrs. Cumberland & Ridout, for their services as architects, and the Public Buildings were insured for £3000'). Haldimand County Museum, doc. X978.1122.11, Treasurer's Book, p. 26, 13 August 1852 (Worthington was paid £630.18.0 for his services, Pim £79, and Cumberland & Ridout £110). Toronto *Globe*, 23 February

1850, p. 95, col. 5 (design competition announcement; closing date 22 March). W.H. Smith, *Canada: Past, Present and Future* (Belleville, Ont.: Mika Publishing 1973 [1851]), 1:165. *Illustrated Historical Atlas of the Counties of Haldimand and Norfolk* (Belleville, Ont.: Mika Publishing 1973 [1877]), 4–15, 38–9 (history and map of Cayuga). Brantford *Grand River Sachem*, 3 January 1877 (report on jailer's house, designed by Brantford firm of Mellish & Sons and constructed in 1876–7; jailer's house depicted in *Illustrated Historical Atlas*). 'Haldimand County Court House: Architectural/Historical Report,' Ministry of Government Services, Heritage Properties Program, n.d. MacRae and Adamson, *Cornerstones of Order*, 156–9
EARLY VIEWS: *Tremaine's Map* (1863), vignette. *Illustrated Historical Atlas of the Counties of Haldimand and Norfolk*, 27; Haldimand County Museum, doc. X976. 451.1 (County buildings after 1922 fire)

St Lawrence Hall, Toronto

Corner of Jarvis and King streets
Temporary fittings. In connection with celebrations held to mark the opening of a new section of the Welland Canal, the governor general made a trip of Buffalo. Dignitaries from the American city returned the visit some weeks later and St Lawrence Hall was temporarily fitted up in their honour.
Frederic Cumberland and Jacques & Hay
DATE: 1850

The Toronto *Patriot*, 6 August 1850, p. 3, cols. 1–2, reported that 'The St. Lawrence Hall will be fitted up temporarily for the occasion [of the Buffalo visit], and will be connected with the City Hall by a covered arcade, extending throughout the new market and quite across Front Street, thus forming a promenade of over five hundred feet in length, properly lighted and protected from the weather.' The Toronto *British Colonist*, 9 August 1850, p. 2, col. 7, commented after the visit that

Much praise is due to Mr. Cumberland, and Messrs.

Jacques & Hay, for the very tasteful way in which the room was decorated; and considering the very short time these gentlemen had allowed them for their several tasks, the general arrangement was judicious and proper in the extreme. We mention that particularly, because it was certainly a matter of some delicacy to arrange matters so as to give the two countries their due place and prominence; but, we are glad to say, that no herald or master of the ceremonies, however skillful, could have made a more appropriate and courteous display of the several flags, armorial bearings, and other insignia of England and America, than they did on this occasion.

Everything seemed to have been studied with the nicest taste, so as to do every honour and pay every consistent compliment due to our distinguished guests. The British and American flags stood lovingly side by side, and long may they remain so. The English lion and the Columbian eagle sat peacefully in each others [sic] embrace as if conscious of their united power, and as if declaring to the whole world that while united 'touch us who dare.'

SEE ALSO: Toronto *Globe*, 16 August 1850, p. 26, cols. 6–7; p. 27, cols. 1–3. Thompson, *Reminiscences*, 344–8

Church of the Ascension, Hamilton

64 Forest Avenue at John Street
Cumberland & Ridout
DATE: 1850–1. This church's cornerstone was laid on 9 May 1850. The church opened its doors in June 1851, although the tower was completed only in 1878. The organ and choir were moved from the west gallery to a new gallery built over the north transept, where they remained until 1884. After 1878 a gallery was built over the south transept, and in 1882 a new organ was built in the northeast corner of the church; the north gallery, where the old one had stood, was subsequently fitted up with pews. On 6 January 1887 a fire destroyed the interior of the church. Reconstruction work began the following June and was completed in March 1888 at a cost of $25,000. The church was rebuilt on the same plan but with a larger chancel; the architects were Darling & Curry.

DRAWINGS: Horwood (73)1–10; sepia elevations, n.d., and associated contract drawings dated 19 January 1850
TENDER: Toronto *British Colonist*, 1 February 1850, p. 3; closing date 15 February
CONTRACTORS: 1) Thomas Jones. 2) Sharp, Houston and Sharp
SEE ALSO: Vestry minutes for 1878 in the church archives. *The Church*, 16 May 1850, 166 (description of cornerstone-laying ceremony: 'the very trees in the neighborhood were crowded to their topmost branches by eager expectants of the unusual ceremony'). *Hamilton Spectator*, 11 May 1850 (description of cornerstone-laying ceremony). *Hamilton City Directory*, 1868–9, 29 (description of church; architects incorrectly identified as Cumberland & Storm). *Canadian Church Magazine and Mission News* (January 1889), 10–11 (history of the church; incorrectly states that the cornerstone was laid in 1849). 'A Historical Sketch of Our Parish,' *The Parish Guide* (Church of the Ascension) 1, no. 1 (January 1849), 5–7 and subsequent issues through October. Rev. Canon Howitt, 'A Historical Sketch of Our Parish,' *The Ascension Messenger* 4, no. 4 (July 1930), [1–3]; 5, no. 5 (September 1930), [1–3] (this and the preceding source are in the church archives). Mary Harrington Farmer, *One Hundred Years: The Church of the Ascension, Hamilton. A Short History, 1850–1950* (Hamilton: Kidner Printing 1950). Farmer, *The Church of the Ascension, Hamilton, Ontario. The Next Twenty-five Years 1950–1975* [Hamilton]: n.p., n.d.). Morriss, 'The Church Architecture of Frederic William Cumberland' (thesis). Morriss, 'The Church Architecture of Frederic William Cumberland' (article). Morriss, 'The Nine-Year Odyssey of a High-Victorian Goth'
EARLY VIEWS: Hamilton Public Library, Special Collections (two poor undated nineteenth-century views). *Hamilton City Directory*, 1868–9, 29 (engraving of church)

St. James's Parochial School, Toronto

East side of Church Street, north of King Street
Cumberland & Ridout
DATE: 1850–1. The school opened on 30 Decem-

ber 1851. A wing was added in 1870, and there were further additions the following year. The school was demolished in 1909 to make way for present parish house, designed by Darling & Pearson.

DRAWINGS: 1) Horwood (71)1–5, signed and dated March 1851; plans, elevations, sections, and details. 2) Horwood (749)1 and (751)2; undated and unsigned perspective drawings, watermarked 1858

SPECIFICATIONS: Horwood (C & R) nos. 10 and 11. No. 10 is a good copy of no. 11. The good copy is dated 31 August 1851 but refers to a contract signed 2 April 1850.

SEE ALSO: *The Church*, 5 June 1851, 353 (reports that a design has been adopted for the parochial school and that work has begun). *The Church*, 3 June 1852, 337 ('The building is of a most substantial character and is much admired for its architectural appearance which reflects great credit upon the accomplished author of the design, F. W. Cumberland Esq.'). Ure, *Hand-Book*, 358 (the building is 'An ornament to the Street, but is somewhat disfigured by a very disproportionate bell-tower, of certainly antediluvian style'). Elliot Grasett Strathy, *A Guide to the Cathedral Church of St. James* (Toronto: n.p. 1932), 40–1

EARLY VIEW: MTL/BR, Picture Collection, T-10,744–5, T-30,685, Photographs by Armstrong Beere & Hime, c. 1859

Lunatic Asylum, Toronto

999 Queen Street West
Gatekeeper's lodge, outbuildings (including a 'Cowhouse & Other Farm Building'), fences, gates, and walls
Cumberland & Ridout; Cumberland alone
DATE: 1850–2. Designed by John Howard and constructed in 1846–9, the building was demolished in 1976; only portions of a fence survive.

DRAWINGS: Horwood (72)1–6, signed and dated Cumberland & Ridout, 15 August 1850; additions to outbuildings, grounds, and fences

SPECIFICATIONS: 1) Horwood (C & R) no. 12, n.d.,

iron railing. 2) Horwood (FWC) no. 2, boundary wall, 23 July 1852

TENDER: Toronto *Globe*, 28 June 1851, p. 1; closing date 5 July; for front wall, iron railing, lodge, and entrance gates

SEE ALSO: NAC, MG 29, B1, Sir Sandford Fleming Papers, vol. 12, folder 79, Fleming to FWC, 1 January 1852, enclosing a plan of the Lunatic Asylum property, as requested by Cumberland

Normal School, Toronto

St James's Square, Gould Street, between Church and Victoria streets
Cumberland & Ridout; Cumberland & Storm for some later works
DATE 1850–2. The Normal School, an institution for the training of public school teachers, began operations on 1 November 1847 in temporary quarters in Old Government House. Classes were moved in 1849 to the temperance hall on Temperance Street, where they were held until 24 November 1852, when the new premises on Gould Street opened. The cornerstone was laid on 2 July 1851, but construction was slowed by difficulties in procuring stone and by the business failure of the contractors. The south block of the building was where teachers received classroom instruction. The north block housed a Model School, where student teachers could practise their skills. Play-sheds were added in the late 1850s. In 1869 a government architect reported that the building was in poor repair ($227,000 was expended on repairs from 1867 to 1904). In 1881 changes were made to the east front of the south block to accommodate the Ontario School of Art and Design. In 1888 a second storey was added to the south block, and in 1896 a third. The latter change resulted in the loss of the original cupola and the substitution of a tower. Wings were added on the east and west sides of the south block in 1902, reorienting the Normal School's main axis from north-south to east-west. The complex was demolished (with the exception of the central portico) in 1963.

DRAWINGS: Horwood (79)1–23, 1850–2; elevations, plans, perspectives, sections, details, watercolour sketch, and design for gas lamps by Cumberland & Ridout. Drawings (79)9–11 in this suite are by William Mundie, the landscape architect responsible for the grounds. They are signed and dated William Mundie, Hamilton, 1853.

SPECIFICATIONS: 1) Horwood (C & R) no. 8, n.d. 2) Horwood (C & R) nos. 7–8, n.d.

TENDERS: Toronto *Globe*, 12 December 1850, p. 595; closing date 15 January 1851

CONTRACTORS: Metcalfe, Wilson and Forbes

SEE ALSO: Thomas Fisher Rare Book Library, University of Toronto, Royal Canadian Institute Papers, MS 230, vol. 8, Ordinary Minutes, p. 31, 7 December 1850 and later entries up to 8 February 1851, which relate to claims made by various Toronto architects and surveyors, including Cumberland, William Thomas, Thomas Young, Kivas Tully, John G. Howard, F.F. Passmore, and Sandford Fleming, that George Browne's entry, which had been awarded second place in the Normal School design competition, had been plagiarized. On 1 October 1850 Browne's critics placed a notice to this effect in the Toronto *Patriot*, but nothing further came of the matter. Toronto *Weekly Globe*, 4 October 1850, p. 55, col. 5 (refers to Cumberland's winning the design competition and includes a letter of his objecting to comments the *Globe* made concerning tendering and construction). Upper Canada, Department of Public Instruction, *Annual Reports of the Normal, Model, Grammar and Common Schools in Upper Canada*, 1848–62. *Journal of Education for Upper Canada* 4, no. 7 (July 1851), 97–102 (describes cornerstone-laying ceremonies; front elevation and two plans included); 5, no. 12 (December 1852), 177–84 (lengthy description of opening ceremony); 6, no. 1 (January 1853), 12–13 (quoting the press on Cumberland's design); 170–1 (discussion of plans for cultivation of the grounds). J. George Hodgins, *The School House; Its Architecture, External and Internal Arrangements, with Additional Papers on Gymnastics, the Use of Apparatus, Discipline,*

Methods of Teaching, etc., etc. (Toronto: Lovell and Gibson 1857), especially 5–10 (includes plans of first and second storeys). Hodgins, ed., *Documentary History of Education in Upper Canada*, 28 vols. (Toronto: various publishers 1893–1910), 10:1–14 (history and description). Hodgins, *The Establishment of Schools and Colleges in Ontario, 1792–1910*, 3 vols. (Toronto: L.K. Cameron 1910), 1:32–3 (brief history), 1:36–7 (description by visitors in 1858). *General Report of the Commissioner of Public Works for the Year Ending 30th June, 1867* (Ottawa: Hunter, Rose & Company 1868), 543. Sylvester, *Sketches of Toronto*, 73–7 (history). *Toronto Normal School 1847–1947* (Toronto: School of Graphic Arts 1947), especially 21–30 (history). Robertson, *Landmarks*, 3:35–9 (history). Leong, 'Frederick William Cumberland.' The Ryerson Polytechnic University Archives maintains clipping files on the Normal School.

EARLY VIEWS AND OTHER VISUAL SOURCES: AO, Picture Collection, Cumberland Papers, Photographs (Misc.) E-1, box 40, undated daguerreotype in red velvet presentation box, with 'Sandford Fleming, del[ineator]' clearly marked on the plate. *Journal of Education for Upper Canada* 5, no. 12 (December 1852), 177. Toronto *Globe*, 13 December 1856, p. 3 (front and rear views). Hodgins, *The School House*, 6–7 (front and rear views). *Tremaine's Map* (1863), marginal vignette. *Toronto in the Camera*, plate 5. *Canadian Illustrated News*, 14 March 1872, p. 211 (reproduced in Charles Patrick de Volpi, *Toronto, a Pictorial Record: Historical Prints and Illustrations of the City of Toronto, Province of Ontario, 1813–1882* (Montreal: Dev-Sco 1965), plate 86). Hodgins, *Establishment of Schools and Colleges in Ontario*, 1:32–5 (p. 32 shows south front as it appeared in 1891, following additions; p. 34 shows south front as it appeared from 1851 to 1890; p. 35 shows the ground-floor plan; p. 37 shows upper-floor plan; p. 38 shows Model School plan). *Toronto Normal School, 1847–1894: Jubilee Celebration* (Toronto: Warwick Brothers & Rutter 1898) (frontispiece shows Normal School after third storey added). Hodgins, ed., *Documentary History*, 10: 11, 13 (front and rear elevations). Robertson, *Landmarks*, 3:37. *Globe Magazine*, 15 May 1909, p. 2 (views of interior of museum). Ryerson Archives, Ryerson Hall Document File (numerous photographs of both exterior and interior of Normal School, including photographs of the interior taken in 1963 and others documenting the building's demolition)

Common School, Toronto

Cumberland & Ridout
DATE: 1851 (not built)
SPECIFICATIONS: Horwood (C & R) nos. 1 and 2 (no. 2 is dated December 1851). No. 1, titled 'Report on Design for Common School Bldgs Toronto, draft by T. Ridout,' is a detailed explanation of the proposed building's technical and stylistic features. In this specification the architects in fact provided two designs, one Gothic and one Italianate. They thought the Italianate design more appropriate, remarking that it 'may be made effective and complete at a small cost no decoration of an expensive nature being required in carrying out the style for this purpose and the whole being plain and simple [and] may be constructed altogether with brick so as to produce an extremely good effect.' For the Italianate design they recommended the addition of a campanile – their grand term for a tiny tower – even though this had not been asked for. They also strongly encouraged the inclusion of a cellar in which a furnace could be placed. The architects estimated that without the campanile and cellar the building could be constructed for £755; the extra features would add £825 to the cost.

No. 2 refers to seven drawings of the school, which have not been located.

Main Office of the Bank of Upper Canada, Toronto

252 Adelaide Street East (formerly Duke Street) at George Street

Additions to bank (including residential portion for the Cashier, Thomas Gibbs Ridout)
Cumberland & Ridout (?)
DATE: 1851 (still standing). Cumberland was Ridout's brother-in-law and lived across the street from the bank's main office. There is evidence to suggest that Cumberland oversaw some additions to the bank's main office in 1851, but no drawings have surfaced. In AO, MU 3909, CFP, A-1-a, env. 3, FWC to Wilmot, 25 October 1851, Cumberland wrote, 'I am anxious about the Bank which I do hope will be finished to Mr. Ridout's satisfaction. Tell them not to spoil the place for want of a pennyworth of paint.'
SEE ALSO: Ure, *Hand-Book*, 237 (mentions that an addition had been built, but does not name the architect). Robertson, *Landmarks*, 1:268–70 (early history of the bank building, but no mention of Cumberland). Sheldon Godfrey and Judy Godfrey, *Stones, Bricks, and History: The Corner of 'Duke & George,' 1798–1984* (Toronto: Lester & Orpen Dennys 1984), 21–3 (with drawings showing the sequence of building on the site). Although the evidence for Cumberland's involvement presented by the Godfreys is circumstantial, it is convincing. Notable is the reference to the City of Toronto assessment records of 1852, which show that the value of the buildings on the lot owned by the Bank of Upper Canada increased by 25 per cent in that year. The Godfreys' attribution of the work to Cumberland is repeated in Margaret McKelvey and Merilyn McKelvey, *Toronto Carved in Stone* (Toronto: Fitzhenry & Whiteside 1984), 12, and by Dendy and Kilbourn, *Toronto Observed*, 25–7 (Dendy and Kilbourn also discuss the building's earlier architectural history).
EARLY VIEW: Robertson, *Landmarks*, 1:269

Opera House, Toronto

Cumberland & Ridout
DATE: 1851 (not built)
SPECIFICATIONS: Horwood (C & R) no. 6, signed and dated 15 December 1851

This was a project to convert John Ewart's jail of 1824 into an opera house. In 1852 William Thomas converted the building to other uses.

Trinity College, Toronto

Queen Street West
Cumberland & Ridout
DATE: 1851 (competition entry; not built)
DRAWINGS: Horwood (748)1–2, watermarked 1858; unsigned perspectives. These drawings can be attributed to William G. Storm on stylistic grounds.

During a visit to England in 1850, John Strachan was impressed by the building plans for St Aiden's Theological College, Birkenhead, which was constructed in 1850–3 to the designs of the English architects Thomas Wyatt and David Brandon (the plans are illustrated in *The Builder*, 6 April 1850, 162, and described on p. 163). The Trinity College minutebook shows that the college (which then did not have a building of its own) asked both Kivas Tully and Cumberland & Ridout to prepare plans modelled on those for St Aiden's (Trinity College Archives, Trinity College Minutebook, p. 22, 23 January 1851). Tully's design was chosen. The cornerstone was laid on 30 April 1851 and the building opened on 15 January 1852. The contractors were Metcalfe, Wilson and Forbes.

The college did not include a chapel, however, and in 1857 William Hay submitted proposals to build one. See Trinity College Archives, Documents and Correspondence, 1854–72, 986-0001/019(03)005a, comprising several letters from April 1857 to November 1861 and a lithograph after Hay's design, printed by Maclear & Co. and dated April 1858. The lithograph is accompanied by an explanation of the project and a list of possible subscribers: 'Such an addition to the College is greatly needed, Divine Service having been hitherto conducted in a room, ill-fitted for its celebration, and designed for another purpose.' The college archives also hold Hay's drawings. See also the college minutebook, p. 237, 13 March 1858, reporting that 'Mr. Denison & Mr. Hay attended with plans &c. with respect to the Chapel.' There was no money to build the chapel, however (the MTL/BR holds a broadsheet from 1858 appealing for funds). It fell to Frank Darling (1850–1923), a graduate of the college, to prepare a new design in 1884, which was built. (Darling had been appointed college architect in 1878 and later designed the college's new buildings on Hoskin Avenue, which still stand.)

The drawings here attributed to Storm, watermarked 1858, superficially resemble the 1858 lithograph of Hay's chapel design. The 1858 watermarks, however, rule out a connection with Hay, and there are, moreover, no references to Cumberland or his partners in the college minutebook after 1851. It therefore seems most likely that the two perspective drawings listed here are later drawings of Cumberland & Ridout's 1851 designs. This supposition is not so far-fetched as it sounds. We know that in 1858 Cumberland & Storm prepared a number of perspective drawings for the Provincial Exhibition of that year. A Cumberland & Storm drawing of St James's Parochial School – a project executed by Cumberland in 1851 – also has an 1858 watermark. In addition, stylistic evidence can be mustered to support the attribution of this project to the Trinity College competition of 1851, for the pepper-pot Elizabethan towers shown on the drawings are more in keeping with St Aiden's, the model for Trinity College, than with any known Cumberland & Storm project.

SEE ALSO: Trinity College Minutebook, p. 26, 13 February 1851; p. 28, 20 February 1851. Trinity College Archives, Original Documents, 1843–51, 986-0001/017, Cumberland & Ridout to Thomas Champion, 21 February 1851. AO, MU 1050, env. 34, Sir Sandford Fleming diary, 7 and 20 February 1851. Sylvester, *Sketches of Toronto*, 77–80. MTL/BR, T.A. Reed Papers, p. F5. John George Hodgins, *The Establishment of Schools and Colleges in Ontario, 1792–1910*, 3 vols. (Toronto: L.K. Cameron 1910), 113–36 (historical sketch and reprints of texts documenting the ceremonies surrounding Trinity College's construction and opening). Robertson, *Landmarks*, 3: 4–13 (history; no mention of Cumberland). J.K.H. Henderson, 'The Founding of Trinity College, Toronto,' *Ontario History* 44, no. 1 (January 1952), 7–14. Graham W. Owen, 'Projects for Trinity College, Toronto,' *Journal of Canadian Art History/ Annales d'histoire de l'art Canadien* 4, no. 1 (spring 1977), 61–72. Dendy, *Lost Toronto*, 122

Christian Guardian Newspaper Office, Toronto

Cumberland & Ridout (?)
Extensions
DATE: c. 1851; demolished. The *Christian Guardian*, which operated from 1829 to 1925, was the moderate voice of the Wesleyan Methodists. Its founder and most famous editor was Egerton Ryerson.
DRAWINGS: Horwood (78a)1–2, 'Proposed extension to Guardian Office'; Printing Office No. 2; watermarked 1851; unsigned

The attribution to Cumberland & Ridout is based on the fact that these drawings are found among bundles of identifiable Cumberland materials.

W. Teefy Store, Richmond Hill

Cumberland & Ridout (?)
DATE: c. 1851
DRAWINGS: Horwood (79a)1–7, watermarked 1851; plans, elevations, and sections
SPECIFICATIONS: n.d.

'W. Teefy' is possibly Richmond Hill postmaster Matthew Teefy (1842–92). Teefy's papers (AO, MU 2925-55) do not appear to mention Cumberland. The attribution to Cumberland & Ridout is based on the fact that these drawings are found among bundles of identifiable Cumberland materials.

Central School, Hamilton

75 Hunter Street West
Cumberland & Ridout; Cumberland & Storm
DATE: 1851–3 (extant in much altered form). In 1850 the first elected Board of Trustees of the provincial Department of Education visited several schools in Canada West to look for school design models. Among these was Toronto's Normal School, which attracted the board's praise. Cumberland & Ridout was asked to prepare plans for a Hamilton School of similar design. The plans were approved in March 1851, but because of construction delays the school did not open until 2 May 1853. Designed to accommodate one thousand students, it was the only public school in Hamilton and the largest school in Canada West.

The school's original architectural character was lost as a result of extensive alterations in 1890 by Hamilton architect James Balfour, who added a third storey, a tower, new windows and doors, and gables to the elevation, and also altered the interior. Balfour also modified the austere Greek Revival window-surrounds so that they would be more in keeping with late Victorian tastes. Further renovations were undertaken in 1919 and 1930. In 1952 George T. Evans designed an obtrusive playroom/assembly area for the west side of the building; the concrete blocks used to construct his addition clashed with the original stone. In 1979–80 the building, still in use as a school, closed for extensive renovations. It reopened in September 1980, with the insurance company that had paid for some of the renovations as its second-storey tenant.
DRAWINGS: Horwood (70)1–12, 'New Central Schools [*sic*] Hamilton'; contract drawings (and some tissues on which they are based), signed and dated Cumberland & Ridout, Hamilton, 8 April 1851, except for sheet (70)5, which is signed Cumberland & Storm and undated. These drawings show a second building linked to the main building by a covered passageway – as in the Toronto Normal School – but this was never constructed.
CONTRACTORS: 1) Messrs. Horne (£1800 for masonry work; the firm failed to complete the job and Faulknor [*sic*] and Thorpe took it on for £1400). 2) John Adison [*sic*] (£1197 for

carpentry). 3) Mr Lewis (£1340 for general site work)

SEE ALSO: Upper Canada, Department of Public Instruction, *Annual Reports of the Normal, Model, Grammar and Common Schools in Upper Canada*, 1848–62. *Hamilton Spectator*, 22 March 1851 (report of board of trustees meeting during which Cumberland & Ridout's plans were approved; description of plans for building); 4 May 1853 (description of opening ceremony). *Hamilton Gazette*, 5 May 1853 (description of opening ceremony). *Journal of Education for Upper Canada* 6, no. 5 (May 1853), 75 (brief description of opening ceremony); 6, no. 10 (October 1853), 156–7 ('This institution ... is now in full operation, and is visited with intense interest and admiration by all intelligent strangers who visit the city'). L.T. Spalding, *The History and Romance of Education (Hamilton) 1816–1950* (Hamilton: Board of Education for the City of Hamilton n.d.), 1–3. J.H. Smith, *The Central School Jubilee Reunion: An Historical Sketch* (Hamilton: Spectator Printing Co. 1905). John George Hodgins, *The Establishment of Schools and Colleges in Ontario, 1792–1910*, 3 vols. (Toronto: L.K. Cameron 1910), 1:83–107 (especially 83–91) (description and history; cites articles from the Hamilton *Canadian*, 27 August 1853, and the *Dundas Warder*, 2 September 1853). Lois C. Evans, *Hamilton: The Story of a City* (Toronto: The Ryerson Press 1970), 125–9. Ian E. Davey, 'School Reform and School Attendance: The Hamilton Central School, 1853–1861' (master's thesis, University of Toronto, 1972)

EARLY VIEWS: Hamilton Public Library, Special Collections (reproductions of early views). MTL/BR, Picture Collection: a) T-15,379 (archivist dates to 1853, but probably a later view); b) T-15,380 (1903). *Canadian Illustrated News*, 16 May 1863, p. 7 (description on p. 8). *Sutherland's Hamilton Directory*, 1870, 29. Smith, *Central School Jubilee Reunion* (frontispiece). Hodgins, *Establishment of Schools and Colleges in Ontario*, 1:84 (photograph, 1903); 1:87 (photograph dated 1853, but possibly later)

Seventh Post Office, Toronto

10 Toronto Street
Cumberland & Ridout; Cumberland & Storm
DATE: 1851–3. The post office opened in May 1853, but further works were undertaken until 1854, and repairs in 1856. The building was altered in 1874 by Henry Langley and renovated in 1959.
DRAWINGS: Horwood (76)1–9, dated 1851; elevations, details, and details of joiners' work
SPECIFICATIONS: Horwood (C & R) nos. 4 and 5, signed and dated July 1851 by architects and contractors
TENDER: Toronto *Globe*, 24 June 1851, p. 299; closing date 5 July
CONTRACTORS: 1) Metcalfe, Wilson and Forbes. 2) Thomas Storm
SEE ALSO: NAC, RG 11, A1, DPW, vol. 17, item 16,842, FWC to Thomas A. Begley, secretary of the Board of Public Works, 25 May 1852 (refers to bankruptcy of original contractors and assumption of their duties by Thomas Storm); vol. 20, item 21,277, FWC to Begley, 21 November 1853 (describes addition of porches, casting £110). *Public Accounts for the Province of Canada for the Year 1854* (Quebec: Rollo Campbell 1855), 116–17 (where the firm name is misspelled 'Chamberlin and Storm'). *General Report of the Commissioner of Public Works for the Year Ending 30th June, 1867* (Ottawa: Hunter, Rose & Company 1868), 263–4, 538–9. Sylvester, *Sketches of Toronto*, 16–21. Ure, *Hand-Book*, 244. Robertson, *Landmarks*, 1:163. Dendy and Kilbourn, *Toronto Observed*, 63
EARLY VIEWS: Toronto *Globe*, 13 December 1856, p. 4; *Toronto in the Camera*, plate 1. Robertson, 1:165

York County Courthouse, Toronto

57 Adelaide Street East
Cumberland & Ridout; Cumberland & Storm
DATE: 1851–3. Dendy and Kilbourn in *Toronto Observed*, 61, remark that 'the Courthouse continued in use until 1898–9 and the com-

pletion of the Third City Hall ... which contained far more spacious court facilities. In succeeding years York County, and then Metro Toronto, treated the building with slight regard. In 1903 the wings were unceremoniously severed from the centre, the west wing to be remodelled by F. H. Herbert as showroom and office space for the Consumers' Gas Company. In the 1950s and 1960s the Courthouse was maligned as dark, dirty, and ugly – like many other buildings that Toronto had prized a century before.

'In 1977–8, however, the centre block was renovated by Lett-Smith Architects, with generous government support, as the Adelaide Court Theatres and Restaurant.'

DRAWINGS: 1) Horwood (83)1–7; contract drawings ((77)4 is signed and dated Cumberland & Ridout per William G. Storm, 1 March 1852). 2) Horwood (77)1–7, n.d.; comparative plans, sections, and details (no principal elevations)

TENDERS: 1) Toronto *Globe*, 27 September 1851, p. 463; closing date 7 October. 2) Toronto *British Colonist*, 4 March 1853, p. 3; closing date 5 March

CONTRACTOR: John Ritchey

SEE ALSO: Four progress reports on the construction are found in the minutes of the United Counties of York, Ontario, and Peel (AO, RG21, Municipal Documents Collection). The first, and most detailed (it includes a description of the design and information on tendering) is dated 31 December 1851 and appears on pp. 37–9 of the minutes for that year (the minutes for each year are separately paginated). The second report is dated 8 May 1852 (pp. 69–71). The third report, which describes how construction was delayed by problems with delivery of stone from Ohio, is dated January 1853 (pp. 30–1). The final report, dated 29 June 1853 (p. 68), reports (somewhat exasperatedly) that the works are still not complete. The minutes for 24 January 1855 (pp. 5, 13–14) note that Cumberland claimed and was paid an additional £120 for his services. *Anglo-American Magazine* 1 (July–December 1852), 362 (quoting *Montreal Herald*: 'In the

order of Civil Architecture, the new Court House deserves notice. It promises to be as fine a structure, in its own kind, as the Church [St James's Cathedral]'). Sylvester, *Sketches of Toronto*, 37–8 (description). Ure, *Hand-Book*, 243. Robertson, *Landmarks*, 1:325 (brief description). Toronto *Globe*, 17 November 1930. MacRae and Adamson, *Cornerstones of Order*, 159–61. Crossman, *Early Court Houses of Ontario*, 1:39–46. Carter, comp., *Early Canadian Courthouses*, 221

EARLY VIEWS: MTL/BR, Picture Collection, T-12,418, c. 1860. Robertson, *Landmarks*, 1:322

Irish Presbyterian Church, Toronto

Queen and Mutual streets
Cumberland & Storm (competition entry; not built)
DATE: 1852

The Canadian Journal 1 (1853), reported that Cumberland & Storm, William Thomas, and Joseph Sheard submitted entries to the design competition for this church, which Thomas won. The church was not constructed until 1857, however, and though we know that Thomas was the architect in that year, it is unclear whether he followed his design of 1852.

John Hawkins Hagarty House, Toronto

William (now Simcoe) Street
Frederic Cumberland (drawings prepared and signed by Storm)
DATE: 1852 (demolished)
DRAWINGS: Horwood (81)1–7, some dated 20 June 1852, others 12 July 1852
SPECIFICATIONS: Horwood misc. no. 28, n.d., for stable
CONTRACTOR: John Richey (signs drawings)

T. Brunskill Hotel and Store, Toronto

Front Street
Cumberland & Storm
DATE: 1852

SPECIFICATIONS: Horwood (C & S) no. 3, n.d.
(dated 1852 by archivist)

W.H. McFarlane House, Toronto

Jarvis and Shuter streets
Cumberland & Ridout
DATE: c. 1852
SPECIFICATIONS: Horwood (C & R) no. 9, n.d.

The date and location are known from a letter
from Cumberland to H. Thompson of the
Consumers' Gas Co., Toronto 7 May 1852 (in
the company's archives), asking that gas be
connected to the house without delay, as the
'floors are now being laid and the plasterers
about to commence.'

Ontario County Courthouse and Jail, Whitby

416 Centre Street South
Cumberland & Storm
PARTNER-IN-CHARGE: Storm (replaced by
Cumberland after client complained that the
work was not making satisfactory progress)
DATE: 1852–4. On 24 June 1852 a report to the
Ontario County Council 'beg[ged] to recommend that the Design submitted by Mr.
Cumberland be adopted and that he be
directed to prepare working drawings for the
same with a view to obtaining tenders for one
and two storey wings the latter to be erected if
within the proposed expenditure [of £6000].'
James Wallace won the contract and began
construction; Storm was assigned to superintend the work. The cornerstone was laid on 30
June 1853. But progress was dilatory, and on 6
November James Rowe, the provisional
county warden, wrote William Pawson, the
provisional county clerk, that 'Mr.
Cumberland was here yesterday and is very
much disappointed to find the County buildings in so backward a state and talks of taking
the Buildings out of the Contractor's hands.'
Cumberland made good on his threat by
bringing William H. Pim in to replace James
Wallace, despite notice of a lawsuit from
Wallace. A final accounting took place on
3 April 1854, by which time Cumberland &

Storm had authorized payments totalling
£6102.8.0, including £2410 to Pim.

According to information provided by
local historian Brian Winter, the courtroom
was renovated in 1864 and 1882, a third
storey added to the north end of the building
in 1867, and a second storey added to each
wing in 1910. The building was renovated in
1966 and reopened as the Whitby Centennial
Building in February 1967. The contractors
for the renovations were Totten Sims Hubicki
and Associates, Whitby.
DRAWINGS: 1) Horwood (82)1–41, some signed
and dated Cumberland & Storm, September
1862; contract drawings, paper drawings, and
linens. 2) Horwood (88)1–27, 1853; plans,
elevations, sections, and details. 3) MTL/BR,
Pim Papers, undated and unsigned sheet of
full-scale carpenter's details
SPECIFICATIONS: Horwood (C & S) no. 2, signed
and dated 30 August 1852
TENDER: Toronto *Globe*, 26 August 1852, p. 411;
closing date 8 September
CONTRACTORS: 1) James Wallace. 2) William H.
Pim.
SEE ALSO: AO, MS 600, reel 1, Ontario County
Minutebooks. AO, MS 600, reel 9, Ontario
County By-laws. AO, RG 21, Municipal
Documents Collection, Ontario County
General Accounts, 1852–9; Ontario County
Clerk's Files, box 1, 1853–4. The most substantial information concerning this commission is contained in the clerk's files,
which include building committee reports,
letters (some from Cumberland), and other
items. Toronto *Leader*, 12 July 1853 (description of cornerstone-laying ceremony). *Illustrated Historical Atlas of the County of
Ontario* (Belleville, Ont.: Mika Publishing
1972 [1877]), ii–iii (some of this material was
reprinted by the atlas's author, W.H. Higgins,
in his *The Life and Times of Joseph Gould*
(Belleville, Ont.: Mika Publishing 1972 [1877])
(see pp. 10–11 of the atlas for a plan of
Whitby). Brian Winter, *A Town Called Whitby*
(Whitby: Raymond Huff Productions 1967), 2,
15–16, 26 (illustration). MacRae and
Adamson, *Cornerstones of Order*, 162–4.
Crossman, *Early Court Houses of Ontario*, 1:

122–9. Carter, comp., *Early Canadian Court-houses*, 222

EARLY VIEWS: *Tremaine's Map* (1863), vignette. *Illustrated Historical Atlas of the County of Ontario*, 54. *Saturday Globe*, 26 October 1889. The Whitby Historical Society has a copy of the *Saturday Globe* view, as well as views from 1904, 1905, 1907, 1908, 1914, and later.

Frame Hotel, Liverpool

On the Kingston Road, eighteen miles east of Toronto
Cumberland & Storm
DATE: 1853
TENDER: Toronto *Leader*, 3 August 1853, p. 3; no closing date ('for the erection of a Frame Building, for an Hotel at Liverpool, 18 miles from Toronto, on the Kingston Road. Plans & specs. may be seen at the office of the under-signed. Cumberland & Storm')

James Duggan Wholesale Store, Toronto

North side of Wellington Street just west of Yonge Street
Renovations
Cumberland & Storm
DATE: 1853 (demolished)
DRAWINGS: Horwood (87)1–8; 8 February 1853; contract drawings

Messrs Moffat, Murray & Co. Wholesale Store, Toronto

7 (later 36) Yonge Street
Cumberland & Storm
DATE: 1853 (demolished)
DRAWINGS: 1) Horwood (85a)1–4 (85a)1 is dated 14 June 1853; 2) Horwood (86)1, signed and dated Cumberland & Storm, June 1853; cornice and pilaster details and shop front elevation
SEE ALSO: MTL/BR, Pim Papers, box 2, 13 July 1853, plan of alterations. AO, MU 2321, Pim Papers, Tenders & Estimates 1851–3, folder 3, 'Estimate of sundry alterations for Messrs Moffat Murray &c.,' 12 July 1853 (tender amounting to £294)

Although the Pim documents refer to 'altera-tions,' it appears that Cumberland & Storm designed the entire store.

Reuben A. Parker Wholesale Stores, Toronto

Yonge Street
Cumberland & Storm
DATE: 1853 (demolished)
DRAWINGS: Horwood (637)1–7, September 1853; contract drawings
SPECIFICATIONS: Horwood (C & S) no. 30, n.d.

Trinity Parsonage House, Toronto

South side of King Street, east of Parliament Street
Cumberland & Storm
DATE: 1853 (still standing)
DRAWINGS: Horwood (84)1–5, July 1853; build-ing plans, site plan, elevations, sections, and details
SPECIFICATIONS: Horwood (C & S) no 4, signed and dated 11 July 1853; for fences, shed, and privies

A report in the Toronto *United Empire*, 12 Sep-tember 1853, stated that the parsonage was under construction and would cost £1200.

Wesleyan Methodist Bookstore and Printing Office, Toronto

Wellington Buildings, 9 King Street East
Cumberland & Storm
DATE: 1853
SPECIFICATIONS: 1) Horwood misc. no. 30, signed and dated 18 November 1853. 2) MTL/BR, Pim Papers, box 2, September 1853 (printing office)
TENDER: AO, MU 2321, Pim Papers, folder 4, Tenders & Estimates, 1851–3, 'Tender for Printing office Back of Wesleyan Bookstore,' n.d. No. 1 (North Building), £224; no. 2 (South Building), £175

Houses, Toronto

Yonge Street at Adelaide Street East
Cumberland & Storm

DATE: 1853–4 (demolished)
DRAWINGS: Horwood (85)1–3, signed and dated
Cumberland & Storm, May 1853, but signed
by contractor 27 February 1854; elevations
and plans
CONTRACTOR: Benjamin Walton

The clients may have been the Rick Bell,
Charles Dowson, and John Sterling who signed
the drawings.

Legislature and Governor General's Resident, Toronto

University Park (now Queen's Park). The
legislature was to be located at the north end of
College Avenue (now University Avenue) and
the governor general's residence to its northeast. Five porters' lodges were to be built at the
north, east, and south ends of the site. The
design also called for gardens north and east of
the governor general's residence (see the maps
listed below).

Cumberland & Storm
DATE: 1853–5 (not built)
DRAWINGS: 1) Horwood (54)2, 5, 8, 9, 11–13.
(54)2, 9, 11, and 13 are undated. (54)5 is an
undated survey drawing of the legislature by
F.F. Passmore. (54)12, also by Passmore, is
signed and dated 29 March 1854. (54)8 is an
undated drawing by William Mundie of a
proposed 'Grape Winery Green House' to be
attached to the governor general's residence.
2) Horwood (97)24, 'Tracings and sketches,
Plans, Parliament Buildings & Department
Offices, University Park, Toronto,' n.d.
3) Horwood (97)34, 'Block Plan, Parliament
Buildings, Toronto,' n.d.
TENDER: Toronto *Globe*, 6 March 1854, p. 3;
closing date 10 April
SEE ALSO: NAC, RG 11, A1, DPW, vol. 19, item
20,133, FWC to Thomas A. Begley, secretary
of the Board of Public Works, 13 July 1853
(asks for return of drawings for the governor
general's residence; these bore the motto
'Kitchee Hogeeman Endaut' ('The Home of
the Great Chief'); on the back of the letter is a
notation that the plans were returned on
17 July); vol. 19, item 20,572, FWC to Begley,
30 August 1853 (the site for the legislature has
been transferred from the university to the
government; Cumberland requests information from government department heads
regarding office space needs in the new
legislature, such information to be delivered
'with the least possible delay, as it is obvious
that the works are delayed for its want'); vol.
19, item 20,515, FWC to Begley, 30 August
1853, and vol. 20, item 20,689; FWC to Begley,
15 September 1853 (Cumberland objects
strenuously to government proposal that he
be paid a flat fee for his work rather than a
sum calculated as a percentage of total
construction costs); vol. 20, item 20,626, FWC
to Begley, 12 September 1853 (Cumberland
has had the site surveyed and a 'plan is now
in the course of preparation'; he has also had
a fence built around the property and has
put William Mundie, the Toronto Normal
School's landscaper, in charge of the site; he
still requests information regarding departmental office space – 'As the season is rapidly
passing away we recur to this subject lest we
might be held responsible for the delay'); vol.
20, item 21,039, FWC to Begley, 19 October
1853, and vol. 20, item 21,357, FWC to Begley,
28 November 1853 (progress reports); vol. 20,
item 21,479, FWC to Begley, 22 December
1853 (telegram requesting contract forms);
vol. 20, item 21,533, FWC to Begley, 29 December 1853 (progress report; 'The working
plans and details for the Governor's
Residence are complete and ready for contract; those for the Parliament buildings are
rapidly progressing to completion'). AO, MS
537, Thomas Gibbs Ridout Papers, Thomas
Gibbs Ridout to Matilda Ridout, 10 June 1853
and 24 June 1855. Toronto *Weekly Leader*,
13 October 1852 (Cumberland & Storm put in
charge of maintaining Toronto's Parliament
Building until the provincial government
returns from Quebec). Toronto *Semi-Weekly
Leader*, 2 November 1852 (call for submission
of plans for governor general's residence;
deadline 1 December). Toronto *Weekly
Leader*, 3 November 1852 (comment on

tenders). Toronto *Daily Leader*, 2 August 1853 (report that new government buildings are to go ahead under Cumberland & Storm); 6 August 1853 (notice sent to university authorities to vacate the property); 22 November 1853 (doubts exist whether new government buildings will go ahead); 16 January 1854 (long article on new government buildings; closing of College Avenue). *Toronto Examiner* (quoting Toronto *Daily Leader*), 24 May 1854 (Cumberland proceeds to Quebec with tenders for Toronto's government buildings). Toronto *Daily Colonist*, 3 June 1854 (long and sarcastic article on the delay in constructing the new legislature; particularly pointed on Cumberland). 16 Vict. (1853), c. 161 (Can.) (royal assent 14 June 1853) (act authorizing construction of legislature at a cost of £50,000 and governor general's residence at a cost of £10,000). Province of Canada, Sessional Papers, 1862, no. 3 (letter from government engineer and architect F.P. Rubidge describing Cumberland's project). Sylvester, *Sketches of Toronto*, 21–3. Robertson, *Landmarks*, 1:351–9; 3:318. Frank Yeigh, *Ontario's Parliament Buildings* (Toronto: Williamson Book Co. 1893), 49–50

MAPS: In 1854 land surveyor J. Stoughton Dennis was asked (by whom is unknown) to prepare two subdivision plans for lands adjacent to the new government buildings. In both, the siting and shape of the buildings corresponded with Horwood 54(9). See NAC, National Map Collection 22835, 'Plan of the City of Toronto showing the Town Lots on Bellevue ...,' March 1854, and University of Toronto, Thomas Fisher Rare Book Library, map 3524 T625 1854 D4, 'Plan of Part of the City of Toronto Shewing the Villa Lots on College St. ...,' March 1854. Another plan, prepared by John Tully and dated 27 June 1853, and titled 'Plan of new village of Seaton.' This subdivision was advertised as being 'near [the] New Parliament Buildings,' even though it was more than a mile distant, on lands north and west of Bloor and Bathurst streets. See NAC, National Map Collection 22833 (copy in MTL/BR).

Royal Magnetical Observatory, Toronto

Cumberland & Storm

DATE: 1853–6. The observatory was founded in 1846. In 1853 the imperial government ceded land for an observatory to the University of Toronto. Construction began in 1854 and was completed in 1856. Originally standing southeast of present-day Convocation Hall, in 1908 the observatory was re-erected (with some changes in plan) on a site south of Hart House and east of University College.

DRAWINGS: 1) Horwood (84a)1–9, signed and dated by contractor John Worthington, September 1853; contract drawings. 2) MTL/BR, S117, Pim Papers; elevation, fragmentary window detail, and a larger sheet showing partial elevations and sections

SPECIFICATIONS: 1) Horwood (C & S) nos. 5 and 10. The dating of these is inconsistent. No. 10, dated 1854, is the rough draft of no. 5, dated 1853. No. 5 also has an additional six pages titled 'General Clauses and Conditions,' the last page of which is dated 5 September 1853 and signed by the contractor, with Storm as witness.

TENDERS: 1) Toronto *Leader*, 20 August 1853, p. 3; no closing date; for fencing and gates around site. 2) Toronto *Leader*, 22 August 1853, p. 3; for additions and alterations to the site

CONTRACTOR: John Worthington

SEE ALSO: Toronto *Globe*, 16 November 1859 ('The University Grounds'). *Public Accounts for the Province of Canada for the Year 1855* (Toronto: Rollo Campbell 1856), 121. *Public Accounts for the Province of Canada for the Year 1856* (Toronto: Rollo Campbell 1857), 106. *Illustrated London News*, 5 November 1859, pp. 452, 454 ('Education in Canada – The New University'). *General Report of the Commissioner of Public Works for the Year Ending 30th June, 1867* (Ottawa: Hunter, Rose & Company 1868), 258, 536. T.A. Reed, 'The Observatory of Toronto, 1840–1908,' *Canadian Geographic Journal* 55, no. 6 (December 1957), 234–43

Upper Canada College, Toronto

Site bounded by present-day King, Simcoe,
Adelaide, and John streets
Additions, alterations, and repairs
Cumberland & Storm

DATES: 1853, 1856–7. The original college, now
demolished, was built in 1829–31. Occupa-
tion of the present site north of St Clair
Avenue on Avenue Road dates from 1891.
Richard B. Howard, *Upper Canada College,
1829–1979: Colborne's Legacy* (Toronto:
Macmillan 1979), 62–4, identifies two phases
of building in which Cumberland & Storm
was involved. During the first phase, in 1853,
the firm executed badly needed repairs, for
which it was paid £1250 (Howard states that
the architects were 'severely rebuked' for cost
overruns). During the second phase in 1856–
7, the firm designed an enlarged 'Resident
School House' (student residence) and playground as well as a new study and dining
hall. From records now in the UTA, cited
below, it would appear that Howard's account is substantially correct. Cumberland &
Storm also designed a porter's lodge and
bursar's office for the college and prepared a
plan for subdividing the East Master's Residence.

DRAWINGS: 1) Horwood (109)1–10, 1856; plans,
elevations, and sections of Resident School
House. 2) Horwood (111)2, 1857; plans of
Resident School House and plan of playground. 3) Horwood 632(11), n.d.; subdivision of East Master's Residence

SPECIFICATIONS: Horwood (C & S), nos. 14
(1856), 15 (1856), 19 (1857); Resident School
House

TENDERS: 1) Toronto *Globe*, 8 September 1857,
p. 3; no closing date; for Resident School
House, including yards and walks, playshed,
woodshed, fencing, paving, and drains.
2) Toronto *Globe*, 23 September 1857, p. 3;
closing date 30 September 1857; for two-
storey brick porter's lodge. 3) Toronto *Leader*,
4 October 1857, p. 4; no closing date; for
additions and alterations to Resident School
House

CONTRACTORS: 1) William H. Pim. 2) John Snarr.
3) Others

SEE ALSO: Because Upper Canada College was
linked administratively with the University of
Toronto during these years, its earliest
financial records are found among the
university's financial records in the UTA.
UTA, A68-0010, Office of the Chief Accountant, Upper Canada College, Section II, Group
B, Letterbooks C, D, and E (see finding aid
pp. 23–4, nos. 312, 317–18). Letterbook C
is a record of incoming correspondence;
letterbooks and D and E contain copies of
outgoing correspondence. Letterbook C,
p. 270, Cumberland & Storm to UCC (concerning repairs to college buildings); p. 270,
Cumberland & Storm to UCC, 26 February
1855 (concerning residence of Rev. G.
Maynard); p. 271, Cumberland & Storm to
UCC, 28 February 1855 (concerning repairs);
p. 303, Cumberland & Storm to UCC, 10 July
1855 (applying for payment for services
performed with respect to repairs); p. 426,
Cumberland to UCC, 4 September 1857,
(concerning measurement of UCC grounds
to be leased); p. 433, Cumberland to UCC,
16 October 1857 (enclosing plan of college
lots on King Street). Letterbook D, pp. 316–
17, David Buchan, bursar, to Cumberland,
11 October 1853 (requesting that Cumberland come and determine the work needed
to effect urgent repairs); p. 321, Buchan to
Cumberland, 28 October 1853 (Buchan now
has an order-in-council to effect the works,
pending the governor general's signature);
p. 322, Buchan to Cumberland, 1 November
1853 (official approval received); p. 419,
Buchan to Cumberland & Storm, 27 May
1854 (concerning complaints from owner of
an adjacent property about works in
progress); p. 539, Buchan to Cumberland &
Storm, 9 February 1855 (the firm's report and
bill have been forwarded to the governor
general). Letterbook E, p. 49, Buchan to
Cumberland & Storm, 23 July 1855 (the firm's
bill '*is still under the consideration of the
government*'); p. 308, Buchan to Cumberland,
22 September 1857 (concerning Fleming,

Ridout & Schreiber's subdivision plan of college lots); pp. 315–16, Buchan to Cumberland, 14 October 1857 (same subject); p. 433, Buchan to Cumberland & Storm, 11 October 1858 (asking the architects to supply a bill for work on the bursar's office, which was built by Pim). For additional letters, see UTA, Office of the Chief Accountant, A68-0010, Cumberland to UCC, 27 February 1855 (concerning his firm's report on the college fabric, he would like to see certain additional reports from college teaching masters on the state of the college fabric); Cumberland & Storm to UCC, 10 July 1855 (calling attention to the firm's unpaid bill for services); Cumberland to UCC, 21 September and 16 October 1857 (concerning Fleming, Ridout & Schreiber's subdivision plan); Cumberland & Storm to Buchan, 12 June 1857 (because the contractor Snarr has completed his work, they want to be paid). UTA, A70-0024/058, Board of Governors, UCC Council Minutes, 1850–3, p. 106, 22 March 1853 (call for repairs to drain in playground). UTA, A70-1124/052(2), Board of Governors, Chancellor's Incoming Correspondence, E.A. Meredith (?) to David Buchan, 24 October 1856 (concerning new buildings for the college; he includes a copy of the order-in-council authorizing the work, and mentions the bid of John Snarr for £2223. (UCC says that it has sufficient funds to pay for the works on its own.) UTA, A68-0010, Office of the Chief Accountant, Section II, UCC, Bursar's Quarterly and Yearly Statements, vol. 272, Quarterly Account, quarter ending 31 March 1854 (£452.11.0 spent on college repairs; payees not named); quarter ending 31 March 1855 (£2149.4.11 spent on repairs; payees not named); quarter ending 30 June 1857 (£173.11.3 paid to Cumberland & Storm, being a commission of 5 per cent on cost of repairs; but statement for quarter ending 30 September 1857 states that the payment is for superintending repairs made in *1853*); quarter ending 30 June 1858 (£140.6.3 paid to Cumberland & Storm, being the 'Balance of a/c for superintending various works'); quarter ending 31 December

1858 (£36.8.0 paid to Cumberland & Storm, being the 'balance of commission as architects' – probably for bursar's office). UTA, A70-0024-004(01), Board of Governors, Copies of Orders-in-Council, 1853–87, p. 9, 'Extract from a Report of a committee of the Honorable the Executive Council on matters of state dated 24 October 1853 ... On a memorandum dated 24th inst. from the Hon. the Inspector General transmitting a report from Mr. Cumberland, Civil Engineer on the state of the Buildings used by Upper Canada college, from which it appears that it is absolutely necessary with a view to the preservation of the buildings that immediate repairs be made'; pp. 23–4, copy of an order-in-council, 2 February 1855, regarding Cumberland & Storm's claim for payment of commission (from provincial secretary's covering letter to bursar David Buchan: 'His Excellency (in view of the very great excess of the actual cost above the estimated cost of the repairs and of the fact that a considerable portion of the repairs appears to have been wholly unauthorized) desires before paying the account to obtain from you all the information you can procure in reference to the matter to guide the Government in coming to a decision as to the amount of remuneration to which the architects are fairly entitled ... I am further directed to state that the course pursued by the Architects in not keeping you advised of the very great excess of the expenditures over the estimated cost appear to His Excellency in Council to call for very severe censure & I have to direct you to inform those Gentlemen [that the government] require[s] some more satisfactory explanation of the reasons for their unexpected and unauthorized excess'); pp. 72–3, 19 June 1856, item 3 ('And whereas the building used at present as a Resident School House is too small, and is in these respects unsuited to the purpose, and ought to be enlarged & improved so as to accommodate from 100 to 150 pupils, Be it enacted that the Resident School house shall be forthwith enlarged and improved'). MTL/BR, Pim Papers, box 3, 22 and 30 September and other dates (references to works at Upper Canada College, including porter's lodge). MTL/BR, Broadsides Collection, three-page brochure, 1 August 1857, announcing the opening of the 'College Boarding House' (Resident School House). Sylvester, *Sketches of Toronto*, 72–3 (description). J.G. Hodgins, *The Establishment of Schools and Colleges in Ontario, 1792–1910*, 3 vols. (Toronto: L.K. Cameron 1910), 2:188–200 (history, by John Ross Robertson)

EARLY VIEWS: Toronto *Globe*, 13 December 1856, p. 3. *Toronto in the Camera*, plate 7 (with description). *Canadian Illustrated News*, 18 June 1870, 524. Howard, *Upper Canada College*, between 46 and 47 (plan of Resident School House). UTA, A74-0018 (site plan, n.d.)

Protestants' Orphans' Home, Toronto

North side of Sullivan Street, between Beverley and Huron streets
Cumberland & Storm
DATES: 1853 (building constructed) and 1860 (third storey added). The building was demolished.
SPECIFICATIONS: Horwood (C & S) no. 41, n.d. For third storey. Includes an article of agreement between contractor James Worthington and the Building Committee of the Protestants' Orphans' Home
TENDERS: 1) Toronto: *Semi-Weekly Leader*, 5 July 1853. 2) Toronto *Globe*, 15 May 1860, p. 3; closing date 26 May; for third storey
CONTRACTOR: James Worthington (1860)

Mechanics' Institute, Toronto

East side of Church Street at Adelaide Street East
Cumberland & Storm
DATE: 1853–61. This building included a music hall. The cornerstone was laid on 17 April 1854. Financial problems necessitated renting the unfinished building to the provincial government for use as office space from 1855 to 1861, after which construction was completed. The building was demolished in 1949.

DRAWINGS: Horwood (93)1–25, signed and dated June 1855; elevations, plans, sections, and details
SPECIFICATIONS: Horwood (C & S) no. 6, n.d.
TENDERS: 1) Toronto *Globe*, 14 July 1853, p. 355; closing date 11 August. 2) Toronto *Globe*, 16 July 1853, p. 359; closing date 1 August; for heating and ventilation. 3) Toronto *Leader*, 3 August 1853, p. 3. 4) AO, MU 2321, Pim Papers, Tenders and Estimates 1851–3, 7 September 1853; for all carpentry and joiner's work, £2734. 5) MTL/BR, Pim Papers, 10 July 1857; for government library, £220
CONTRACTOR: William H. Pim
SEE ALSO: The land for the Mechanics' Institute building was purchased from Upper Canada College, at a time when Cumberland was president of the Mechanics' Institute and also doing work for Upper Canada College: see UTA, A70-0024/058, Board of Governors, UCC Council, Minutes, 1850–3, p. 113, Third Annual Report by the Board of Endowment to the Council of Upper Canada College and Royal Grammar School, 1852 (dated 17 February 1853), concerning the sale to the Mechanics' Institute 'of the three lots at the Corner of Church and Adelaide Streets, part of Block D, measuring together 90 feet on Church Street, by 104 feet on Adelaide Street.' The report noted that 'This piece of ground was exposed to Sale at Public Auction, and after a spirited competition was knocked down to a private party at £18.2.6 p. foot for the frontage on Church Street or £1,631 for the three lots.' This unnamed purchaser later 'transferred his interest to the Institute.' UTA, A68-0010, Office of Chief Accountant, Section II, UCC Books, Letterbook C, Correspondence 1851–9 (see finding aid p. 23, no. 312), especially p. 182, Corresponding Secretary of the Mechanics' Institute to UCC, 20 March 1854 (concerning a possible loan from the college), and p. 193, Cumberland & Storm in UCC, 19 May 1854 (concerning improvements by the Mechanics' Institute to the lands purchased from the college). MTL/BR, Toronto Mechanics' Institute Papers. MTL/BR, Broadsides Collection, circular dated 12 April 1855 asking for

financial assistance to complete the new building. *Canadian Family Herald*, 16 October 1852, p. 367 (copy in MTL/BR) (lengthy article reporting on purchase of land for the Mechanics' Institute two weeks previously and on attempts to find £3000 to finance construction; reprints address signed by Cumberland, the Institute's president, and others). Sylvester, *Sketches of Toronto*, 31–3. Ure, *Hand-Book*, 242–3. *Canadian Illustrated News*, 18 June 1870, p. 519 (description). *General Report of the Commissioner of Public Works for the Year Ending 30th June, 1867* (Ottawa: Hunter, Rose & Company 1868), 544. Robertson, *Landmarks*, 1:756–60 (history)

EARLY VIEWS: *Toronto in the Camera*, plate 7 (with description). *Canadian Illustrated News*, 18 June 1870, p. 524 (after a Notman photograph). Robertson, *Landmarks*, 1:756

George William Allan House, Toronto (1)

Pembroke Street
DATE: 1854
Cumberland & Storm
PARTNER-IN-CHARGE: Storm
DRAWINGS: Horwood (90)1–10, signed and dated W.G. Storm, 27 October 1854; contract drawings
CONTRACTOR: John Worthington (signs drawings)
SEE ALSO: Toronto *Globe*, 4 August 1856, p. 2 (house nearing completion)

George William Allan House, Toronto (2)

Wilton Crescent
Cumberland & Storm
DATE: 1854–5
PARTNER-IN-CHARGE: Storm
DRAWINGS: 1) Horwood (90)12–23, signed by Cumberland & Storm September 1854 and by Storm and contractor 30 October 1854; plans, elevations, and sections (very full suite of drawings). 2) Horwood (90)28–31, signed and dated Cumberland & Storm October 1855; Stable and coach-house. 3) Horwood (90)33,

n.d.; gates. (Note: Horwood (90)25–7, 32 are drawings of Allan's earlier residence, 'Homewood,' by H.B. Lane.)
CONTRACTOR: John Worthington (1854)

House and Outbuildings, Toronto

Sumach Street
Cumberland & Storm
DATE: 1854
TENDER: Toronto *Leader*, 16 January 1854; closing date 20 January

Provincial Assurance Co. Building, Toronto

Toronto Street
Additions and alterations (including fireproof vaults and rear addition)
Cumberland & Storm
DATE: 1854
DRAWINGS: Horwood (628)1–11, unsigned and undated
SPECIFICATIONS: Horwood (C & S) no. 40, n.d., but watermarked 1853 and calling for tenders on 'Friday, 5 May.' 5 May fell on a Friday in 1854.

Mrs Radenhurst House, Toronto

Duke Street (now Adelaide Street East)
Cumberland & Storm(?)
DATE: c. 1854
DRAWING: Horwood, verso of (90)31, n.d.; rough pencil sketch of front elevation, executed on back of plan for G.W. Allan Mansion on Wilton Crescent

It seems unlikely that the project was executed – and certainly not from this drawing.

Shepley House, Toronto

Corner of North (now Bay) Street and St Mary's Street
Additions and alterations
Cumberland & Storm
DATE: c. 1854
DRAWINGS: 1) Horwood (91a)1–5, watermarked

1854; plans, elevations, and one sheet of interior details

Casimir Stanislaus Gzowski House, Toronto ('The Hall')

Facing 396 Bathurst Street, north of Queen
  Street (now the site of Alexandra Park)
Cumberland & Storm
DATE: c. 1854–5 (demolished 1904)
DRAWINGS: 1) Horwood (638)1–42, unsigned and
  undated, but by virtue of drawing style,
  handwriting, size and brand of paper, and
  presentation techniques, almost certainly by
  Cumberland & Storm. (638) 3, 4, 6, 8, and 9
  are Kivas Tully's drawings for a house for
  Gzowski on Beverley Street, signed and dated
  1 August 1854; (638)6 is labelled 'C.S.
  Gzowski's Mansion K. Tully's Design Dupli-
  cate Drawings.' It is conceivable that
  Cumberland & Storm vied with Tully in a
  formal competition for the Gzowski commission. 2) Horwood (639a)1, 'Sketch of Plan for
  Mansion for C.S. Gzowski, William Storm,
  Architect &c., Toronto 1855,' showing in fact
  three plans
EARLY VIEWS: MTL/BR, T-11,255-62 (photo-
  graphs of interior and exterior, c. 1896). AO,
  Picture Collection, S 2903-4, c. 1901

Before the drawings for this house surfaced in
the Horwood Collection in 1979, two authors
proposed that it had been designed by
Cumberland & Storm: see Eric Arthur, *Toronto:
No Mean City*, 2nd ed. (Toronto: University of
Toronto Press 1974), 145, figs. 232–5; Martyn,
Toronto, 139–47. The Gzowski Papers in the AO
(MU 1188-92) contain no references to the
house, but this could simply be because they are
mostly later in date and consist largely of scrap-
books of invitations, letters congratulating
Gzowski on his knighthood, and so on. However,
in a letter to Wilmot in June 1854, Cumberland
writes, 'Gzowski is here [Toronto] and we have
been talking over house building. He has purchased five acres close to Cayley and has enclosed and fenced two acres intending to sell
the remainder – probably to McPherson. He
[–] Gzowski [–] estimates his expenditure

including planting and furniture at £8,000': AO,
MU 3909, CFP, A-1-a, env. 4, FWC to Wilmot,
4 June 1854.

Post Office, Hamilton

72 James Street North
Cumberland & Storm
PARTNER-IN-CHARGE: Cumberland
DATE: 1854–6. This stone-covered Italianate
  building opened officially on 4 February
  1856. A view in the *Hamilton City Directory* of
  1868–9 shows the building constructed as
  the Horwood drawings indicate, but later
  nineteenth-century photographs show that
  the bays were eventually filled in. In 1888–9
  the building served briefly as Hamilton's city
  hall. In 1899 it was enlarged and substantially
  renovated, becoming the regional office of
  the Sun Life Assurance Company. In 1926 it
  was renamed the Federal Building and now
  accommodates stores, offices, and apartments. The only original portions of the
  building still extant are the pedimented
  second-storey windows with their distinctive
  floral-motif surrounds and keystones.
DRAWINGS: Horwood (91)1–19, signed and dated
  Cumberland & Storm, March 1854; elevations, sections, and plans
SPECIFICATIONS: Horwood (C & S) no. 9, 1854–5
TENDER: Toronto *Leader*, 19 April 1854, p. 3,
  closing date 3 May
CONTRACTORS: 1) G. Sharpe. 2) William Houston
  (also spelled Huston)
SEE ALSO: NAC, Isaac Buchanan Papers, MG 24,
  D16, vol. 22, pp. 18889–18901 (correspondence relating to purchase of land for the post
  office, 11 July 1853 to 20 June 1854). *Journals
  of the Legislative Assembly of the Province of
  Canada*, 1854–5, appendix F.F.F. ('The New
  Post Office'). *Hamilton Gazette*, 3 July 1854,
  p. 3, col. 1 (foundation-stone about to be
  laid). *Hamilton Spectator*, 28 January 1856,
  p. 2 ('This elegant and commodious edifice,
  one of the best in the city, and probably the
  most perfect of the kind in the province, is
  now nearly completed, and is expected to be
  opened to the public on Monday next, the
  4th February'). *Public Accounts for the Prov-*

ince of Canada for the Year 1855 (Toronto: Rollo Campbell 1856), 124. Province of Canada, Sessional Papers, 1867, appendix 8, p. 264 (description and construction cost estimate of $51,650). *General Report of the Commissioner of Public Works for the Year Ending 30th June, 1867* (Ottawa: Hunter, Rose & Company 1868), 264, 538. *Hamilton City Directory*, 1868–9, 21 (brief description). J. Brian Henley, 'Today's Federal Building First Opened as Post Office,' *Hamilton Spectator*, 10 May 1986

EARLY VIEWS: Hamilton Public Library, Special Collections (various undated views, before and after renovations). *Hamilton City Directory*, 1868–9, 21

British North American Assurance Co. Building, Toronto

Church Street
Additions and alterations
Cumberland & Storm
DATES: 1854, 1856
TENDERS: 1) Toronto *Globe*, 20 April 1854, p. 3; closing date 29 April. 2) MTL/BR, Pim Papers, box 2, May 1854, bid of £2239 (see also AO, MU 2321, Pim Papers, Notebooks 1854, 5 May 1854). 3) MTL/BR, Pim Papers, 17 March 1856, bid of £95

Bank of Upper Canada Building, Windsor

Southeast corner of Pitt and Goyeau streets
Cumberland & Storm
DATE: 1855 (demolished)
DRAWINGS: Horwood (99)1–10, n.d.; plans, elevations, and sections (contract drawings)
TENDER: *Windsor Herald*, 21 July 1855, p.2, col. 7
SEE ALSO: The first volume of Windsor Council minutes, which begins in 1854 and is held by the Windsor Public Library (RG 2, AIV-1/1), yields three early references to the Bank of Upper Canada. In 1855 there are two references to the bank. In 1858 the bank requests a municipal loan to establish a branch in Windsor. As the bank had already been operating in Windsor for four or five years, it is clear that this is a reference to the bank's

plan to move to a new site and put up a new building, which in fact happened soon after. *Windsor Herald*, 17 October 1856, p. 2, col. 4 ('Among the buildings worthy of notice [in Windsor], we think the Bank of Upper Canada stands first, which, for beauty of architecture and internal finish, might lay a fit ornament for a metropolis – showing that no want of confidence in the growth of Windsor exists in the minds of the Directors of this establishment. It is now occupied, and "Bank Open" from 10 to 3')

EARLY VIEW: *Bird's Eye View of Windsor* (1878) (copy in Windsor Public Library)

David Lewis Macpherson House, Yorkville ('Chestnut Park')

Additions and alterations
East side of Yonge Street between Roxborough Street and Rowanwood Avenue
Cumberland & Storm
DATE: 1855 (demolished)
DRAWINGS: Horwood (92)1–30, signed and dated Cumberland & Storm, 6 June 1855; plans, elevations, sections, and details
EARLY VIEWS: *Canada Farmer* 2 (1865), 364 (conservatory) and 365. MTL/BR, Picture collection, T-11,413, c. 1900 (identification uncertain)

Canada Company Building, Toronto

Bay Street
Cumberland & Ridout
DATE: c. 1855. The richness of ornament in the design would seem to link it with the firm's residential commissions of c. 1855, but nothing precludes an earlier date.
DRAWINGS: Horwood (69)1–9, n.d.; plans, elevations, and sections, and details for outbuildings
SPECIFICATIONS: Horwood misc. no. 29, 'Specification of work to be done and material to be provided in erecting and completing furnishing a two-story Building in Bay Street in the City of Toronto,' n.d. The specifications identify the client as the Canada Company, per Thomas Beckett.

George Moberly House, Barrie

Including coach-house, stable, and woodshed
Cumberland & Storm
DATE: c. 1855 (demolished?)
DRAWINGS: 1) Horwood (139e)1–11, unsigned
and undated; ten linens of house, one paper
sheet of millwork details. 2) Horwood (139f) 1,
unsigned and undated; a linen of the coach-
house. (139e)1–11 are lettered in a different
hand from (139f)1, but all of the drawings
may reasonably be assigned to Cumberland's
firm. Horwood Add. Accession 13607 is a
paper duplicate of (139f)1 transferred to the
AO from the Simcoe County Archives.

The date of c. 1855 is a conjecture based on the
fact that Walter Moberly, originally from Barrie,
was employed by Cumberland at that time.
Walter's relationship to George Moberly is
unclear (Walter's father was named John).

Canadian Institute Building, Toronto

Pembroke Street
Cumberland & Storm
DATE: 1855–6. The cornerstone was laid by
Governor General Sir Edmund Walker Head
on 14 November 1855, but the building was
not constructed.
DRAWINGS: Horwood, (110)1–17, n.d.; plans,
elevations, sections, and details. These
undated drawings bear witness to three
different design schemes and to an evolution
from a less elaborate to a more elaborate
design. (110)16–17 are dimensioned sepia
plans and appear to be preliminary drawings.
(110)2, 4–7, 9 constitute a more elaborate
second scheme. (110)4–6 are elevations; the
others are plans and sections. The most
elaborate scheme, which has strong
Ruskinian polychromatic elements, is seen
in (100)1, 11–14.
TENDER: Toronto Globe, 28 August 1857, p. 3; no
closing date
SEE ALSO: University of Toronto, Thomas Fisher
Rare Book Library, Royal Canadian Institute
Papers, 'Annual Report of the Council, 1857'
(referring to the building plans, provided

without charge by Cumberland & Storm).
Toronto Globe, 4 August 1856, p. 2 (building
about to be erected). Toronto Daily Colonist,
23 December 1855, p. 1 (wood engraving of
cornerstone-laying ceremony) (copy in MTL/
BR, Picture Collection, T-30,108)

J. Lukin Robinson Law Chambers, Toronto
('The Wellington Law Chambers')

Jordan Street
Cumberland & Storm
DATE: 1855–6
DRAWINGS: Horwood (95)1–12, n.d.; elevations,
plans, and sections
SEE ALSO: Toronto Globe, 12 September 1855,
p. 872 ('Mr James Lukin Robinson is erecting
a large building at the corner of Jordan and
Melinda Streets, to be let out as Law chambers. It is a handsome structure'); 4 August
1856, p. 2 (construction has been completed;
'a three story brick building, with stone
dressings')

J. Lukin Robinson Town Houses, Toronto

Front and Windsor streets. The Toronto Globe,
4 August 1856, p. 2, reported that two town
houses had just been completed, and were
part of 'an intended range of six.' The others
were never built.
Cumberland & Storm
DATE: 1855–6 (demolished)
DRAWINGS: Horwood (94)1–15, March 1855;
elevations, plans, and sections
SPECIFICATIONS: Horwood (C & S) no. 33, n.d.
(watermarked 1852)
SEE ALSO: Arthur, Toronto (3rd ed.), 133

John Ross House, Toronto

Davenport Road
Cumberland & Storm
DATE: 1855–6 (building designed and con-
structed) and 1860 (additions and altera-
tions). The building was demolished.
DRAWINGS: Horwood (96)1–18, n.d.; plans,
elevations, and sections
SPECIFICATIONS: Horwood misc. no. 5, 1860

TENDERS: 1) Toronto *Globe*, 5 June 1855, p. 3, col. 2; closing date 13 June; for 'House at the end of Cruikshank's Lane [Bathurst Street] adjoining Davenport.' 2) Toronto *Globe*, 1 Sep-tember 1855, p. 3; closing date 5 September; for 'first-class house, Davenport Road' (Ross identification uncertain). 3) MTL/BR, Pim Papers, tender dated 2 February 1860, for additions and alterations to north and south wings at a cost of $2910

SEE ALSO: Toronto *Globe*, 4 August 1856, p. 2 (house rapidly approaching completion and 'forms a commanding object on the Davenport Road, which, from its altitude, ensuring a bird's-eye view of the Lake and City, seems to be growing in favour for suburban dwellings')

William Hume Blake House, Toronto

'Adjoining Davenport near the head of Crookshanks [Bathurst Street]' (according to the specifications)
Cumberland & Storm
DATE: 1855–6 (demolished)
DRAWINGS: Horwood (100)1–8, signed and dated Cumberland & Storm 1 June 1855; contract drawings
SPECIFICATIONS: Horwood (C & S) no. 27, n.d.
CONTRACTOR: Long & Johnson (signs drawings, 19 July 1856)

Bank of Upper Canada Building, Port Hope

Northwest corner of John and Augusta streets
Cumberland & Storm
PARTNER-IN-CHARGE: Cumberland
DATE: 1855–8 (still standing, although renovated for other uses)
SPECIFICATIONS: Horwood (C & S) no. 11, n.d.
CONTRACTOR: William H. Pim (preceded by others whose names are unknown)
TENDERS: 1) Toronto *Globe*, 30 September 1855, p. 3. 2) MTL/BR, Pim Papers, box 2, 16 December 1857; for finishing bank at a cost of £1016
SEE ALSO: MTL/BR, Pim Papers, box 2, FWC to Pim, 19 December 1857 (explains why work was suspended by previous builders); FWC to Pim, 6 March 1858 (concerning extras for bank)

Halton County Courthouse, Milton

Additions(?)
Cumberland & Storm
DATE: 1856
DRAWINGS: Horwood (108)1–8, n.d.; plans, elevations, and sections
TENDER: Toronto *Globe*, 15 May 1856, p. 3; closing date 2 June; for registrar's office and other additions

Whether the additions went ahead is unknown.

William Benjamin Robinson House, Toronto

'Nearly opposite the Canadian Institute' (Toronto *Globe*, 4 August 1856)
Cumberland & Storm
DATE: 1856
DRAWINGS: Horwood (106)1–11, n.d.; plans, elevations, sections, and details
SEE ALSO: Toronto *Globe*, 4 August 1856, p. 2 (announcement of planned construction)

Wesleyan Church, Toronto

321 Queen Street east of Brock Street (now Spadina Avenue)
Cumberland & Storm
DATE: 1856–7 (demolished)
PARTNER-IN-CHARGE: Storm
DRAWINGS: Horwood (101)6, signed and dated Cumberland & Storm, 9 February 1856; plans, elevations, and details
SPECIFICATIONS: Horwood (C & S) no. 12, 1856. Attached is a contract for £2653 between the church trustees and Abel Wilcock, builder, dated 27 February 1856. As Wilcock was also a church trustee, his name was replaced on the list of trustee signatories by James Robertson on 24 April 1856.
CONTRACTOR: Abel Wilcock
SEE ALSO: Toronto *Globe*, 4 August 1856, p. 2 (progress report; construction almost finished). Sylvester, *Sketches of Toronto*, 51 ('[The church] is designed in the Norman style, by Messrs. Cumberland & Storm, having a bell cote in the main gable. It is now a large and handsome building; it was opened on 4th January, 1857'). Thomas

Champion, *The Methodist Churches of Toronto* (Toronto: G.M. Rose & Sons 1899), 138–51 (p. 139: 'Mr. Storm of the firm of Cumberland & Storm, was the architect in charge, and received an extra £100 for superintendence'). Robertson, *Landmarks*, 4:370–3

EARLY VIEWS: Champion, *Methodist Churches of Toronto*, facing 138. Robertson, *Landmarks*, 4:372

Thomas Gibbs Ridout House, Toronto ('Sherborne Villa')

495 Sherborne [*sic*] Street (the present-day street name is Sherbourne)
DATE: 1856–8 (demolished 1964). Ridout was married to a sister of Cumberland's wife.
Cumberland & Storm
DRAWINGS: Horwood (633)1–22, 8 November 1856; contract drawings
TENDER: Toronto *Globe*, 24 October 1856, p. 3; no closing date; for a Brick house on Sherborne Street near Carleton [*sic*] Street (may be for another house)
CONTRACTORS: Worthington Brothers
SEE ALSO: AO, MS 537, Ridout papers, letters from Thomas Gibbs Ridout to his wife Matilda: 25 April 1857 (excavation of property); 3 May 1857 (seventy workmen on site); 10 May 1857 (foundations excavated; stone up to ground level; 'We shall have to keep a pair of horses and carriages to go from one room to another'); 19 July 1857 (roof); 26 July 1857 (roof completed, chimneys built). Toronto *Globe*, 30 June 1857, p. 2 (mentions only that the house, 'one of the largest in the city,' is being erected; no mention of architect). London *Building News*, 20 August 1858, 846 (reportedly quoting the Toronto *British Colonist*, although the original article has not been located) ('Of the private residences in course of erection, the mansion of T.G. Ridout, Esq., Sherborne House, will be considered one of the most substantial seats in the vicinity of Toronto. It is built on the rising ground in the northern part of the city, having a magnificent prospect towards the lake, and also commanding the pine-crested eminences to the eastward, which add considerably to the picturesque character of

Toronto. The mansion has been built by Worthington Brothers, from the plans of Messrs. Cumberland & Storm, and is constructed of white brick, with Ohio cut stone dressings. The handsome stone porch, steps, and landing is an attractive feature, and the interior arrangements embrace every convenience which is essential to a first-class mansion'). Martyn, *Toronto*, 128–32. Marion MacRae and Anthony Adamson, *The Ancestral Roof: Domestic Architecture of Upper Canada* (Toronto and Vancouver: Clarke, Irwin 1963), 154–6
VIEW: MacRae and Adamson, *The Ancestral Roof*, 155

University College, Toronto

King's College Circle
Cumberland & Storm
DATE: 1856–9. The cornerstone for this building was laid on 4 October 1856. The topping-off ceremony took place exactly two years later. A fire devastated the building on 14 February 1890, but it was rebuilt over the next two years. D.B. Dick, the university's architect, was in charge of the rebuilding. University College is Cumberland's best-known work and the variety and quality of the surviving documentation is unmatched in any of his other projects.
DRAWINGS:
A) UTA: Seventy-four drawings by Cumberland & Storm were donated to the archives by the architectural firm of Horwood & White in 1922. Some are now missing. The remaining drawings include sections, plans, elevations, and details for all parts of the building.
B) Horwood: Horwood 125(8) appears to have been prepared for the original 1856 scheme and shows regular fenestration across the façade and no chemical laboratory. Other drawings are as follows: 1) (135)1–28; details, plans, and other items, 1856–9(?). 2) (125)1–10; sundry sketches. 3) (114)1–17; elevations and sections (on canvas), c. 1857–8. 4) (119)1–3; sections of southeast and east wings, design for library fittings, details for main doorway, and College Street porter's lodge, 1858. 5) (118)1–149; masonry details,

full-scale window details, and columns.
6) (115)1–162; various masonry details (some full-size). 7) (107a)1–2; perspective views. 8) (103)1–123; plans, details of carved masonry, and ironwork. 9) (104)1–25; foundation plans, details of moulded brick, roof plan, section through grounds, and details of elevations. 10) (104a)1; sketch of tower (Cumberland & Storm or D.B. Dick?). 11) (105)1–187; full-scale details of masonry. 12) (138)1; 'Toronto University, Plan of Lecture Rooms' (cf. (137)1, a longitudinal section of a classical scheme, probably the winning entry by Thomas Yonge of 1851, but not built). 13) (107)1–2, c. 1857–8; plans, elevations, sections, and perspective for geological museum, library, and other buildings. 14) (747a)1, n.d., perspective of library interior. See also section 5 of this *catalogue raisonné*, which lists reference plans purchased or commissioned by Cumberland while in Europe in 1856 researching designs for the college.

SPECIFICATIONS: One large leather-bound volume of general specifications survives in Horwood (no call number). Other specifications relate to specific aspects of the work: 1) Horwood (C & S) no. 13, 1856; 'U. of T. Draft specs to be embraced in Contract no. 1.' 2) Horwood (C & S) no. 28, n.d.; university gas service. 3) Horwood (C & S) no. 39, n.d. for plumbing (chemical school, students' lodgings, dean's house, and stewards' premises). 4) Horwood (C & S) no. 49, n.d.; steam-heating service

TENDERS: 1) Toronto *Globe*, 5 September 1856, p. 3; closing date 20 September; for excavations, masonry, brickwork and drains. 2) Toronto *Globe*, 23 February 1857; p. 3; no closing date; for additional works. 3) *The Builder*, 23 May 1857, 293; no closing date; for south and east sides of building (lists contractors and their bids, including those of subtrades; states that Worthington and Brother's bid of £49,470 for entire works was accepted). 4) Toronto *Globe*, 27 April 1858, p. 3; no closing date; for completion of student quarters. 5) Toronto *Globe*, 21 July 1858; p. 1; closing date 23 July; for glazing

CONTRACTORS: 1) Worthington Brothers (general works). 2) Jacques & Hay (woodwork). 3) Wellington & Co. 4) William H. Pim (site works). 5) Maw & Co. (tiles)

SEE ALSO: UTA, university financial records, Senate minutes, and letters from Cumberland to various university officials. Horwood, MU 3984, Add. 1, sixteen items relating to the restoration of University College, including William G. Storm's letters. Toronto *Globe*, 4 August 1856, p. 2 ('every preparation has been made for the immediate commencement of these buildings'); 30 June 1857, p. 2 (progress report; chemical school advancing rapidly; main building just rising above the foundations); 5 October 1858, p. 2, cols. 5–9 ('The New University Buildings'); 28 July 1859, p. 2, cols. 7–9 (progress report; describes main door and laying of tiles by Maw & Co.); 16 November 1859 (laying out of grounds; 'Mr. Edwin Taylor, a pupil of [Sir Joseph] Paxton's, has the work in hand, and promises well' [Paxton was the designer of the Crystal Palace]). *Journals of the Legislative Assembly of the province of Canada*, 15 (1857), appendix 28 ('The New University Buildings'). *Report of the Commissioners Appointed to Enquire into the Expenditure of the Funds of the University of Toronto ...* (Quebec: G.T. Cary 1862). *Final Report of the Commissioners of Inquiry into the Affairs of King's College University, and Upper Canada College* (Quebec: Rollo Campbell 1862). John Langton to his brother William, 12 November 1856, in *Early Days in Upper Canada*, 277–97, especially 291–6. Sylvester, *Sketches of Toronto*, 37–47. *Dominion Illustrated*, 22 February 1890, 119–20; 3 March 1890, 145, 148–50. Cumberland, 'The Story of a University Building.' A.H. Harkness, 'The Architecture of a University Building,' *Canadian Magazine* 17 (1901), 244–53. W.H. van der Smissen, 'The Building,' *University of Toronto Monthly* 5, no. 9 (June–July 1905), 209–17. *The University of Toronto and Its Colleges, 1827–1906* (Toronto: University Library 1906). John George Hodgins, *The Establishment of Schools and Colleges in Ontario 1792–1910*, 3 vols. (Toronto: L.K. Cameron 1910), 3:28ff. (topping-off ceremony described on 33–46). *Journal of Education for Upper Canada* 11, no. 11 November 1858), 161–6 (topping-off ceremony). Hodgins, *Documentary History of Education in Upper Canada*, 28 vols. (Toronto: various publishers 1893–1910), 14:37 (topping-off ceremony). Robertson, *Landmarks*, 1:34–6 (early history). W. Stewart Wallace, *A History of the University of Toronto, 1827–1927* (Toronto: University of Toronto Press 1927) G. Steven Vickers, 'Building,' in Claude T. Bissell, ed., *University College: A Portrait, 1853–1953*, (Toronto: University of Toronto Press 1953), 22–34. Walker, 'A Doorway Made Him Famous.' Lochnan, 'Victorian Tiles in Toronto.' Bain, 'William Mundie.' Dendy and Kilbourn, *Toronto Observed*, 64–70. Richardson, *A Not Unsightly Building*

EARLY VIEWS: Nearly every nineteenth-century publication on Toronto includes a view of University College. Notable among these is an engraving that appeared in the *Illustrated London News*, 5 November 1859, 454 (reproduced in Charles Patrick de Volpi, *Toronto, a Pictorial Record: Historical Prints and Illustrations of the City of Toronto, Province of Ontario, 1813–1882* (Montreal: Dev-Sco 1965), plate 43). Somewhat unusual is the photograph in Hodgins, *Establishment of Schools and Colleges in Ontario*, 3:47, which shows the college from the east, on its original entrance axis. The college's archives possess valuable early watercolours, including some by Governor General Head, and also photographs of the 1890 fire and its aftermath. Horwood Add. 5, box 1, also has photographs of the building after the fire, as well as views of the reconstructed woodwork. Of considerable interest are the photographs of the building's reconstruction accompanying Barlow Cumberland's 1901 *Canadian Magazine* article. The MTL/BR has photographs that show the site in the 1850s. The 1854 Passmore map of the site is another important source (NAC, National Map Collection, fiche 11452; copies in MTL/BR and Robarts Library, University of Toronto).

Toronto in the Camera, plate 17. *Tremaine's map* (1863), marginal vignette. *Canadian Illustrated News*, 8 November 1862 (copy in Royal Ontario Museum, Canadiana Collection, 978.359.221) (poor with regard to architectural detail); 22 January 1870, 188. *The Saturday Reader*, 29 December 1866 copy in Royal Ontario Museum, Canadian Collection, 978.359.253). *Canadian Architect and Builder* 9, no. 3 (January 1898), 22 (south elevation). Robertson, *Landmarks*, 1:35

Osgoode Hall, Toronto

Northeast corner of Queen Street and University Avenue
Cumberland & Storm
DATE: 1856–62. The east wing of Osgoode Hall, designed by John Ewart, was built in 1829–32. A west wing, designed by W.W. Baldwin, was added in 1833. In 1844 Henry Bowyer Lane was commissioned to alter the east wing and create a new west wing; the old west wing, which became Osgoode Hall's centre block, was also altered. Cumberland & Storm was chosen in November 1856 to rebuild the centre block, work on which was completed in 1860. Other, smaller, projects by Cumberland & Storm followed.
DRAWINGS: 1) Horwood (102)1–41, 1856–7 and 1861; site plan, plans and sections, and presentation drawings (all 1857); plans of outbuildings (1861). 2) Horwood 117(1–32), 1856–61; plans, elevations, details. 3) Horwood 128(1), 1861; plan of grounds and outbuildings. 4) Horwood (129)1–4, c. 1861; details of stained glass, marble floors, etc. 5) Horwood (130), c. 1861; details. 6) Horwood (131)1–66, c. 1861; details. 7) Horwood, 1861; joinery details. 8) Horwood (649)1, n.d.; fence. 9) Horwood (747), n.d.; perspectives. 10) Horwood (unclassified), five bundles of undated drawings, probably by Storm and related to his Osgoode Hall work of 1880
SPECIFICATIONS: 1) Horwood (C & S) no. 1, signed and dated Cumberland & Storm, 24 March 1862; boundary wall. 2) Horwood (C & S) no. 23, n.d.; heating service. 3) Horwood (C & S) no. 24, c. 1862; restoration of

east wing. 4) Horwood (C & S) no. 38, n.d.; additions to west wing. 5) Horwood (C & S) no. 42, n.d.; heating. 6) Horwood (C & S) no. 43, n.d.; restoration of west wing. 7) Horwood (C & S) no. 48, 1860; list of tradesmen with cost of work and materials, figures pertaining to the cost of restoring the east wing, and correspondence pertaining to the fittings on the bronze screens in the Convocation Room. 8) Horwood (misc.) nos. 2 and 3, n.d.; steam-heating. 9) Horwood (misc.) nos. 8 and 9, n.d.; heating and library fittings. 10) Horwood (misc.) no. 25, 1861; gatekeeper's lodge

TENDERS:

A) *The Builder*, 11 July 1857, 395. Bids listed as follows: 1) for excavation, masonry, and brickwork: Worthington Brothers, £15,229; Benjamin Walton £13,571. States that Walton was awarded the contract, but a statement of expense in the Law Society of Upper Canada Archives (Toronto), Index to Minutes of Convocation, vol. 1, 28 May 1859, indicates Worthington Brothers. 2) for carpentry and joinery work: William H. Pim, £9093; Thomas Storm, £8722; George Netting, £8492; Jacques & Hay, £7728 (Jacques & Haw awarded the contract). 3) for plasterwork: T. Teddan, £2524; J. Loftus, £2390; J. Foster, £2195; Hynes Brothers, £2070 (Hynes Brothers awarded the contract). 4) for glazing and painting: J. Carr, £2300; A. Hamilton, £2097 (Hamilton awarded the contract). *The Builder* added that 'The plastering of the library (estimated to cost about £1,800) is not included in the above [list of tenders]. The sum of £2,350 has to be added to the stonecutter's tender for the erection in Caen Stone of the arcade in the centre hall.'

B) Toronto *Globe*: 1) 28 May 1857, p. 3; closing date 6 June; for additions and alterations. 2) 8 February 1858, p. 3; closing date 10 February; for gas piping and steam-heating in the additions. 3) 18 April 1859, p. 3; closing date 21 April; for plumbing, gas-fitting, and heating. 4) 27 July 1861, p. 3; closing date 10 August; for fences, woodshed, coalshed, boundary wall, and gatekeeper's lodge.

5) 22 March 1862, p. 3; closing date 29 March; for boundary wall

CONTRACTORS: See 'Tenders,' section A, above.

SEE ALSO: Queen's University Archives (Kingston, Ontario), MG 20, 232, David Stirling Notebook. Stirling was an architect who worked for Cumberland & Storm during the 1850s. According to the Toronto *Leader*, 25 May 1859, he was clerk of the works for the Osgoode Hall project (the newspaper incorrectly spells his name as Sterling). His notebook contains a list of the firm's Osgoode Hall drawings with their reference numbers. Toronto *Globe*, 30 June 1857, p. 2 (description of works to be undertaken; construction about to begin). London *Building News*, 20 August 1858, 846 (detailed account of work completed). Toronto *Globe*, 28 July 1859, p. 2 (description and progress report); 7 February 1860, p. 2, cols. 4–5 (description of opening ceremony); 8 February 1860, p. x, cols. 3–4 (Chief Justice Draper's remarks on the building). Sylvester, *Sketches of Toronto*, 29–31 (description). Eric Arthur, 'Osgoode Hall,' *Law Society of Upper Canada Gazette* 6 (December 1972), 24–6. Crossman, *Early Court Houses of Ontario*, 1: 79–91. MacRae and Adamson, *Cornerstones of Order*, especially 153–5. Johnson and Maitland, 'Osgoode Hall.' Dendy and Kilbourn, *Toronto Observed*, 71–7 (includes discussion of earlier architectural history). Carter, comp., *Early Canadian Courthouses*, 109–11, 221. Angela Carr, 'The Architecture of Osgoode Hall' (independent studies paper, Department of Fine Art, University of Toronto, 1984) (includes extensive bibliography and appendixes listing early views and maps of the property). Carr, 'Hopkins, Lawford & Nelson.' Arthur, *Toronto*, 100–8, 114

EARLY VIEWS: MTL/BR, Picture Collection, T-12,015, Armstrong, Beere & Hime photographs (1856). *Tremaine's* Map of the County of York, 1869, marginal vignette. *Toronto in the Camera*, plate 25. *Canadian Illustrated News*, 23 April 1870, 393 (description), 394 (view); 20 September 1879, 180 (library interior). Arthur, 'Osgoode Hall,' 21 (1857 perspective drawing showing proposed renovations). Carr, 'Architecture of Osgoode Hall'

Masonic Hall, Toronto

18–20 Toronto Street, third floor
Furniture arrangements
Cumberland & Storm (?)
DATE: c. 1856–7. The Masonic Hall was designed by William Kauffmann in 1856–7 and was demolished in 1962.
DRAWING: Horwood (135b)1, n.d.; floor plans and details

Dendy, *Lost Toronto*, 61, claims that Cumberland & Storm was responsible for designing furniture for the Masonic Hall. Both architects were Masons, and the firm did design furniture for University College, but there is no evidence that strongly supports Dendy's claim.

The provenance of the drawing itself is uncertain. Although the lettering seems to be in Storm's hand, the fine detailing is not, and the sheet is not of a size typically used by the firm.

Frederic William Cumberland House, Toronto ('Pendarves')

East side of St George Street, north of College Street
Cumberland & Storm
DATE: c. 1856–60. The house, which has been added to many times, still stands, and is now the International Student Centre at the University of Toronto. It has also been known as Maplehearn House and Baldwin House.
DRAWINGS: 1) Horwood (59)1–10, n.d.; plans, elevations, sections, and site plan. 2) Horwood (133), n.d. 3) Horwood (701)1–8, 1883; Storm's additions
SPECIFICATIONS: Horwood (C & S) nos. 17 and 20, 1857
CONTRACTOR: William H. Pim

The Pendarves property was in Cumberland's hands by 1854: see AO, MU 3911, CFP, Wilmot Diary, 1 March 1854; AO, MU 3909, CFP, A-1-a, env. 4, FWC to Wilmot, 4 June 1854. On 19 August 1856 Cumberland wrote to his wife, Wilmot, that he was 'At [the] bank submitting the sketches for the house' (AO, MU 3909, CFP, A-1-a, env. 6). It is impossible to know, however, how closely those sketches resembled the finished house. On 21 July 1857 Wilmot recorded in her diary that 'The digging commenced at Pendarves.' Sometime in 1857 Cumberland and Pim signed a contract for construction of the house (see MTL/BR, Pim Papers, which also contain letters between the two men concerning the house). A subcontract between the painter Alexander Hamilton Pim, dated 24 August 1857, refers to 'the house you are now building.' Thomas Gibbs Ridout wrote to his wife Matilda on 19 July 1857 that Cumberland had said that Pendarves would cost more than Gibbs's Sherborne Villa, then being constructed. Gibbs also mentioned that 'I told you before he had altered his plan.'

Two years later, in a letter from Cumberland to Pim dated 29 October 1859 (MTL/BR, Pim Papers), Cumberland complained that Pim had stopped work on the house unnecessarily. An entry dated 6 February 1860 in one of Pim's notebooks (AO, MU 2321, Pim Papers, Notebooks 1859–60) shows that Pim was then working on the locks for the house. A little later he was constructing the fireplaces, and on 14 April he drew up a bill of extras (MTL/BR, Pim Papers). He died a few weeks later, and a letter from his executor to Cumberland, dated 5 July 1860, indicated that Cumberland still owed Pim $2535.82.

The Cumberlands probably moved into the house in 1859, but because there is no documentation on this point (there are no Wilmot diary entries for 1859), we cannot be sure. The 1861 *Toronto City Directory* confirms that Cumberland was then living on College Street.

Bank of Upper Canada Building, Sarnia

Cumberland & Storm
DATE: 1857
DRAWINGS: Horwood (112)1–8, signed and dated Cumberland & Storm, July 1857; plans, elevations, and sections (contract drawings)

TENDERS: 1) Toronto *Globe*, 13 July 1857, p. 3; closing date 20 July. 2) *London Free Press*, 15 July 1857, p. 3, col. 2

Frederick Widder House, Toronto ('Lyndhurst')

Wellington Place (south side of Wellington Street West, west of Spadina Avenue)
Additions and alterations
Cumberland & Storm
DATE: 1857 (demolished 1961). According to Eric Arthur, *Toronto: No Mean City* (Toronto: University of Toronto Press 1974), 70–1, 'A very complicated interlocking collection of buildings grew on a property bounded by Front and Wellington Streets, west of Spadina. It began with Vice-Chancellor Jameson's house (1837–44), which became part of "Lyndhurst," the house of Mr. Frederick Widder (1844–65). In 1860 the house was bought by Loretto Abbey and many changes took place.'
DRAWINGS: Horwood (116)1–26, signed and dated Cumberland & Storm, 30 July 1857; site plan, details, elevations, sections and plans
SPECIFICATIONS: Horwood (C & S) nos. 36–7, n.d., additions and alterations. No. 36 is the corrected version of no. 37.
TENDERS: 1) Toronto *Globe*, 10 July 1857, p. 3; closing date 18 July; additions and alterations. 2) MTL/BR, Pim Papers, 22 July 1857; tender for additions and alterations in accordance with Cumberland & Storm's plans and specifications. 3) AO, MU 2321, Pim Papers, Tenders, 1857, 'Tender for Mr. Widder's House,' £1804
SEE ALSO: Robertson, 5: *Landmarks*, 5: 446–8 (history)
EARLY VIEWS: MTL/BR, Picture Collection, T-10,091, T-11, 346–9. Robertson, *Landmarks*, 5:447 (two pen-and-ink views of the interior)

Bank of Upper Canada Building, Lindsay

Cumberland & Storm
DATES: 1857–8, 1861(?)
SPECIFICATIONS: 1) Horwood (C & S) no. 16,

1857; 'Works to Bank Agency'. 2) Horwood (C & S) nos. 21 and 22, 1858. 3) Horwood (C & S) no. 26, 1861 (Lindsay identification uncertain)

Model Grammar School, Toronto

North of Normal School
Cumberland & Storm
DATE: 1857–8 (demolished). The Model Grammar School was a short-lived teacher-training institution.
DRAWINGS: Horwood (100a)1–10, watermarked 1855; plans, elevations, sections, and details
SPECIFICATIONS: 1) Horwood (C & S) nos. 18(a) and 18(b). Horwood (C & S) no. 35 is a rough draft of 18(a) and 18(b), and 18(b) is a good copy of 18(a). Both 18(a) and 18(b) are signed by contractors William Storm and Thomas Snarr and dated 20 April 1857.
TENDERS: 1) Toronto *Globe*, 29 June 1855, p. 3, col. 2. 3) MTL/BR, Pim Papers, box 2, bid of £2444 for erection of Model Grammar School, 20 April 1857. 4) *The Builder*, 23 May 1857, 293 (lists contractors and their bids but does not say which bid was selected). 2) AO, Pim Papers, Tenders 1857, 'Tender for Model School,' 14 April 1857, amounting to £2444. Overleaf are notes showing Pim's own bid compared with those of other builders, and here he gives a different amount (£3202). The other builders listed are Snarr, Walton, Storm, Ellis, Netting, and Carroll.
CONTRACTORS: 1) Thomas Snarr. 2) Thomas Storm. 3) Alex Hamilton
SEE ALSO: Toronto *Globe*, 30 June 1857, p. 2 ('in course of erection'). *Toronto in the Camera*, p. 5 ('In 1857, a handsome new building, facing Gerrard Street, was erected for the Normal School'). *Toronto Normal School 1847–1947* (Toronto: School of Graphic Arts [1947]), 42–3 ('in 1857 a Model Grammar School, costing $39,269, was erected north of the Model Schools, and facing Gerrard Street. The project was never a success. Few students attended, the opinion being that the holding of a university degree was sufficient evidence in itself of ability to teach in a grammar school. The institution closed in

1863'). John George Hodgins, *The Establishment of Schools and Colleges in Ontario, 1792–1910*, 3 vols. (Toronto: L.K. Cameron 1910), 1:33, 36 (brief history; incorrectly dates construction to 1858)

St James's Cemetery Chapel, Toronto

635 Parliament Street, south of Bloor Street
Cumberland & Storm
DATE: 1857–61. The cemetery grounds were laid out by John G. Howard in 1844. Main entrance gates, an office, and a caretaker's lodge were constructed in 1905.
DRAWINGS: 1) Horwood (132)1–57, [1857]; complete suite of drawings. 2) Horwood (56)1, n.d.; pencil perspective. 3) Horwood (750)1, ink perspective
SPECIFICATIONS: 1) Horwood (C & S) no 32, n.d.; plasterwork. 2) Horwood (C & S) no. 46, n.d.; foundations and vaults
TENDERS: Toronto *Globe*, 16 September 1858, p. 3; no closing date; for excavation, brickwork, and masonry for foundations and vaults
CONTRACTORS: Worthington Brothers
SEE ALSO: Toronto *Globe*, 30 June 1857, p. 2 (brief description and notice of impending construction); 28 July 1859, p. 2 (brief progress report; chapel under construction); 26 February 1862 (description of chapel, recently opened). Sylvester, *Sketches of Toronto*, 33–4 (description of cemetery before chapel built). Robertson, *Landmarks*, 4:33–6. AO, MU 3984, University College Restoration Papers, *St. James's Cemetery, Toronto: Rules and Regulations* (1906) (this pamphlet describes recent changes to the property, including construction of the main entrance gates and the caretaker's lodge). Toronto *Telegram*, 23 June 1938 ('Chapel Near Forgotten Rededicated for Prayer'; reports on extensive renovations under cathedral architect F. Hilton Wilkes). Toronto *Globe*, 2 June 1945 (centennial article). Morriss, 'The Church Architecture of Frederic William Cumberland' (thesis). Morriss, 'The Church Architecture of Frederic William Cumberland' (article). Morriss, 'The Nine-Year Odyssey of a High-Victorian Goth.' MacRae and Adamson, *Hallowed Walls*, 158–9

(design of chapel incorrectly attributed to George and Edward Radford, through the mediation of Storm). Dendy and Kilbourn, *Toronto Observed*, 81–4
EARLY VIEWS: MTL/BR, Picture Collection, T-10,746–8, T-32,040

Plans for a cemetery chapel were first drawn up in the early 1840s. A memorandum in the St James's Cathedral Archives, prepared by rector Henry James Grasett, records the following on 30 June 1844 (p. 23): Cemetery recently purchased by church wardens. The ground, 60 acres, lying between Mr. Cayley's property and the Park, was bought of Mr. W.H. Boulton for £250 & £2,500 more will probably be expended on it. In the few weeks since purchase more than 1,000 stumps have been taken out: tastefully laid out, winding walks [footnote: 'Under the superintendence of J.G. Howard Esq.'] ... Will be planted in the spring. Bishop originated idea some years ago. Twenty already buried in it [footnote: 'On a little knoll, a short distance fm. the entrance, timber being prepared for erection of a small chapel 23 X 40 ft.']. The ground was consecrated on 5 June 1845. The memorandum records (p. 23): 'Morn'g p'r in Cath'l at 11. Bishop, Clergy & large Cong'n proceeded to Cemetery. Procession made circuit while Bishop at intervals repeated verse of 49th psalm, the rest respond'g then sentence of consecration.'

Plans for the chapel were then shelved for some years. The Toronto *Daily Leader*, 23 May 1855, mentioned that a 'Cemetery Chapel and Catacombs, St. James's Cemetery,' were then 'in progress,' but it is not until 1857 that we have firm evidence of Cumberland & Storm's being commissioned to design the building. At the vestry meeting of 11 May 1857 (p. 82), we find that 'The design of the Cemetery Chapel was submitted by Mr. Cumberland and discussed,' and on 19 May (p. 83) – a meeting at which Cumberland acted as secretary – it was ordered 'That the Cemetery chapel be erected according to the sketches submitted by Mr. Cumberland, but without outside vaults & that the Rector & Churchwardens be authorized to proceed immediately to the erection thereof in conformity therewith the best terms as to price what they may be able to make & provided that the Cemetery funds are appropriate therefore.'

The chapel opened for funeral services in 1861. On 21 April 1862 the minutebook records (pp. 98ff.) that it 'will be shortly opened for Divine Service on Sundays.' That the chapel's functions expanded to include regular church services is confirmed by a reference in the minutebook on 6 April 1863 (p. 104) to 'the labors of the Rev. Samuel J. Boddy, M.A., who has [been] transferred to the Pastoral Charge of the Cemetery Chapel' and has made 'praise-worthy efforts to establish an additional Church of England congregation in this City [that is, a chapel congregation].'

Edinburgh Life Assurance Company Building, Toronto

17–19 Wellington Street West
Cumberland & Storm
DATE: 1858 (demolished)
DRAWINGS: 1) Horwood (90a)1–10; unsigned and undated, but watermarked 1854; contract drawings. 2) Horwood (90b)1–2; floor plans, elevations
SPECIFICATIONS: Horwood (C & S) nos. 31 and 45, n.d.
CONTRACTOR: Worthington Brothers (see Worthington's obituary in *The Mail*, 27 December 1873)
SEE ALSO: Dendy, *Lost Toronto*, 66–7
EARLY VIEWS: *Toronto in the Camera*, plate 23 (includes description). *Construction* (December 1913), 466. Dendy, *Lost Toronto*, 67

University of Toronto Porter's Lodge, Toronto

University of Toronto grounds, near College Street gates
Cumberland & Storm
DATE: unknown, but presumably c. 1858
DRAWINGS: 1) Horwood (119)3, n.d.; paper sheet of details (project is identified on the back of the sheet; the sheet is erroneously filed with the drawings for the observatory director's house). 2) Horwood (120)5, n.d.; tissue drawing showing plan, elevation, and details
SPECIFICATIONS: Horwood (120)6, n.d.; three

pages of rough specifications in longhand, corresponding to the drawings listed above

This was a modest building, a morning's work for a clerk in Cumberland & Storm's office. Its importance lies in the conclusion that may be drawn from it, namely that Cumberland & Storm designed even the smallest buildings that were constructed for the university during the later 1850s.

Staff Quarters, Royal Magnetical Observatory, Toronto

University of Toronto grounds
Cumberland & Storm
DATE: c. 1858–9 (demolished). These buildings were usually called the Observatory Cottages. There was one single cottage and one double cottage.
DRAWINGS: 1) Horwood (120)1–8, 27. 2) Drawings in private collection, Toronto. All of these drawings are undated perspective elevations, c. 1858.
SPECIFICATIONS: Horwood (misc.) no. 14, n.d.; 'Three cottages (one double and one single) to be attached to the Magnetical Observatory in the City of Toronto on the western boundary of the University Grounds'
TENDERS: 1) Toronto *Globe*, 9 July 1857, p. 3; closing date 17 July; for three observatory cottages. 2) Toronto *Leader*, 27 December 1858, p. 3; closing date 3 January 1859 (attribution uncertain)
SEE ALSO: Toronto *Globe*, 30 June 1857, p. 2 ('The assistants to the observatory will be lodged in new and ornamented cottages, the grounds of which will be thrown open, and the out-door instruments will have handsome wooden coverings erected over them')
EARLY VIEW: MTL/BR, Picture Collection, T-12,964 (labelled 'Gardener's Cottage, 1890s')

Director's House, Royal Magnetical Observatory, Toronto

University of Toronto grounds
Cumberland & Storm

DATE: 1858–60. This house, built for George Templeman Kingston, the observatory's director and professor of meteorology at the University of Toronto, stood until 1901.

DRAWINGS: Horwood (120)9–26; plans, elevations, sections, details, and blueprints. (120)20 is signed and dated Cumberland & Storm, November 1858. (Erroneously mixed in with this group are drawings for the observatory cottages.)

TENDERS: 1) MTL/BR, Pim Papers, tender dated 17 December 1858 (to build the house for £1050, before 1 August 1859. 2) MTL/BR, Pim Papers, tender dated 1859 (to build the house for $2284, including subcontractors' work). 3) MTL/BR, Pim Papers, tender dated February 1859 (to build the house for £1050, excluding subcontractors' work)

CONTRACTOR: probably William H. Pim

SEE ALSO: UTA, A68-0012, Senate Minutes, vol. 2, p. 471, 20 September 1858 ('Read a letter from Messrs. Cumberland & Storm accompanied by a sketch for proposed residence for the Director of the Magnetic Observatory'; senate approves appropriation of £1085 from the University Income Fund for the erection of the house), vol. 2, p. 525, 30 May 1860 ('Read a letter from the Provincial Secretary, dated May 26, stating that the Governor-General in Council had been pleased to order that the Bursar be authorized to advance out of the Permanent Fund the sum of $10,000 to meet expenses incurred in buildings attached to the Observatory [i.e. the staff cottages as well as the director's house], and in the removal to the New Buildings')

EARLY VIEWS: MTL/BR, Picture Collection, T-11,374–8. *Canadian Architect and Builder* 9, no. 3 (March 1898), n.p.

Parliament Buildings, Ottawa

Cumberland & Storm
DATE: 1859 (competition entry under the pseudonym 'Odawah'; not built). The competition was advertised on 17 May 1859; the deadline date was 17 August.

DRAWINGS: 1) Horwood (121)1–5, n.d.; large competition drawings on linen. 2) Horwood (122)1–2, n.d.; slightly variant perspective water-colours. 3) Horwood (124)1–3, n.d.; site plan, interior perspective view of legislative chamber, and sepia perspective on linen in oval frame. 4) Horwood (125)1–10, n.d.; sundry pencil sketches

SEE ALSO: Letters from architects who requested particulars of the competition (but none from Cumberland & Storm) are preserved in NAC, RG11, A1, DPW vol. 105. Standard letters of rejection were sent out on 17 September 1859, notifying the losing candidates that their drawings would be returned to them (Cumberland & Storm did not receive one, although they were among the losers). Those are found in NAC, RG11, A1, DPW vol. 131, December 1858–October 1859. The entries were described and assessed in the *Report of the Commission Appointed to Inquire into Matters Connected with the Public Buildings at Ottawa* (Quebec: Josiah Blackburn 1862), 10–11. *Documents Relating to the Construction of the Parliamentary and Departmental Buildings at Ottawa* (Quebec: Hunter, Rose and Lemieux 1862), 5–18. Province of Canada, Sessional Papers, 1860, no. 2, 13; no. 11, 31–3; 1862, no. 3, 5–18. Young, '"Odahwah,"' and *The Glory of Ottawa*

Governor General's Residence, Ottawa

Cumberland & Storm
DATE: 1859–61 (competition entry; not built). This proposed building was commonly called Government House. Although Cumberland & Storm's 'Norman' design finished second in the competition to Fuller & Jones's 'Grecian' design, the government chose the former for construction. Before construction could begin, however, the project was abandoned, and the government eventually decided to renovate Rideau Hall for use by the Queen's representatives.

DRAWINGS: 1) Horwood (122)1–2, perspective water-colours. 2) Horwood (122a)1, pencil sketch of elevation. 3) Horwood (123)1–48, complete set of drawings. 4) Horwood (123a)1–20, more drawings. 5) Horwood (124)1–3, elevations and perspectives

TENDER: Toronto *Leader*, 9 January 1860, p. 3; closing date 22 February (other calls give closing date of 10 March)

SEE ALSO: NAC, RG 11, B1(c), DPW, vol. 769, no. 30,784, letter to Cumberland & Storm from the secretary of the Board of Public Works, 7 February 1860 (in response to incoming letter 45,160). The firm's plans were originally to have been ready for viewing on 8 January. The secretary wrote back 'to convey ... the very great dissatisfaction felt by the Government at this delay.' For a designation of the premiated designs, see *Documents Relating to the Construction of the Parliamentary and Departmental Buildings at Ottawa* (Ottawa, 1862), 12a.

D. Crawford House, Toronto

Cumberland & Storm
DATE: 1860 (demolished)
DRAWINGS: Horwood (126)1–3, n.d.; plans, elevations, and sections

House, Toronto

Isabella and Huntley streets
Cumberland & Storm
DATE: 1860
TENDER: Toronto *Globe*, 1 May 1860, p. 3; closing date 9 May

Three Commemorative Arches, Toronto

DATE: 1860

These arches were erected in September 1860 to commemorate the visit of the young Prince of Wales (later Edward VII) to Canada, an event that evoked a high degree of patriotic fervour in Toronto. The city's fraternal societies (and other groups) entered into a spirit of friendly competition to see who could build the most splendid arch. Prominent Torontonians who designed these arches included William Hay and Sandford Fleming. The Toronto *Globe*, 8 September 1860, p. 3, col. 6, had this to say: 'In the whole history of Toronto ... never before has she been dressed in such a profusion of decorations as in every street, almost on every house, she exhibited yesterday. All our citizens vied with each other [to see] who should do the most to indicate the joyous enthusiasm with which all classes were eager to greet the advent of the Prince of Wales; and the result was a display of evergreens and flowers, banners and bannerets, shields, drapery, and gorgeous illuminations such as never before have been equalled in Upper Canada.'

1) St George's Society Arch

Opposite the Globe Hotel, Yonge Street
A triumphal 'triple arch' (an arch with a centre opening flanked by smaller side openings)

The Toronto *Globe*, 8 September 1860, described the arches designed by Cumberland & Storm on p. 2, col. 5. The following is a description of the St George's Society arch: 'It is a very pretty and substantial structure, the design being from the pencil of Mr. F.W. Cumberland. This arch belongs to the Gothic order, and rests on two piers twenty feet in height, covered with evergreens. In the centre of the arch is a large and well[-]painted transparency of St. George and the Dragon, surrounded by a trophy, of the red ensigns of Old England. The two side arches are also covered with evergreens and flowers, and on their faces are the words "Albert Edward." From the embattlements of these arches rise a number of flags ... On the piers of the centre arch are shields, with Prince of Wales plumes and arms of England emblazoned on them. This structure has been much admired by visitors, and is highly creditable to the "Sons of St. George" who so proudly marched under it yesterday.'

2) Masonic Arch

King Street East, east of Leader Lane

From the *Globe*: 'It is a floral structure, and presents a very fine appearance. The arch proper springs from two massive piers covered entirely with evergreens, and rising to a height of twenty-five feet. On each side of the piers are shields with the compass and square, the level, the cornucopia, the mallet and trowels, and other Masonic emblems ... The arch is after the gothic style of architecture, and springs from the tops of the piers to a height of fifty feet from the ground ... The designers of this handsome structure are Messrs. Cumberland & Storm.'

3) Arch (Sponsor Unknown)
Foot of John Street
DRAWINGS: Horwood (641)1–8. (641)3 is dated 20 July 1860 and signed by Storm. It is one of the few drawings signed by him while still in partnership with Cumberland, and its style therefore provides a means of analysing (unsigned) drawings that one suspects are his.
VIEW: For a photographic reproduction of a water-colour rendering see MTL/BR, Picture Collection, T-10,246.

This was by far the most splendid of the arches erected for the prince's visit. From the *Globe*: 'This triple arch, the most beautiful erected in Toronto, or in fact in Canada or the Lower Provinces, according to the opinion of gentlemen well able to judge, and who have visited every city through which the Prince has passed, was designed by W.G. Storm, Esq. It is of a mixed style of architecture and is beautifully proportioned. It is sixty-five feet in height from the base to the apex, and, being situated at the top of the [temporary] amphitheatre and fronting the reception platform, the effect produced is brilliant in the extreme. The arch has a span of 27 feet and springs from piers 30 feet in height.'

Louis Shickluna(?) Frame Dwelling House, St Catharines

Cumberland & Storm (?)
DATE: 1861 (watermark)
DRAWINGS: Horwood (80)1–2; general plan, floor plans, and front elevation

The drawings read 'for Chickalunia' of St Catharines. Louis Shickluna (1808–80) was a St Catharines shipbuilder. Whether this project was executed is unclear. The Cumberland & Storm identification is based on the fact that the drawings are found with other Cumberland Horwood materials.

Victoria County Courthouse and Jail, Lindsay

26 Francis Street
Cumberland & Storm
PARTNER-IN-CHARGE: Storm
DATE: 1861–3. Soon after Victoria County was created in 1861, Cumberland & Storm, in an astute business move, submitted designs for a courthouse and jail to the new county council without being asked. The initial presentation was made by Cumberland, but much of the construction was supervised by Storm.
  The courthouse was renovated and the belltower removed in 1971. Further renovations were undertaken in 1986–7 by C.A. Ventin Architects, Simcoe, Ontario.
DRAWINGS: 1) Horwood (127)1–16, n.d.; for courthouse: plans, elevations, sections, and details. 2) Horwood (133)1–12 and fourteen unnumbered drawings, n.d.; for jail: plans, elevations, and sections
TENDER: Toronto *Globe*, 12 February 1862, p. 3; closing date 6 March
CONTRACTOR: John Kestevan
SEE ALSO: Province of Canada, Sessional Papers, 1862, no. 19, 'Second Report of the Board of Inspectors of Asylums, Prisons, &c.' (confirms that the plans were prepared by Cumberland & Storm). *Journal of the Proceedings and By-laws of the Provisional Council of the County of Victoria* (Lindsay: Victoria Herald 1863), especially 18–19 (meeting of 15 October 1861); 33–4 (warden's address of 9 December 1861); 57 ('Report of Committee on Building and County Property,' 6 February 1862); 118 (building committee reports on 31 October 1862 that since their last communication to council 'the progress of our Buildings has been so marked as to exceed our most sanguine expectations'); 122 (building committee reports on 16 January 1863 its 'extreme satisfaction of [*sic*] congratulating you [council] upon the near completion of your public buildings, and of your unparalleled success in obtaining so speedy a separation of this County from the County of Peterboro'). The first meeting of council in its new chambers was held on 15 May 1863. The total cost of the new buildings was recorded as $29,065.12.

MacRae and Adamson, *Cornerstones of Order*, 187–9. Crossman, *Early Court Houses of Ontario*, 3:551–60. Carter, comp., *Early Canadian Courthouses*, 218

EARLY VIEWS: AO, Picture Collection, two undated views of courthouse (S 14,274–5) and an undated view of the jail (S 14,279)

Lincoln County Jail, St Catharines

Cumberland & Storm
DATE: 1863
DRAWINGS: Horwood (134)1–44; plans, elevations, and sections. One set is signed Cumberland & Storm, 12 September 1863. Another is signed William G. Storm, September 1863.
TENDERS: 1) Toronto *Globe*, 21 August 1863, p. 3; closing date 14 September; for adding courthouse and offices to town hall (no architect cited, so Cumberland & Storm attribution is uncertain). 2) Toronto *Globe*, 8 December 1863, p. 3; closing date 28 December

Carter, comp., *Early Canadian Courthouses*, 220, cites sources showing that work was undertaken on the Lincoln County Courthouse in 1864, but there is no mention of Cumberland & Storm.

Norfolk County Courthouse and County Buildings, Simcoe

Cumberland & Storm
DATE: 1863 (competition design; not built)

The *Brant Expositor*, 5 June 1863, p. 3, col. 2, reported that

The Competition Designs for the erection of the Court House and County Buildings for the County of Norfolk was [sic] submitted on Monday last, at Simcoe. There were 12 designs sent in, some of which were very artistically executed particularly those prepared by Messrs. Cumberland & Storm, and the Messrs. Gundry & Mr. T. Thomas, and Mr. Pully, all of Toronto, also those sent in by Messrs. Fuller & Jones, the Architects of the Parliament Buildings in

Ottawa, and those sent by Mr. Horsy of the latter city, and those of Mr. John Turner, of Brantford. When hung on the wall they presented a very imposing appearance. The Committee after some time spent in investigating the designs called on the several architects to explain their plans, after which the interested parties were requested to withdraw. The Council after duly conceding the merits of the each [sic] awarded the first premium to Mr. John Turner of this town, and the second premium to Mr. T. Thomas of Toronto. This award, when it is considered with how many distinguished competitors he had to contend, reflects high credit on him as an architect, and adds another laurel to the town.

No Cumberland & Storm drawings for this project are known to have survived.

Colonel George Lawman House (Location Unknown)

Probably not Toronto
Cumberland & Storm
DATE: unknown
DRAWINGS: Horwood (136a)1–16, n.d.; working drawings on paper and tissues on linen (include many details)
SPECIFICATIONS: Horwood (C & S) no. 47, n.d.

Egerton Ryerson House, Toronto

East side of Victoria Street, north of Dundas Street
Cumberland & Storm
DATE: unknown
DRAWINGS: Horwood (136)1–13, n.d.; plans, elevations, and sections
EARLY VIEW: possibly MTL/BR, Picture Collection, T-11,481 (obscured view from 1886)

*Model School, Hamilton

DATE: supposedly 1848

Cumberland's obituary in the Toronto *Telegram*, 5 August 1881, p. 4, claimed that 'in 1848 the Model School at Hamilton was erected from his designs,' but no corroborating evidence has been found. The 1848 *Journal of*

Education for Upper Canada makes no mention of a new school in Hamilton, nor does the 1848 *Annual Report of the Normal, Model, Grammar and Common Schools in Upper Canada.* The 1848 *Report* (21) and the 1849 *Report* (29) state that no new schools were built in Hamilton during those years.

*Duncan Campbell House, Simcoe ('Lynnwood')

21 Lynnwood Avenue
DATE: c. 1850–1. The building, renovated by C.A. Ventin Architects, now serves as the Lynnwood Arts Centre. On 9 August 1975 it was designated a National Historic Site by the Historic Sites and Monuments Board of Can-ada. Drawings were prepared in 1965 and are now in the AO, Picture Collection, D 1341–3.
CONTRACTORS: John and George Jackson
SEE ALSO: Lewis Brown, *A History of Simcoe 1829–1929* (Simcoe: Pearce Publishing Co. 1929), 9–10 (no mention of Cumberland). 'Campbell Residence, Lynnwood Arts Centre, Criteria for Designation,' n.d., prepared by C. Smale for the Simcoe Local Architectural Conservation Advisory Committee, n.d. (tentative attribution to Cumberland)

No extant drawings or specifications connect Cumberland with this house, although local tradition attributes it to him. Cumberland was working in the area in the early 1850s on the Haldimand County Court House, and William H. Pim, one of the courthouse contractors, knew Campbell (there are some scattered references to Campbell in AO, MU 2321, Pim Papers, but nothing that can definitely be tied to the house). Cumberland may have known Campbell, who was a prominent figure in Simcoe. It is worth noting that the entrants in the courthouse design competition were asked to address themselves to Campbell, who would 'point out the spot,' according to a report in the *Toronto Globe*, 23 February 1850, p. 95, col. 5. There was later to be a family connection: Cumberland's daughter, Helen, married Campbell's son, Archibald Frederick, in Toronto on 20 February

1873. (AO, Office of the Registrar-General, master number 569037/rg.)

*University of Victoria College, Cobourg

Proposed additions
DATE: 1861
DRAWINGS: Two perspective drawings in the collections of Cumberland descendants Nancy Redner of Port Hope and Gordon de Saint Wotherspoon of Uxbridge

Because the drawings were passed down in the family, they were thought to have been Cumberland's work (variant designs for University College). However, a comparison of these drawings with Storm's Victoria College drawings in the Horwood Collection ((642)1–10; plans and interior and exterior perspectives) proves they were done by Storm.

*Schools (Location Unknown)

Toronto (?)
Cumberland & Storm (?)
DATE: c. 1861 (watermark on drawings)
DRAWINGS: Horwood (133a)1–4; plans, elevations, and sections

Although found among the Horwood drawings associated with Cumberland's practice, the paper and style of draftsmanship of these drawings are significantly different from drawings known to have been prepared by Cumberland & Storm.

*Church Spire (Location Unknown)

Cumberland & Storm (?)
DATE: unknown
DRAWING: Horwood (135a)1, n.d.; pencil sketch for spire of an Anglican church

A mere scrap. Although found among the Horwood drawings associated with Cumberland's practice, the paper and style of draftsmanship of these drawings are significantly different from drawings known to have been prepared by Cumberland & Storm.

3. NORTHERN RAILWAY PROJECTS

Newmarket Railway Bridge and Other Designs

Includes designs for other bridges, culverts, a
  sleeping-car, and a cattle-guard
Architect/designer unknown
DATE: c. 1850 (watermark)
DRAWINGS: Horwood (66)1–16, n.d.; mostly
  engineering details

Lower Credit River Bridge

Architect unknown (probably not Cumberland
  or his partners)
DATE: 1850s (?)
DRAWINGS: Horwood (79b)1, n.d. (watermark
  illegible)

Esplanade and Railway Terminus, Toronto Waterfront

Cumberland & Storm (?) (for Horwood (62)3–4;
  Frederic Cumberland and Sandford Fleming
  (?) (tentative identification from annotations
  on back of Horwood (68)1)
DATE: 1853
DRAWINGS: 1) Horwood (62)3–4, n.d., tissue
  plans. 2) Horwood (68)1, n.d.; 'Design for
  Railway Quay and Esplanade Services for the
  Frontage of the City of Toronto'
SEE ALSO: A petition from the City of Toronto for
  authorization to construct an esplanade was
  presented to the Legislative Assembly in 1852–
  3, and a bill granting the request was passed as
  16 Vict. (1853), c. 219 (later amended several
  times). There were frequent reports in the
  newspapers concerning the plans for the
  esplanade, for which the sum of £100,000 was
  set aside. See, for example, Toronto *Weekly
  Leader*, 27 July 1853; 3 August 1853; 24 August
  1853; 21 September 1853. The MTL/BR has a
  manuscript titled 'A New Plan of Esplanade
  and City Railway Accommodation.' This is a
  report by Cumberland as the railway's chief
  engineer to the president and directors, dated
  23 July 1853. In the MTL/BR are two relevant

plans from 1853, one titled 'General Plan of
  Arrangements for Railway Terminii in the City
  of Toronto with Provisions for Public Walks,'
  and the other, 'Plan of Proposed Railway
  Terminii in Connection with the Harbour of
  the City of Toronto.'

Wharf, Toronto

Cumberland & Ridout
DATE: c. 1853
DRAWING: Horwood (62)1, watermarked 1850;
  plan on paper

The wharf can probably be dated to the railway's expansion of its Toronto operations in
1853.

Engine-House, Car-Shed, Freight-House, and Two Tank Houses, Collingwood and Other Locations along the Line

Huron Street, Collingwood, and other locations
  along the line between Collingwood and
  Barrie
Frederic Cumberland (?)
DATE: 1854–5 (Collingwood buildings destroyed
  by fire, 1865)
TENDER: Toronto *Globe*, 9 January 1855, p. 3;
  closing date 18 January; for one-and-a-half
  storey frame freight-house in Collingwood
  (and other railway works in Toronto)
CONTRACTOR: William H. Pim
SEE ALSO: MTL/BR, Pim Papers, FWC (signing as
  chief engineer of the Ontario, Simcoe and
  Huron Railroad Union Company [the Northern Railway's predecessor]) to William H.
  Pim, 6 July 1854 ('You are hereby authorized
  to construct the following buildings for the
  service of the company. At Collingwood: An
  Engineer House of six bays, as per drawing; a
  Car Shed, 180 feet long, as per drawing. On
  the line between Barrie & Collingwood: a
  3rd-class Freight House; Two Tank Houses.
  The latter to be prepared & constructed with
  all possible despatch. The Collingwood
  buildings to be furnished in the 1st September next'). Huron Institute *Papers and
  Records* 2 (1914), 10 ('about ... 1855–56, the

railway built a hotel, and covered the tracks with a large shed, having three arched entrances for trains; the waiting room and ticket office were attached to the shed, and passengers could board the train without exposure to the weather. The railway hotel was rather a pretentious affair, roomy, large, three stories, with two rows of Dormer Windows in the roof. It was known as the "Armstrong House" [also as Week's Hotel and Ryley House], after the name of the landlord. It stood on the east side of the track, and two large willow trees still on the grounds, are the only marks left showing where this costly structure once stood. All these buildings were wood, and nearly all were destroyed by fire'); 3 (1939), 39 ('Ryley House was burned about 1881–82 by navvies on their way west to work on C.P.R. construction').

EARLY VIEWS: The City of Toronto Archives contains two photographic views of the Collingwood complex of buildings (SC 347 nos. 7–8). AO, CFP, Picture Collection, misc. E-1, box 40, folder 108 (photograph of Northern Railway elevator at Collingwood). Ten early views held by the Collingwood Museum are described in the Huron Institute *Papers and Records* 3 (1939), 30 (items 820–30). Two of them, of the car-shed and railway hotel, are reproduced in Arp, ed., *Reflections*, 8, 39.

Blacksmith's Shop, Toronto

Brock Street (now Spadina Avenue)
Additions
William G. Storm
DATE: 1861
SPECIFICATIONS: Horwood (misc.) no. 7, 1861

Company Offices, Toronto

Front Street and Brock Street (now Spadina Avenue)
William G. Storm (some drawings by Sandford Fleming)
DATE: 1861–2. In the Toronto *Globe*, 26 February 1862, Storm is described as the sole architect of the new company offices, which are to be

'of red brick with stone facings ... very substantially built, and fitted up with every necessary convenience.'
CONTRACTORS: 1) George Carroll (signs 1861 drawings). 2) Edward Galley
DRAWINGS: 1) Horwood (409)1–12, 11 November 1861. No. 1 is a paper sheet of details; no. 2 is a cover scrap; nos. 3–7 are dated linens; nos. 8–12 are paper originals of the linens, signed and dated by Sandford Fleming in his capacity as engineer of the Northern Railway. 2) Horwood (643)1–3, signed and dated 'William Storm, Architect, Romaine Buildings, 12 February 1862'; 'No. 2 Northern Railway offices. Yard, wall, shed, etc.'
EARLY VIEW: City of Toronto Archives, SC 347, no. 5 (exactly as in drawing (409)5, photograph c. 1862)

4. NON-ARCHITECTURAL WORKS

Harbour Works, Pickering (1)

Dredging and crib work, entrance to Frenchman's Bay
Cumberland & Ridout
DATE: 1850–1. These works were done for the Pickering Harbour and Road Joint Stock Company.
SPECIFICATIONS: Horwood (C & R) no. 3, 1851. Signed by R.A. Parker (president of the Pickering Harbour Company), Cumberland, and A[lfred] Brunel. Parker may have been the Reuben A. Parker for whom Cumberland prepared designs for the stores on Yonge Street listed in section 2 of this catalogue.
SEE ALSO: *Toronto Examiner*, 18 December 1850, p. 3. Toronto *Globe*, 22 March 1851, p. 139. An undated testimonial letter from Parker, included in a group of letters Cumberland attached to his 1852 application for the position of professor of engineering at the University of Toronto, remarks, 'I beg to state, as President [of the Pickering Harbour Company], that the Company has every reason to be well satisfied with the manner in

which your duties on its behalf have been executed; and that, as far as the work has yet progressed, it is highly satisfactory, and gives hope of being well fitted to its purpose, and an evidence of engineering skill' (AO, MU 3910, CFP, box 2, env. 2).

Harbour Works, Pickering (2)

Wharf and warehouse
Probably not by Cumberland & Ridout, but perhaps produced for the firm
DATE: 1851
DRAWINGS: Horwood (79c)1–5, n.d.
SPECIFICATIONS: Horwood (C & R) no. 7, November 1851; 'Specification of the several works necessary to be done in the construction of a wharf and Warehouse for the Pickering Harbour Company agreeably to the drawings furnished by the Engineers Messrs. Cumberland & Ridout'

Harbour Works, Port Hope

Crib work, east and west piers
Cumberland & Ridout
DATE: c. 1851–3
DRAWINGS: Horwood (79d)1–7, n.d.; details

The *General Report of the Commissioner of Public Works for the Year Ending 30th June, 1867* (Ottawa: Hunter, Rose & Company 1868), 89, notes that 'On the 3rd of January, 1852, the stockholders [of the Port Hope Harbour and Wharf Company, founded in 1829], sold the harbor to the town council of Port Hope.' The drawings might be connected with surveys for, or works anticipated from, this sale.

Subdivision Plan of Thomas Gibbs Ridout's Lots, Toronto

Between Duke Street (now Adelaide Street East), Duchess Street (now Richmond Street East), Caroline Street, and Ontario Street
Cumberland & Ridout
DATE: c. 1853–5 (although drawing is watermarked 1843)
DRAWING: Horwood (79f)1

Subdivision Plan of Building Lots, Toronto

Sherborne [*sic*] and Carleton [*sic*] streets
Cumberland & Ridout
DATE: c. 1853–5
DRAWINGS: Horwood (79g)1, n.d.

This appears to have been connected with Thomas Gibbs Ridout's lots on Sherbourne Street, about which he observed in a letter to his wife in 1853, 'there are several parties after my Sherborne Street properties – I would sell it, I think, for $16,000' (AO, MS 537, Ridout to Matilda, 3 June 1853). He was eventually forced to sell this property after the market crashed in 1857 (see DCB, vol. 9, 661–3).

Boat in Drydock and Drydock Facilities (Location Unknown)

Architect unknown
DATE: unknown
DRAWING: Horwood (79c)1, n.d.; pencil sketch

Subdivision Plan of Lots 3 and 4, First Concession, Township of York

Between Yonge and Parliament streets, Toronto
Cumberland & Ridout (?)
DATE: unknown
DRAWING: Horwood (79h)1, watermarked 1843

Cumberland worked on subdivision plans only during his early years in Toronto.

Subdivision Plan of Waterfront Lots, Toronto

South of King Street
Architect unknown
DATE: unknown
DRAWING: Horwood (62)2, n.d.; tissue plan

5. REFERENCE DRAWINGS

John Street School, Toronto

John and Mercer streets
Cumberland & Storm
DATE: 1855
DRAWING: Horwood (98)1, signed and dated
Cumberland & Storm, 12 March 1855; tissue
plan
SEE ALSO: Toronto Board of Education Records
Archive and Museum, Toronto Board of
Education Minutes, 1854–5. *Report of the Past
History, and Present Condition, of the Common or Public Schools of the City of Toronto*
(Toronto: Lovell and Gibson 1859), 48.
Honora M. Cochrane, ed., *Centennial Story:
The Board of Education for the City of Toronto, 1850–1950* (Toronto: Thomas Nelson
& Sons 1950), 36

The John Street School was one of three identical schools designed by Joseph Sheard and erected in 1855–6. It is unclear why Cumberland & Storm should have drawn up a plan for the school, unless it was for reference purposes connected with the firm's educational designs.

British and Continental Buildings

BUILDING AND LOCATION	HORWOOD NUMBER	DESCRIPTION
Bibliothèque Ste Geneviève, Paris, and Musée Nationale d'Histoire Naturelle (here identified as Museum of Natural History), Paris	(137a)1	Two plans on one sheet
Museum of Practical Geology, London	(138a)1–6	Watermarked 1856
Oxford University colleges	(1641)1–2	Magdalen, Christ Church, Brazen-Nose [Brasenose], Jesus, Lincoln, and Corpus Christi
Queen's College, Belfast	(1639)1, (1640)1	Plans
Queen's College, Galway	(1644)1–2	Floor plans
Trinity College, Dublin	(1643)1	Plan of student quarters
University College, London	(1642)1–13	Plans, elevations, and sections

Additional plans of Queen's College, Belfast, and Queen's College, Cork, are also found in the Horwood Collection, but had not been assigned catalogue numbers at the time they were consulted by the author.

Cumberland's Principal Executed Works

BUILDING AND LOCATION	FIRM	DATE	CURRENT CONDITION
Cathedral Church of St James, Toronto	Cumberland; Cumberland & Ridout; Cumberland & Storm	1849–53	Extant in good condition. Many changes to interior
Church of the Ascension, Hamilton	Cumberland & Ridout	1850–1	Interior destroyed by fire in 1887 and rebuilt in 1887–8 on same plan but with a larger chancel. Extant
Haldimand County, Courthouse and Jail, Cayuga	Cumberland & Ridout	1850–1	Courthouse destroyed by fire in 1922. Jail extant
St James's Parochial School, Toronto	Cumberland & Ridout	1850–1	Demolished in 1909
Normal School, Toronto	Cumberland & Ridout; Cumberland & Storm For some later works	1850–2	Demolished in 1963 except for central portico
Central School, Hamilton	Cumberland & Ridout; Cumberland & Storm	1851–3	Third storey and tower added in 1890. Other changes then and later. Interior no longer in original state
Seventh Post Office, Toronto	Cumberland & Ridout	1851–3	Exterior extant in good condition. Interior renovated for office use

BUILDING AND LOCATION	FIRM	DATE	CURRENT CONDITION
York County Courthouse, Toronto	Cumberland & Ridout; Cumberland & Storm for later works	1851–3	Wings remodelled, but centre block exterior remains as originally designed. Centre block interior renovated in 1977–8 for theatre and restaurant use
Ontario County Courthouse and Jail, Whitby	Cumberland & Storm	1852–4	Third storey added to the north end of the building in 1867. Many other changes since 1860s. Interior no longer in original state
Mechanics' Institute, Toronto	Cumberland & Storm	1853–5	Demolished in 1949
Royal Magnetical Observatory, Toronto	Cumberland & Storm	1853–6	Moved from original location in 1908 and renovated. Now University of Toronto Students' Administrative Council headquarters
Post Office, Hamilton	Cumberland & Storm	1854–6	Only the pedimented second-storey windows remain
Houses for William Hume Blake, Cumberland himself, Casimir Stanislaus Gzowski, David Lewis Macpherson, Thomas Gibbs Ridout, and John Ross, Toronto. Director's house and staff cottages, Royal Magnetical Observatory, Toronto	Cumberland & Storm	c. 1854–60	Only 'Pendarves,' Cumberland's own house, remains, though extensively renovated. Now University of Toronto International Student Centre
University College, Toronto	Cumberland & Storm	1856–9	Badly damaged by fire on 14 February 1890. Rebuilt in 1890–2 and renovated many times since
Centre block (and other works), Osgoode Hall, Toronto	Cumberland & Storm	1856–62 (centre block 1856–60)	Extant in excellent condition. Many additions since 1860s
St James's Cemetery Chapel, Toronto	Cumberland & Storm	1857–61	Extant in good condition, with renovations
Victoria County Courthouse and Jail, Lindsay	Cumberland & Storm	1861–3	Extensively renovated in 1971 and 1986–7

Cumberland's Architectural Library

Cumberland was a bibliophile with a large professional library. Some of these books he brought with him when he emigrated, others he purchased on his frequent trips back to England. What follows is not a full list of the books in Cumberland's library, but it includes most of the significant architectural works he owned. The University of Toronto's Thomas Fisher Rare book Library is the source of most of the items listed here.

As for other books formerly in Cumberland's library, in 1896 Cumberland's son, Barlow, compiled a list of the 1041 books in his own library; some of these were works on architecture, presumably inherited from his father (Barlow was not an architect).[1] A handful of Cumberland's books remained with Storm after 1872, later passed to Edmund Burke, and ultimately were deposited in the Horwood Collection of the Archives of Ontario.[2] Storm's library has been donated to the Thomas Fisher Rare Book Library by the Ontario Association of Architects (Storm was its first president).[3] To gain a fuller understanding of the books Cumberland may have drawn on when designing buildings, one should consult Storm's library; at the very least one may assume that both Cumberland and Storm had access to Storm's books, and possibly owned many of them jointly. Toronto bookseller Hugh Anson-Cartwright generously provided information about Cumberland-owned volumes formerly in his possession. Finally, the Metropolitan Toronto public library system has eight books with Cumberland's book-plate, relating to railways and other non-architectural subjects.

The following is a list, with library call numbers where applicable, of all the books known to contain Cumberland's book-plate or signature, except for the eight books just mentioned. There is also one volume that can be linked to Cumberland because it contains a handwritten dedication to the architect. Unless otherwise noted, the books listed here are found in the Thomas Fisher Rare Book Library.

Barry, Charles. *The Travellers' Clubhouse.* London: J. Weale 1839. (F-10 814)

Beauvallet, Pierre Nicolas. *Fragmens d'ornemens dans le style antique ...* 2 vols. in 1. Paris: Bance 1820. (FO-1 128)

Brandon, Raphael, and J. Arthur Brandon. *Parish Churches; Being Perspective views of English Ecclesiastical Structures ...* 2 vols. London: D. Bogue 1851. (G-10 427)

Britton, John. *Historical and Descriptive Essays Accompanying a Series of Engraved Specimens of the Architectural Antiquities of Normandy.* London: J. Britton 1828. (G-10 428)

– *The History and Antiquities of the Cathedral Church of Salisbury ...* London: Longman, Hurst, Rees, Orme and Brown 1814. (G-10 430)

[Bury, Jean Baptiste Marie]. *Modèles de serrurerie choisis parmi ce que Paris offre ...* Paris: Bance aîné [18—]. (M-10 39)

Bury, Thomas Talbot. *Remains of Ecclesiastical*

Woodwork. London: J. Weale 1847. (F-10 1140)

Caveler, William. *Architectural Illustrations of Warmington Church, Northamptonshire* ... Oxford: J. Parker 1850. (G-10 426)

Chambers, William. *A Treatise on the Decorative Part of Civil Architecture*. 2 vols. London: Priestley and Weale 1825. (E-10 2798)

Colling, James Kellaway. *Gothic Ornaments*. 2 vols. London: George Bell 1848. (G-10 479)

[Combe, Thomas]. *Illustrations of Baptismal Fonts*. London: J. Van Voorst 1844. (RB 106.244)

Demont, [—]. *Traité des premiers élémens d'architecture à l'usage des ouvriers en bâtimen*. Paris: Chez Jean 1836. This book was signed by both Cumberland and Storm and is found among Storm's books in the Thomas Fisher Rare Book Library. (stor/039)

Ecclesiological Society. *Instrumenta Ecclesiastica*. London: J. Van Voorst [1847–56]. 2 vols. in 1. Trinity College Library, University of Toronto (NA 4950 I 57 1847)

Flaxman, John. *Oeuvres* ... Paris: Bance aîné [1821?]. (F-10 648)

Gibbs, James. *Bibliotheca Radcliviana; or, a Short Description of the Radcliffe Library at Oxford Containing Its Several Plans, Uprights, Sections and Ornaments, on 23 Copper Plates, Neatly Engraved, with the Explanation of Each Plate*. London: The Author 1747. F-10 687

Gourlier, Charles Pierre. *Choix d'édifices publics projetés et construits en France depuis le commencement du XIXᵉ siècle*. 3 vols. Paris: L. Colas 1825–50 (G-10 499)

Grier, William. *The Mechanic's Pocket Dictionary: Being a Note Book of Technical Terms, Rules, and Tables, in Mathematics and Mechanics. For the Use of Millwrights, Engineers, Machine Makers, Founders, Carpenters, Joiners, and Students of Natural Philosophy*. 8th ed. Glasgow: Blackie & Son 1846. (Formerly owned by Hugh Anson-Cartwright)

Haviland, James. *Tables of Specific Gravity of All Substances* ... New ed. London: John Weale 1846. Although this book is signed 'Fred Cumberland,' it is found among Storm's books in the Thomas Fisher Rare Book Library. (RB 123603 P.O. Sci.)

Neufforge, Jean François de. *Recueil élémentaire d'architecture; plusieurs planches*. Paris: The Author 1757–68. (F-10 925)

Pugin, Augustus Charles. *Pugin's Gothic Ornaments Selected from Various Buildings in England and France*. [London: The Author 1831]. (G-10 422)

Pugin, Augustus Welby Northmore. *A Glossary of Ecclesiastical Ornament and Costume*. London: Henry G. Bohn 1844. (E-10 4434)

Ryde, Henry T. *Illustrations of the New Palace of Westminster*. London: Warrington 1849. (L-10 81)

Scott, W[illiam] B[ell]. *The Ornamentist, or, Artisan's Manual in the Various Branches of Ornamental Art: Being a Series of Designs Selected from the Works of Dietterlin, Berain, Blondell [sic], Meisonier, Le Pautre, Zahn, Boetticher, and the Best French and German Ornamentalists, with an Introductory Essay on Ornamental Art*. London: A. Fullarton 1853. (F-10 1138)

Soyer, L. Ch. *Modèles d'orfévrerie, choisis aux expositions des produits de l'industrie française* ... Paris: Bance aîné 1839. (F-10 645)

Strickland, William, ed. *Reports, Specifications, and Estimates of Public Works in the United States of America*. London: John Weale 1841. Although this book is signed 'Fred Cumberland, Toronto,' and has Cumberland's bookplate, it is found among Storm's books in the Thomas Fisher Rare Book Library. (stor/115)

Stuart, James, and Nicholas Revett. *The Antiquities of Athens, Measured and Delineated*. New ed. 4 vols. London: Priestly and Weale 1825–30. (G-10 423)

Thiollet, François. *Nouveau recueil de menuiserie et de décorations intérieures et extérieures* ... Paris: Bance aîné 1837. (F-10 655)

– *Serrurerie et fonte de fer récemment exécutées* ... Paris: Bance aîné 1832. (G-10 336)

Transactions of the Institute of Civil Engineers. Vols. 1–2. London: John Weale 1838. (sci per ff 1–2)

Vasi, Giuseppe Antonio. *Delle magnificenze di Roma antica e moderna* ... 10 vols. in 3.

Rome: Stamperia del Chracas 1747–69. (F-10 951)

Views of Rome. Bound volume of fifty views of Rome. No publisher, date, or text. The front flylead reads, 'In testimony of friendship to Frederick Cumberland Esq. Toronto from John Joseph Lynch Arbp. of Toronto,' 1 January 1872. Lynch was the Catholic arch-bishop of Toronto. (Formerly owned by Hugh Anson-Cartwright)

[Vignola, Giacomo Barozzi da]. *Règle des cinq ordres d'architecture selon Jacques Barozzio de Vignole. Dessiné et gravé par J. Michelinot.* Paris: Chez Jean 1836. (Horwood Add. 1, MU 3985)

NOTES

Note: See the Selected Bibliography for items cited in abbreviated form in the notes.

Preface

1 AO, MU 3909, CFP, A-1-a, env. 4, letters of 1854.
2 Charles Dickens, *Hard Times*, David Craig (Harmondsworth: Penguin Books, 1969 [1854]), 65.

PART ONE: LIFE AND TIMES

Chapter One: Early Life in Ireland and England

1 This is known as the 'Cuba Diary' and is found in AO, MU 3913, CFP, misc. A-5, env. 1 (with it is an envelope of sketches associated with his trip). Another manuscript relating to the Cuba trip is held by the MTL/BR. The jocular tone and oratorical quality of the diary suggest that it was written as a speech, with a view to publication.
2 AO, 'Cuba Diary,' n.d.
3 Fred Cumberland seems to have believed that the family was descended from Richard Cumberland, Bishop of Peterborough (1691–1718). This may be true, but no evidence has been found to substantiate it.
4 I would like to thank my aunt, Susette Simmins, who conducted research in Kippax and in the West Yorkshire Archives on my behalf.
5 See *Cumberland's British Theatre*, several editions of which may be found in the British Library.
6 The marriage record of Thomas Cumberland and Elizabeth Stevens is taken from an abstract of the register of Kippax Parish Church, Yorkshire: see *Publications of the Yorkshire Parish Register Society* 10(1901), n.p.
7 Cumberland's eldest sibling was Elizabeth Jessie, whose place and date of birth are uncertain. She may have been born at Old Wolverton on 31 March 1811, although this would mean that she arrived only three months after her parents married. The other siblings were Frances Sarah, born on 19 October 1812 and baptized on 7 March 1813; Thomas James, born on 2 April 1814 and baptized on 27 November 1814; John Charles, born on 25 March 1816 and baptized on 4 August 1816; and Caroline, born on 12 January 1818 and baptized on 15 February 1818.
8 Some sources erroneously give his birthday as 10 September. The sources also indiscriminately spell his name with or without the terminal 'k.' In those instances where Cumberland himself signed documents, he preferred the spelling without the 'k,' which is the choice that has been adopted here. His son Frederick Barlow's name was always spelled with the 'k.'
9 A misleading record concerning a Thomas Cumberland has led to some confusion about the family's economic and social status. On 30 September 1833 a Thomas Cumberland was appointed as an office-keeper in the Colonial Office at an annual salary of £100. Thomas resigned from this position on 5 February 1839. This Thomas, however, was not Fred's father, but Fred's *brother* Thomas, who was later incapacitated by mental illness. Unfortunately, the

coincidence of first names between father and son led the authors of the *DCB* entry on Cumberland to infer that Fred's father Thomas was the office-keeper in question. See J.C. Sainty, *Office-Holders in Modern Britain, vol. 6, Colonial Office Officials* (London: University of London Institute of Historical Research 1976), 29, 39. The Colonial Office was located among the government offices of Whitehall, near Downing Street: Sir Charles Jeffries, *The Colonial Office* (London: George Allen & Unwin [1956]), 113.

10 Lord Stanley's political career is sketched out by D.M. Young in *The Colonial Office in the Early Nineteenth Century* ([London]: Longmans 1961), 108–9.

11 The closest to an original source that I have found for this information comes from an 1852 document that Cumberland prepared in support of an application to the University of Toronto for the position of professor of engineering. See AO, MU 3910, CFP, box 2, env. 2.

12 Cumberland reserved his most acid remarks of any to be found in his letters for his stepmother, who, on the death of Cumberland's father, apparently took all the family money into her new marriage. See AO, MU 3909, CFP, A-1-a, env. 3, FWC to Wilmot, 16 October 1851, where he described her in the following terms: '[I saw] Mrs Cumberland's [*sic*] at Brompton. She has grown particularly stout & full in the bust & looks better than ever I saw her. Her mean pinched up starvation mouth is as cold and chilling as ever. She dresses most wretchedly, is positively dirty in her person & yet in the remains of old finery believes herself in the height of fashion. Did I tell you that she was now applying for a divorce from her husband & that she has ceased to use his name[?]'

13 See Gordon Huelin, *King's College London, 1828–1978* (London: King's College, University of London 1978).

14 Information concerning Cumberland's schooling comes from a 1984 letter from Frank Miles, then archivist of King's College. Cumberland's father gave as his address 14 Downing Street, and was able to call on Lord Gower to support Cumberland's application to the school, which suggests that the social standing of Cumberland's father was fairly high.

15 In 1863 Cumberland sent his son Frederick Barlow to Cheltenham College, where Alfred Barry, one of Charles Barry's sons, was headmaster.

16 See Adele M. Holcomb, *John Sell Cotman* (London: British Museum Publications Series 1978), 15–16. For a discussion of Cotman's career at King's College see Frank Miles, 'Boy's Own Artist,' *Country Life*, 26 October 1989, 80–3.

17 The papers have survived. See the AO, MU 3910, CFP Legal Papers, 1840–71, env. 1.

18 See Howard Colvin, *A Biographical Dictionary of English Architects, 1600–1840* (London: John Murray 1954), 622. Little is known about Tress. *The Builder*, a contemporary trade journal, contains three references to Tress: 13 December 1845, 603 (a tender call for building the Fever Hospital, which is described as being 'in the Land of Promise, Hoxton, for the parochial authorities of St. Leonard's, Shoreditch'); 19 August 1848, 407 (tenders for addition to the workhouse of St Leonard's, Shoreditch); 31 October 1857, 631 (Tress tenders unsuccessfully for the post of surveyor to St Leonard's, Shoreditch). In a report on the opening of the railway line from Tunbridge Wells to Hastings, the *Illustrated London News* of 14 February 1852 noted that 'the architect of the stations and the lodges for gate-keepers at level crossings is Mr William Trees [*sic*] of Finsbury-Square, who also designed the St. Leonard and Hastings stations.'

19 See Samuel Lewis Jr, *Islington as It Was and as It Is* (London: Henry Jackson 1854), 48, 59.

20 Cited by Nikolaus Pevsner, ed., *The Buildings of England, vol. 2, London* (1952 ed.), 226.

21 See the memorandum of agreement between William Tress and Cumberland in AO, MU 3910, CFP, Legal Papers 1840–71, env. 1.

22 F.W. Cumberland, 'To the Caput of the University of Toronto,' 2 February 1852, in support of an application for the position of professor of engineering at the University of Toronto. A copy is found in AO, MU 3910, CFP, box 2, env. 2. Unless otherwise noted, additional material concerning Cumberland's early career also comes from this document. The entry on Cumberland in Rose's *Cyclopaedia of Canadian Biography*, 705–7, suggests that the author had access to the 1852 document, but his account of Cumberland's early career is so muddled that it is

useless. Rose probably received his information from Frederick Barlow Cumberland.

23 See Biddle and Nock, *The Railway Heritage of Britain*, 193–7. A reference to Tress's designs for the Tunbridge Wells and Hastings Railway are found in the *Sussex Advertiser*, 3 February 1852, 5, where he is described as the company's architect and surveyor. A similar report appears in the *Hastings and St. Leonard's News*, 2 February 1852, 4.

24 The sketch-books are in Horwood Add. 5, box 8. See the introduction to the *catalogue raisonné* for a description of the Horwood Collection and an explanation of its classification system.

25 This letter is found in AO, MU 3910, CFP, box 2, env. 2, Testimonials, 1839–53.

26 The letter is in the collection of Nancy Redner of Port Hope, who is a descendant of the Cumberland family.

27 AO, MU 3910, CFP, box 2, env. 2, Testimonials, 1839–53.

28 Public Record Office (London), ADM 12/411, 41–18.

29 Wilmot was born on 17 August 1818 and died on 9 May 1899.

30 The letters are in AO, MU 3909, CFP, A-1-a, and other series. There are twenty-nine letters from 1843 and seventeen from 1844. Fred and Wilmot's correspondence appears to have tapered off after their marriage in 1845, but they continued to write whenever one or the other – usually Fred – was travelling. The earliest letters were crisscrossed – in some cases three times – to save on postage; as a result, some are virtually illegible. In later life, when Cumberland's finances had improved and he did not have to worry about postage costs, he wrote letters that were up to twenty sheets long. The letters supply a great deal of information on Cumberland's interests, and discuss architecture as well as family matters. They are particularly lengthy – and correspondingly valuable for historical purposes – in 1851 (when Cumberland was a delegate to the Great Exhibition in London), and in 1856, when Cumberland was conducting research in Europe in preparation for designing University College.

31 AO, MU 3909, CFP, A-1-a, env. 1, FWC to Wilmot, [19 August 1843].

32 According to A.W. Ward and A.R. Waller, eds., *The Cambridge History of English Literature*, vol. 12, pt. 1, *The Nineteenth Century* (Cambridge, England: University Press 1915), 246, '*The Vicar of Wrexhill* is a book of virulent malignity, in which the chief character is a clergyman of evangelical beliefs. He is licentious, suave, cold and cruel; and the force with which his vices are shown to be mingled with his religion could only have been displayed by a novelist of courageous and forceful mind.'

33 AO, MU 3909, CFP, A-1-a, env. 1, FWC to Wilmot, [28 August 1843].

34 AO, MU 3909, CFP, A-1-a, env. 1, FWC to Wilmot, [23 December 1843].

35 AO, MU 3909, CFP, A-1-a, env. 1, FWC to Wilmot, [postmarked 3 July 1843].

36 AO, MU 3909, CFP, A-1-a, env. 1, FWC to Wilmot, [postmarked 26 July 1843].

37 AO, MU 3909, CFP, A-1-a, env. 1, FWC to Wilmot, [17 July 1843].

38 AO, MU 3909, CFP, A-1-a, env. 1, FWC to Wilmot, [7 August 1843]. In the same letter he swore her to secrecy regarding a pending operation on his brother Tom, whose health had continued to decline.

39 AO, MU 3909, CFP, A-1-a, env. 1, FWC to Wilmot, [9 August 1843 (morning)].

40 AO, MU 3909, CFP, A-1-a, env. 1, FWC to Wilmot, [9 August 1843 (evening)].

41 Edward George Bulwer-Lytton (1803–73). In 1859 the Pre-Raphaelite follower Arthur Hughes painted a poignant work titled *The Long Engagement* (Birmingham Museums and Art Gallery, England).

42 Probably Hamilton Hartley Killaly (1800–74), who in 1841 was appointed chairman of the Board of Public Works of the Province of Canada. Killaly was born in Dublin and emigrated to Upper Canada in 1834. Cumberland may have met Killaly when Killaly returned to England during the 1840s.

43 AO, MU 3909, CFP, A-1-a, env. 1, FWC to Wilmot, [2 November 1843].

44 AO, MU 3909, CFP, A-1-a, env. 1, FWC to Wilmot, [13 November 1843].

45 AO, MU 3909, CFP, A-1-a, env. 2, FWC to Wilmot, [11 September 1844].

46 AO, MU 3909, CFP, A-1-a, env. 2, FWC to Wilmot, [12 September 1844].

47 AO, MU 3909, CFP, A-1-a, env. 2, FWC to Wilmot, [postmarked 23 September 1844].

48 Cumberland provided a number of drawings that were engraved for publication in the *Papers on Subjects Connected with the Duties of the Corps of Royal Engineers* 9 (1847). He also wrote an article on this work: 'Iron Roofs Erected over Building Slips, Nos. 3 and 4, in Her Majesty's Dockyard, Portsmouth,' in the same volume, pp. 59–65.

49 This genealogical information comes from the records of the Church of Jesus Christ of Latter-Day Saints.

50 In 1848 the Cumberlands had a second son, Walter Ridout, who was born on 30 October, but died on 5 February 1850: Toronto *British Colonist*, 8 February 1850, p. 3. The records of St James's Cemetery, however, give his name as Walton Rideout.

51 For Thomas Gibbs Ridout, see *DCB*, vol. 9, 661–3.

52 For Joseph Davis Ridout (1809–84), see *DCB*, vol. 9, 735–6. Ridout was a director of the Bank of Upper Canada and also on the board of the Northern Railroad. It is not known when Joseph and Julia married. Julia died in 1852, and Joseph married Cumberland's sister Caroline on 16 November 1854.

53 This letter, dated 30 March 1847, is in AO, MU 7176, CFP, Correspondence Series F, which contains Cumberland's letters of 1847.

54 Some of the copies mentioned are with F.B. Cumberland's business papers in AO, MU 3921, CFP, box 13, env. 1. Others are found in AO, MU 7176, CFP, Testimonials. The testimonials were indeed glowing.

55 This is the only reference we have to Cumberland undertaking private commissions in England. Although it reasonably allows us to infer that he had already begun private architectural practice before emigrating, how many commissions he obtained, and of what sort, is impossible to determine.

56 AO, MU 7176, CFP, Correspondence Series F, FWC to Thomas Ridout Sr, 17 June 1847.

57 Shawbridge, an Englishman, was later an important board member and bondholder of Canada's Northern Railway, an enterprise with which Cumberland had a long association (see chapter 5).

58 AO, MS 537, Ridout Papers, Thomas Ridout Jr to his mother, 18 June 1847. Ridout, apparently, was studying architecture while in London, but it is not known with whom and for how long. On his return to Toronto, the newspapers mentioned an absence of 'several years.'

59 It seems likely that they came to Canada on the *Victoria* because Cumberland mentioned in an 1851 letter to Wilmot that they had once sailed together on that ship. See AO, MU 3909, CFP, A-1-a, env. 3, FWC to Wilmot, 18 September 1851.

60 *DCB*, vol. 9, 225. The original source for this information is Rose's *Cyclopaedia of Canadian Biography*, 705. Rose provides the most ample discussion of Cumberland's early career, although the details are often muddled. Given that he seems to have derived his information from Barlow, the assertion concerning the route the Cumberlands took might very well be correct.

Chapter Two: Constructing a Canadian Career

1 *Toronto Examiner*, 15 September 1847, p. 3, col. 1.

2 *Toronto Examiner*, 22 September 1847, p. 2, cols. 2–3, 6. Of course, immigrant living conditions had long concerned people interested in public health reform. One worry was insanitary water supplies, which led to cholera epidemics in Canada from 1832 to 1871. See Geoffrey Bilson, *A Darkened House: Cholera in Nineteenth-Century Canada* (Toronto: University of Toronto Press 1980)

3 *Toronto Examiner*, 27 October 1847, p. 2, col. 2.

4 The *Herald* reprinted its entire report on the visit (with some additions) on 21 October 1847, p. 2, cols. 1–7, and p. 3, cols. 1–2, and noted that Cumberland and his wife had been presented to the Countess of Elgin, the governor general's wife.

5 Smith, ed., *Young Mr. Smith in Upper Canada*, 111. Smith also described the Toronto immigrant sheds, which were filled mostly with unfortunates who had fled the Irish potato famine.

6 See, in particular, Greer and Radforth, eds., *Colonial Leviathan*, which has chapters on transportation, education, and railways, and McCalla, *Planting the Province*.

7 For a discussion of some of these developments, see Bruce Curtis, *True Government by Choice Men?*

8 Despite its age, Stephen Leacock, *Baldwin, Lafontaine, Hincks: Responsible Government* (Toronto: Morang & Co. 1911), 292ff., contains much useful information on the government initiatives of these years and on the men behind them.

9 For the history of the University of Toronto, see Richardson, *A Not Unsightly Building*.

10 For a discussion of the controversy over the location of the Province of Canada's seat of government, see Knight, *Choosing Canada's Capital*.

11 AO, RG21, Municipal Documents Collection, Home District Council Minutes, 1848, 20, and Appendix, 42.

12 Copies of some of these are found in AO, MS 385, reel 4, Calendar to Toronto City Council Papers, 26 February–13 November 1849.

13 Howard's diaries are in the MTL/BR and in AO, MU 855. For references to Cumberland, see MTL/BR, John G. Howard Papers, Office Journals, 10, 18, 19, 25, 26, 27, 30 April, 2, 3, 10, 15, 26, 28 May, 5 June 1849.

14 Howard's journal entries on Cumberland took on a negative tone after Cumberland won the St James's Cathedral competition. See AO, MU 855, John G. Howard Work Journal, vol. 3, 12 September 1849: 'Mr. Young and Johnson [the judges] awarded the premiums [for St James's] according to their own views but contrary to what I consider just.' Also 10 October 1849: 'Saw Mr. Cumberland on the corner of King & Church Street had words with him.'

15 AO, RG 21, Municipal Documents Collection, York County Council Minutes, 1850, [15].

16 AO, York County Council Minutes, 1853, [12], 58–9.

17 For records of this competition, see AO, GS 2022, St Catharines, Lincoln County Minutebooks, 1845–55.

18 AO, MS 74, vol. 8, William Hamilton Merritt Papers, miscellaneous letter 160, Thomas G. Ridout to Merritt, 10 June 1848.

19 Robert W.S. Mackay, *The Canada Directory ...* (Montreal: John Lovell 1851), 426. According to this source, Cumberland & Ridout's office was located on the corner of Nelson and King streets.

20 Toronto *British Colonist*, 9 August 1850, p. 2, col. 7. See the *catalogue raisonné* for other sources.

21 There are many histories of Toronto during this period. One source that provides convenient references to earlier literature is Careless, *Toronto to 1918*.

22 AO, Home District Council Minutes, 1848, 72.

23 *Rowsell's City of Toronto and County of York Directory, for 1850–1*.

24 *British Colonist*, 9 April 1850, p. 2, col. 7.

25 See *Toronto Examiner*, 2 January 1850, p. 3. See also *British Colonist*, 8 March 1850, p. 4; *Toronto Examiner*, 20 March 1850, p. 1; *Globe*, 9 April 1850, p. 172, col. 5.

26 For more details concerning these architectural commissions, see the *catalogue raisonné*.

27 AO, York County Council Minutes, 1851, p. [19].

28 Young, *Early Engineering Education at Toronto*, 11–14. For the testimonials in support of his application, see AO, MU 3910, CFP, box 2, env. 2.

29 *British Colonist*, 23 July 1852, p. 2, col. 5. (The railway had been founded in 1849 as the Ontario, Toronto, Simcoe, and Huron Railroad Union Company.) Other sources also widely report this development. See NAC, MG 29, B1, Sandford Fleming Papers, vol. 12, folder 79. The *Canadian Institute Journal* 1 (1852–3), 23, reported that H.C. Seymour, the railway's Chief engineer, had resigned, that Cumberland was his successor, and that Cumberland had 'already entered upon his duties.'

30 The documentary sources for Storm are in chapter 9.

31 See *Globe*, 26 August 1852, p. 411; and *Daily Colonist*, 25 August 1852, p. 3, col. 3.

32 Cumberland's service was actually with the United Counties of York, Ontario, and Peel, which had been united on 1 January 1852. On 30 December 1853 Ontario County was separated from the United Counties, and on 1 January 1867 Peel County was separated from York County.

33 As quoted in the *Anglo-American Magazine* 1 (July–December 1852), 362.

34 See the entry in the *catalogue raisonné*. Some discussion of the various schemes for an esplanade can be found in G.P. deT. Glazebrook, *The Story of Toronto* (Toronto: University of Toronto Press 1971), 121–3.

35 According to Cumberland's obituary in the Toronto *Telegram*, 5 August 1881, 4, he was initiated as a Mason on 16 August 1853.

Chapter Three: Cumberland and the Canadian Interpretation of the Victorian Concept of Progress

1 On this subject, see Berger's brilliant *Science, God, and Nature in Victorian Canada*, and McKillop, *A Disciplined Intelligence*.

2 On Victorian science generally, see Barber, *The Heyday of Victorian Science*.

3 For a discussion of the mechanics' institutes, and references to earlier literature, see Geoffrey Simmins, *The Ontario Association of Architects: A Centennial History, 1889–1989* (Toronto: Ontario Association of Architects 1989), 21–2. The Toronto Mechanics' Institute was established in 1832.

4 MTL/BR, Toronto Mechanics' Institute Papers, E1, Members, vol. 1, 1833–48. W.G. Storm is shown as a junior member in 1845, and as a life member by 1848.

5 The Mechanics' Institute building was used by the provincial government while it was in Toronto from 1855 to 1859, and then returned to the Mechanics' Institute. Cumberland was not always available to complete necessary renovations. In 1860 a committee found that the architects were not paying proper attention to the work, according to a report in the Toronto *Daily Leader*, 31 August 1860, p. 2, col. 2. Although Cumberland addressed a public meeting 'in a very animated manner' in support of his firm, the Institute eventually relieved him of the remaining work and gave it to William Thomas, as can be inferred from the notice relating to tender calls to be delivered to Thomas, which appeared in the *Daily Leader*, 21 November 1860, p. 3, col. 6.

6 The manuscript of Cumberland's lecture, and a copy of the printed version that appeared in the *Hamilton Spectator* on 13 December 1848, can be found in AO, MU 3910, CFP, box 2, env. 1. The printed version differs significantly from the manuscript, although the differences are not crucial for the purposes of the discussion that follows.

7 AO, MU 3910, CFP, box 2, env. 1, manuscript of Cumberland lecture, 6.

8 Ibid.

9 Ibid., 2.

10 Ibid., 2–3.

11 Ibid., 3

12 Ibid., 20.

13 Ibid., 21.

14 Ibid., 29.

15 The precise source or sources of Cumberland's quotations from McCulloch have not been identified, but presumably the quotations come from such publications as *A Descriptive and Statistical Account of the British Empire: Exhibiting Its Extent, Physical Capacities, Population, Industry, and Civil and Religious Institutions*, 3rd ed. (London: Longman, Brown, Green and Longmans 1847), or *A Discourse on the Rise, Progress, Peculiar Objects, and Importance, of Political Economy: Containing an Outline of a Course of Lectures on the Principles and Doctrines of That Science* (Edinburgh: A. Constable 1824).

16 Cf. John Ramsey McCulloch, ed., *An Inquiry into the Nature and Causes of the Wealth of Nations, by Adam Smith* (Edinburgh: Adam and Charles Black 1850), p. xxxi: 'Hobbes seems to have been one of the first who was fully impressed with a conviction of the paramount importance of labour in the production of wealth. At the commencement of the 24th chapter of the *Leviathan*, published in 1651, he says, "The *nutrition* of a commonwealth consisteth in the *plenty* and *distribution* of *materials* conducing to life. As for the plenty of matter, it is a thing limited by nature to those commodities which, from (the two breasts of our common mother) *land* and *sea*, God usually either freely giveth, or for labour selleth to mankind. For the matter of this nutriment, consisting in animals, vegetables, minerals, God hath freely laid them before us, in or near the face of the earth; so as there needeth no more but the labour and industry of receiving them. Insomuch that *plenty dependeth* (next to God's favour) *on the labour and industry of men.*"

'Locke, however, had a much clearer apprehension of this doctrine. In his *Essay on Civil Government*, published in 1639, he has entered into a discriminating and able analysis to show that is from labour that the products of the earth derive almost all their value. "Let any one consider," says he, "what the difference is between an acre of land planted with tobacco or sugar, sown with wheat or barley, and an acre of the same land lying in common, without any husbandry upon it, and he will find that the improvement of labour makes the far greater part of the value. I think it will be but a very modest computation to say, that of the products of the earth useful to the life of man, *nine-tenths* are the effects of labour; nay, if we will rightly consider things as they come to our use, and cast up the several expenses about them, what in them is purely owing to nature, and what to labour, we shall find, that in most of them *ninety-nine hundredths* are wholly to be put on the account of labour."'

I have used the 1850 edition, but Cumberland would have consulted the 1838 edition.

17 AO, MU 3910, CFP, box 2, env. 1, manuscript of Cumberland lecture, 23.

18 See Wallace, ed., *The Royal Canadian Institute Centennial Volume.*

19 'Notes and Queries,' *Canadian Institute Journal* 1 (1852–3), 42.

20 The Royal Canadian Institute Papers are now in the Thomas Fisher Rare Book Library, University of Toronto (MS 230).

21 William G. Storm, Cumberland's future partner, was also active in the Canadian Institute. The records show that Storm attended its meetings as early as 1850.

22 This information comes from the masthead of the *Canadian Institute Journal.* See also Wallace, ed., *Royal Canadian Institute Centennial Volume*, 186, where Cumberland is listed as a charter member and as a member of the standing committee appointed in 1849. The *Centennial Volume* also records that he was corresponding secretary from 1851 to 1852, vice-president from 1852 to 1853, and recording secretary from 1854 to 1856.

23 Cumberland was also a Canadian delegate to the New York Exhibition in 1852 (Toronto *Weekly Leader*, 6 October 1852, p. 3, col. 4) and to the Paris Exhibition in 1855. Next to nothing is known about Cumberland's involvement in the Paris Exhibition. The papers of the organizing committee for the Canadian delegation to the Paris Exhibition are in MTL/BR, and show that on 9 December 1854 Cumberland was one of twelve men present at a meeting of the organizing committee. Cumberland was also appointed to serve on the subcommittee concerned with architecture and engineering, but whether that subcommittee met is unclear. The subcommittee had thirteen members, including Alfred Brunel and Sandford Fleming.

24 See NAC, MG 24, D16, Isaac Buchanan Papers, vol. 22, 18881–901, FWC to Isaac Buchanan, 6 March 1851.

25 AO, MU 3909, CFP, A-1-a, env. 3, FWC to Wilmot, 25 October 1851.

26 Ibid.

27 AO, MU 3909, CFP, A-1-a, env. 3, FWC to Wilmot, 25 October 1851.

28 AO, MU 3909, CFP, A-1-a, env. 3, FWC to Wilmot, 11 November 1851.

29 Ibid.

30 AO, MU 3909, CFP, A-1-a, env. 3, FWC to Wilmot, 5 November 1851.

31 AO, MU 3909, CFP, A-1-a, env. 3, FWC to Wilmot, 11 November 1851.

32 AO, MU 3909, CFP, A-1-a, env. 3, FWC to Wilmot, 11 December 1851.

Chapter Four: Midcareer, Full Stride

1 AO, MU 3909, CFP, A-1-a, env. 4, FWC to Wilmot, 21 July 1854.

2 This was the Toronto Pressed Brick Company, a venture whose principal partners were Cumberland, John Worthington, Thomas C. Bramley (Wilmot's brother), and John Hillyard Cameron. Cumberland, Worthington, and Cameron were its directors. The firm was operating by 1855, according to a report in the *Daily Colonist*, 20 June 1855, p. 2, cols. 2–3, although it was unincorporated at that time. It was incorporated on 27 May 1857: 20 Vict. (1857), c. 177 (Can.). In the preamble it was mentioned that the investors had 'expended large sums of money in the purchase of machinery.' Cumberland's business papers in the AO make it clear that by

1860 the company had lost substantial amounts of money, and no more is heard of it after 1860.

3 Two other children did not survive infancy: Ernest August was born in May 1855 and died on 26 October 1857. Evelyn Matilda was born on 24 January 1860 and died on 4 April 1861.

4 AO, MU 3909, CFP, A-1-a, env. 4, FWC to Wilmot, 4 June 1854. On 1 March 1854 Wilmot recorded, 'Drove out to see our place Pendarves': AO, MU 3911, CFP, Wilmot Diary.

5 These will be discussed in Part Two.

6 AO, MU 3909, CFP, A-1-a, env. 4, FWC to Wilmot, 9 June 1854.

7 AO, MU 3909, CFP, A-1-a, env. 4, FWC to Wilmot, 2 July 1854.

8 AO, MU 3909, CFP, A-1-a, env. 4, FWC to Wilmot, 6 August 1854.

9 AO MS 527, Ridout Papers, Thomas Ridout to Matilda Ridout, 24 June 1855. 'That partnership with Worthington' was the Toronto Pressed Brick Company.

10 AO, MU 3909, CFP, A-1-a, env. 4, FWC to Wilmot, 26 August 1854.

11 AO, MU 3909, CFP, A-1-a, env. 4, FWC to Wilmot, 17 September 1854.

12 AO, MU 3909, CFP, A-1-a, env. 4, FWC to Wilmot, 14 May 1854.

13 AO, MU 3909, CFP, A-1-a, env. 4, FWC to Wilmot, 4 June 1854.

14 AO, MU 3909, CFP, A-1-a, env. 4, FWC to Wilmot, August 1854.

15 Wilmot's diary is catalogued as AO, MU 3911–13.

16 As in other instances, there may have been letters that have since gone astray. Wilmot recorded in her diary receiving many letters from Cumberland, but only a few remain among the family papers. Frank Walker's works (listed in the bibliography) contain many quotations from letters written by Cumberland in the 1850s, the originals of which cannot be located today. Walker published his research more than thirty-five years ago. Perhaps the letters he used will eventually resurface.

17 And not for an entire year, as stated, for example, in Rose's *Cyclopaedia of Canadian Biography*, 706.

18 AO, MU 3909, CFP, A-1-b, env. 4, FWC to Wilmot, 14 March [1856] (this and several other letters of 1856 are incorrectly filed in envelope 4 with letters of 1853).

19 Ryerson entrusted his daughter to Cumberland, who was to show her the sights. Later, Cumberland offered Ryerson advice concerning the development of his museum for the Normal School in Toronto. For a history of the museum, see Johnson, 'A Colonial Canadian in Search of a Museum.'

20 AO, MU 3909, CFP, A-1-b, env. 4, FWC to Wilmot, 14 March [1856].

21 AO, MU 3909, CFP, A-1-b, env. 4, FWC to Wilmot, 21 March [1856].

22 Also known as the Tractarians. This was a religious movement named after its founder, the theologian George Pusey (1800–82).

23 AO, MU 3909, CFP, A-1-b, env. 4, FWC to Wilmot, [21 March 1856].

24 AO, MU 3909, CFP, A-1-b, env. 6, FWC to Wilmot, 28 March 1856.

25 The story is recorded in his letter of 28 March 1856.

26 AO, MU 3909, CFP, A-1-b, env. 6, FWC to Wilmot, 25 April [1856].

27 Ibid.

28 AO, MU 3909, CFP, A-1-b, env. 6, FWC to Wilmot, 8 May [1856].

29 AO, MU 3911, CFP, Wilmot Diary, 2 June 1856.

30 Wilmot's diary is missing for 1860, but it seems most likely that they moved into the house in late 1859 or early 1860.

Chapter Five: Life on the Railway

1 For statistics and references to recent literature, see Douglas McCalla, 'Railways and Provincial Development, 1850–1870,' in *Planting the Province*, 199–216. Greer and Radforth, eds., *Colonial Leviathan.*

2 Douglas McCalla, 'Railways and the Development of Canada West,' in Greer and Radforth, eds., *Colonial Leviathan*, 197.

3 Quoted in S.J.R. Noel, *Patrons, Clients, Brokers: Ontario Society and Politics, 1791–1896* (Toronto: University of Toronto Press 1990), 115.

4 The 1857 and 1858 statistics are from Province of Canada, *Report of Railway Commissioners for Canada.*

5 AO, MU 3909, CFP, A-1-a, env. 3, FWC to Wilmot, 5 November 1851.

6 For Capreol's remarkable history, see *DCB*, vol. 11, 150 n. 1.

7 The papers of the Northern Railway are found in the NAC, RG 30, IG. An excellent guide to the statutes relating to the Northern is Robert Dorman, comp., *A Statutory History of the Steam and Electric Railways of Canada, 1836–1937* (Ottawa: King's Printer 1938), 430–2. The numerous secondary studies on the Northern include Smith, 'The Northern Railway'; Stevens, *Canadian National Railways*, vol. 1; and Thompson, *A History of Canadian Railways to 1876.*

8 Cumberland's limited involvement with the architectural designs for the Northern's buildings is discussed in more detail in the *catalogue raisonné.*

9 See Williams, 'Shipping on the Great Lakes.' Vol. 3 of the Huron Institute *Papers and Records* (1939) gives detailed histories of ships that sailed on the Great Lakes, including the *Cumberland.* For a more recent work, see Ashdown, *Railway Steamships of Ontario.*

10 Toronto *Mail*, 15 June 1874, p. 4, col. 3.

11 Pennington, *Railways and Other Ways*, 120.

12 Baskerville, 'Professionalism vs. Proprietor.' For an assessment of the work that American contractors performed on Canadian railways during this period, see the same author's 'Americans in Britain's Backyard.'

13 That Cumberland took cash from the contractors is confirmed by a reference to the bribe in AO, MU 3909, CFP, A-1-a, env. 4, FWC to Wilmot, 21 July 1854. See also Alfred Brunel's 1857 memorandum on the Northern Railway in Baskerville, 'Americans in Britain's Backyard,' 68 n. 58.

14 Peter Baskerville, 'Transportation, Social Change, and State Formation, Upper Canada, 1841–1861,' in Greer and Radforth, eds., *Colonial Leviathan*, 230–56 (quotation at 247).

15 AO, MU 3909, CFP, A-1-a, env. 8, FWC to Wilmot, 6 December 1866.

16 AO, MU 3914, CFP, env. 5, FWC to Wilmot, 3 January 1872 (misfiled among Barlow Cumberland's papers).

17 AO, MU 3909, CFP, A-1-b, env. 5, FWC to Wilmot, 2 July 1872.

18 See the *Report of the Commission Appointed for investigating the Books, Accounts, and Vouchers of the Northern Railway Company of Canada.* The commission was appointed on 22 July 1876. Cumberland was interviewed at length on 25 and 26 August, after which the commission was refused permission to examine the company's books. In September Cumberland was too ill to continue testifying, or at least claimed to be.

19 In total he testified for fifteen days during the period from 16 March to 17 April.

20 Throughout his testimony Cumberland rationalized his own position by analogy to the activities of other railway men.

21 *Report of the Select Committee on the Affairs of the Northern Railway.*

22 Ibid., 39.

23 AO, MU 3909, CFP, A-1-a, env. 10, FWC to Wilmot, 5 November 1876.

24 AO, MU 3909, CFP, A-1-a, env. 10, FWC to Wilmot, 11 April 1877.

25 See *Report of the Select Committee on the Affairs of the Northern Railway*, especially the initial summary.

26 See the *Journals of the House of Commons of the Dominion of Canada*, vol. 12 (1878).

27 Toronto *Mail*, 6 August 1881.

28 Those curious about these regional railway disputes can find much of interest in the columns of the partisan and feisty *Barrie Northern Advance.*

Chapter Six: Political Career

1 On the 1867 election see Debra Forman, ed. and comp., *Legislators and Legisatures of Ontario, A Reference Guide* ([Toronto]: Legislative Library, Research and Information Services 1984), 2: 4, as well as other sources cited below.

2 J.K. Johnson, ed., *The Canadian Directory of Parliament, 1867–1967* (Ottawa: Public Archives of Canada 1968), 146.

3 Newspaper reports of the speeches are assembled in University of Toronto, Robarts Library, Government Documents Collection, Newspaper Hansard, 1 (30 December 1867–29 March 1873).

4 Toronto *Globe*, 31 December 1867.

5 Toronto *Globe*, 14 January 1868.

6 Since this was based in Orillia its interests were tied to the Northern.

7 Toronto *Globe*, 25 January 1871, quoted in C.B. Sissons, ed., *Egerton Ryerson: His Life and Letters*

(Toronto: Clarke, Irwin & Company 1947), 2:584 n. 4.

8 Cumberland also gained a considerable reputation as a witty after-dinner speaker. See, for instance, Clarke, *Sixty Years in Upper Canada*, 159.

9 AO, MU 3909, CFP, A-1-b, env. 5, FWC to Wilmot, 2 July 1868.

10 *History of the Federal Electoral Ridings, 1867–1980* (Ottawa: Library of Parliament Information and Reference Branch n.d.), 2:3. Johnson, ed., *Canadian Directory of Parliament*, 146, is incorrect in stating that Cumberland contested the riding of Cardwell.

11 NAC, MG 26A, Macdonald Papers, reel C-1710, FWC to Macdonald, 10 May 1871.

12 See the *Journals of the House of Commons of the Dominion of Canada*, vol. 5 (1872).

13 Walker, ed. *Daylight through the Mountain*, 357. Unfortunately, much of the information contained in this book is unreliable. As is frequently the case in publications by Walker, he refers to copies of letters in his possession that have not yet been deposited in public collections. Thus many of the more colourful of Walker's assertions cannot be confirmed. The Pacific Railway is not mentioned in the letters between Cumberland and Macdonald among the Macdonald Papers in the NAC.

14 See NAC, MG 2GA, Macdonald Papers.

15 NAC, MG 26A, Macdonald Papers, reel C-1695, FWC to Macdonald, 5 May 1868.

16 NAC, MG 26A, Macdonald Papers, reel C-1709, FWC to Macdonald, 23 May 1868.

17 NAC, MG 26A, Macdonald Papers, reel C-1709, FWC to Macdonald, 13 October 1869.

18 NAC, MG 26A, Macdonald Papers, reel C-27, Macdonald to FWC, 10 February 1869.

19 NAC, MG 26A, Macdonald Papers, reel C-29, Macdonald to FWC, 1 February 1871.

20 NAC, MG 26A, Macdonald Papers, reel C-1710, Macdonald to FWC, 9 February 1872.

21 Forman, *Legislators and Legislatures of Ontario*, 2:14. The dual-representation law was enacted as 35 Vict. (1872), c. 15 (Can.). Its passage can be traced in the *Journals of the House of Commons of the Dominion of Canada*, vol. 5 (1872).

22 NAC, MG 26A, Macdonald Papers, reel C-1711, FWC to Macdonald, 28 August 1873.

23 NAC, MG 26A, Macdonald Papers, reel C-1711, FWC to Macdonald, 16 October 1873.

24 Robinson was able to win this seat in 1875 when Moss was appointed a judge.

Chapter Seven: Later Personal Life

1 Canada, Army Historical Section, *The Regiments and Corps of the Canadian Army*, 138. See also Chambers, *The Royal Grenadiers*; Champion, *History of the 10th Royals*; Goodspeed, *Battle Royal*, Stacey, *Canada and the British Army*.

2 There are twenty-six letters (from 1861–5) relating to the founding and operations of the 10th Royals in NAC, RG9, IC1, Department of Militia and Defence, Correspondence, 1846–69.

3 There might have been a bit of good-natured rivalry here. About two weeks previously, Mrs Gzowski had presented a bugle to the 2nd Rifles on the cricket ground.

4 Ross, *History of the Canadian Bank of Commerce*, 2:75–6.

5 Toronto *Daily Leader*, 30 October 1869, p. 3, col. 2.

6 According to a letter dated 27 August 1881 from the board of St Andrew's Lodge, Toronto, offering condolences to Mrs Cumberland on the occasion of Cumberland's death: AO, MU 3910, CFP, A-1-c, env. 1, Condolences.

7 According to the obituary in the Toronto *Telegram*, 5 August 1881, p. 4. The newspaper's Ross Robertson, was himself a prominent Mason. For Freemasonry in Ontario see Robertson, *The History of Freemasonry*; Smith, *History of St. Andrew's Lodge*; McLeod, ed., *Whence Come We?*

8 The partnership was not legally dissolved until 1871. See Alexander Grant, *Reports of Cases Adjudged in the Court of Chancery of Ontario*, vol. 18 (Toronto: Rowsell & Hutchison 1872), 245–53.

9 *The Builder*, 9 August 1862, 573.

10 AO, MU 3909, CFP, A-1-a, env. 8, FWC to Wilmot, 6 December 1866.

11 One later source erroneously states that Cumberland himself enrolled as a student at Osgoode Hall in 1864. See James Hamilton Cleland, *Osgoode Hall: Reminiscences of the Bench and Bar* (Toronto: The Carswell Company 1904), 27: 'In Easter Term 1864, Mr. Frederick W. Cumberland, who, with Mr. Storm as architect,

had almost rebuilt the hall six years before, applied for admission as a student ... Mr. Cumberland, though he passed with credit, did not proceed further in his law course. He was a man of affairs and became President of the Northern Railway Company.'

12 AO, MU 3909 CFP, A-1-a, env. 7, FWC to Wilmot, 19 August 1864. Wilmot noted in her diary on 22 August, 'Nice letter from Fred.'

13 AO, MU 3909, CFP, A-1-a, env. 8, FWC to Wilmot, 21 June 1868.

14 AO, MU 3909, CFP, A-1-a, env. 8, FWC to Wilmot, 26 December 1866.

15 AO, MU 3909, CFP, A-1-b, env. 5, FWC to Tom Bramley (copy), 2 September 1869. Wilmot saw this letter, and on the back she rebutted some of his points: 'Since that time he has treated me with coldness & sternness & has left my bedroom in toto.' There is no mention of any of this in her diary.

16 Her diary frequently mentions being ill and staying in her bedroom. But 'illness' was euphemistically used to describe several conditions – even confinement! One more undated letter paints a similarly bleak picture of relations between them. The contents speak for themselves: 'Being obliged to find some excuse for putting off my friends, & as you are the cause, I have attributed it to your being unwell, & therefore if you wish further to compromise me & heap on more unmerited trouble upon me, you will shew yourself to my friends by coming into town, & thus secure the luxury of adding "Liar" to the many other bad attributes you – and thank God only you – attach to my character. FWC.' See AO, MU 3910, CFP, A-1-b, env. 11, FWC to Wilmot, n.d.

17 AO, MU 3909, CFP, A-1-b, env. 5, FWC to Wilmot, 12 November 1874.

18 AO, MU 3914, CFP, env. 8, Barlow Cumberland Papers, Barlow to Wilmot, 30 September [1875]: 'The Dad is well and hearty doing wonders in the way of work and cheery as a lark – when he will be leaving is as yet uncertain but it will be before long ... The dad seems to enjoy her [a cook's?] housekeeping and is a great deal at home i.e., on an average 3 nights a week.' The following spring, Barlow wrote to Wilmot that his father had lodgings in Richmond Street: 'Last Evening Julia Nell Archie [Helen's husband, Archie Campbell]

Fin [Seraphina Fraser, Barlow's wife] & myself took tea with the Dad in his new lodgings in Richmond St. He has a bedroom & sitting room. Takes breakfast at home and the rest of his meals at the Club.'

19 Côté, ed., *Political Appointments, Parliaments, and the Judicial Bench in the Dominion of Canada*, 9, which notes that Cumberland was one of three aides-de-camp to Lord Monck from 2 October to 13 November 1868 (when Monck's appointment terminated). His cordial relations with Lord and Lady Dufferin are clearly spelled out in Lady Dufferin, *My Canadian Journal*. See also *Narrative. Visit of the Governor-General and the Countess of Dufferin to the Six Nations Indians. August 25, 1874* in AO, MU 3914, CFP Misc. Pamphlets, D-2, env. 6. At the Six Nations visit Cumberland, as aide-de-camp, was on the dais with the other notables. J.K. Johnson, ed., *The Canadian Directory of Parliament, 1867–1968* (Ottawa: Public Archives of Canada 1968), 146, records that Cumberland was provincial aide-de-camp from 1865 to 1878.

20 H.H. Langton, *Sir Daniel Wilson*, 208–12.

21 As quoted in ibid., 280. Again, the original of this letter has not been located.

22 Ibid.

23 These letters are not known to have survived.

24 NAC, MG 26A, Macdonald Papers, reel C-1714, FWC to Macdonald, 2 December 1878.

25 NAC, MG 26A, Macdonald Papers, reel C-1715, FWC to Macdonald, 13 March 1879.

26 *DCB*, vol. 12, 395.

27 AO, MU 3913, CFP, Wilmot Diary.

28 The *Hamilton Spectator*, in its obituary of 5 August 1881, described Cumberland's illness as 'fatty degeneration of the heart.'

29 AO, MU 3914, CFP, B-1-a, env. 9, Wilmot to FWC, 29 May [1881]. The letter is filed with Barlow Cumberland's papers, but the envelope is addressed to Colonel Cumberland.

30 The principal obituaries were *Toronto World*, 6 August 1881, 2; Toronto *Globe*, 6 August 1881, 9; Toronto *Telegram*, 5 August 1881, 4; Toronto *Mail*, 6 August 1881, 8 and 8 August; *Hamilton Spectator*, 5 and 8 August 1881; *Barrie Northern Advance*, 11 August 1881, 2.

31 Toronto *Globe*, 6 August 1881, 6.

32 Toronto *Mail*, 6 August 1881, 8.

33 AO, MU 3910, CFP, A-1-c, Condolences. There was nothing from William Storm.

34 Another cast of the bust is held by the Ontario Association of Architects.

35 AO, GS 1-984, York County Surrogate Court Papers, #3122, Will and Inventory of Fred Cumberland.

36 AO, MU 3910, CFP, box 2, env. 4–5, 'Position of Trust Account, 1 August 1881.'

37 Barlow, Julia, and Florence were also buried in St James's: Barlow on 1 September 1913, at age 66; Julia on 6 September 1925, at age 74; and Florence on 11 March 1929, at age 71. They joined their siblings Walter, Ernest, and Evelyn, all of whom did not survive infancy. I have not been able to determine where Helen and Constance were buried.

PART TWO: ARCHITECTURAL CASE STUDIES

Chapter Eight: Assessing the English Heritage

1 These testimonials are all found in the AO, but are, confusingly, intercalated among the papers of Cumberland and his son Barlow. MU 3910, CFP, box 2, env. 2 (manuscript originals and printed versions from 1852, when Cumberland applied for the position of professor of engineering at the University of Toronto); MU 3921, CFP, box 13, env. 1 (undated manuscript copies of testimonials); MU 7176, CFP (abbreviated manuscript copies of testimonials).

2 The source of this erroneous assertion appears to be Frank Walker, who made the claim in *Four Whistles to Wood-up*, 19. For another instance, see Leggatt, 'Engineer, Architect, Actor.' I think it likely that the confusion stems from the fact that Cumberland employed an Alfred Brunel on the Northern Railway. It is not known whether Alfred was related to the more famous engineer of the same surname.

3 This statement seems to have first been made by his son in an article following Cumberland's death. See Cumberland, 'The Story of a University Building.'

4 Gwilt's 1842 *Encyclopaedia of Architecture* became a minor classic.

5 See appendix B for a list of the books known to have been in Cumberland's library. It is quite likely that there were other books that we do not know about.

6 See, for example, plate x, 'Grecian Ionic Capital,' or plate xii, 'Ionic Order.' The book was published by Thomas Kelly of London.

7 See David Watkin, *The Rise of Architectural History* (Chicago: University of Chicago Press 1983).

8 Robinson, *Rural Architecture*. Robinson's dates are 1776–1858.

9 See Thomas Roscoe, *The London and Birmingham Railway* ... (London: Charles Tilt [1839?]), 82–3, where Wolverton Station is described.

10 See Cumberland's article, 'Iron Roofs Erected over Building Slips, Nos. 3 and 4, in Her Majesty's Dockyard, Portsmouth,' 59–65.

11 AO, MU 3909, CFP A-1-a, env. 1, FWC to Wilmot, [21 August 1843].

12 AO, MU 3909, CFP A-1-a, env. 1, FWC to Wilmot, [24 August 1843].

13 AO, MU 3909, CFP A-1-a, env. 1, FWC to Wilmot, [4 December 1843].

14 AO, MU 3909, CFP A-1-a, env. 2, FWC to Wilmot, 28 April 1844.

15 AO, MU 3909, CFP A-1-a, env. 3, FWC to Wilmot, 25 October 1851.

16 Ibid.

17 AO, MU 3909, CFP A-1-a, env. 3, FWC to Wilmot, 27 November 1851.

18 For Thomas Ellis Owen (1804–62), see Howard Colvin, *A Biographical Dictionary of British Architects, 1600–1840* (London: John Murray 1978), 603–4.

19 AO, MU 3909, CFP A-1-a, env. 3, FWC to Wilmot, 19 November 1851.

20 Cumberland was referring to William Thomas (c. 1799–1860), a rival Toronto architect who had had differences of opinion with him regarding the St James's Cathedral competition and the Normal School.

21 AO, MU 3909, CFP A-1-a, env. 3, FWC to Wilmot, 21 December 1851. The reference to a *real noble* was a sarcastic jibe: the house's owner was a parvenu.

22 See, for instance, AO, MU 3909, CFP A-1-a, env. 3, FWC to Wilmot, 2 December 1851.

Chapter Nine: 'The Beautiful Medium' and Other Topics

1 See Andrew Saint, 'The Architect as Professional: Britain in the Nineteenth Century,' and 'The Architect as Businessman: The United States in the Nineteenth Century,' in *The Image of the Architect* (New Haven: Yale University Press 1983), 51–95.
2 Drummond (1813–82) was a lawyer, politician, and judge.
3 AO, MU 3909, CFP, A-1-a, env. 4, FWC to Wilmot, 8 May [1856].
4 There are forty relevant letters in NAC, RG11, A1, DPW, vols. 14–20.
5 NAC, RC 11, A1, DPW, vol. 14, item 10,996, FWC to Thomas Begley, 5 March 1850.
6 NAC, RG 11, A1, DPW, vol. 15, item 11,309, FWC to William H. Merritt, 17 April 1850. In Cumberland's defence, some of the other letters show that he wrote for approval even for the most minor expenditures, such as fire buckets: see, for example, NAC, RG 11, DPW, vol. 14, item 10,610, FWC to Commissioner of Public Works, 15 January 1850.
7 NAC, RG 11, A1, DPW, vol. 14, item 11,263, FWC to William H. Merritt, 10 April 1850. Cumberland objected strenuously, but apparently to no avail.
8 The newspapers included Toronto's *Globe*, *Leader*, and *British Colonist*, as well as newspapers from other cities, including the Oshawa *Freeman* and the Kingston *Daily News*.
9 Supplies were bought from Henry Rowsell and paid for semi-annually.
10 The principals eventually went to court to settle who owned what. See Alexander Grant, *Reports of Cases Adjudged in the Court of Chancery of Ontario*, vol. 18 (Toronto: Rowsell & Hutchison 1872), 245–53. Storm objected to a ruling that the partnership be held jointly responsible for its real estate losses. Storm argued, among other things, that improper charges – including lawyer's fees – had been added to the accounting, leading to a false picture of the firm's finances.
11 See, for instance, NAC, RG 11, A1, DPW, vol. 15, item 11,644, Cumberland to Thomas Begley, 4 June 1850. This letter is noteworthy because

Cumberland signed it 'for Cumberland & Ridout,' whereas he usually omitted his partner's name.
12 AO, MU 3909, CFP, A-1-a, env. 3, FWC to Wilmot, 25 October 1851.
13 For an overview of Storm's life and career, see *DCB*, vol. 12, 991–4. Storm's obituary in the *Canadian Architect and Builder* 5, no. 8 (August 1892), 81, claimed that their association began in 1848 and that Storm first worked for Cumberland on the St James's Cathedral competition. This is possible, but there is no evidence to support such a claim.
14 According to the *DCB* entry on Ridout, vol. 9, 661–3.
15 AO, MU 3910, CFP, box 2, A2, env. 1, 'Articles of Co-Partnership.' The partnership was officially dissolved on 23 August 1871.
16 AO, RG 21, Municipal Documents Collection, Ontario County, Clerk's Files, 1853–4, box 1, Communications, James Rowe to William Dawson, 6 November 1853.
17 See AO, RG 21, Municipal Documents Collection, *Proceedings and By-Laws of the County of Victoria, 1861–1864*, Appendix, [33]–4, which reports that Cumberland presented the plans on 9 December 1861.
18 See AO, RG 21, Municipal Documents Collection, *Proceedings and By-Laws of the County of Victoria, 1861–1864*, Appendix, 43–6, where it is reported that Storm presented the specifications to council on 5 February 1862.
19 See Deborah Nevins and Robert A.M. Stern, *The Architect's Eye: American Architectural Drawings from 1799–1978* (New York: Pantheon Books 1979), 92.
20 Ibid., 88.
21 For illustrations, see John Zukowsky, ed., *Chicago Architecture, 1872–1922: Birth of a Metropolis* (Munich: Prestel Verlag 1987), catalogue nos. 230–6.
22 Storm was away from 13 August 1857 to 3 February 1858. The dates are recorded in Wilmot's diary.
23 See Horwood, MU 3984, Add. 1, comprising sixteen items relating to the restoration of University College, including letters from William G. Storm.

Chapter Ten: A Selection of Schools

1 John Earl, 'Canada,' in *A Sketch of the County of Norfolk*, 24.

2 Cumberland also conducted such extensive renovations on Upper Canada College in Toronto during the mid-fifties that to all intents and purposes the design of the school after that time can be credited to him. The renovations were so prosaic, however, that they need no comment.

3 The literature on Ryerson is immense, that on the Toronto Normal School less extensive. Recent discussions of Ryerson include Curtis, *Building the Educational State* and *True Government by Choice Men?*; Gidney and Millar, *Inventing Secondary Education*; and Houston and Prentice, *Schooling and Scholars*. The best early source on the Ontario schools designed and constructed during this period is Hodgins, *Establishment of Schools and Colleges in Ontario*. See the *catalogue raisonné* for additional sources.

4 For a discussion of the ways that government became actively involved in education in Canada West during the 1840s, see Bruce Curtis, 'Class Culture and Administration: Educational Inspection in Canada West,' in Greer and Radforth, eds., *Colonial Leviathan*, 103–33.

5 Hodgins, *The School House*, 5.

6 Toronto *Weekly Globe*, 4 October 1850, p. 55, col. 5.

7 Later Cumberland and the other Toronto architects complained that Browne's design was plagiarized from published sources.

8 'Ceremony of Opening the New Buildings of the Normal and Model Schools for Upper Canada,' *Journal of Education for Upper Canada* 5, no. 12 (December 1852), 177–84. Documents relating to the official opening of the Normal School are found in Hodgins, *Historical and Other Papers and Documents*, 2:29–42.

9 Toronto *Semi-Weekly Leader*, 26 November 1852, quoted in 'Ceremony of Opening the New Buildings,' 177.

10 Ibid.

11 Quoted in Hodgins, *Historical and Other Papers and Documents*, 2:36.

12 Egerton Ryerson, 'The Chief Superintendent's Annual Report for 1852,' ibid., 5:131–52.

13 The general histories of schools as building types consulted by the author contained nothing useful. Schools are not mentioned in Nikolaus Pevsner, *A History of Building Types* (Princeton, N.J.: Princeton University Press 1976).

14 Hodgins, *The School House*, 5.

15 See Hodgins, *Historical and Other Papers and Documents*, 2:145: 'A number of pamphlets, containing plans of School Houses, were obtained from the Massachusetts State Board of Education, for distribution to School Trustees. An extensive series of wood cuts of School House plans was procured from Mr. H.C. Hickok, Deputy Superintendent of Education in the State of Pennsylvania, and from Doctor Henry Barnard, of Hartford, Connecticut.' See Barnard, *School Architecture*, 3rd ed. The first edition was published in 1841 and reprinted in 1842. There is nothing in Barnard's book on the scale of the Normal School.

16 For Ryerson's letters concerning his plans for the museum, and his purchases in 1855, see Hodgins, *Historical and Other Papers and Documents*, 2:2–19. It took Ryerson several years to make all the purchases necessary for the museum, and it did not open until 1857. See also Johnson, 'A Colonial Canadian in Search of a Museum,' and Carter, 'Ryerson, Hodgins, and Boyle.'

17 It is curious that the contemporary sources talk about style but never mention how the building actually worked.

18 Cumberland favoured south-facing libraries; the Osgoode Hall library and the University College library also faced south.

19 See Bain, 'William Mundie.'

20 *Toronto Normal School Jubilee Celebration* (Toronto: Warwick Brothers & Rutter 1898), 41.

21 Cumberland and Mundie had to cut back their original plans extensively. This was also Cumberland's experience at University College, where plans for a beautiful park were never executed.

22 Ryerson's guests included Canada's governors general, who quizzed the students on a variety of subjects. Lord Dufferin even gave a demonstration of perspective drawing: Hodgins, *Historical and Other Papers and Documents*, 4:233–4.

23 Cited in note 20 above.

24 The buildings are described in an unsigned article, 'Ryerson Athletic Facilities, Toronto,' *Canadian Architect* 34, no. 2 (February 1989), 28–32.
25 See the *catalogue raisonné* for sources relating to this building.
26 *The Church*, 3 June 1852, 337.
27 Ure, *The Hand-Book of Toronto*, 358. It appears that Ure was not a disinterested observer. He may have called on a competitor of Cumberland's, William Hay, to write the architectural descriptions for this book: see UCA, TS, Douglas S. Richardson, 'The Politics of Architecture in 1858: A Note on William Hay as G.P. Ure's Architectural Ghost-Writer for *The Hand-Book of Toronto*,' 3 March 1986.
28 For a history of the Hamilton Central School, see Hodgins, *Establishment of Schools and Colleges in Ontario*, 1:69–71. See the *catalogue raisonné* for sources relating to this building.
29 Barnard, *School Architecture*, 241, shows a 'Grammar School House' in a Greek Revival idiom, whose battered pilasters may be compared with those of the Hamilton Central School, but whether it was a source of inspiration for the Central School is unknown. Barnard, *School Architecture*, 265, shows a Perpendicular Gothic school that bears some stylistic comparison with the St James's Parochial School.
30 For a history of the Grammar School, see Hodgins, *Establishment of Schools and Colleges in Ontario*, 1:33, 36. For a discussion of the complex legislative background to the creation of the grammar schools in Ontario, see Gidney and Millar, *Inventing Secondary Education*, 155 and passim.
31 See Houston and Prentice, *Schooling and Scholars*, 319 and passim.
32 *Toronto Normal School Jubilee Celebration*, 42–3.

Chapter Eleven: University College

1 See the *catalogue raisonné* for a list of sources relating to this building. For an extensive discussion of the history and architecture of University College see Richardson, *A Not Unsightly Building*. Readers interested in the social and institutional history of the University of Toronto should consult Richardson and the following sources: *The University of Toronto and Its Colleges, 1827–*

1906 (Toronto: University Library 1906); Wallace, *A History of the University of Toronto*, and Bissell, ed., *University College: A Portrait*.
2 In an amusing coincidence, Trollope was the son of the Mrs Trollope whose *Vicar of Wrexhill* Cumberland had excoriated. His reactions to the book are discussed in chapter 1.
3 Trollope, *North America*, 73–4.
4 Lady Dufferin, *My Canadian Journal*, 35. The speech is reprinted in full in Hodgins, *Historical and Other Papers and Documents*, 4:234–7. Similarly positive reactions to University College are found in the writings of many others of the time. For instance, Charles MacKay in *Life and Liberty in America, or Sketches of a Tour in the United States and Canada in 1857–8* (London: Smith, Elder 1859), 2: 273–4, wrote 'Toronto possesses a well-endowed University, several colleges and public schools, and may be said to have set an example to all Canada, in the cause of public education. The "showplaces" of Toronto, after the Houses of Parliament, are the University, the Normal and Model School, under the Superintendent of The Rev. Dr. Egerton Ryerson, to whom education in Canada owes much.'
5 For a comprehensive discussion of the history of universities in Ontario, see McKillop, *Matters of Mind*.
6 *The Origin, History and Management of the University of King's College, Toronto* (Toronto: George Brown 1844), 62.
7 There are many discussions of Strachan and his involvement with Canadian cultural institutions. One of the most thorough is Purdy, 'John Strachan.' See especially chapter 6, 'University of King's College, 1843–49.' Egerton Ryerson termed the university problem in Upper Canada the 'question of questions' (quoted in ibid., 268).
8 Quoted in Bethune, *Memoir of the Right Reverend John Strachan*, 260.
9 Ibid., 263.
10 The book concentrates on diocesan administration, the epic struggles over the Clergy Reserves, the amending of the King's College charter and the founding of Trinity College.
11 See McKillop, *Matters of Mind*, and Hodgins, *Establishment of Schools and Colleges in Ontario*, 3:28ff.

12 Quoted in UTA B65–0014/004, John Langton Papers, 'Letters and Journals of Sir Daniel Wilson' (typescript), unpaginated sheet headed 'Notes.'

13 Blake resigned from the committee before Cumberland presented his designs for the college.

14 William Henry Draper (1801–77), chief justice of the Court of Common Pleas of Upper Canada (1856–63) and chief justice of Upper Canada (1863–77).

15 Wallace, *A History of the University of Toronto*, 73; Richardson, *A Not Unsightly Building*, 53 n. 10.

16 UTA, A70-0024/053(2), Board of Governors Papers, Correspondence, John Langton to David Buchan, 9 February 1856. The correspondence files show that as early as 13 October 1852 Cumberland was trying to assess the state of the university grounds, which suggests that the university was contemplating commissioning him to design a building: UTA, A68-0010, Office of the Chief Accountant, Correspondence, box 24, FWC to David Buchan (?), 13 October 1852.

17 All the financial records of Upper Canada College for this period are housed in the UTA. Cumberland & Storm did a great deal of work on the college buildings in the 1850s. See UTA, Office of the Chief Accountant, Correspondence, Section II, Group B, Letterbook D, finding aid, p. 23, no. 317. See also the financial records listed in the Upper Canada College entry in the *catalogue raisonné*. The letters show that Cumberland & Storm conducted these works with dispatch. Because the governor general approved the payments for college work, he would have known the architects to be reliable and efficient – a fact that may have assisted them in obtaining the commission for University College.

18 UTA, A68-0012, Senate Minutes. At this meeting the manner of remunerating Cumberland & Storm was discussed, but it was agreed to defer a decision until an estimate of the cost of the buildings could be made, 'upon the understanding that he shall be allowed in full payment of all charges a commission of four per cent on the cost or a fixed sum equivalent to it at the option of the Senate.' The senate continued to discuss this topic throughout the fall of 1856. The minutes show (vol. 2, p. 544) that on 7 November 1856 Chancellor Blake fixed the remuneration at £3000, 'being four per cent upon the largest sum, which the Senate was authorized to expend.' The senate thereafter refused to grant additional payements, even though construction costs far exceeded the original estimate. The architects then brought a claim against the university, as described in the minutes, vol. 2, pp. 567–8. The outcome of the claim is unclear.

There is an index to the minutes that lists all references to Cumberland in vols. 1–2.

19 UTA, Senate Minutes, vol. 1, p. 328.

20 During the 1980s, when the finalists in the National Gallery of Canada design competition were taken to see existing art galleries, they were doing essentially what Cumberland had done more than one hundred years previously.

22 AO, MU 3909, CFP, A-1-b, env. 6, FWC to Wilmot, [21 March 1856] (misfiled with letters of 1853).

23 AO, MU 3909, CFP, A-1-b, env. 6, FWC to Wilmot, 28 March 1856.

24 Craig, *Architecture of Ireland*, 302–4.

25 For a discussion of the Gothic Revival in Ireland, see Richardson, *Gothic Revival Architecture in Ireland*, and Blau, *Ruskinian Gothic*.

26 UTA, Senate Minutes, vol. 2, p. 418.

27 AO, MU 3909, CFP, A-1-b, env. 6, FWC to Wilmot, 13 April 1856.

28 Ibid.

20 AO, MU 3909, CFP, A-1-b, env. 6, FWC to Wilmot, 25 April [1856].

30 AO, MU 3909, CFP, A-1-6, env. 6, FWC to Wilmot, 8 May [1856].

31 These drawings were of the Museum of Practical Geology, Jermyn Street, London: Queen's College, Galway; Trinity College, Dublin; Oxford's Magdalen College, Christ Church College, Brasenose College, Jesus College, Lincoln College, and Corpus Christi College; University College, London; Queen's College, Belfast; Queen's College, Cork (now University College). There were also reference plans of two Parisian buildings: the Musée Nationale d'Histoire Naturelle and the Bibliothèque Ste Geneviève (the plans were combined on one sheet).

32 Richardson, *A Not Unsightly Building*, 55.

33 Ibid., 56–7.

34 As regards religious architecture, he knew of these theoretical issues as early as the 1840s, as was shown in chapter 8.

35 Maw & Co. sent a skilled workman to ensure that the tiles were properly installed. The design used was no. 226 in a late 1860s catalogue entitled *Encaustic Tile, Geometrical Mosaic and Plain Tile Pavements.* It is illustrated in Richardson, *A Not Unsightly Building*, 91. See generally Lochnan, 'Victorian Tiles in Toronto.'

36 Blau, *Ruskinian Gothic*; Brooks, *John Ruskin.*

37 Papworth and Papworth, *Museums, Libraries, and Picture Galleries.* William Storm's library included a copy of this book. For a listing of the contents of Storm's library, see Richardson, comp., *William G. Storm.*

38 In 1848 the Oxford-educated Sir Edmund Walker Head was the first civilian appointed lieutenant governor of New Brunswick. He presided over the introduction of responsible government to the colony and became governor general of British North America in 1854. In this post he influenced Queen Victoria's choice of Ottawa as the capital of the Province of Canada. As governor general he was a strong champion of Confederation, a cause he had been advocating for some years. He returned to his native England in 1861. See Kerr, *Sir Edmund Head.* Kerr's book contains no mention of Cumberland or University College.

39 Langton, *Early Days in Upper Canada*, 292. Langton's statement has been cited in every publication on the founding of University College.

40 Hodgins, *Establishment of Schools and Colleges in Ontario*, 3:44.

41 Richardson, *A Not Unsightly Building*, 59 n. 40.

42 For an etymological analysis of the word Gothic, see Paul Frankl, *The Gothic: Literary Sources and Interpretations through Eight Centuries* (Princeton: Princeton University Press 1960).

43 Wallace, *A History of the University of Toronto*, 73. Langton had this to say about the governor general's interference in the laying out of the building (Langton, *Early Days in Upper Canada*, 293–5): 'It seems that His Excellency had all along thought that the South front was to face the East [West?] [W.A. Langton's editorial interpolation], and nothing would satisfy him but so it must be, and under his superintendence we proceeded to measure and stake out, Cumberland's face exhibiting blank despair, for it brought his chemical laboratory where no sun would ever shine into it, his kitchens, etc., into the prettiest part of the grounds, and several other inconveniences which His Excellency said could be easily remedied. However there stands on the ground an elm tree, a remnant of the old forest, with a long stem as such trees have and a little bush on top of it, not unlike a broom with its long handle stuck in the ground, and it soon became evident that the tree would fall a sacrifice. This he would not permit and when I hinted that it would certainly be blown down before long, he told me that it was the handsomest tree about Toronto (as it is certainly one of the tallest), and politely added "But you Canadians have a prejudice against trees." He then stalked off the ground followed by his A.D.C. I thought Cumberland would have thrown the whole thing up that day, he was so annoyed, but we took up the stakes and staked it out our way with the South front facing the South, and by a little stuffing and squeezing we got the tree in such a position that it may be saved ... However, I bless that tree and hope its shadow may never be less, for it got us out of the scrape. When the Governor paid us a visit the next day he was quite satisfied and complimentary, and in congratulating us upon the safety of the tree he said to Cumberland, with that impertinence which governors general can so well indulge in, "For I am sure you can never put anything up half as pretty."' There is no reason to doubt that the substance of this statement is true, but Langton's evident irony suggests that he may have exaggerated the situation somewhat. Note that there is no indication that Storm was involved in this design phase.

44 UTA, Langton Papers, 'Letters and Journals of Sir Daniel Wilson,' unpaginated sheet headed 'Notes.' Much of this information is repeated in H.H. Langton, *Sir Daniel Wilson*, 76.

45 See David Watkin, *Morality and Architecture: The Development of a Theme in Architectural History and Theory from the Gothic Revival to the Modern Period* (Oxford: Clarendon Press 1977).

46 Hodgins, *Establishment of Schools and Colleges in Ontario*, 3:43–4.

47 Ibid., 3:38–9.

48 For a full description of this event, see ibid., 3:33–46. Much of the same ground is covered in Hodgins, ed., *Documentary History of Education in Upper Canada*, 14:24–38.

49 Hodgins, *Establishment of Schools and Colleges in Ontario*, 3:37.

50 Ibid., 3:43–4.

51 UTA, Langton Papers, 'Letters and Journals of Sir Daniel Wilson,' 14 February 1890.

52 Ibid., 14 February 1892.

53 Henry-Russell Hitchcock, *Architecture: Nineteenth and Twentieth Centuries*, 3rd ed. (Harmondsworth: Penguin 1971), 278.

54 Blau, *Ruskinian Gothic*; Brooks, *John Ruskin*.

Chapter Twelve: Steeples for the People

1 For a discussion of these developments, see James F. White, *The Cambridge Movement: The Ecclesiologists and the Gothic Revival* (Cambridge, England: Cambridge University Press 1962). For a discussion of the crucial decade of the 1840s, see Brownlee, 'The First High Victorians.'

2 Cumberland owned this book (see appendix B to the present work).

3 This article is reprinted in Simmins, ed., *Documents*, 33–42.

4 See Stanton, 'Christ Church Cathedral and the Chapel of St. Anne, Fredericton, New Brunswick,' in *The Gothic Revival & American Church Architecture*, 127–58.

5 Frank Wills, *Ancient English Ecclesiastical Architecture and Its Principles, Applied to the Wants of the Church at the Present Day* (New York: Stanford and Swords 1850). Wills (1822–57) designed some fifty churches before his early death. See *DCB*, vol. 7, 941–5.

6 For the Canadian Gothic Revival generally, see Brosseau, *Gothic Revival in Canadian Architecture*. In a stimulating article that discusses why Gothic Revival became so popular in Ontario, William Westfall and Malcolm Thurlby argue that the style became a means of emphasizing the difference between the sacred and the secular. By commissioning a building in Gothic Revival style, religious authorities were able to reassert the importance of Christian values in the face of Victorian secular materialism. See 'The Church in the Town.' The authors also argue convincingly that the province's architects manipulated sometimes modest Gothic features to make them more conspicuous in the increasingly urban landscape of nineteenth-century Ontario. The use of prominent corner towers, for instance, may be considerd a specifically Ontario adaptation of the Gothic Revival aesthetic. See Thurlby and Westfall, 'Church Architecture and Urban Space'; Thurlby, 'Nineteenth-Century Churches in Ontario'; idem, 'Medieval Toronto.'

7 William Thomas (1799–1860) designed some thirty churches, twelve in Toronto alone: *DCB*, vol. 8, 872–8.

8 The letter was dated 10 September 1849 and cited A.W.N. Pugin's *The True Principles of Pointed or Christian Architecture* (1841). The letter is in the correspondence files of the St James's Cathedral Archives.

9 The most important discussions of Cumberland's churches are by Shirley Morriss. See her master's thesis, 'The Church Architecture of Frederic William Cumberland,' and her two articles, 'The Church Architecture of Frederic William Cumberland,' and 'The Nine-Year Odyssey of a High-Victorian Goth.'

10 In addition to the architects mentioned in the text, other Canadian architects working along Ecclesiological lines included Joseph Connolly, Thomas Fuller, Thomas Gundry, Henry Langley, Augustus Laver, Thomas Seaton Scott, and Thomas Stent.

11 It is not known whether these pews were rented or free. At St James's the pews were all rented, and this would appear to have been the more common practice.

12 According to Mary Harrington Farmer, *One Hundred Years: The Church of the Ascension, Hamilton. A Short History, 1850–1950* (Hamilton: Kidner Printing 1950), 10–11. Darling & Curry's involvement is noted in the vestry minutes, 85 (unfortunately for our purposes, the church's first extant minutebook dates from 1878). The works were completed by 4 March 1888, at a cost of $25,000. The minutebooks are found in the Church of the Ascension Archives. See the *catalogue raisonné* for further references.

13 Morriss, 'Nine-Year Odyssey,' figs. 1–3, between pp. 42 and 43.

14 The St James's Cathedral Archives provide most of the sources on which the following section is based. The documents are somewhat idiosyn-

cratically organized, but reward the persistent.

15 These earlier churches are described by MacRae and Adamson, *Hallowed Walls*, 39–41.

16 See Frederick Armstrong, 'The First Great Fire of Toronto,' *Ontario History* 53, no. 3 (September 1961), 201–21.

17 McRae and Adamson, *Hallowed Walls*, 156.

18 *The Church*, 13 September 1849, 26.

19 In an undated letter probably from September 1849, Cumberland observed that a committee of the Mechanics' Institute wanted to exhibit elevations and perspectives. William Thomas said the same thing in a letter of 25 September 1849. These letters are found in the St James's Cathedral Archives.

20 *Memorandum for the Congregation of St. James' Church*, 12 December 1849. Copies of this and other pamphlets concerning St James' are found in the MTL/BR Broadsides Collection.

21 'Bramhill's' pamphlet is found in the MTL/BR broadsides collection and in the cathedral archives.

22 Four sources in the cathedral archives provide the information related here. In addition to the correspondence files, there are the vestry minutebooks of 1842–1907; the building committee minutebooks of 1849–54; and a book entitled (on its spine) 'A Church Journal. March 1842 to February 1907,' and (on its front cover) 'Journal of St. James's Cathedral. Toronto.' This latter source also contains a number of pasted-in printed documents, including a letter from 'F.R.S.' to the *Globe* in 1849, which explains in detail why the Cumberland design was not approved immediately and how Smith managed to insinuate himself into the competition.

23 [Strachan], *Thoughts on the Rebuilding of the Cathedral Church of St. James.*

24 The date recorded in the building committee minutebooks is 1 November 1849, but presumably 1 December is meant.

25 The vestry actually went to the expense of printing a pamphlet entitled *Resolutions and Amendments, to Be Submitted to the Vestry of St. James's Church, at the Meeting to Be Held on Friday, December 14, 1849* [Toronto: n.p. 1849]. A copy of this can be found in vol. 1 of the vestry minutebooks.

26 *Second Report of the Building Committee Appointed by the Vestry of St. James' Church to Report on the Rebuilding of the Church* (Toronto: n.p. 1849).

27 Ibid., 7–8.

28 The resolutions of the 21st are in ibid., 8–9. The decision to rent out church land was rescinded on 9 March 1850 by a close vote of thirty-one to twenty-nine. That the church officials took all of this very seriously can be seen from a story reported in an unidentified newspaper clipping of 14 June 1855 in the vestry minutes. One Francis H. Heward had promised to donate £20 to the church, provided that it was rebuilt on the old foundations. When the church was rebuilt on new foundations, the bones of Heward's father had to be disinterred. Heward's condition not being met, he did not hand over the promised money, whereupon the churchwardens Moffatt and Harris sued, won their case, and seized twelve barrels of flour as payment! The minutes also contain a copy of a *Globe* article of 12 May 18[54?] concerning a lawsuit over pews.

29 A mere parish church was not what most people had in mind. Many people thought to have the new church serve as a cathedral until such time as a more lavish structure could be built. During the meeting of the 21st a motion was passed stating 'That it is greatly to be desired that the parish church of St. James's should continue to be as it has hitherto been[:] The Cathedral Church of the Diocese.' This was amended to read: 'That when the Parish Church of St. James's shall have been reerected his Lordship the Bishop be respectfully invited to establish his throne therein until such time as a Cathedral of the Diocese be constructed the congregation being desirous of maintaining the Honor and advantage of his presence.' This passed by a majority of five, a slight majority for a meeting at which at least forty-eight people were present.

30 See the letter from Wilmot to T.D. Harris, 25 March 1850, in the St James's Cathedral Archives.

31 *The Church*, 21 November 1850, 132.

32 The verse from 2 Samuel reads, 'And it was told King David, saying, the Lord hath blessed the house of Obed-edom, and all that pertaineth unto

him, because of the ark of God. So David went and brought up the ark of God from the house of Obed-edom into the city of David with gladness.'

33 The minutebooks do not record another meeting until 1866.

34 See Thurlby, 'Medieval Toronto.'

35 Ibid., 30.

36 See Jean Bony, *The English Decorated Style: Gothic Architecture Transformed, 1250–1350* (Ithaca: Cornell University Press 1979), and Nikolaus Pevsner and Priscilla Metcalf, *The Cathedrals of England: Southern England* (Harmondsworth: Penguin 1985).

37 Interestingly, *The Church* in its description of the cornerstone-laying ceremony on 20 November 1850 alluded to this combinatin of stylistic sources, as follows: 'The edifice will be of the early English style of Gothic Architecture, of a somewhat later period, approachinig, and indeed, in some parts attaining that known as "the transition" – or in other words that which being more decorative is less classically severe than the earlier system.'

38 The gallery was removed in 1889, when the choir was also moved from the organ loft in the south gallery.

39 See the *catalogue raisonné* for further details.

40 This church is also known as St-James's-the-Less, but the sources refer to it as the St James's Cemetery Chapel. MacRae and Adamson, *Hallowed Walls*, 158, suggest that the brothers George and Edward Radford, architects of St Paul's Yorkville (1860), may have had a hand in the design of the chapel. But the evidence shows that only Cumberland was involved, and there are stylistic similarities to the earlier Church of the Ascension.

41 'I would give my ears to be asked to build a *Small Stone Church* in Canada, but unfortunately with small resources they always will insist upon large accommodation and thus reduce us to the necessity of something very near a kin [*sic*] to four bare walls': AO, CFP, MU 3909, A-1-a, env. 3, FWC to Wilmot, 25 October 1851.

42 A newspaper account from 1855 reported that a 'cemetery chapel and catacombs' were 'in progress' at St James's, but the report was premature: Toronto *Daily Leader*, 23 May 1855.

43 See the *catalogue raisonné* for further information.

44 Bishop Strachan was more generous-spirited than is sometimes credited. He does not seem to have objected to Cumberland's obtaining this commission, even though Cumberland had designed University College, whose very name was anathema to the bishop.

45 Raphael Brandon and J. Arthur Brandon, *Parish Churches; Being Perspective Views of English Ecclesiastical Structures ...* (London: David Bogue 1851), vol. 2, facing p. 41. This book, with a scrap of paper marking the drawing of Marston Church, was in Cumberland's library (see appendix B).

46 According to an article in the Toronto *Telegram*, 22 June 1938.

Chapter Thirteen: Post Offices, Courthouses, and Other Public Buildings

1 Illustrated in Stewart, *Stones of Manchester*, 19.

2 Illustrated in ibid., 42.

3 NAC, Picture Collection, PA46463.

4 Cumberland's courthouses are discussed in Crossman, *Early Court Houses of Ontario*; MacRae and Adamson, *Cornerstones of Order*; Carter, comp., *Early Canadian Courthouses*.

5 See the *catalogue raisonné* for sources relating to these designs.

6 For a discussion of prisons as a building type, see Nikolaus Pevsner, *A History of Building Types* (Princeton: Princeton University Press 1976), 159–68.

7 See MacRae and Adamson, *Cornerstones of Order*, 156–9.

8 Whether other architects entered the competition, and if so how the Cumberland & Ridout design was chosen, has not been determined.

9 The main contractor was John Worthington. William H. Pim also did some work on the site.

10 W.H. Smith, *Canada: Past, Present and Future*, 1:165.

11 *Illustrated Historical Atlas of the Counties of Haldimand and Norfolk*, 15.

12 For a description of this building, see MacRae and Adamson, *Cornerstones of Order*, 159–62.

13 The most significant cutback resulted from the decision to use brick instead of stone in the flanking offices, but this did not alter substantially the architectural character of the project.

14 At least two different plans of the main floor were prepared.

15 For an official account of the slow development of the design see AO, RG 21, Municipal Documents Collection, United Counties of York, Ontario, and Peel, *Annual Report*, 1852, 37–9.

16 Illustrated in MacRae and Adamson, *Cornerstones of Order*, 161.

17 The county reports chronicling the progress of construction are listed in the *catalogue raisonné*.

18 See MacRae and Adamson, *Cornerstones of Order*, 187–9. I disagree, however, with MacRae and Adamson's unproven attribution of all the work to Storm.

19 See the record of the meetings of 1861–3 in *Journal of the Proceedings and By-laws of the Provisional Council of the County of Victoria* (Lindsay: Victoria Herald 1863), 18–19, 33–5, 57.

20 In 1863 the firm prepared one other jail design, for Lincoln County. This was essentially an adaptation of the firm's earlier jail designs. See the *catalogue raisonné* for sources relating to this project.

21 See the *catalogue raisonné* for sources relating to the building. For recent articles, see Johnson and Maitland, 'Osgoode Hall,' and Carr, 'Hopkins, Lawford & Nelson.' See also Maitland, *Neoclassical Architecture in Canada*. For general histories of the building, see MacRae and Adamson, *Cornerstones of Order*, 120–55, and Arthur, *Toronto*, 100–8, 114.

22 The Four Courts were principally the work of James Gandon (1743–1823), who was responsible for the neo-classical elevation and the interior (1786–1802). The interior was destroyed by fire in 1922.

23 Trollope, *North America*, 73–4.

24 The Court of Chancery was abolished in 1881.

25 See Carr, 'Hopkins, Lawford & Nelson,' appendix.

26 'It is true that the main cornice is continuous, but the band course and the base below ignore the wings, and the new windows are totally unrelated to the old. In short, the new centre is a frontispiece that seems to have been inserted without apology or acknowledgments of any kind to the graceful pavilions of 1829 or 1844': Arthur, *Toronto*, 108.

27 Ibid.

28 Johnson and Maitland, 'Osgoode Hall,' 14. The authors have noted, however, that Somerset House was a monumental single-block structure, whereas Osgoode Hall had a tripartite design, which they have tentatively attributed to unidentified American sources.

29 *The Builder*, 25 July 1857, 419, ran an illustration of Somerset House.

30 Arthur, *Toronto*, 108.

31 MacRae and Adamson, *Cornerstones of Order*, 155.

32 For the Palazzo Tursi-Doria see Richardson, *Gothic Revival Architecture in Ireland*, 2:401–3 and figs. 250–1. Fig. 250 shows the plan and is taken from the *Enciclopedia italiana*, vol. 15. Fig. 251 shows the entrance court and is taken from M.P. Gauthier, *Les plus beaux édifices de la ville de Gênes*, vol. 1.

33 Depicted in the *Illustrated London News*, 2 March 1850, 148. For a discussion of Bridgewater House, see Sykes, *Private Palaces*, 289.

34 See ibid., 293.

35 See Carr, 'Hopkins, Lawford & Nelson,' 24.

36 In pleasant contrast to Cumberland's usually frugal clients, the Law Society chose Caen stone even though it was the most expensive option proposed by the architect. See Carr, 'Hopkins, Lawford & Nelson,' 24.

37 MacRae and Adamson, *Cornerstones of Order*, 155. They have made these comments partly to refute Eric Arthur's doubts about the practicality of a south-facing library.

38 The original site of Campbell's house was on Adelaide Street East. The building was moved to University Avenue in 1972.

39 In the Broadsides Collection at the MTL/BR is a circular dated 12 April 1855 asking for assistance to complete the new hall, construction on which had been suspended for some time for lack of funds.

40 Illustrated in Stewart, *Stones of Manchester*, 43.

41 Illustrated in ibid., 41.

42 See the *catalogue raisonné* for sources relating to these designs.

43 An engraving of this event was printed in the Toronto *Daily Colonist*, 28 December 1855, 1. A copy of this engraving is found in the MTL/BR, Picture Collection, T-30,108.

44 Horwood (110)16–17.

45 Horwood (110)2, 4, 6, 7, 9.

46 Horwood (110)1, 11–14. These drawings must be for a third design because they are working drawings. The earlier designs exist only as presentation drawings.

Chapter Fourteen: Private Commissions

1 *DCB*, vol. 8, 845–50.
2 *DCB*, vol. 8, 399–400.
3 *DCB*, vol. 10, 631–3.
4 *DCB*, vol. 10, 622–3.
5 *DCB*, vol. 9, 55–60.
6 *DCB*, vol. 11, 783–95.
7 For Gzowski, see *DCB*, vol. 12, 389–96. For a brief discussion of Cumberland's designs for Ridout and Gzowski, see Martyn, *Toronto*, 128–32 and 139–47, respectively. See also MacRae and Adamson, *The Ancestral Roof.*
8 *DCB*, vol. 12, 682–9.
9 As noted in the *catalogue raisonné*, there is no evidence to support the assertion that Cumberland designed 'Lynnwood,' Duncan Campbell's house in Simcoe, Ontario, erected in 1850–1.
10 The Hagarty house was very similar to a design Cumberland & Storm prepared in September 1854 for George William Allan.
11 In 1855 Cumberland designed law offices for J. Lukin Robinson on Jordan Street. The building was a three-storey heavily ornamented block with a segmental-arched centre bay crowning a very impressive front elevation.
12 This information was graciously provided by Stephen Otto.
13 MacRae and Adamson, *The Ancestral Roof,* 155.
14 The drawings show that Cumberland & Storm were adding a new house to an existing structure. A photograph in the MTL/BR Picture Collection (T-11,256), although identifed as Chestnut Park, is probably Gzowski's house.
15 Cumberland designed the Bank of Upper Canada's offices in Port Hope, Sarnia, Windsor, and Lindsay.
16 For a discussion of the forms that Canadian bank buildings have taken, see Howard Shubert, 'Cumberland & Storm and Mies van der Rohe: The Problem of the Banking Hall in Canadian Architecture,' *Journal of Canadian Art History* 12, no. 1

(1989), 7–21, as well as his 'The Development of the Banking Hall in Canadian Architecture' (master's thesis, University of Toronto, 1983).
17 See Baskerville, ed., *The Bank of Upper Canada.*
18 The Henning comparison is drawn from a design for a £1550 villa published in a pattern-book in 1855. See Hitchcock, *Early Victorian Architecture,* vol. 2, plate XIII–22.
19 See appendix B to the present work.
20 Drawings for several schemes exist for these cottages, including some showing two separate cottages under a single roof, and another showing them as free-standing structures. A photograph indicates that the latter scheme was likely the one chosen. It also shows that the cottages had wooden roofs instead of the slate ones called for in the drawings. This was likely due to budgetary considerations.
21 The building stood at 17–19 Wellington Street West, between Bay and Yonge streets. It has been demolished. For a brief discussion, see Dendy, *Lost Toronto,* 66–7.
22 *Building News,* 20 August 1858, 86.
23 See Richardson, *Gothic Revival Architecture in Ireland,* 1:414ff. The New Bridge Street branch is depicted in fig. 256 and the Fleet Street branch in fig. 257.

Chapter Fifteen: Proposals for Building a National Capital

1 See Knight, *Choosing Canada's Capital.*
2 Nothing beyond the plans exists for the 1853 project. Perhaps Cumberland decided to hold off preparing detailed drawings until he could be sure that funding would be approved. If so, this was a prudent decision.
3 For the history of the governor general's residences, see Hubbard, *Rideau Hall.*
4 In its general character this design was reminiscent of the 1841 King's College plan by long-time Toronto architect Thomas Young, portions of which had been executed in the same park, although Cumberland's plan was more complex spatially and less symmetrical.
5 AO, MU 3909, CFP, A-1-a, env. 4, FWC to Wilmot, 23 May [1853 or 1854]. Cumberland could have been referring either to James Morris (postmaster

general from 22 February 1851 to 16 August 1853) or Malcolm Cameron (postmaster general from 17 August 1853 to 10 September 1854).

6 AO, MU 3909, CFP, A-1-a, env. 4, FWC to Wilmot, 4 June 1854.

7 AO, MU 3909, CFP, A-1-a, env. 4, FWC to Wilmot, 2 July 1854.

8 The sources also identify Rubidge as departmental architect.

9 See *Documents Relating to the Construction of the Parliamentary and Departmental Buildings at Ottawa*, 3ff., reprinted in Simmins, ed., *Documents*, 59–76.

10 The government reports concerning Cumberland & Storm's Ottawa designs can be found in *Documents Relating to the Construction of the Parliamentary and Departmental Buildings at Ottawa*; Province of Canada, Sessional Papers, 1862, no. 3; Province of Ontario, Sessional Papers, 1881, no. 23, 4–6. The quoted portion is from the 1881 publication.

11 Ontario, Sessional Papers, 1881, no. 23, 4–6.

12 See Knight, *Choosing Canada's Capital*, for further information. See also Alan H. Armstrong, 'Profile of Parliament Hill,' *Journal of the Royal Architectural Institute of Canada* 34 (September 1957), 327–31.

13 See Young, '"Odahwah,"' and *The Glory of Ottawa*. The main printed sources for documents relating to the 1859 competition *Report of the Commission Appointed to Inquire into Matters Connected with the Public Buildings at Ottawa* (Quebec: Josiah Blackburn 1862), 10–11; *Documents Relating to the Construction of the Parliamentary and Departmental Buildings at Ottawa* (Quebec: Hunter, Rose, and Lemieux, 1862), 5–18; Province of Canada, Sessional Papers, 1860, no. 2, 13; no. 11, 31–3; 1862, no. 3, 18.

14 For Thomas Fuller, see *DCB*, vol. 12, 243–6, and for Augustus Laver, see *DCB*, vol. 12, 534–5.

15 *Documents Relating to the Construction of the Parliamentary and Departmental Buildings at Ottawa*, in Simmins, ed., *Documents*, 64–5.

16 Photographs of perspective drawings of both designs are held by the Parliamentary Library in Ottawa. The whereabouts of the original drawings are unknown. Fuller & Jones's design was an elegant and sophisticated one based on classical vocabulary. Its main feature was a magnificent colossal order above a rusticated ground storey. It was a more integrated design, albeit not as closely connected with current fashions as Cumberland & Storm's.

17 The correspondence chronicling all the delays is available in RG 11, B1(a), DPW, Correspondence, vol. 425, subject 1028, and vol. 428, subject 1029.

18 A nonsensical calumny. Cumberland design was approved on its merits, *despite* its extravagant projected cost.

19 *Quebec Morning Chronicle*, n.d., reprinted in the *Ottawa Union*, 25 January 1860, p. 3, col. 1.

20 RG 11, B1(a), DPW, Correspondence, vol. 425, subject 1028, FWC to Samuel Keefer, 27 August 1861.

21 See Hubbard, *Rideau Hall*.

Epilogue: Cumberland's Legacy

1 See *Report of the Commission Appointed to Inquire into Matters Connected with the Public Buildings at Ottawa* (Quebec: Josiah Blackburn 1862).

2 Toronto *Mail*, 6 August 1881, 8.

PART THREE: CATALOGUE RAISONNÉ

Introduction

1 Among the most comprehensive newspaper articles on Toronto buildings of the 1850s were those published by the *Globe*: see 12 September 1855, p. 2, cols. 3–5 ('Growth in the City'); 4 August 1852, p. 2; 13 December 1856; 30 June 1857, p. 2; 5 October 1858, p. 2, cols. 5–9 ('The New University Buildings'); 28 July 1859, p. 2, cols. 7–9 ('Building in Toronto').

2 In a letter to William H. Pim of 6 July 1854, Cumberland, signing as chief engineer of the Ontario, Simcoe and Huron Railroad Union Company, authorized Pim to erect an engine-house, car-shed, and other minor buildings at Collingwood and elsewhere. This letter is in the Pim Papers in the MTL/BR.

3 AO, MU 2321, William H. and Henry Pim Papers; MTL/BR, [William H. and] Henry Pim Papers.

4 The letters are found in NAC, RG 11, A1, DPW, vols. 14–20.

5 *General Report of the Commissioner of Public Works for the Year Ending 30th June, 1867* (Ottawa: Hunter, Rose & Company 1868), especially appendix no. 23, by G.F. Baillargé, 'Description and Cost of the Public Buildings Constructed or Improved by the Department of Public Works,' 247–64, 280, 324; see also 534–6.

6 Hodgins, ed., *Documentary History of Education in Upper Canada*, 28 vols. Hodgins produced an abridgement of this work under the title *The Establishment of Schools and Colleges in Ontario, 1792–1910*, 3 vols.

7 Ure, *Hand-Book of Toronto*.

8 UCA, Douglas S. Richardson, 'The Politics of Architecture in 1858: A Note on William Hay as G.P. Ure's Architectural Ghost-Writer for *The Hand-Book of Toronto*,' 3 March 1986.

Appendix B: Cumberland's Architectural Library

1 See AO, MU 3913, CFP, misc. A-5, env. 1, latter half of 'Cuba Diary.'

2 These are identified in a list of books in Burke's library prepared in 1925 (Horwood Add. 5, box 8).

3 See Richardson, comp., *William G. Storm*. This is a catalogue of Storm's library.

SELECTED BIBLIOGRAPHY

MANUSCRIPT COLLECTIONS

Archives of Ontario, Toronto
Historical Plaque Descriptions
Horwood Collection (including Horwood Additional
    and MU 3984, items relating to the restoration of
    University College)
Map Collection (map of Port Hope, Wall & Forrest,
    1853, D-8)
Pamphlet Collection
Picture Collection (including Cumberland Family
    Papers, Photographs, misc. E-1, box 40)
Railway and Navigation Collection
GS 1-984 York County Surrogate Court Papers,
    #3122, Will and Inventory of Fred Cumberland
GS 2022 St Catharines, Lincoln County Minute-
    books
MS 74 William Hamilton Merritt Papers
MS 76b Colonel Charles Clarke Papers
MS 385 Toronto City Council Papers
MS 537 Ridout Papers
MS 600 Ontario County Council Papers
MU 20 J.C. Baily Papers
MU 211 Miscellaneous Collection
MU 279–80 Board of Arts and Manufactures
    Minutebooks
MU 304 Andrew Norton Buell Papers
MU 470 Alexander Campbell Papers
MU 855 John G. Howard Papers (office journals)
MU 1050 Sandford Fleming Papers
MU 1188–92 Casimir Gzowski Papers
MU 1379 John George Hodgins Papers
MU 2321 [William H. and] Henry Pim Papers

MU 3909–14, 3918, 3921, 3940–1, 7176 Cumberland
    Family Papers
RG 21 Municipal Documents Collection

Baker Library, Harvard University
R.G. Dun Credit Ledgers Collection

Cathedral Church of St James Archives, Toronto
Drawings
Pamphlets
'Rebuilding of St. James's Cathedral 1849–1854'
    (folder)
Vestry Building Committee Minutebooks,
    1849–54
Vestry Minutebook, 1842–1907 ('Church Journal')

**Church of the Ascension Archives, Hamilton,
Ontario**
Vestry Minutebooks

City of Toronto Archives, Toronto
Assessment Rolls
City of Toronto Directories

Consumers' Gas Company Archives, Toronto
Minutes and correspondence

Haldimand County Museum, Cayuga, Ontario
X978.1122.11 Treasurer's Book
X978.1122.16 Extracts of Minutes of Council
    Meetings
X980.71.9 Correspondence and Original Minutes of
    Council Meetings

Hamilton Public Library, Hamilton, Ontario
Special Collections

Law Society of Upper Canada Archives, Osgoode Hall, Toronto
Minutes of Convocation, 1846–56

Metropolitan Toronto Library, Toronto (Baldwin Room unless otherwise stated)
Banting Collection (architectural plans)
Broadsides Collection
City of Toronto Directories
H.J. Grasett Scrapbook on St James's Cathedral
John G. Howard Papers (office journals)
John Harvey Papers
Map Collection (in main library holdings)
Northern Railway Papers
Paris Exhibition, 1855. Central Committee for Upper Canada Minutes
Picture Collection
T.A. Reed Papers
Toronto Mechanics' Institute Papers
William H. and Henry Pim Papers

National Archives of Canada, Ottawa
Map Collection
MG 24, B29 Joseph Howe Papers
MG 24, B30 John Sandfield Macdonald Papers
MG 24, D16 Isaac Buchanan Papers
MG 26A Sir John A. Macdonald Papers
MG 29, A21 John McIntyre Papers
MG 29, B1 Sir Sandford Fleming Papers
MG 29, F13 George Denison Papers
RG 5, B9 Bonds, Licences, Certificates, and Related Documents, Upper Canada, 1801–67
RG 9, IC1 Department of Militia and Defence, Correspondence, 1846–69
RG 11 Department of Public Works, Correspondence (various series)
RG 12 Department of Transport Papers (Northern Railway of Canada)
RG 30, IG Northern Railway Group Papers
RG 43 Old Railways and Canals Papers

Private Collection, Barrie, Ontario
Cumberland & Storm Business Records, 1852–62

Queen's University Archives, Kingston, Ontario
MG 20, 232 David Stirling Notebook

Royal Ontario Museum, Toronto
Canadiana Collection (views of Toronto buildings)

Ryerson Polytechnic University Archives, Toronto
Museum of Education File
Normal School File
Ryerson Hall File

Simcoe County Archives, Minesing, Ontario
Simcoe County Council Minutes, 1848–54

Toronto Board of Education Records Archive and Museum, Toronto
Toronto Board of Education Minutes

University College Archives, Toronto
Photographs and other items

University of Toronto Archives, Toronto
A65-0004/1-2 Photographs
A68-0010 Office of the Chief Accountant, Upper Canada College
   Section II, Bursar's Quarterly and Yearly Statements, vol. 272, Quarterly Accounts, 1854–8
   Section II, Group B, Letterbooks C, D, and E, 1851–9
   Section III, Correspondence, 1851–6
A68-0012 Senate Minutes
A70-0024/004(01) Board of Governors, Copies of Orders-in-Council
A70-0024/053(2) Board of Governors, Correspondence)
A70-0024/058 Board of Governors, Upper Canada College Council Minutes
A73-0026/075 (26–7, 29) Clipping Files
A74-0018 Upper Canada College Papers, Miscellaneous (including undated drawings)
A76-0003 Upper Canada College Papers, cash disbursement journal
B65-0014/004 John Langton Papers, 'Letters and Journals of Sir Daniel Wilson'

University of Toronto Libraries, Toronto
Government Documents Collection, Newspaper Hansard (Robarts Library)
Map Collection (Robarts Library)
MS 230 Royal Canadian Institute Papers (Thomas Fisher Rare Book Library)

University of Trinity College Archives, Toronto
Minutebooks, 1850–68
986-0001/019(03) Documents and Correspondence,
1854–72

**University of Western Ontario Archives, London,
Ontario**
Thomas Swinyard Papers (Regional Collection)

Windsor Public Library, Windsor, Ontario
RG 2, AIV-1/1 Windsor Council Minutes

OTHER SOURCES

*Annual Report of the Common Schools in Upper
    Canada ... 1845–6.* Montreal: Rollo Campbell 1847
    (and subsequent reports).
Archibald, William Currie. *The Grand Trunk Railway
    of Canada.* Toronto: University of Toronto Press
    1957.
Armstrong, Frederick H[enry]. *A City in the Making:
    Progress, People & Perils in Victorian Toronto.*
    Toronto: Dundurn Press 1988.
– 'Fred's Buildings.' *Canadian Heritage* 3, no. 3
    (summer 1977), 44–7.
– 'Toronto's First Railway Venture, 1834–1838.'
    Ontario History 58, no. 1 (March 1966), 21–41.
Armstrong, Frederick H[enry], and Peter Baskerville.
    'Frederick William Cumberland.' *Dictionary of
    Canadian Biography*, vol. 11. Toronto: University
    of Toronto Press 1982, 225–9.
Arp, Barbara, ed. *Reflections: An Historical Anthology
    of Collingwood.* Collingwood: Corporation of the
    Town of Collingwood [1983].
Arthur, Eric. 'Talks about University College.'
    University of Toronto Graduate 3, no. 3 (June
    1970), 36–9, 100–7.
– *Toronto: No Mean City.* 3rd ed. Revised by Stephen
    A. Otto. Toronto: University of Toronto Press 1986.
Ashdown, Dana, *Railway Steamships of Ontario.*
    Erin, Ont.: Boston Mills Press 1988.
Bain, David. 'William Mundie, Landscape Gardener.'
    Journal of Garden History 5, no. 3 (1985), 298–308.
Barber, Lynn. *The Heyday of Victorian Science, 1830–
    1870.* London: Victoria and Cape 1972.
Barnard, Henry. *School Architecture: or, Contribu-
    tions to the Improvement of School-Houses in the
    United States.* 3rd. ed. Edited by Jean McClintock

and Robert McClintock. New York: Teachers
    College Press 1970 [1849].
Baskerville, Peter. 'Americans in Britain's Backyard:
    The Railway Era in Upper Canada, 1850–1880.'
    Business History Review 55 (autumn 1981),
    314–36. Reprinted in Douglas McCalla, ed. *The
    Development of Canadian Capitalism: Essays in
    Business History.* Toronto: Copp Clark Pitman
    1990, 57–77.
– 'Professionalism vs. Proprietor: Power Distribution
    in the Railway World of Upper Canada/Ontario,
    1850–1881.' Canadian Historical Association
    Historical Papers 60 (1978), 47–63.
– ed. *The Bank of Upper Canada: A Collection of
    Documents.* Toronto: Champlain Society 1987.
Berger, Carl. *Science, God, and Nature in Victorian
    Canada.* Toronto: University of Toronto Press 1983.
Bethune, Alexander Neil. *Memoir of the Right
    Reverend John Strachan ... First Bishop of Toronto.*
    Toronto: Henry Rowsell 1870.
Biddle, Gordon, and O.S. Nock. *The Railway Heritage
    of Britain: 150 Years of Railway Architecture and
    Engineering.* London: Michael Joseph 1983.
Binney, Marcus, and David Pearce, eds. *Railway
    Architecture.* London: Bloomsbury Books 1975.
Bishop, Olga Bernice. *Publications of the Govern-
    ment of the Province of Canada 1841–1867.*
    Ottawa: National Library of Canada 1963.
Bissell, Claude T., ed. *University College: A Portrait,
    1853–1953.* Toronto: University of Toronto Press
    1953.
Blau, Eve. *Ruskinian Gothic: The Architecture of Dean
    and Woodward, 1845–1861.* Princeton: Princeton
    University Press 1982.
Boase, Frederic. 'Frederick William Cumberland.'
    Modern English Biography. Truro: Netherton and
    Worth 1892, 782.
Bouchier, Michelle Frances. 'Impact of the Northern
    Railroad on Sense of Place in Canada West, 1850–
    1865.' Master's thesis, York University, 1979.
'Bramhill.' *To the Vestry-men of the Parish of St.
    James.* Toronto: n.p. 1849 (copy in Metropolitan
    Toronto Library, Baldwin Room).
Breckenridge, Roeliff Morton. *The History of Banking
    in Canada.* Washington: Government Printing
    Office 1910.
Breihaupt, William H. 'The Railways of Ontario.'
    Ontario Historical Society *Papers and Records* 25
    (1929), 12–25.

Brooks, Michael W. *John Ruskin and Victorian Architecture.* London: Thames and Hudson 1989.

Brosseau, Mathilde. *Gothic Revival in Canadian Architecture.* Ottawa: Parks Canada 1980.

[Brown, George]. *The Origin, History and Management of the University of King's College, Toronto.* Toronto: The Author 1844.

Brownlee, David B. 'The First High Victorians: British Architectural Theory in the 1840s.' *Architectura: Zeitschrift für Geschichte der Baukunst/Journal of the History of Architecture* 15, no. 1 (1985), 33–46.

Burpee, Lawrence J. *Sandford Fleming: Empire Builder.* London: Oxford University Press 1915.

Cameron, Christina. *Charles Baillargé, Architect & Engineer.* Montreal and Kingston, Ont.: McGill-Queen's University Press 1989.

Cameron, Christina, and Janet Wright. *Second Empire Style in Canadian Architecture.* Ottawa: Parks Canada 1980.

Canada. Army Historical Section. *The Regiments and Corps of the Canadian Army.* Ottawa: Queen's Printer 1964.

Careless, J.M.S. *The Pre-Confederation Premiers: Ontario Government Leaders, 1841–1867.* Toronto: University of Toronto Press 1980.

– *Toronto to 1918: An Illustrated History.* Toronto: James Lorimer & Company 1984.

– *The Union of the Canada: The Growth of Canadian Institutions, 1841–1857.* Toronto: McClelland and Stewart 1967.

Carr, Angela, 'Hopkins, Lawford & Nelson at Osgoode Hall: The Debacle of 1855.' SSAC *Bulletin* 13, no. 4 (December 1988), 17–25.

Carter, John C. 'Ryerson, Hodgins, and Boyle: Early Innovators in Ontario School Museums.' *Ontario History* 76, no. 2 (June 1994), 119–32.

Carter, Margaret, comp. *Early Canadian Courthouses.* Ottawa: Parks Canada 1983.

Chambers, Captain Ernest J. *The Royal Grenadiers: A Regimental History of the 10th Infantry Regiment of the Active Militia of Canada.* Toronto: E.L. Ruddy 1904.

Chambers, Sir William. *A Treatise on the Decorative Part of Civil Architecture, by Sir William Chambers, with Illustrations, Notes, and an Examination of Grecian Architecture by Joseph Gwilt.* 2 vols. London: Priestley and Weale 1825.

Champion, Thomas Edward. *History of the 10th Royals and of the Royal Grenadiers from the Formation of the Regiment until 1896.* Toronto: Hunter, Rose Company 1896.

– *The Methodist Churches of Toronto.* Toronto: G.M. Rose & Sons 1899.

Clarke, Colonel Charles. *Sixty Years in Upper Canada, with Autobiographical Recollections.* Toronto: William Briggs 1908.

Clerk, Nathalie. *Palladian Style in Canadian Architecture/Le style palladien dans l'architecture au Canada.* Ottawa: Parks Canada 1984.

Cochrane, Honora M., ed. *Centennial Story: The Board of Education for the City of Toronto, 1850–1950.* Toronto: Thomas Nelson & Sons 1950.

'Colonel F.W. Cumberland.' *History of Toronto and County of York, Ontario,* vol. 2. Toronto: C. Blackett Robinson 1885, 36–7.

Côté, N. Omer, ed. *Political Appointments, Parliaments and the Judicial Bench in the Dominion of Canada, 1867 to 1895.* Ottawa: Thorburn & Co. 1896.

Craig, Maurice. *The Architecture of Ireland from the Earliest Times to 1880.* London: B.T. Batsford 1892.

Crossman, Kelly. *The Early Court Houses of Ontario.* 3 vols. Ottawa: Parks Canada 1978.

'Cumberland. Toronto's High Priest of Victorian Eclectic Architecture Has Left a Legacy Carved in Stone.' *Equinox* 1, no. 1 (January–February 1982), 94–103.

[Cumberland, Frederic William]. 'Engineering and Architecture.' *Canadian Journal of Industry, Science and Art* n.s., 1 (January 1856), 203.

[–] 'Engineering and Architecture. Preservation of Timber.' *Canadian Journal of Industry, Science and Art* n.s., 6 (November 1856), 559–61.

– 'Iron Roofs Erected over Building Slips, Nos. 3 and 4, in Her Majesty's Dockyard, Portsmouth.' *Papers on Subjects Connected with the Duties of the Corps of Royal Engineers* 9 (1847), 59–65.

– *Letter to the Hon. John Quincy Adams, Jr., Relating to Through Traffic Connections for Season 1878. Between the Ogdensburg & L.C. Ry. Co. and the Northern Railway Company of Canada (Collingwood Line).* Toronto(?): n.p. 1878(?) (CIHM microfiche no. 25,143).

– *Memorandum Relative to the Present Position of the Ontario, Simcoe and Huron Railroad Union Company: And Suggestive of Parliamentary Measures of Relief.* Toronto: Blackburn's 1858 (CIHM microfiche no. 43,434).

– *A New Plan of Esplanade and City Railway Accom-*

modation, 23 July 1853. Metropolitan Toronto Library, Map Collection. Printed version of manuscript entitled 'Report on City Frontage' in the Metropolitan Toronto Library, Baldwin Room.

– *The Queen's Wharf Depot Lands: The Corporation of Toronto and the Northern Railway Co.: Report of a Submission Made by Frederic Cumberland, Managing Director of the Northern Railway, to the Committee of Enquiry into the Matter of the Valuation of the Corporation Property.* Toronto(?): n.p. 1872(?) (CIHM microfiche no. 25,157).

– *Railways to Grey: Being a Letter to the Warden, Reeves and Deputy Reeves, of the South Riding of the County of Grey.* Toronto: Globe Printing Co. 1867.

– *Report by the Chief Engineer to the Directors of the Ontario, Simcoe & Huron Railway Company, February 1853.* Toronto: Hugh Scobie [1853].

– 'On Science and Art, and the Influence Which They Exercise on the Wealth and Character of Nations.' Lecture delivered before the Mechanics' Institute of Hamilton, 4 December 1848. Archives of Ontario, MU 3910, Cumberland Family Papers, box 2, env. 1. A different version of this lecture was printed in the *Hamilton Spectator of Commerce*, 13 December 1848.

– 'Some Notes of a Visit to the Works of the Grand Trunk Railway, West of Toronto, February 1855.' *The Canadian Journal: A Repertory of Industry, Science and Art* 3, no. 10 (May 1855), 225–7.

Cumberland, F[rederick] Barlow. 'The Story of a University Building.' *Canadian Magazine* 17, no. 3 (July 1901), 235–43.

– ed. *The Esplanade of Toronto: A Forecast Made in 1853; Report of Col. Fred. Cumberland to the Directors of the Osgoode Hall, Simcoe and Huron Railway.* N.p.: n.p. 1889(?) (CIHM microfiche no. 2237).

– ed. *The Northern Lakes of Canada ...* 2nd ed. Toronto: Hunter Rose & Co. 1886.

– ed.(?) *Northern Railway of Canada and Great Rail & Lake Connections. Toronto, Canada Summer Excursion Routes ...* [Toronto]: Bell & Co. [1878].

Curtis, Bruce. *Building the Educational State: Canada West, 1836–1871.* London, Ont.: Althouse Press 1988.

– *True Government by Choice Men? Inspection, Education, and State Formation in Canada West.* Toronto: University of Toronto Press 1992.

Davey, Ian I. 'School Reform and School Attendance: The Hamilton Central School, 1853–1861.' Master's thesis, University of Toronto, 1972.

Dendy, William. *Lost Toronto.* Toronto: Oxford University Press 1978.

Dendy, William, and William Kilbourn. *Toronto Observed: Its Architecture, Patrons, and History.* Toronto: Oxford University Press 1986.

Dent, John Charles. *The Last Forty Years: Canadian Politics, Railways, and Finance in the Nineteenth Century.* Toronto: University of Toronto Press 1943.

de Volpi, Charles Patrick. *Toronto, A Pictorial Record: Historical Prints and Illustrations of the City of Toronto, Province of Ontario 1813–1882.* Montreal: Dev-Sco 1965.

Documents Relating to the Construction of the Parliamentary and Departmental Buildings at Ottawa. Ottawa: Hunter, Rose and Lemieux 1862.

Dufferin, Lady. *My Canadian Journal 1872–1878.* Edited by Gladys Chantler Walker. Don Mills, Ont.: Longmans Canada 1969.

Earl, John. *A Sketch of the County of Norfolk.* Simcoe, Ont.: Norfolk Messenger 1857.

Ellis, Hamilton. *British Railway History, 1830–1870.* London: G. Allen & Unwin 1954–9.

Farmer, Mary Harrington. *One Hundred Years: The Church of the Ascension, Hamilton. A Short History, 1850–1950.* Hamilton, Ont.: Kidner Printing 1950.

Final Report of the Commissioners of Inquiry into the Affairs of King's College University, and Upper Canada College. Quebec: Rollo Campbell 1862.

Fleming, Sir Sandford. 'The Early Days of the Canadian Institute.' Canadian Institute *Transactions* 6 (1899), 1–24.

'Frederic William Cumberland.' *Appleton's Cyclopaedia of American Biography.* Edited by James Grant Wilson and John Fiske. New York: D. Appleton and Company 1888, 29.

'Frederic William Cumberland.' *A Cyclopaedia of Canadian Biography: Being Chiefly Men of the Time.* Edited by George Maclean Rose. Toronto: Rose Publishing Company 1886, 705–7.

'Frederic William Cumberland.' *Dictionary of Hamilton Biography*, vol. 1. Edited by Thomas Melville Bailey. Hamilton: W.L. Griffin 1981, 56–7.

'Frederic William Cumberland, Esq.' *Canadian Illustrated News*, 25 July 1863, 121–2.

'Frederick William Cumberland.' *The Canadian*

Directory of Parliament, 1867–1967. Edited by J.K. Johnson. Ottawa: Public Archives of Canada 1968, 146.

General Report of the Commissioner of Public Works for the Year Ending 30th June, 1867. Ottawa: Hunter, Rose & Company 1868.

Gidney, Robert Douglas, and W.P.J. Millar. *Inventing Secondary Education: The Rise of the High School in Nineteenth-Century Ontario.* Montreal and Kingston, Ont.: McGill-Queen's University Press 1990.

Goodspeed, D[onald] J. *Battle Royal: A History of the Royal Regiment of Canada, 1862–1962.* Toronto and Brampton, Ont.: Charters Publishing Company 1962.

Gough, Thomas Bunbury. *Boyish Reminiscences of His Majesty the King's Visit to Canada in 1860.* London: John Murray 1910.

Greer, Allan, and Ian Radforth, eds. *Colonial Leviathan: State Formation in Mid-Nineteenth-Century Canada.* Toronto: University of Toronto Press 1992.

Grier, Crawford. 'The Right Place.' *Varsity Graduate* [University of Toronto] 12 (Christmas 1965), 97–101.

Harkness, A.H. 'The Architecture of a University Building.' *The Canadian Magazine* 17 (1901), 244–53.

Hay, William. 'Architecture for the Meridian of Canada.' *Anglo-American Magazine* 2 (January–June 1853), 253–5.

History of the Federal Electoral Ridings, 1867–1980, vol. 2: *Ontario.* [Ottawa]: Library of Parliament Information and Reference Branch 1980.

Hitchcock, Henry-Russell, Jr. *Early Victorian Architecture in Britain.* 2 vols. New Haven: Yale University Press 1954.

Hodgins, John George. *The Establishment of Schools and Colleges in Ontario, 1792–1910.* 3 vols. Toronto: L.K. Cameron 1910.

– *Historical and Other Papers and Documents Illustrative of the Educational System of Ontario ...* 5 vols. Toronto: L.K. Cameron 1911–12.

– ed. *Documentary History of Education in Upper Canada, from the Passing of the Constitutional Act of 1791 to the Close of the Reverend Doctor Ryerson's Administration of the Education Department in 1876: Forming an Appendix to the Annual Report of the Minister of Education.* 28 volumes.

Toronto: various publishers 1893–1910 (subtitle varies).

– ed. *The School House; Its Architecture, External and Internal Arrangements, with Additional Papers on Gymnastics, the Use of Apparatus, School Discipline, Methods of Teaching, etc. etc. Together with Selections for Public Recitations in Schools.* Toronto: Lovell and Gibson 1857.

– ed. *The Story of My Life: Being Reminiscences of Sixty Years' Public Service in Canada by Egerton Ryerson ...* Toronto: William Briggs 1883.

Houston, Susan E., and Alison Prentice. *Schooling and Scholars in Nineteenth-Century Ontario.* Toronto: University of Toronto Press 1988.

Howell, Peter. *Victorian Churches.* England: Country Life Books 1968.

Hubbard, R.H. *Ample Mansions: The Viceregal Residences of the Canadian Provinces.* Ottawa: University of Ottawa Press 1989.

– *Rideau Hall: An Illustrated History of Government House, Ottawa, from Victorian Times to the Present Day.* Montreal and London: McGill-Queen's University Press 1977.

Huelin, Gordon. *King's College London, 1828–1978.* London: University of London, King's College 1978.

Hulse, Elizabeth. *A Dictionary of Toronto Printers, Publishers, Booksellers and the Allied Trades, 1798–1900.* Toronto: Anson-Cartwright Editions 1982.

Illustrated Historical Atlas of the Counties of Haldimand and Norfolk. Belleville, Ont.: Mika Publishing 1973 [1877].

Illustrated Historical Atlas of the County of Ontario. Belleville, Ont.: Mika Publishing 1972 [1877].

'Incorporation Dates for Ontario Counties.' *Library Bulletin,* 11 December 1978 (copy in Archives of Ontario).

'Incorporation Dates for Regional Municipalities, District Municipalities and Metropolitan Corporations.' *Library Bulletin,* 7 December 1978 (copy in Archives of Ontario).

James, Ellen. *John Ostell: Architect, Surveyor.* Catalogue of an Exhibition held at the McCord Museum, Montreal, 1985.

Johnson, Dana, and Leslie Maitland. 'Osgoode Hall and the Development of Public Architecture in Canada.' SSAC *Bulletin* 10, no. 4 (December 1985), 14–18.

Johnson, F. Henry. 'A Colonial Canadian in Search of

a Museum.' *Queen's Quarterly* 77, no. 2 (summer 1970), 217–30.

Jordan, Robert Furneaux. *Victorian Architecture.* Harmondsworth: Penguin Books 1966.

Journal of the Proceedings and By-laws of the Provisional Council of the County of Victoria. Lindsay, Ont.: Victoria Herald 1863.

Journals of The House of Commons, vol. 11 (1877), appendix 5: *Report of the Select Committee Appointed to Enquire into the Affairs of the Northern Railway and the Northern Extension Railways.*

Keefer, T.C. *Philosophy of Railroads and Other Essays.* Edited by H.V. Nelles. Toronto: University of Toronto Press 1972 [1853].

Kerr, D.G.G. *Sir Edmund Head: A Scholarly Governor.* Toronto: University of Toronto Press 1954.

Knight, David B. *Choosing Canada's Capital: Conflict Resolution in a Parliamentary System.* 2nd. ed. Ottawa: Carleton University Press 1991.

Landmarks of Canada. A Guide to the J. Ross Robertson Canadian Historical Collection in the Toronto Public Library. Toronto: Toronto Public Library 1967.

Laidlaw, George. *Cheap Railways: A Letter to the People of the Bruce and Grey Railway.* Toronto: Globe Printing Company 1867.

Langton, H[ugh] H[ornby]. *Sir Daniel Wilson: A Memoir.* Toronto: Thomas Nelson 1929.

– *The University of Toronto and Its Colleges, 1827–1906.* Toronto: University Library 1906.

Langton, John. *Early Days in Upper Canada; Letters of John Langton from the Backwoods of Upper Canada and the Audit Office of the Province of Canada.* Edited by W.A. Langton. Toronto: Macmillan 1926.

Langton, John, and Daniel Wilson. *University Question: The Statements of John Langton, Esq., M.A., Vice-Chancellor of the University of Toronto and Professor Daniel Wilson, L.L.D. of University College, Toronto, with Notes and Extracts from the Evidence Taken before the Committee of the legislative Assembly on the University.* Toronto: Rowsell & Ellis 1860 (CIHM microfiche no. 22,836).

Leggatt, Robert F. 'Engineer, Architect, Actor ... F.W. Cumberland Rich in Talent.' *Canadian Consulting Engineer* (April 1981), 61–2.

Leong, Yew-Thong. 'Frederick William Cumberland and the Toronto Normal and Model Schools Building.' SSAC *Bulletin* 9, no. 3 (October 1984), 10–11.

'Lieut.-Col. Fred. Wm. Cumberland.' *The Dominion Annual Register and Review for ... 1880–1881.* Edited by Henry S. Morgan. Montreal: John Lovell & Son 1882, 404.

Lochnan, Katherine. 'Victorian Tiles in Toronto.' *Canadian Collector* 16, no. 5 (September/October 1981), 54–9.

MacRae, Marion, and Anthony Adamson. *The Ancestral Roof: Domestic Architecture of Upper Canada.* Toronto and Vancouver: Clarke, Irwin. 1963.

– *Cornerstones of Order: Courthouses and Town Halls of Ontario 1784–1914.* Toronto and Vancouver: Clarke, Irwin 1983.

– *Hallowed Walls: Church Architecture in Upper Canada.* Toronto and Vancouver: Clarke, Irwin 1975.

Maddick, Heather, comp. *County Maps: Land Ownership Maps of Canada in the 19th Century.* Introduction by Joan Winearls. Ottawa: Public Archives of Canada 1976.

Maitland, Leslie. *Neoclassical Architecture in Canada/L'architecture néo-classique au Canada.* Ottawa: Parks Canada 1984.

Martyn, Lucy Booth. *Toronto: One Hundred Years of Grandeur. The Inside Stories of Toronto's Great Homes and the People Who Lived There.* Toronto: Pagurian Press 1978.

Masters, D.C. *The Rise of Toronto, 1850–1890.* Toronto: University of Toronto Press 1947.

McCalla, Douglas. *Planting the Province: The Economic History of Upper Canada, 1784–1870.* Toronto: University of Toronto Press 1993.

McHugh, Patricia. *Toronto Architecture: A City Guide.* 2nd. ed. Toronto: McClelland and Stewart 1989.

McKelvey, Margaret E., and Merilyn McKelvey. *Toronto Carved in Stone.* Toronto: Fitzhenry and Whiteside 1984.

McKillop, A.B. *A Disciplined Intelligence: Critical Inquiry and Canadian Thought in the Victorian Era.* Montreal: McGill-Queen's University Press 1979.

– *Matters of Mind: The University in Ontario, 1791–1951.* Toronto: University of Toronto Press 1994.

McLeod, Wallace, ed. *Whence Come We? Freemasonry in Ontario, 1764–1980.* Hamilton: Masonic Holdings 1980.

Melville, Henry. *The Rise and Progress of Trinity College, Toronto; With A Sketch of the Lord Bishop of Toronto, as Connected with Church Education in Canada.* Toronto: Henry Rowsell 1852.

Miles, Frank. 'Boy's Own Artist.' *Country Life*, 26 October 1989, 80–3.

Millard, J. Rodney. *The Master Spirit of the Age: Canadian Engineers and the Politics of Professionalism, 1887–1922*. Toronto: University of Toronto Press 1988.

Morriss, Shirley G. 'The Church Architecture of Frederic William Cumberland.' Master's thesis, University of Toronto 1976.

– 'The Church Architecture of Frederic William Cumberland (1820/21–1881).' *Ontario Museum Association Newsletter* 4, no. 3 (1975), 17–25.

– 'The Nine-Year Odyssey of a High-Victorian Goth: Three Churches by Fred Cumberland.' *Journal of Canadian Art History* 2 (summer 1975), 42–53.

Murray, Henry A. *Lands of the Slave and the Free*. London: G. Routledge & Co. 1857.

Narrative. Visit of the Governor-General and the Countess of Dufferin to the Six Nations Indians. August 25, 1874. 2nd ed. N.p.: n.p. 1865 (copy in Archives of Ontario, MU 3941, CFP, misc. pamphlets, D-2, env. 6).

Northern Railway of Canada. *'The Barrie Switch.' Reply by the Directors to a 'Brief Statement' Circulated in the Legislature*. Toronto: n.p. 1862.

Papworth, John W., and Wyatt Papworth. *Museums, Libraries, and Picture Galleries, Public and Private: Their Establishment, Formation, Arrangement, and Architectural Construction*. London: Chapman and Hall 1853.

Pennington, Myles. *Railways and Other Ways: Being Reminiscences of Canal and Railway Life during a Period of Sixty-five Years: with Characteristic Sketches of Canal and Railway Men ...* Toronto: Williamson & Co. 1894.

Public Accounts for the Province of Canada for the Year 1855. Toronto: Rollo Campbell 1855 (and subsequent reports).

Public Schools, City of Toronto. Report of the Past History, and Present Condition, of the Common or Public Schools of the City of Toronto. Toronto: Lovell & Gibson 1859.

Purdy, Judson D. 'John Strachan and Education in Canada 1800–1851.' Ph.D. diss., University of Toronto 1962.

Read, David B[reckenridge]. *The Lives of the Judges of Upper Canada and Ontario, from 1791 to the Present*. Toronto: Rowsell & Hutchison 1888.

Reed, T.A. 'The First Fifty Years of U.C.' University of Toronto *Bulletin* (March–April 1954), 114–16.

– *A History of the University of Trinity College*. Toronto: University of Toronto Press 1952.

– 'The Observatory of Toronto, 1840–1908.' *Canadian Geographic Journal* 55, no. 6 (December 1957), 234–43.

Report of Railway Commissioners for Canada. Report of Samuel Keefer, Esq., Inspector of Railways, for the Year 1858. Hamilton: G. Vespy & Robertson 1859 (and subsequent reports).

Report of the Chief Engineer to the Directors of the Ontario, Simcoe and Huron Railroad Union Company. Toronto: Hugh Scobie 1852 (also 1853).

Report of the Commission Appointed for Investigating the Books, Accounts, and Vouchers of the Northern Railway Company of Canada, and the Disbursements and Expenditures of the Said Company. Together with the Evidence Taken by Said Commission. Ottawa: Maclean, Roger & Co. 1877.

Report of the Commissioners Appointed to Enquire into the Expenditure of the Funds of the University of Toronto, and into the State of Its Financial Affairs; and to Enquire into the Annual Expenditure of the Appropriations for University College, and the General State of Its Financial Affairs, &c., &c. Quebec: G.T. Cary 1862.

Report Submitted by the Board of Directors of the Ontario, Simcoe and Huron Railroad Union Company, to the Annual Meeting of the Proprietors, Held at the Company's Offices, Monday, 17th July 1854. Toronto: The Globe Book and Job Office 1854 (and subsequent annual reports).

Richardson, Douglas Scott. *Gothic Revival Architecture in Ireland*. 2 vols. New York: Garland 1983.

– *A Not Unsightly Building: University College and Its History*. [Oakville, Ont.]: Mosaic Press 1990.

Richardson, Marianna May, comp. *William G. Storm: A Catalogue of His Library*. [Toronto: Ontario Association of Architects 1990].

Robertson, J[ohn] Ross. *The History of Freemasonry in Canada from Its Introduction in 1793*. 2 vols. Toronto: George N. Morang & Company 1900.

– *Landmarks of Toronto; A Collection of Historical Sketches of the Old Town of York from 1792 to 1833, and of Toronto from 1834 to 1914 ...* 6 vols. Toronto: The Author 1894–1914.

Robinson, Peter Frederick. *Rural Architecture; or, a Series of Designs for Ornamental Cottages*. London: Rodwell 1823.

Rose, George Maclean, ed. *A Cyclopaedia of Canadian Biography: Being Chiefly Men of the Time.* Toronto: Rose Publishing Company 1886.

Ross, Dunbar. *The Seat of Government of Canada.* Quebec: E.R. Fréchette 1856 [1843].

Ross, Victor. *A History of the Canadian Bank of Commerce, with an Account of the Other Banks Which Now Form Part of Its Organization*, vol. 2. Toronto: Oxford University Press 1922.

Rutherford, James H. 'Early Navigation on the Georgian Bay.' Ontario Historical Society *Papers and Records* 18 (1920), 14–20.

Scadding, Henry. *Toronto of Old.* 2nd. ed. Edited by Frederick H. Armstrong. Toronto: Dundurn Press 1987 [1878].

'Shareholder, A.' *Ontario, Simcoe, and Huron Railroad Union Company. Eight Letters on Matters in Connection with the Affairs of the Above Company.* Toronto: George E. Thomas & Co. 1853.

Simmins, Geoffrey, ed. *Documents in Canadian Architecture.* Peterborough, Ont.: Broadview Press 1992.

Simmins, Geoffrey, and Shirley Morriss. *Frederic Cumberland (1820–1881): An Exhibition of Architectural Drawings.* Catalogue of an exhibition held at the Lynwood Arts Centre, Lynnwood, Ontario, 5 October–4 November 1990.

Small, J.T., comp. *A Consolidation of the Statutes Relating to the Northern Railway of Canada, with an Index. For the Use of the Company [and prepared] under the Direction of Frederic Cumberland, Esq., Managing Director.* Toronto: Hunter, Rose & Co. 1876.

Smith, Henry T. *History of St. Andrew's Lodge ... 1822–1922.* Toronto: The Macoomb Press 1922.

Smith, Mary Larratt, ed. *Young Mr. Smith in Upper Canada.* Toronto: University of Toronto Press 1987.

Smith, Russell D. 'The Northern Railway: Its Origin and Construction, 1834–1855.' *Ontario History* 48, no. 1 (winter 1956), 24–36.

Smith, W.H. *Canada: Past, Present and Future.* Belleville, Ont.: Mika Publishing 1973 [1851].

Special Report of the Measures Which Have Been Adopted for the Establishment of a Normal School ... Montreal: Lovell and Gibson 1846.

Stacey, C.P. *Canada and the British Army, 1846–1871: A Study in Responsible Government.* Imperial Studies Series No. 11 (Toronto 1936).

Stanton, Phoebe. *The Gothic Revival & American Church Architecture: An Episode in Taste, 1840–1856.* Baltimore: The Johns Hopkins Press 1968.

Steegman, John. *Victorian Taste: A Study of the Arts and Architecture from 1830 to 1870.* Foreword by Nikolaus Pevsner. Cambridge: MIT Press 1970.

Stevens, G.R. *Canadian National Railways*, vol. 1. Toronto: Clarke, Irwin and Company 1960.

Stewart, Cecil. *The Stones of Manchester.* London: Edward Arnold 1956.

[Strachan, John]. *Thoughts on the Rebuilding of the Cathedral Church of St. James.* Toronto: Diocesan Press 1850.

Strathey, Elliot Grasett. *A Guide to the Cathedral Church of St. James.* Toronto: n.p. 1932.

Sykes, Christopher Simon. *Private Palaces: Life in the Great London Houses.* London: Chatto & Windus 1985.

Sylvester, Alfred. *Sketches of Toronto, Comprising a Complete and Accurate Description of the Principal Points of Interest in the City, Its Public Buildings &c., Together with Necessary Details in Connection with the Provincial Exhibition.* Toronto: Charles E. Holiwell 1858.

Tausky, Nancy Z., and Lynne D. DiStefano. *Victorian Architecture in London and Southwestern Ontario: Symbols of Aspiration.* Photographs by Ian MacEachern. Toronto: University of Toronto Press 1986.

Thomas, Christopher. 'Architectural Image for the Dominion.' *Journal of Canadian Art History*, nos. 1–2 (fall 1976), 83–94.

Thompson, John Beswick. *A History of Canadian Railways to 1876.* [Ottawa]: Parks Canada 1977.

Thompson, Samuel. *Reminiscences of a Canadian Pioneer for the Last Fifty Years: An Autobiography.* Toronto: Hunter, Rose & Company 1894.

Thurlby, Malcolm. 'Medieval Toronto.' *Rotunda* 24, no. 4 (spring 1992), 27–33.

– Nineteenth-Century Churches in Ontario: A Study in the Meaning of Style.' *Historic Kingston* 35 (January 1987), 96–110.

Toronto in the Camera: A Series of Photographic views of the Principal Buildings in the City of Toronto. Toronto: O[ctavius] Thompson 1868.

Toronto Normal School. Centennial Committee. *Toronto Normal School 1847–1947.* Toronto: School of Graphic Arts [1947].

Toronto Normal School, 1847–1895: Jubilee Celebration ... Biographical Sketches and Names of Suc-

cessful Students, 1847 to 1875. Toronto: Warwick Brothers & Rutter 1898.

Tremaine, George R. *Tremaine's Map of Upper Canada Compiled & Drawn by Geo. R. Tremaine; Assisted by A. Jones, Esq. From Original Surveys & Government Plans.* Toronto: George C., George R., and G.M. Tremaine 1863 (copy in Map Library, University of Toronto) (and this firm's Ontario county maps of the period).

Trollope, Anthony. *North America.* New York: Harper & Brothers 1862.

Trout, J.M., and Edward Trout. *The Railways of Canada for 1870–1, Shewing the Progress, Mileage, Cost of Construction, the Stocks, Bonds, Traffic, Earnings, Expenses, and Organization of the Railways of the Dominion.* Toronto: Coles Canadiana Collection 1970 [1871].

Tully, Kivas. *Memorandum for the Congregation of St. James's Church ...* Toronto: n.p. 1849 (copy in Metropolitan Toronto Library, Baldwin Room).

Unitt, Doris J., et al., comps. *Sir Sandford Fleming.* Peterborough, Ont.: Review Printing Co. 1968.

Ure, George P. *The Hand-Book of Toronto: Containing Its Climate, Geology, Natural History, Educational Institutions, Courts of Law, Municipal Arrangements, &c. &c.* Toronto: Lovell and Gibson 1858 (CIHM microfiche no. 37,020).

Van der Smissen, W.H. 'The Building [University College, Toronto].' *University of Toronto Monthly* 5, no. 9 (June–July 1905), 209–17.

Vaughan, Carol Lawrie. 'The Bank of Upper Canada in Politics, 1817–1840.' *Ontario History* 40, no. 4 (December 1968), 185–204.

Walker, Frank N. 'A Doorway Made Him Famous.' University of Toronto *Bulletin* 54, no. 3 (March–April 1954), 99–100.

– *Four Whistles to Wood-up: Stories of the Northern Railway of Canada.* Toronto: Upper Canada Railway Society 1960.

– ed. *Daylight through the Mountain: Letters and Labours of Civil Engineers Walter and Francis Shanly.* [Montreal]: Engineering Institute of Canada 1957.

Wallace, W. Stewart. *A History of the University of Toronto, 1827–1927.* Toronto: University of Toronto Press 1927.

– ed. *The Royal Canadian Institute Centennial Volume, 1849–1949.* Toronto: The Royal Canadian Institute 1949.

Warr, George Winter. *Canada as It Is; or, The Emigrant's Friend and Guide to Upper Canada: Being a Sketch of the Country, Climate, Inhabitants, Professions, Trades, etc.: Taken During a Residence in 1843, 1844, 1845, 1846 ...* London: William Edward Painter 1847.

Weaver, John C. 'Crime, Public Order, and Repression: The Gore District in Upheaval, 1832–1851.' *Ontario History* 78, no. 3 (September 1986), 175–208.

– *Hamilton: An Illustrated History.* Toronto: Lorimer 1982.

Westfall, William E. 'The Dominion of the Lord: An Introduction to the Cultural History of Protestant Ontario in the Victorian Period.' *Queen's Quarterly* 83, no. 1 (spring 1976), 47–70.

– *Two Worlds: The Protestant Culture of Nineteenth-Century Ontario.* Montreal and Kingston, Ont.: McGill-Queen's University Press 1989.

Westfall, William, and Malcolm Thurlby. 'Church Architecture and Urban Space: The Development of Ecclesiastical Forms in Nineteenth-Century Ontario,' in David Keane and Colin Read, eds., *Old Ontario: Essays in Honour of J.M.S. Careless.* Toronto: Dundurn Press 1990, 118–47.

– 'The Church in the Town: The Adaptation of Sacred Architecture to Urban Settings in Ontario.' *Études Canadiennes/Canadian Studies* 20 (June 1986), 49–59.

Williams, David. 'Shipping on the Great Lakes.' Huron Institute *Papers & Records* 1 (1909), 43–59.

Winter, Brian. *A Town Named Whitby.* Whitby: Raymond Huff Productions 1967.

Wise, S.F. *God's Peculiar Peoples: Essays on Political Culture in Nineteenth-Century Canada.* Edited by A.B. McKillop and Paul Romney. Ottawa: Carleton University Press 1993.

Woods, N.A. *The Prince of Wales in Canada and the United States.* London: Bradbury & Evans 1861.

Yeigh, Frank. *Ontario's Parliament Buildings; or, a Century of Legislation, 1792–1892.* Toronto: Williamson Book Company 1893.

Young, Carolyn. *The Glory of Ottawa: Canada's First*

Parliament Buildings. Montreal and Kingston, Ont.: McGill-Queen's University Press 1995.

– '"Odahwah": The Competition of 1859 for the Canadian Parliament Buildings.' Master's thesis, University of Toronto, 1989.

Young, C[larence] R[ichard]. *Early Engineering Education at Toronto, 1851–1919*. Toronto: University of Toronto Press 1958.

Zeller, Suzanne. *Inventing Canada: Early Victorian Science and the Idea of a Transcontinental Nation*. Toronto: University of Toronto Press 1987.

INDEX

Page numbers in italics indicate illustrations.